HUGH DE LACY
FIRST EARL OF ULSTER

Irish Historical Monograph Series

ISSN 1740–1097

Previous titles in this series

I. Ruling Ireland 1685–1742: Politics, Politicians and Parties, *D. W. Hayton*, 2004

II. Lord Broghill and the Cromwellian Union with Ireland and Scotland, *Patrick Little*, 2004

III. Irish Migrants in New Zealand, 1840–1937: 'The Desired Haven', *Angela McCarthy*, 2005

IV. The Fenian Ideal and Irish Nationalism, 1882–1916, *M. J. Kelly*, 2006

V. Loyalism in Ireland, 1789–1829, *Allan Blackstock*, 2007

VI. Constructing the Past: Writing Irish History, 1600–1800, *edited by Mark Williams and Stephen Forrest*, 2010

VII. The Making of the Irish Protestant Ascendancy: The Life of William Conolly, 1662–1729, *Patrick Walsh*, 2010

VIII. The Militia in Eighteenth-Century Ireland: In Defence of the Protestant Interest, *Neal Garnham*, 2012

IX. The Anglo-Irish Experience, 1680–1730: Religion, Identity and Patriotism, *D. W. Hayton*, 2012

X. The Presbyterians of Ulster, 1680–1730, *Robert Whan*, 2013

XI. The Welsh and the Shaping of Early Modern Ireland, 1558–1641, *Rhys Morgan*, 2014

XII. The Irish in the Spanish Armies in the Seventeenth Century, *Eduardo de Mesa*, 2014

XIII. Consumption and Culture in Sixteenth-Century Ireland: Saffron, Stockings and Silk, *Susan Flavin*, 2014

XIV. Elite Women in Ascendancy Ireland, 1690–1745: Imitation and Innovation, *Rachel Wilson*, 2015

XV. The Stuart Restoration and the English in Ireland, *Danielle McCormack*, 2016

XVI. Charity Movements in Eighteenth-Century Ireland: Philanthropy and Improvement, *Karen Sonnelitter*, 2016

HUGH DE LACY FIRST EARL OF ULSTER

Rising and Falling in Angevin Ireland

Daniel Brown

THE BOYDELL PRESS

First published 2016
The Boydell Press, Woodbridge

ISBN 978-1-78327-134-4

The Boydell Press is an imprint of Boydell & Brewer Ltd
PO Box 9, Woodbridge, Suffolk IP12 3DF, UK
and of Boydell & Brewer Inc.
668 Mt Hope Avenue, Rochester, NY 14620–2731, USA
website: www.boydellandbrewer.com

A CIP catalogue record for this title is available from the British Library

This publication is printed on acid-free paper

Typeset by Fakenham Prepress Solutions, Fakenham, Norfolk NR21 8NN

Printed and bound in Great Britain by
TJ International Ltd, Padstow, Cornwall

MIX
Paper from responsible sources
FSC www.fsc.org FSC® C013056

For my wife, Gemma

Contents

Illustrations

Acknowledgements

It was Professor Marie Therese Flanagan (Queen's University Belfast) who first suggested the younger Hugh de Lacy as a suitable topic for a doctoral thesis. Since then I have profited immeasurably from her meticulous critical eye, boundless patience and personal friendship, without which this book would be very much the poorer. I am also grateful to Dr James Davis (Queen's University Belfast) and Professor Seán Duffy (Trinity College Dublin) for their support and encouragement, and for reading and commenting on various stages of my research. To Dr Colin Veach (University of Hull) and Paul Duffy (Grassroots Archaeology) I am thankful for stimulating discussion and correspondence on the de Lacys, and for so graciously sharing their own ideas and expertise. Professor David Crouch (University of Hull), Professor Nicholas Vincent (University of East Anglia), Professor Daniel Power (Swansea University) and Professor Dauvit Broun (University of Glasgow) have all been extraordinarily generous with their advice and time, pointing me towards useful archival material and saving me from grievous error. I also wish to acknowledge the Arts and Humanities Research Council (AHRC) and Irish Research Council (IRC) for respectively funding my doctoral and postdoctoral research on Hugh de Lacy. Lastly, I want to thank my family, and in particular my wife, without whose love and support this book could not have been written.

Abbreviations

AC	*Annála Connacht: the annals of Connacht, A.D. 1224–1544*, ed. A. M. Freeman (Dublin, 1970)
AClon.	*The annals of Clonmacnoise, being annals of Ireland from the earliest period to A.D. 1408*, ed. Denis Murphy, trans. Conell Mageoghagan (Dublin, 1896)
AD	Archives Départementales
AFM	*Annala rioghachta Eireann: annals of the kingdom of Ireland by the Four Masters from the earliest period to the year 1616*, ed. John O'Donovan (7 vols, Dublin, 1851)
AI	*The annals of Inisfallen (MS Rawlinson B 503)*, ed. Seán Mac Airt (Dublin, 1951)
ALC	*The annals of Loch Cé. A chronicle of Irish affairs from A.D. 1014 to A.D. 1590*, ed. W. M. Hennessy, Rolls Series (2 vols, London, 1871)
Anal. Hib.	*Analecta Hibernica, including the reports of the Irish manuscripts commission* (Dublin, 1930–)
Ann. mon.	*Annales monastici*, ed. H. R. Luard, Rolls Series (5 vols, London, 1864–9)
ANS	*Anglo-Norman studies*, ed. R. A. Brown, Christopher Harper-Bill, Marjorie Chibnall *et al.* (Woodbridge, 1978–)
Archiv. Hib.	*Archivium Hibernicum: or Irish historical records* (Maynooth, 1912–)
AU	*Annala Uladh. Annals of Ulster, otherwise annala Senait, annals of Senat; a chronicle of Irish affairs, A.D. 431–1131, 1155–1541*, ed. Bartholomew Mac Carthy (4 vols, Dublin, 1893)
Bib. Mun.	Bibliothèque Municipale
BL	British Library
Bréifne	*Bréifne: journal of Cumann Seanchais Bhreifne* (Cavan, 1958–)
Cal. Carew MSS	*Calendar of the Carew manuscripts preserved in the archiepiscopal library at Lambeth, 1515–74* [etc.] (6 vols, London, 1867–73)
Cal. papal letters	*Calendar of entries in the papal registers relating to Great Britain and Ireland: papal letters, 1198–1304* [etc.] (12 vols, London, 1893–1933)

CCHR	*Calendar of the charter rolls, 1226–57* [etc.] (6 vols, London, 1903–1927)
CCR	*Calendar of the close rolls, 1272–9* [etc.] (47 vols, London, 1892–1963)
CDI	*Calendar of documents relating to Ireland preserved in Her Majesty's Public Record Office, London, 1171–1251* [etc.], ed. H. S. Sweetman and G. F. Handcock (5 vols, London, 1875–86)
CDS	*Calendar of documents relating to Scotland preserved in Her Majesty's Public Record Office, London,* 1108–1272 [etc.], *ed. Joseph Bain (4 vols, Edinburgh, 1881–8)*
CPR	*Calendar of the patent rolls, 1232–47* [etc.] (London, 1901–16)
Chartul. St Mary's, Dublin	*Chartularies of St Mary's Abbey, Dublin: with the register of its house at Dunbrody and annals of Ireland, 1162–1370*, ed. J. T. Gilbert, Rolls Series (2 vols, London, 1884–6)
Christ Church deeds	*Christ Church deeds*, ed. M. J. McEnery and Raymond Refaussé (Dublin, 2001)
Chron. Houedene	*Chronica magistri Rogeri de Houedene*, ed.William Stubbs, Rolls Series (4 vols, London, 1869–71)
Chron. maj.	Matthew Paris, *Chronica majora*, ed. H. R. Luard, Rolls Series (7 vols, London, 1872–83)
Chron. Mann	*Chronicle of the kings of Mann and the Isles*, ed. and trans. George Broderick and Brian Stowell (Edinburgh, 1973)
Early sources, ed. Anderson	Early sources of Scottish history, A.D. 500–1286, ed. A. O. Anderson (2 vols, Edinburgh, 1922)
EHR	*English Historical Review* (London, 1886–)
Éigse	*Éigse: a journal of Irish studies* (Dublin, 1939–)
Ériu	*Ériu: founded as the journal of the School of Irish Learning* (Dublin, 1904–)
Expug. Hib.	Giraldus Cambrensis, *Expugnatio Hibernica: the conquest of Ireland*, ed. A. B. Scott and F. X. Martin (Dublin, 1978)
Flores hist.	*Rogeri de Wendover liber qui dicitur Flores historiarum*, ed. H. G. Hewlett, Rolls Series (3 vols, London, 1886–9)
G.E.C. *Peerage*	G. E. Cockayne, *The Complete Peerage of England, Scotland, Ireland, Great Britain and the United Kingdom*, ed. Vicary Gibbs, H. A. Doubleday, Duncan Warrand, Lord Howard de Walden, G. H. White and R. S. Lea (2nd edn, 8 vols, London, 1910–59).
Gir. Camb. op.	*Giraldi Cambrensis opera*, ed. J. S. Brewer, J. F. Dimock and G. F. Warner, Rolls Series (8 vols, London, 1861–91)

Gorm. reg.	*Calendar of the Gormanston register: from the original in the possession of the Right Honourable the viscount of Gormanston*, ed. James Mills and M. J. McEnery (Dublin, 1916)
Hist. Albigensis	Peter des Vaux-de-Cernay, *Historia Albigensis*, trans. W. A. Sibly and M. D. Sibly (Woodbridge, 1998)
Hogan, *Onomasticon*	Edmund Hogan, *Onomasticon Goedelicum: locorum et tribuum Hiberniae et Scotiae. An index, with identifications, to the Gaelic names of places and tribes* (Dublin, 1910)
HWM	*The history of William Marshal, ed. A. J. Holden, Stewart Gregory and David Crouch (3 vols, London, 2002–6)*
IER	*Irish Ecclesiastical Record* (Dublin, 1864–)
IHS	*Irish Historical Studies: the joint journal of the Irish Historical Society and the Ulster Society for Irish Historical Studies* (Dublin, 1938–)
Ir. cartul. Llanthony	*The Irish cartularies of Llanthony Prima and Secunda*, ed. Eric St. John Brooks (Dublin, 1953)
JLAS	*Journal of the County Louth Archaeological Society* (Dundalk, 1904–)
JRSAI	*Journal of the Royal Society of Antiquaries of Ireland* (Dublin, 1892–)
MCB	*Miscellaneous Irish annals, A.D. 1114–1437 (MacCartaigh's book)*, ed. Séamus Ó hInnse (Dublin, 1947)
Med. relig. houses	Aubrey Gwynn and R. N. Hadcock, *Medieval religious houses: Ireland* (London, 1970)
Mon. Ang.	*William Dugdale, Monasticon Anglicanum (6 vols in 8, London, 1846)*
NA	*The National Archives*
NHI	T. W. Moody, T. D. Williams, J. C. Beckett and F. X. Martin (eds), *A new history of Ireland, under the auspices of the Royal Irish Academy* (9 vols, Dublin, 1968–2008)
NLI	National Library of Ireland
NRS	National Records of Scotland
ODNB	*Oxford dictionary of national biography* (60 vols, Oxford, 2004)
Ormond deeds	*Calendar of Ormond deeds*, ed. Edmund Curtis (6 vols, Dublin, 1932–43)
Orpen, *Normans*	G. H. Orpen, *Ireland under the Normans, 1169–1333* (4 vols, Oxford, 1911–20; 1 vol. repr., Dublin, 2005)
Otway-Ruthven, *Med. Ire.*	*A. J. Otway-Ruthven, A history of medieval Ireland (2nd edn, London, 1980)*

Past & Present	*Past & Present: a journal of historical studies* (London, 1952–)
Pat. rolls	*Patent rolls of the reign of Henry III, 1216–25* [etc.] (2 vols, London, 1901–3)
Pipe roll 3 [etc.] *John*	*The great roll of the pipe for the third* [etc.] *year of the reign of King John*, ed. D. M. Stenton, P. M. Barnes, Sidney Smith (Pipe Roll Society, new ser., London, 1936–55)
Pipe roll Ire. 1211–12	'The Irish pipe roll of 14 John, 1211–1212', ed. Oliver Davies and D. B. Quinn, *UJA*, 3rd ser., 4, suppl. (1941), 53–69
Pont. Hib.	*Pontificia Hibernica: medieval papal chancery documents concerning Ireland, A.D. 640–1261*, ed. M. P. Sheehy (2 vols, Dublin, 1962–5)
PRIA C	*Proceedings of the Royal Irish Academy, section C: archaeology, Celtic studies, history, linguistics and literature* (Dublin, 1902–)
PRO	Public Record Office
PRONI	Public Record Office of Northern Ireland
Red bk Kildare	*The red book of the earls of Kildare*, ed. Gearóid Mac Niocaill (Dublin, 1964)
Reeves, *Eccl. ant.*	William Reeves (ed.), *Ecclesiastical antiquities of Down, Connor and Dromore* (Dublin, 1850)
Reg. St Thomas	*Register of the abbey of St. Thomas, Dublin, ed. J. T. Gilbert, Rolls Series (London, 1889)*
Rev. Celt.	*Revue Celtique (41 vols, Paris and London, 1870–1924)*
RLC	*Rotuli litterarum clausarum, 1204–24 [etc.], ed. T. D. Hardy (2 vols, London, 1833–44)*
RLP	*Rotuli litterarum patentium, 1201–16, ed. T. D. Hardy (London, 1835)*
Rot. chart.	*Rotuli chartarum in Turri Londinensi asservati, 1199–1216* (London, 1837)
Rot. lib.	*Rotuli de liberate ac de misis et praestitis regnante Johanne*, ed. T. D. Hardy (London, 1844)
Rot. oblatis.	*Rotuli de oblatis et finibus in Turri Londinensi asservati tempore Regis Johannis*, ed. T. D. Hardy (London, 1835)
Rot. pat. Hib.	*Rotulorum patentium et clausorum cancellariae Hiberniae calendarium*, ed. Edward Tresham (4 vols, Dublin, 1828)
Rymer, *Foedera*	*Foedera, conventiones, litterae, et cujuscunque generis acta publica, inter regis Angliae et alios quosvis imperatores, reges, pontifices, principes, vel communitates*, ed. Thomas Rymer (4 vols in 7, London, 1816–30)

Scot. Hist. Rev.	*Scottish Historical Review* (Glasgow, 1903–28; 1947–)
Seanchas Ard Mhacha	*Seanchas Ard Mhacha: a journal of the Armagh Diocesan Historical Society (Armagh, 1954–)*
Speculum	*Speculum: a journal of medieval studies* (Cambridge, Mass., 1926–)
St A. lib.	*Liber cartarum prioratus Sancti Andree in Scotia, ed. Thomas Thomson, Bannatyne Club (Edinburgh, 1841)*
TDGNHAS	*Transactions of the Dumfriesshire and Galloway Natural History and Antiquarian Society* (Dumfries, 1862–)
UJA	*Ulster Journal of Archaeology* (Belfast, 1853–)

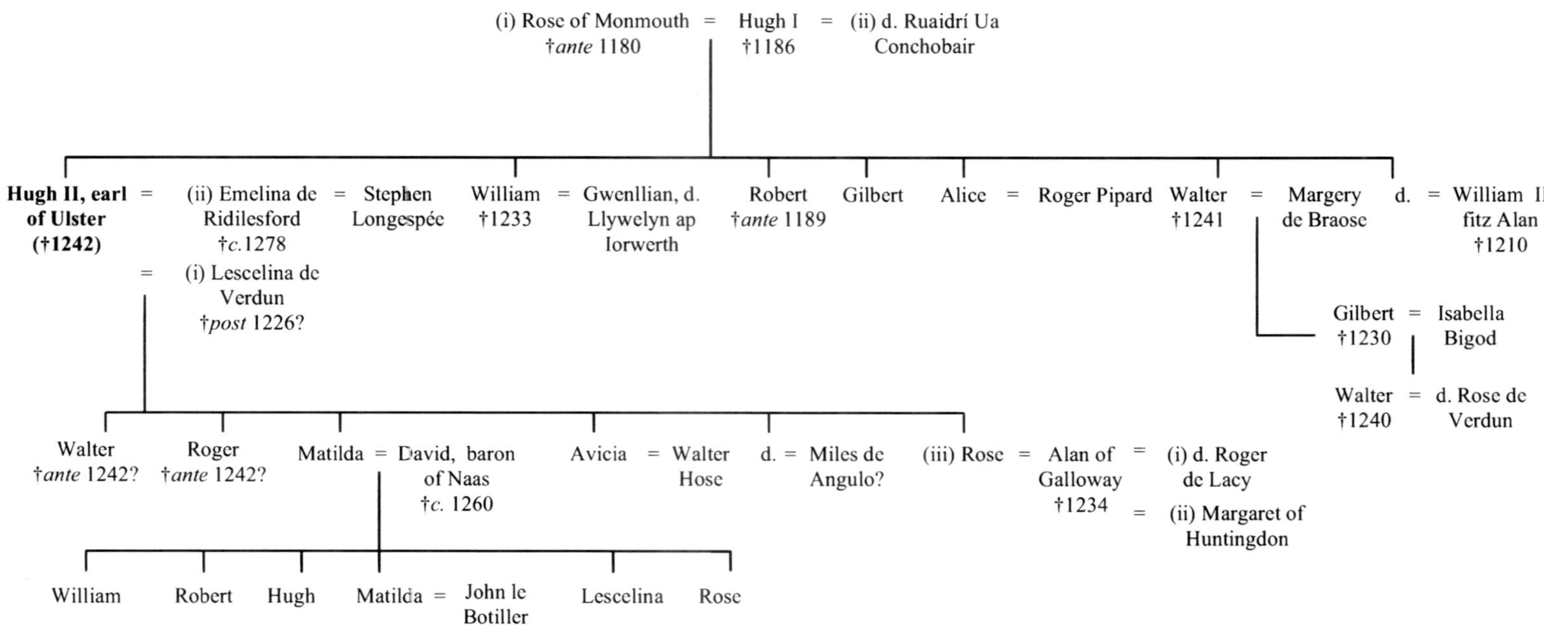

Figure 1: the family of Hugh II de Lacy (I)

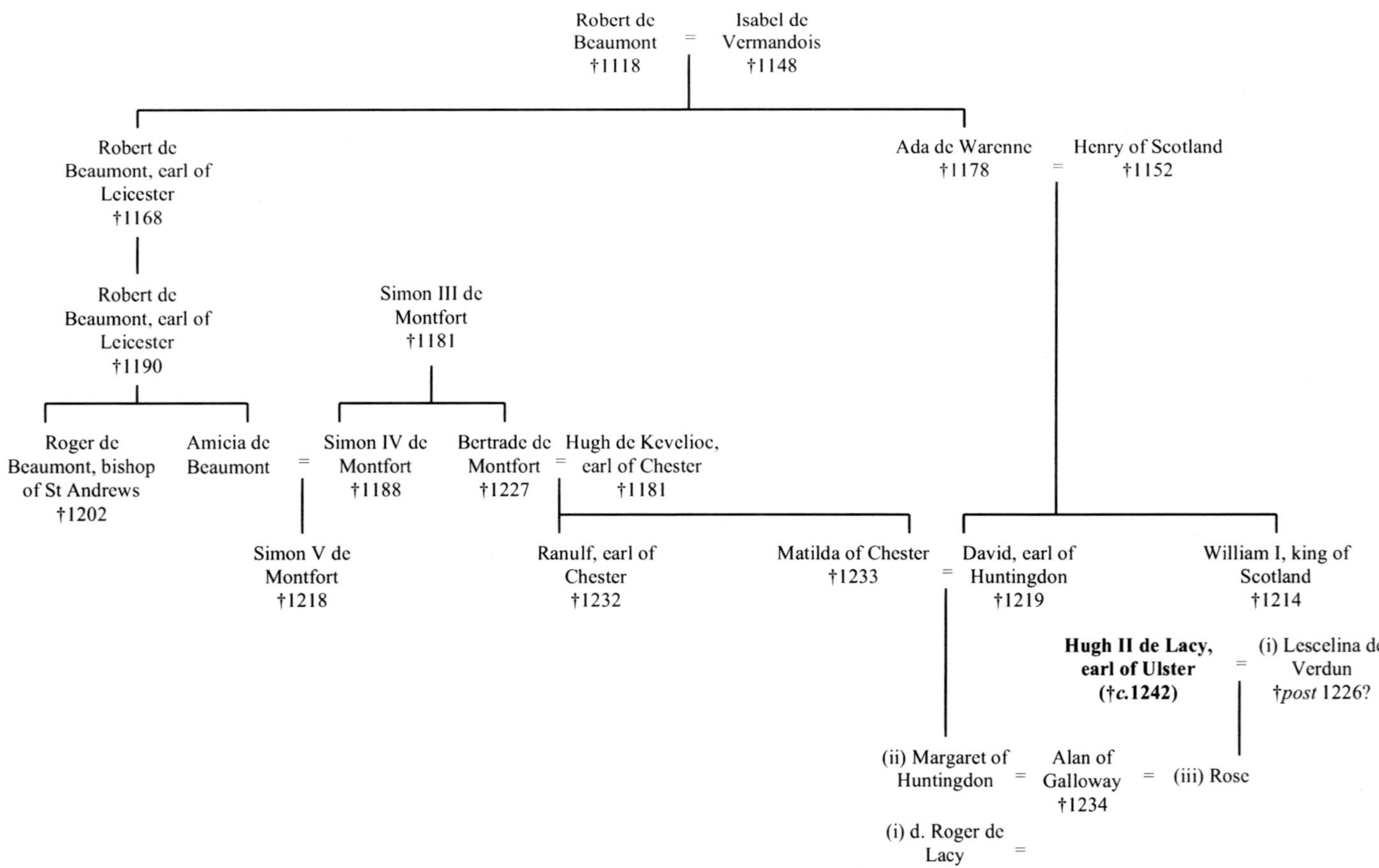

Figure 2: the family of Hugh II de Lacy (II)

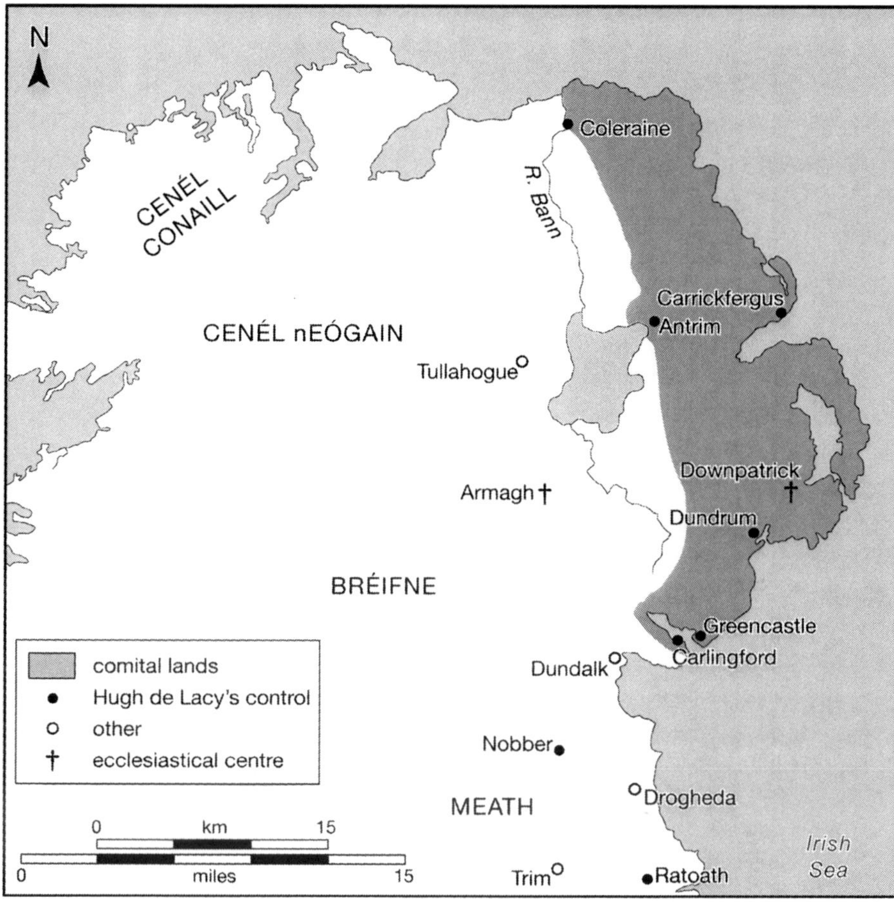

Map 1: The earldom of Ulster, c.1230

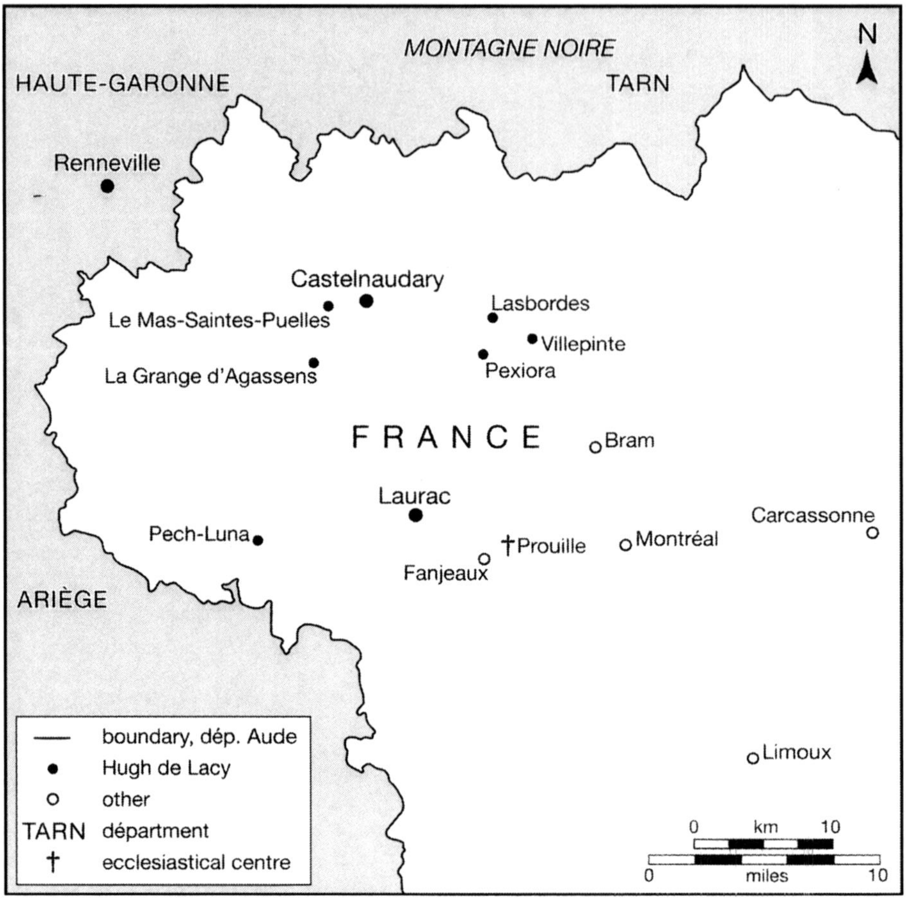

Map 2: De Lacy's French lands in context

Introduction

> Fellow soldiers, it is not a call to luxury and ease that has brought us to this land. Rather have we come to make trial of the vicissitudes of Fortune and to test the strength of our valour at the risk of our lives. For a while we were at the top of Fortune's wheel. Now we are sinking towards the bottom, but by reason of its very mutability we are destined to rise again to the top.[1]

A ubiquitous image in the Middle Ages, used by writers to make the course of events more intelligible, was the 'wheel of Fortune', raising men and women up to the apex of fame, wealth and power, or casting them back to earth and the terrestrial realities of ignominy, poverty and disgrace. Whether depicted in manuscript illustrations, narrative structures or literary trajectories, life was reduced to the three stages: ascent, supremacy and decline. All enjoyed highs and suffered lows, but it was the fates of the highborn which held most interest for a medieval audience. 'Nothing so interested the general populace, then as now, as to watch an individual fall, especially from great heights', writes James Bothwell.[2]

Few aristocratic lives in medieval Britain and Ireland displayed greater degrees of success and reversal than that of Hugh II de Lacy. Ascending from modest beginnings as a younger son of a celebrated Anglo-Norman adventurer, Hugh was the recipient of the first earldom in Angevin Ireland when he was created earl of Ulster by King John on 29 May 1205. But almost as swiftly as he had risen to prominence, Hugh fell foul of the crown and was banished from Ireland in 1210, joining the Albigensian crusade in southern France. Rise, supremacy and fall – except that de Lacy's story contained a fourth act. If the momentum of the *rota Fortunae* was beyond human control, on occasion the wheel could complete more than one revolution.[3] After two decades in the

1 Attributed by Giraldus Cambrensis to Maurice fitz Gerald (†1177) during the siege of Dublin (1171): *Expug. Hib.*, 80–1. For recurrences of the wheel of Fortune motif in Giraldus's work, see ibid., 26–7, 38–9, 86–7, 160–1, 224–7.

2 James Bothwell, *Falling from grace: reversal of fortune and the English nobility, 1075–1455* (Manchester, 2008), 4. See also, William Cook and Ronald Herzman, *The medieval world view: an introduction* (Oxford, 2004), 117–18; Alexander Murray, *Reason and society in the Middle Ages* (Oxford, 1978), 98–101; R. T. Lambdin and L. C. Lambdin (eds), *Encyclopedia of medieval literature* (Westport, CT, 2000), 379; Leslie Ross, *Medieval art: a topical dictionary* (Westport, CT, 1996), 264–5.

3 'If you try to stop the force of her turning wheel, you are the most foolish man alive': Boethius, *The consolation of philosophy*, trans. Richard Green (Indianapolis, 1962), 21–2.

political wilderness, Hugh was restored to his earldom in 1227 and retained it until his death, in late 1242 or early 1243.[4]

Despite its unique quality, Hugh de Lacy's career has yet to be subjected to a thorough scholarly examination. The sole monograph on Anglo-Norman Ulster, by T. E. McNeill, is now over thirty years old. While it advanced understanding of the earldom's organisation and archaeology, a wide-ranging chronological span and narrow geographical scope allowed the detail of Hugh de Lacy's career to be largely glossed over.[5] The most comprehensive treatment of thirteenth-century Ulster has been found in G. H. Orpen's *Ireland under the Normans*, first published over a century ago and constrained by the relatively shallow investigation permitted by a wide-ranging survey.[6] Recently, Colin Veach has updated and extended the standard work on the eleventh- and-twelfth-century de Lacys, by W. E. Wightman,[7] with his impressive study of Hugh I de Lacy (†1186) and his son, Walter (†1241), successive lords of Meath and heads of the Herefordshire familial branch.[8] What little is said of the earl of Ulster is cogently presented, but framed in relation to his father and elder brother, a 'loose-end' highlighted by one reviewer, in calling for 'a separate account of Anglo-Irish-French relations in the first half of the thirteenth century built around the career and ambitions of this fascinating man'.[9] Veach's focus on the aristocratic *familia* as the source of effective lordship, I would argue, has also led to a misconception concerning the intimacy of the association between Hugh II and his elder brother, Walter. It was fraternal competition, rather than solidarity, which best contextualises the younger Hugh's relentless pursuit of power.

4 News of Hugh's death reached King Henry III by 8 February 1243: *Close rolls, 1242–7*, 60; *CDI*, i, no. 2600; below, 201.

5 T. E. McNeill, *Anglo-Norman Ulster: the history and archaeology of an Irish barony* (Edinburgh, 1980). Other general surveys of the region include Ciaran Brady, Mary O'Dowd and Brian Walker (eds), *Ulster: an illustrated history* (London, 1989); J. P. Mallory and T. E. McNeill, *The archaeology of Ulster: from colonisation to plantation* (Belfast, 1991).

6 G. H. Orpen, *Ireland under the Normans, 1169–1333* (Oxford, 1911–20), 153–60, 409–27; idem, 'The earldom of Ulster (i)', *JRSAI* 43 (1913), 30–46, 133–43; (ii) 44 (1914), 51–66; (iii) 45 (1915), 123–42; (iv) 50 (1920), 167–77; (v) 51 (1921), 68–76.

7 W. E. Wightman, *The Lacy family in England and Normandy, 1066–1194* (Oxford, 1966).

8 Colin Veach, *Lordship in four realms: the Lacy family, 1166–1241* (Manchester, 2014). See also, idem, 'A question of timing: Walter de Lacy's seisin of Meath, 1189–94', *PRIA* C 109 (2009), 165–94; idem, 'King and magnate in medieval Ireland: Walter de Lacy, King Richard and King John', *IHS* 37, no. 146 (2010), 179–202. For other valuable treatments of Walter de Lacy's career, see Joe Hillaby, 'Colonisation, crisis management and debt: Walter de Lacy and the lordship of Meath, 1189–1241' *Ríocht na Mídhe: records of the Meath Archaeological and Historical Society* 8, no. 4 (1992/3), 1–50; idem, 'Hereford gold: Irish, Welsh and English land', *Transactions of the Woolhope Field Club (Herefordshire)* (i) 44, no. 3 (1984), 358–419; (ii) 45, no. 1 (1985), 193–270.

9 Brendan Smith, 'Review of Colin Veach, *Lordship in four realms: the Lacy family, 1166–1241* (Manchester, 2014)', *IHS* 39, no. 154 (2015), 338–9.

In historiography on the Angevin colony in Ireland the focus of scholarship has largely been trained on aristocratic adventurers other than Hugh II de Lacy, including John de Courcy, Ulster's first Anglo-Norman *conquistador*, under whom the fabric of the lordship was woven between 1177 and 1205.[10] The career of de Courcy's usurper, Hugh de Lacy, is hardly less intriguing: he had his own connections with the sea-going lords of the Irish Sea region; battled with heretics in southern France; joined rebellions in Wales and Galloway; and cultivated a network of allies and contacts from the Hebrides to the Pyrenees. Hugh's description in a fifteenth-century Scottish chronicle as 'the most powerful of the English in Ireland' (*potentissimus Anglorum in Hibernia*) was at least periodically fitting.[11]

De Lacy's immediate sphere of operation was Ireland, and his hand can be seen in many of the key set-pieces underpinning the history of the nascent colony: the baronial crisis of 1207–08; King John's Irish expedition of 1210; Hugh's rebellion of 1223–24; the 'murder' of Richard Marshal, earl of Pembroke, in 1234; and the re-conquest of Connacht in 1235–36. Hugh's activities beyond Ireland have also begun to be better understood.[12] An advantage of biography is that it can move through the geographical boundaries constricting regional-specific studies as fluidly as members of the thirteenth-century aristocratic elite itinerated through contemporary territorial limits. Historians of medieval Ireland have long been aware of Ulster's significance as a 'wedge' between the 'old Gaelic world of Erin and Alba',[13] but even after its conquest in the twelfth century and constitution as an earldom under Hugh de Lacy, the north-east of Ireland continued to form part of the 'maritime orbit'[14] encircling the Western Isles, Galloway, Man and parts of northern England.

Through the study of one magnate it is possible to bring a fresh perspective to the much-trampled themes of power and identity. The scholarly neglect of Hugh de Lacy's career may be partly explained by a lingering perception

10 Seán Duffy, 'The first Ulster plantation: John de Courcy and the men of Cumbria', in T. B. Barry, Robin Frame and Katharine Simms (eds), *Colony and frontier in medieval Ireland: essays presented to J. F. Lydon* (London, 1995), 1–27; M. T. Flanagan, 'John de Courcy, the first Ulster plantation and Irish church men', in Brendan Smith (ed.), *Britain and Ireland, 900–1300: insular responses to medieval European change* (Cambridge, 1999), 154–79; Steve Flanders, *De Courcy: Anglo-Normans in Ireland, England and France in the eleventh and twelfth centuries* (Dublin, 2008).

11 *Scotichronicon, by Walter Bower*, ed. D. E. R. Watt (9 vols, St Andrews, 1994), iv, 460–1.

12 See, for example, the recent survey of de Lacy's exile, in Paul Duffy, "*Ung sage et valent home*': Hugh de Lacy and the Albigensian crusade', *JRSAI* 141 (2014), 66–90.

13 Edmund Curtis, cited in Keith Stringer, 'Periphery and core in thirteenth-century Scotland: Alan son of Roland, lord of Galloway and constable of Scotland', in Alexander Grant (ed.), *Medieval Scotland: crown, lordship and community* (Edinburgh, 1998), 82–113, at 87.

14 Robin Frame, 'Lordship and liberties in Ireland and Wales, c. 1170–c. 1360', in Huw Pryce and John Watts (eds), *Power and identity in the Middle Ages: essays in memory of Rees Davies* (Oxford, 2007), 125–52, at 125.

of Ulster as a marginal constituent of the Angevin empire. Robin Frame's recent study of lordship in Ireland and Wales passes over the earldom of Ulster, 'which was remote from the main centres of royal power in Ireland'.[15] This may be true, but the earldom's exclusion from scholarly surveys can only lead to distorted, incomplete or inaccurate conclusions about the definition of royal and seigneurial power. One accepted paradigm is that baronial jurisdictions in twelfth- and thirteenth-century Ireland were being steadily eroded in competition with those of the crown. In being granted the earldom of Ulster in 1205, however, Hugh de Lacy was more liberally enfranchised than any of his peers. If the Irish colony was increasingly moulded by the 'politics of the metropolis',[16] the process of royal encroachment on private enterprise was not unbroken.

It is exactly Ulster's separateness which makes it so valuable for an understanding of crown/noble interaction. Lords of remote outposts in the Plantagenet dominions were unable to attend court regularly, and were often excluded from the 'golden circle' of men surrounding the king.[17] At the same time, a view of royal power atrophying as it rippled to geographical extremities ignores the fact that those closest to the king could be so enthralled in royal control that they were unable to pursue independent courses of action or forge their own fates. In 1224 the royal justiciar in Ireland was prevented from pursuing Hugh de Lacy into Ulster by 'densities of mountains and woods'.[18] This was a place where, by virtue of its topography and geography alone, mechanisms of royal control and discipline broke down. With no lands outside Ireland, a magnate such as Hugh de Lacy could not easily be subjected to distraint or financial exaction. As more strands making up the 'web of proprietorship' connecting noble families are uncovered,[19] we are reminded that landholding in mainland Britain was not a prerequisite for power. Indeed, it was partly the earl of Ulster's agitation beyond the reach of royal institutions that caused King John to cross to Ireland personally in 1210.

The crown remained the principal conduit for advancement in the Irish colony, but power also 'flowed along additional channels'.[20] Colonists usually acted in concert with royal policy, but the expansion or retraction of the Anglo-Norman conquest – the blood-spattered detail of its history – was dictated by individuals pursuing their own agendas and imposing their wills on others, whether *Hibernici*

15 Ibid., 125–38, at 125n.

16 Robin Frame, 'England and Ireland, 1171–1369', in idem, *Ireland and Britain, 1170–1450* (London, 1998), 15–30, at 17.

17 Bothwell, *Falling from grace*, 6.

18 *Ann. mon.*, iii, 91 (Dunstable annals), and below, 159–60.

19 Beth Hartland, 'English landholding in Ireland', in Michael Prestwich, Richard Britnell and Robin Frame (eds), *Thirteenth century England X: proceedings of the Durham conference, 2003* (Woodbridge, 2005), 119–29, at 119.

20 Frame, 'Lordship and liberties', 138.

or *Anglici*. However highly someone was held in royal esteem, he or she could not be considered powerful unless they could make effective alliances, attract supporters, inspire loyalty, subdue opponents and impose military dominance. The expansion or retraction of Hugh de Lacy's influence depended on his ability to fulfil these criteria; despite his endowment with a comital title, Hugh's actual power in Ulster was hamstrung by local conditions, whether a scarcity of allies, the opposition of native Irish or the enmity of churchmen.

The 'postcolonial dilemma' has been defined as 'the inability of those hybrid beings who live in the aftermath of conquest to find a secure category of selfhood to which to belong'.[21] The extent to which such a crisis of identity existed among the settlers in Ireland is questionable. While conscious of different ethnic groupings, many of the early colonists clearly perceived themselves as English.[22] Nevertheless, if John Gillingham may be justified in calling for the idea of a 'Norman' conquest of Ireland to be consigned to the rubbish heap,[23] the career of Hugh de Lacy reminds us that in frontier zones and 'hybrid geographies' such as Ulster,[24] identity could be a fluid concept. In 1237 one of Hugh's charters, to Newry Abbey, referred to the 'coming of the English to Ireland'.[25] But de Lacy was also part of the northern French elite prosecuting the Albigensian crusade, and joined the faction of 'foreign' courtiers surrounding the young Henry III. How confidently could someone who held no land in England, and rarely attended court, identify himself as 'English'?[26]

The attention afforded to Hugh de Lacy in some English chronicles may be partly attributable to his perception as 'other'.[27] Those on the edges of society fascinated contemporary commentators, perhaps most visibly in the miraculous tales of Irish flora and fauna related by Giraldus Cambrensis,[28] but also to a lesser degree in Hugh de Lacy's appearances in 'monastic' chronicles. Bound up in conceptions of the native Irish as a *gens barbara* was the connection of the unfamiliar with immoral behaviour.[29] The same prejudice may be seen in

21 J. J. Cohen, *Hybridity, identity and monstrosity in medieval Britain: on difficult middles* (Basingstoke, 2006), 83.

22 M. T. Flanagan, 'Defining nations in medieval Ireland', in Hirokazu Tsurushima (ed.), *Nations in medieval Britain* (Donington, 2010), 104–21.

23 John Gillingham, 'Normanizing the English invaders of Ireland', in Pryce and Watts (eds), *Power and identity in the Middle Ages*, 85–97.

24 Cohen, *Hybridity, identity and monstrosity*, 2.

25 Appendix I, no. 29.

26 In the absence of a more convincing taxonomy, I shall continue to use the problematic term 'Anglo-Norman', except where 'Hiberno-Norman' is used to differentiate the baronial community in Ireland from that in England.

27 *Ann. mon.*, iii (Dunstable annals), 75, 91–3; *Memoriale fratris Walteri de Coventria*, ed. William Stubbs, Rolls Series (2 vols, London, 1872–3), ii, 202; *Flores hist.*, iii, 80–7; *Chron. maj.*, iii, 365.

28 Cohen, *Hybridity, identity and monstrosity*, 77–109.

29 *Expug. Hib.*, xxvii–xxxi.

Matthew Paris's association of Hugh de Lacy with the Gaelic nobility of Galloway and their blood-drinking rituals,[30] or the salacious report of the Dunstable annalist that de Lacy had cast aside his rightful wife in favour of an 'adulteress'.[31]

By the thirteenth century some of the unity of purpose felt by the early colonists in Ireland had begun to dissipate.[32] Competition for land intensified, exacerbated by the crown's encouragement of factional infighting and the recurring importation of royal *curiales*. The cohesiveness of the aristocratic community was also being undermined by the same factors threatening honorial integrity in England: divided landholding and multiple tenure.[33] As the initial impetus towards conquest subsided, the need for collective identity diminished and it became more important for individuals to fashion their own sense of self. For some living close to centres of culture, identity could be constricting, 'bringing with it immutable rules of behaviour and lifestyle'.[34] Conversely, those existing in cultural margins were at liberty to add layers to the 'self', creating, assuming and cultivating *personae*. Hugh de Lacy presented himself in ways which would connote authority to an Irish audience. A parallel might be drawn between Hugh's violent incursions into central Ulster in 1206–07, for example, and the 'first adventure' expected of inaugurated Irish kings.[35] It was as a member of the Angevin elite, however, that Hugh was most eager to present himself. One of the devices best suited to self-creation was the 'linguistic idiom', and Hugh underlined his comital rank through the conscious manipulation of charter diplomatic, in imitation of royal formulae and protocol.[36]

For the earl of Ulster's career we are unable to rely on the 'rich flotsam of documentation' available to the biographer of the younger Simon de Montfort.[37] Nonetheless, useful material is not in short supply. Hugh de Lacy's political maturity coincided with the proliferation of written records being produced and preserved by the English chancery and exchequer.[38] 'In 1199', writes Nicholas Vincent, 'the documentary floodgates burst, and we are swiftly overwhelmed by a torrent of rolls, registers, schedules and other such wonders'.[39] It is primarily

30 *Chron. maj.*, iii, 365.

31 *Ann. mon.*, iii, 91–2.

32 For the distinctive settler identity, see Flanagan, 'Defining nations', 104–21.

33 See below, 20, 27, 34, 38–9, 49, 165, 184–7, 200.

34 Miri Rubin, 'Identities', in Rosemary Horrox and W. M. Ormrod (eds), *A social history of England, 1200–1500* (Cambridge, 2006), 383–412, at 384.

35 See below, 60.

36 Rubin, 'Identities', 396. For the imitation of royal charter protocols, see below, 53–4.

37 J. R. Maddicott, *Simon de Montfort* (Cambridge, 1994), xiv.

38 D. A. Carpenter, 'The English royal chancery in the thirteenth century', in Adrian Jobson (ed.), *English government in the thirteenth century* (Woodbridge, 2004), 49–69; M. T. Clanchy, *From memory to written record: England, 1066–1307* (3rd edn, Chichester, West Sussex, 2013), ch. 2.

39 Nicholas Vincent, 'Why 1199? Bureaucracy and enrolment under John and his contemporaries', in Jobson (ed.), *English government in the thirteenth century*, 17–49, at 17. For evidence pointing to

through synthesis of these records that interactions between crown and colonist are illuminated. Unfortunately, the fire which destroyed the Public Record Office of Ireland, in 1922, also consumed most extant records of the medieval administration in Ireland,[40] denying us recourse to documents which might have helped to fill the frequent and sizeable lacunae in the English rolls.[41]

Remaining aware of textual traditions, interpolations and inaccuracies, the Irish (as well as Welsh, Manx and Scottish) annals are invaluable in helping to trace de Lacy's military manoeuvrings and encounters with indigenous polities. While at times frustratingly silent, annalistic sources often provide details not found anywhere else. We would be entirely unaware of Hugh's expulsion from Ulster at the hands of the Irish in 1238 were it not for *Mageoghagan's book*, a seventeenth-century compilation probably based on earlier (now lost) material.[42] So-called 'Anglo-Irish' annals from the later colonial period are also useful, but the dubious tradition surrounding Hugh de Lacy's sojourn at the Norman abbey of St Taurin, in 1210, sounds a cautionary note about their authenticity.[43] Narrative sources are a colourful addition to the documentary corpus, but their value tends to be compromised by authors' subjectivity. Hugh's chivalric depiction in the contemporary biography of William Marshal, lord of Leinster and earl of Pembroke (†1219), owes much to the creativity of its chief informant, John of Earley, whom de Lacy rescued from royal forces in 1208.[44] Hugh is also a protagonist in one of the vibrant narratives of the Albigensian crusade, but his literary persona was at least partially constructed as a stylistic device, variously to criticise or advertise the ideals and motives of the crusaders.[45]

Perhaps the most valuable window onto de Lacy's activity is provided by his baronial *acta*. Outside Ireland collections of charters have long been recognised

an earlier genesis for some of the rolls, see D. A. Carpenter, '*In testimonium factorum brevium*: the beginnings of the English chancery rolls', in Nicholas Vincent (ed.), *Records, administration and aristocratic society in the Anglo-Norman realm: papers commemorating the 800th anniversary of King John's loss of Normandy* (Woodbridge, 2009), 1–29. For a rebuttal of this argument, see Nicholas Vincent, 'The record of 1204', in idem (ed.), *Records, administration and aristocratic society*, xvi–iii.

40 A notable exception is the Irish pipe roll from 1211–12, transcribed by Sir James Ware in the seventeenth century, which provides an invaluable snapshot of the Irish colony in the aftermath of King John's Irish expedition of 1210: *Pipe roll Ire. 1211–12*. The reconstruction of the lost records of the Irish chancery, by the CIRCLE project (https://chancery.tcd.ie), unfortunately begins in 1244, just after Hugh de Lacy's death.

41 For King John's reign, the regnal years 1–5, 10–13 are missing in the close rolls; 1–2, 11–13 in the patent rolls; 3–4, 11–13 in the charter rolls; 4–5, 8, 10–14 in the oblate and fine rolls; 1, 4, 6–18 in the liberate rolls; 15, 18 in the pipe rolls; 2–9, 11–18 in the memoranda rolls; 1–6, 8, 10–11, 13 in the prestita rolls; 1–10, 12–13, 15–18 in the misae rolls.

42 *AClon.*, 1238, and below, 199–200.

43 See below, 117–18.

44 *HWM*, ii, ll. 13763–85, and below, 97, 100, 112n.

45 *The song of the Cathar wars: a history of the Albigensian crusade*, ed. and trans. Janet Shirley (Aldershot, 2000); see also, below, ch. 4.

as an invaluable tool for the researcher.[46] It is only through the ordering and comparison of these instruments that patterns emerge, shifting affinities can be traced, sub-tenancies mapped and strategies of lordship analysed. To date there has been no attempt to collate the charters of Hugh de Lacy (or any other earls and lords of Ulster).[47] None of Hugh's original *acta* is extant, but thirty such instruments can be reconstructed using transcripts preserved in ecclesiastical and lay cartularies, royal inspeximuses, records of military orders and the copybooks of antiquarians. These, with the earl's lost *acta*, are provided in an appendix, and represent the foundation upon which the following study is constructed.

46 *Earldom of Gloucester charters: the charters and scribes of the earls and countesses of Gloucester to A.D. 1217*, ed. R. B. Patterson (Oxford, 1973); *The charters of the Anglo-Norman earls of Chester, c. 1071–1237*, ed. Geoffrey Barraclough (Chester, 1988); *The acts of Welsh rulers, 1120–1283*, ed. Huw Pryce (Cardiff, 2005); *Charters of the honour of Mowbray, 1107–91*, ed. D. E. Greenway (London, 1972); *The acts and letters of the Marshal family: marshals of England and earls of Pembroke, 1145–1248*, ed. David Crouch, Camden Fifth Series 47 (Cambridge, 2015).

47 In Ireland we are still 'behind in charter scholarship, and what might be called feudal prosopography', over two decades after the indictment was made: Robin Frame, 'Aristocracies and the political configuration of the British Isles', in R. R. Davies (ed.), *The British Isles, 1100–1500: comparisons, contrasts and connections* (Edinburgh, 1988), 142–59, at 144.

1

Beginnings

Birth, brotherhood and the burden of lineage

'Origins', stated Donnchadh Ó Corráin of the genealogical tradition in medieval Ireland, 'are not simply origins'. Once ignored or dismissed as antiquarian indulgences, this vast body of royal pedigrees, king-lists and poetic panygyric is now recognised as having served a very real service for its patrons as the proving documents of power. In a society where authority was largely based on dynastic credentials, 'an origin is the demand the present makes upon the past, not knowledge for its own sake – a much more recent historical pretence'.[1] This function of historical writing, as architect as well as record of the past, was also easily recognisable to the Anglo-Norman world which provided the incomers to Ireland after 1169, in which prestige and property descended in vertical lines, and for whom *lignage* was an equally pervasive preoccupation. National pseudo-histories gave roots to the authority of post-Conquest kings of England by connecting them with a legendary British past. Genealogies of noble families, fusing romance with record, claimed dignity for their sponsors by emphasising contiguity with their progenitors.[2]

If a burden could be placed on memory by the present, however, so too an origin could be a mandate of the past on the here and now. Individual agency in medieval Britain and Ireland was often shaped by a concern with living up to, or living down, one's ancestors. When inherent characteristics of nobility were believed to pass from generation to generation, consanguinity with an illustrious forebear was still the basic qualification of nobility, and 'no ceremony could make up for the lack of exalted blood-lines'.[3] The inheritance of moral as well as physical qualities was also accepted in Gaelic Ireland. In the first recension of the epic *Táin bó Cúailnge* ('The cattle-raid of Cooley'), the antagonist Medb, queen of Connacht, lists Maine 'Cotageib Uile' ('grasp them all') among her seven sons: *is éside tuc cruth a máthar & a athar & a n-ordan díb*

1 Donnchadh Ó Corráin, 'Creating the past: the early Irish genealogical tradition, Carroll Lecture 1992', *Peritia* 12 (1998), 177–208, quotations at 185.

2 John Spence, *Re-imagining history in Anglo-Norman prose chronicles* (Woodbridge, 2013).

3 Constance Brittain Bouchard, *Those of my blood: constructing noble families in medieval Francia* (Philadelphia, PA, 2001), 5.

línaib ('he it is who has inherited the appearance of his mother and father and the dignity of them both').[4]

Membership of a noble family was in this way double-edged. Deference or allegiance could be claimed simply by virtue of one's name, and even before his leading role in Anglo-Norman intervention in Ireland, Richard de Clare (Strongbow) was already 'set apart by his ancestry, born of the noble stock of the Clare family'.[5] The encumbrance of *gentillece* as a birthright, however, was that an ancestor's characteristics and abilities were expected to be replicated by his progeny.[6] Nobility without works was stillborn, and it was partly the moral imperative of high birth that drove men like Strongbow – who before his acquisition of Leinster had 'a great name rather than great prospects'[7] – to risk their lives along the frontiers of the Angevin empire. Like the 'melodious bardisms' composed for Irish kings,[8] the Anglo-Norman *cantilenae*, immortalising the heroic deeds of fallen kinsmen, could be as much inspirational templates for future action as commemorations of past glories.[9] In light of his own pedigree as son of a major player on the twelfth-century stage, the early career of Hugh II de Lacy must also have been at least partly conditioned by the burden of lineage. The brief genealogical record of the de Lacys in Ireland preserved in the register of the abbey of St Thomas, Dublin, remembers Hugh I de Lacy as *primus conquestor* of Meath and Hugh II as conqueror of Ulster.[10] What the memorandum cannot tell us, however, is to what extent the achievements of the son were inspired by those of the father.

The English dimension of the de Lacys, deriving their name from Lassy in Normandy (dép. Calvados), was added by the brothers, Ilbert (†1093) and Walter (†1085), whose participation in the Norman Conquest of England saw them established with the respective honors of Pontefract (Yorkshire) and Weobley (Herefordshire). It was Walter's descendants who showed the greatest appetite for further conquest, extending their control in the Welsh march from their base at Ewyas (Lacy) and seeking additional rewards across

4 Cecile O'Rahilly, *Táin bó* Cúailnge: recension 1 (Dublin, 1976), 6, 129.

5 *Expug. Hib.*, 54–5.

6 David Crouch, *The birth of nobility: constructing aristocracy in England and France, 900–1300* (Harlow, 2005), 125–8.

7 *Expug. Hib.*, 54–5.

8 'At ale poems are chanted, fine [genealogical] ladders are climbed, melodious bardisms modulate through pools of liquor the name of Áed' (ninth-century poem in praise of a Leinster dynast): Whitley Stokes and John Strachan (eds), *Thesaurus paleohibernicus: a collection of Old-Irish glosses, scholia, prose and verse* (2 vols, Cambridge, 1901–10), ii, 295.

9 Georges Duby, 'Youth in aristocratic society', in idem, *The chivalrous society*, trans. Cynthia Postan (London, 1977), 113–22.

10 *Reg. St Thomas*, 419–20. A more chronologically extensive but inaccurate family genealogy was compiled at the priory of Llanthony Secunda (Gloucester): *Mon. Ang.*, vi, pt 1, 135–6.

the Irish Sea.[11] Head of the Herefordshire branch by 1166, Hugh I de Lacy joined the retinue of Henry II crossing to Ireland in 1171, where in the next year he was granted the Irish kingdom of Mide (anglicised Meath).[12] The success of Hugh's conquest in the Irish midlands and his preeminent position among the first colonists is reflected by his description, in 1184, as *tigearna Gall Eireann* – 'lord of the Foreigners of Ireland'.[13] Hugh's supremacy was fleeting, however, and in 1186, as he inspected one of his castles at Durrow (Co. Offaly), his head was cut off by an axe-wielding Irishman at the instigation of a disgruntled local king, 'and he fell, both head and body, into the ditch of the castle'.[14]

For those aspiring aristocrats without the means to commission genealogies, a link between the living and the dead could be made in that 'most ubiquitous Anglo-Norman document',[15] the Latin charter of property or privilege. Both Hugh II de Lacy and his older brother, Walter, dedicated grants for the souls of their father and mother in the *pro anima* clauses of their early charters.[16] An even clearer statement of contiguity was made by the younger sibling in his employment of the personal style, *Hugo de Lacy filius Hugonis de Lacy*.[17] But if Hugh II could claim distinction from peers by association with his father, the name they shared was also a yardstick against which the son's career would be measured.[18] 'When a man claimed noble lineage', notes David Crouch, 'he had to demonstrate the qualities which he claimed ran in his blood'.[19] Among the merits of the elder Hugh, estimated by Giraldus, were his steadfast and temperate character; careful handling of private and public affairs; and familiarity with *militaribus negociis* – the 'business of war'.[20] The chief currency of nobility was land, and the greatest challenge for Hugh II would be to emulate his father's success as a transnational magnate. Like his kinsman, Strongbow, Hugh 'had

11 The family's Norman estates were held from the bishop of Bayeux: Wightman, *Lacy family*, 136, 195–227.

12 Veach, *Lordship*, ch. 1.

13 MCB, 1184.

14 *ALC*, 1186. The deed was apparently orchestrated by the king of Tethba: *AFM*, 1186. In 1195 Hugh's body was removed from Durrow to Bective abbey in Meath, while his head was interred at the abbey of St Thomas, Dublin, alongside his first wife, Rose of Monmouth (†before 1180): James Grace, *Annales Hiberniae*, ed. Richard Butler, Irish Archaeological Society (Dublin, 1842), *s.a.* 1195; *Chartul. St Mary's, Dublin*, ii, *s.a.* 1195. Following a lengthy dispute between Bective and St Thomas's, in 1205 Hugh's body was translated to Dublin and reunited with his head: *Reg. St Thomas*, 348–50.

15 M. T. Flanagan, 'Strategies of lordship in pre-Norman and post-Norman Leinster', in *ANS* 20, 107–26, at 107.

16 Appendix I, nos 2–3, 5–6; Veach, *Lordship*, 263.

17 Appendix I, no. 2.

18 The name also recalled Hugh, lord of Lassy (†1085), the family's Norman progenitor.

19 Crouch, *Nobility*, 128.

20 *Expug. Hib.*, 192–3.

succeeded to a name rather than possessions'.[21] In seeking the material evidence of nobility, however, he first had to circumnavigate the obstacle presented by his own family.

For three years after his death, Hugh I de Lacy's vast assemblage of estates in Normandy, England, Wales and Ireland was held in wardship by the crown, before descending to the eldest surviving son, Walter, c.1189.[22] By a circuitous route, the de Lacy succession conformed with what is often assumed to have been the dominant mode of inheritance in the twelfth-century insular Angevin dominions, whereby an eldest son took sole charge of his father's lands. In fact, recent scholarship has shown that the triumph of primogeniture was not assured until the late thirteenth century. Before then, it was quite common for property to be partitioned among multiple heirs, as noblemen weighed concerns for the integrity of their estates against the moral responsibility to provide for their children.[23] In 1219, shortly before his death, William Marshal, earl of Pembroke and lord of Leinster, divided the bulk of his transmarine hegemony among three of his five sons.[24] This kind of deathbed planning was a luxury not afforded to Hugh I de Lacy, whose assassination in 1186 disturbed any plans he may have had to provide generously for his younger sons.[25]

Contemporary legal theorists may have stressed the advantages of primogeniture in protecting the integrity of familial lands, but the most effective barrier to the fragmentation of estates remained the hesitation of living heads of aristocratic families to grant away land, and with it, power.[26] After his succession, it was Walter de Lacy's responsibility to allocate his possessions among his younger siblings. The relatively parsimonious manner in which he did so may challenge

21 Ibid., 54–5. Rose, mother of Hugh II, was a daughter of the Welsh marcher lord, Baderon of Monmouth (†1176). Her cousin, Richard de Clare (Strongbow), lord of Striguil, had been deprived of his earldom of Pembroke by Henry II in 1154.

22 Veach, 'A question of timing', 165–94. An elder son, Robert, appears in two of Hugh I's early *acta*, but was presumably deceased before Walter succeeded in 1189: Veach, *Lordship*, 78–9. A younger son, Robert, was active in Meath before his death in 1206: *AClon.*, 1206 ('Robert delacie, son of Hugh delacie, died'). The witness to charters of Hugh II in 1207 must therefore have been the Robert de Lacy (of uncertain relationship to the family) granted Rathwire (Co. Westmeath) by Hugh I: appendix I, nos 12–13; *The deeds of the Normans in Ireland: la geste des Engleis en Yrlande*, ed. Evelyn Mullally (Dublin, 2002), ll. 3148–9; *The song of Dermot and the earl: an Old French poem from the Carew manuscript no. 596 in the archiepiscopal library at Lambeth palace*, ed. and trans. G. H. Orpen (Oxford, 1892), ll. 3150–1.

23 Crouch, *Nobility*, 98–119.

24 'He then provided for his children, dividing up and bequeathing them, as his heart prompted him': *HWM*, ii, ll. 18136–9.

25 Hugh's father, Gilbert, had divided his possessions among his three sons. The reassembling of the patrimony in Normandy, England and Wales under Hugh I was only made possible by the death of his elder brother, Robert, before 1162: Veach, *Lordship*, 22–5.

26 K. B. McFarlane, *The nobility of later medieval England: the Ford lectures for 1953 and related studies* (Oxford, 1973), 63.

some existing scholarly presuppositions about the de Lacy fraternity, at least calling to mind McFarlane's observation that noblemen 'did not often fall into King Lear's error'.[27]

In elite Anglo-Norman society the family could be 'a solidarity, a group which co-operated for the benefit of its members, offering protection and the redress of wrongs, a set of conventions by which land could be transmitted from one generation to the next, and a focus for affective relationships'.[28] Hugh II de Lacy probably took his first political steps as an itinerant member of his elder brother's retinue, and the barons of Meath provided the military support for Hugh's early acquisitive forays in Connacht, Uriel and Ulster.[29] The de Lacys at times functioned as a cohesive political body, most transparently as part of the baronial faction in opposition to the king's justiciar, Meiler fitz Henry, in 1207–08.[30] An emotional bond can also be seen in the name Walter, given to one of Hugh II's sons.[31] This said, treatments of family as a 'self-evident unit' can lead to inattention towards individual agency and identity, and care must be taken not to overstress the depth of kin-feeling.[32] The recent assessment of the de Lacy brothers as 'almost inseparable politically'[33] strays perilously close to the 'vision of unity and cooperation' characterising fictional portrayals of brothers in the medieval period.[34] In the Middle English version of the popular romance, *Amis and Amiloun*, based on a lost Anglo-Norman poem, the physically identical protagonists express the depth of their friendship by entering into a covenant of blood-brotherhood, pledging mutual loyalty and fidelity:

> That bothe bi day and bi night,
> In wele and wo, in wrong and right,
> That thai schuld frely fond
> To hold togider at everi nede,
> In word, in werk, in wille, in dede.[35]

27 Ibid.

28 J. A. Green, *The aristocracy of Norman England* (Cambridge, 1997), 329–30.

29 See below, 33, 50, 59.

30 Crouch, *Nobility*, 141–6. For joint appearances of Hugh and Walter in charters from the period before 1210, see *Ir. cartul. Llanthony*, 33–4, 110; *Ormond deeds*, i, 5–6, 42; *Reg. St Thomas, Dublin*, 42; *Chartul. St Mary's, Dublin*, i, 146–8; *Gorm. reg.*, 163. For appearances of Walter de Lacy in Hugh's *acta*, see appendix III. For Hugh's appearances in early charters of Walter de Lacy, see *Ormond deeds*, i, 359; *Reg. St Thomas*, 11–12.

31 See below, 162, 167, 200–1.

32 Bouchard, *Those of my blood*, 2.

33 Veach, *Lordship*, 265.

34 Matthew Howard, '"We are broderen"': fraternal bonds and familial loyalty within the fifteenth-century romance of Generydes', in Isabel Davis, Miriam Müller and Sarah Rees Jones (eds), *Love, marriage and family ties in the later Middle Ages* (Turnhout, 2003), 129–42, at 129.

35 *Amis and Amiloun, Robert of Cisyle and Sir Amadace*, ed. Edward Foster (2nd edn, Kalamazoo, 1997), ll. 148–52.

When 'wele' turned to 'wo' for the de Lacys, the bond of brotherhood counted for very little. Blood could be thinner than gold or soil, and when his lordship of Meath came under threat of confiscation by the crown, in 1210, Walter de Lacy was prepared to offer up his younger brother in order to divert the king's anger from himself. Hugh's Irish rebellion of 1223–24, during which he and his half-brother, William *Gorm*, forcibly occupied Walter's lordship of Meath, goes little further in sustaining the idea of the de Lacys as an unchangingly cohesive kin-group.[36]

The real paradox of the fraternal relationship, looking to the House of Plantagenet ('the Atreides of the twelfth century'[37]) for an exemplar, is that brothers could be simultaneously one's closest kin and one's greatest competitors for prestige and property.[38] It has been suggested that the medieval fraternal ideal followed an antique model.[39] However, if Plutarch's *De fraterno amore* had celebrated the unique bond between brothers, it also devoted equal space to the fragility of the relationship, identifying the division of a father's property as especially traumatic for some fraternities, being in some cases the 'beginning of friendship and concord' but in others the origin of 'implacable enmity and strife'.[40]

For the de Lacys, it may have been somewhere in the middle. Walter did not overlook his siblings after 1189, but neither did he give them any significant territorial base of a kind to rival his own, reserving the most lucrative and prestigious familial estates in England and Wales for himself.[41] One brother, Gilbert, held the family's ancestral estates in Normandy, at Lassy and Campeaux, until the duchy's loss to Capetian France in 1204.[42] Until the 1230s, the only certain share of the de Lacy inheritance held by William *Gorm*, son of Hugh I by his unlicensed marriage to a daughter of the king of Connacht, Ruaidrí Ua Conchobair, c.1180, was a manor at Ballymagarvey, near Duleek (Co. Meath).[43] The largest share of the de Lacy possessions was

36 See chs 3–4.

37 Martin Aurell, *The Plantagenet empire*, trans. David Crouch (Harlow, 2007), 35–47, at 35.

38 Bouchard, *Those of my blood*, vii–viii.

39 Nada Zečević, 'Brotherly love and brotherly service: on the relationship between Carlo and Leonardo Tocco', in Davis, Müller and Rees Jones (eds), *Love, marriage and family ties*, 143–56, at 146.

40 *Plutarch's Moralia, VI*, ed. and trans. W. C. Helmbold (London, 1939), 277.

41 The English honor included components in Shropshire, Staffordshire, Herefordshire, Wiltshire and Gloucestershire. In the *cartae baronum* survey of 1166 Hugh I de Lacy returned 57¾ fees (52¼ old feoffment, 5½ new feoffment) for all his English lands: Veach, *Lordship*, appendix 2, table 1.

42 In 1203 Philip Augustus gave Richard de Garencières a fee subject to dispute with Gilbert de Lacy: *Cartulaire Normand de Philippe-Auguste, Louis VIII, Saint-Louis et Philippe-le-Hardi*, ed. Léopold Delisle (Paris, 1882), no. 72. In the next year Gilbert's Norman lands were granted by Philip to Andrew Propensée, maire of Falaise: ibid. no. 76.

43 See below, 143. For a recent study of William's career, see Colin Veach and Freya Verstraten

reserved by Walter for his nearest sibling, Hugh II, who was given a sizeable sub-enfeoffment in Meath centred on the baronies of Ratoath (with the grange of Trevet, bar. Skreen) and Morgallion before 1191.[44] In Normandy, Hugh may also have held the honor of Le Pin, bought by his father from Count Robert of Meulan for £200 (Angevin) before 1175, and comprised of a core of estates in the region of Le Pin-au-Haras (dép. Orne), north of Sées, as well as outlying fees in the Cotentin peninsula.[45]

Although *prima facie* a substantial interest, Hugh's territorial ambit appears less impressive on closer inspection. His tenure in Normandy has been inferred from a royal writ from 1203 granting William de Braose the honor of Le Pin, with its appurtenances in the bailiwick of William des Préaux, 'which had been Hugh de Lacy's (*q[ue] fuit Hug[oni] de Lascy*).[46] The qualification of ownership may not refer to Hugh II de Lacy, however, whose tenure in the duchy is otherwise unattested. Rather, it could represent an instruction to William des Préaux to distinguish the parts of the elder Hugh's purchase in his own bailiwick (Exmes) from those satellite fees in the bailiwick of Cotentin, before delivering seisin to de Braose. The younger Hugh was certainly in Normandy in 1199, when on 6 September, at Rouen, he witnessed a charter of King John in favour of William, baron of Naas, alongside his elder brother, Walter.[47] But this is no indicator of a Norman tenure; Hugh might as easily have travelled to the duchy as part of the army which had crossed the Channel with the king in June.[48] Even if the younger Hugh came to control Le Pin before 1203, the honor seems not to have included one of its original components, Mont Ormel (dép. Orne), which was probably the 'land of *Montornium*'

Veach, 'William *Gorm* de Lacy, 'chiefest champion in these parts of Europe'', in Seán Duffy (ed.), *Princes, prelates and poets in medieval Ireland: essays in honour of Katharine Simms* (Dublin, 2013), 63–84. Various meanings were attached to *gorm*, the most likely intended epithets being 'swarthy' or 'illustrious': eDIL (Electronic dictionary of the Irish language), letter G, cols 137–8 (http://www.dil.ie).

44 *Gorm. reg.*, 142, 190. Perhaps as a result of the fragmented political landscape in pre-Anglo-Norman Mide, units of local government in Meath were not the usual cantreds (formed from native *trícha céts* – 'thirty hundred [men]') found elsewhere in Anglo-Norman Ireland, but rather the baronies established at the time of the lordship's sub-infeudation by Hugh I de Lacy, c.1172: Paul MacCotter, *Medieval Ireland: territorial, political and economic divisions* (Dublin, 2008), 196–7. For Ratoath and Morgallion, respectively located in the *trícha céts* of 'Deiscert Breg' (which gave its name to bar. Deece) and 'Gailenga, Luigne, Saithne', see ibid., 203–6.

45 *Rotuli Normanniae in Turri Londinensi asservati*, ed. T. D. Hardy (London, 1835), 74; *Recueil des actes de Henri II, roi d'Angleterre, et duc de Normandie*, ed. Léopold Delisle and Élie Berger (3 vols, Paris, 1923), ii, 333–4; Veach, *Lordship*, 37–8, where the Assevilla and Buesevilla of Hugh's purchase are identified with Azeville and Beuzeville (dép. Manche).

46 *Rot. Norm.*, 74; Veach, Lordship, 80.

47 *Gorm. reg.*, 163.

48 Sidney Painter, *The reign of King John* (Baltimore, MD, 1949), 15–16.

granted by Walter de Lacy to Durand du Pin soon after Walter's succession in 1189.[49]

The scope of Hugh's sub-tenancy in Meath is also somewhat ambiguous. With Ratoath and Morgallion, Walter's grant of 1189×91 had included the 'thueth of fithd Winterwod', all the land of 'Knelene' and the land of 'Knelecwre'.[50] The location of the first fee is obscure, but was probably the 'Fithemunterrody' granted by Hugh II to his daughter, Matilda, on the occasion of her marriage to David, baron of Naas (1227×35).[51] On 4 December 1198 the Lord John confirmed to Hugh II the 'reasonable gift' made to him by his brother Walter, including 'the land of Thomas fitz Alured'.[52] In 1303 one of Thomas's descendants appears as 'late lord of Kenalean', shown by Orpen to have been synonymous with Cenél Enda (Kinalea), near the hill of Uisnech (Co. Westmeath), and which probably represents the 'Knelene' of Walter's grant.[53] 'Knelecrwe' has been connected by Veach with Cenél Láegaire, once roughly coterminous with the baronies of Upper and Lower Navan.[54] Along with Morgallion, Navan had been granted to Gilbert de Angulo by Hugh I de Lacy, and so the inference of 'a wholesale grant of the de Angulo territories' to Hugh II is not inconceivable.[55] Again, the Lord John's confirmation has a bearing on the issue. In 1198 Hugh's 'reasonable gift' included 'the land of Rudi'.[56] This may refer to Adam Rudipat (*alias* Rudepac), whose holdings included Kilberry, in the part of (Lower) Navan bordering on Morgallion.[57]

'Knelecrwe' seems not to have referred to the whole de Angulo grant in Navan, but rather to a northerly portion contiguous with other of Hugh's

49 *Calendar of documents preserved in France, illustrative of the history of Great Britain and Ireland, A.D. 918–1206*, ed. J. H. Round (London, 1889), no. 618. The grant was made to Durand for his service to Walter de Lacy and his father and brother, perhaps indicating that the honor of Le Pin had previously been an appanage for Robert de Lacy, the eldest son of Hugh I: Veach, *Lordship*, 80–1. Soon after his purchase of Le Pin, c.1175, Hugh I had granted to Durand the fee of Neuphe-sur-Dives (dép. Orne) for £25½ (Angevin): ibid., 38.

50 *Gorm. reg.*, 142, 190.

51 Appendix I, no. 20.

52 *Gorm. reg.*, 142, 190.

53 *CDI*, v, no. 167; Orpen, 'The earldom of Ulster (v)', 168–70. Thomas had also held Dengyn (Dangan, Co. Meath) from Hugh I de Lacy: ibid., 170.

54 Edmund Hogan, *Onomasticon Goedelicum: locorum et tribuum Hiberniae et Scotiae. An index, with identifications, to the Gaelic names of places and tribes* (Dublin, 1910), 221.

55 *Song of Dermot*, ll. 3142–5; *Deeds of the Normans*, ll. 3144–7; Colin Veach, 'Nobility and crown: the de Lacy family in Ireland, England and Normandy, 1172–1241', (Ph.D. thesis, University of Dublin, 2010), 93n.

56 *Gorm. reg.*, 142, 190.

57 *CDI*, i, nos 619, 822, 824; *Reg. St Thomas*, 35, 242, 264. Prof. Seán Duffy (Trinity College Dublin) suggested to me that the territory of 'Fithemunterrody', granted to Matilda de Lacy before 1235, and probably synonymous with the 'thueth of fithd Winterwod' given to Hugh II in 1189×91, could have been a corrupt rendering of 'Fid Muintir Rodaigh' ('the wood of the people of Rodaigh'). This in turn might indicate the 'land of Rudi' confirmed to Hugh by Lord John: see appendix I, no. 21.

territories. Even still, Ratoath and Morgallion, with their important seigneurial *capita*, should have been enough to class Hugh as one of Meath's most prominent tenants.[58] In reality, Hugh's freedom of seigneurial movement may have been marginal. Real lordly power entailed the distribution of land or privilege among one's following, but there was little left in these baronies, two decades after their initial settlement, to supply a new programme of patronage. Retained as demesne, Ratoath had been used by Hugh I de Lacy to cultivate links with his preferred religious houses, whose holdings in the barony were extensive.[59] The greater scope for sponsorship may have been in Morgallion, from which the original de Lacy feoffee, Gilbert de Angulo, may have been expelled by Walter de Lacy for mercenary activity in Connacht as early as 1189.[60] It speaks to the limitations on Hugh II's early position, however, that the only novel gift he is known to have made in Meath before 1205 was the grange and land beside Dunshaughlin (bar. Ratoath) to the Dublin abbey of St Thomas.[61] The rest of Hugh's known *acta* from this period are confirmations of anterior grants. Of course, in ratifying a gift of land 'as it was divided and perambulated in the time of my father', the younger Hugh both invoked the memory of his father and laid claim to his qualities of discernment.[62] But other of Hugh's confirmatory charters only serve to underline the fragility of his tenure in Ratoath, the part of Meath closest to the royal city of Dublin, and which became the scene of a power struggle between Walter de Lacy and the Lord John.

After 1172 Hugh I de Lacy's aptitude for conquest had earned him the suspicion of the crown, and his unlicensed marriage to the daughter of Ua Conchobair, king of Connacht and high-king of Ireland, c.1180, did little to dispel the rumours circulating in England to the effect that de Lacy was carving out his own 'kingdom' across the Irish Sea.[63] During his expedition to assume the lordship of Ireland, in 1185, the Lord John is reported to have blamed de Lacy for his failure to procure hostages or tribute from the Irish kings,[64] and Hugh's assassination in the next year allowed John to exploit the minority of

58 B. J. Graham, 'Anglo-Norman settlement in county Meath', *PRIA* C 75 (1975), 223–49, at 226; Margaret Murphy and Michael Potterton (eds), *The Dublin region in the Middle Ages: settlement, land-use, and economy* (Dublin, 2010), 126.

59 Murphy and Potterton (eds), *Dublin region*, 81–2.

60 In 1196 the Irish lands of Gilbert de Angulo, by this time engaged in the service of rival dynasts in Connacht, were confiscated by the Lord John and given to Walter de Lacy. Walter's own grant of de Angulo territory to Hugh II de Lacy (1189×91), however, would seem to indicate that Gilbert de Angulo (*alias* Mac Goisdealbh, later Mac Costello), had already vacated his Meath lands: Veach, 'A question of timing', 176–7.

61 Appendix I, no. 5.

62 Ibid., no. 1 (to Geoffrey Faber).

63 Veach, *Lordship*, ch. 2.

64 *ALC*, 1185 ('The son of the king of the Saxons went across afterwards to complain of Hugo de Laci to his father; for it was Hugo de Laci that was king of Erinn when the son of the king of the

Walter de Lacy (1186–89) to assert his personal control over Meath. Part of John's strategy involved hijacking the de Lacy affiliation with the priories of Llanthony Prima (Gwent) and Secunda (Gloucester), represented in Meath by the cells of Colpe and Duleek.[65] As well as issuing a general protection for the priories' Irish property, and confirming anterior donations of Hugh I de Lacy, John also made a novel endowment to Llanthony of Ballybin, in Ratoath,[66] and installed his associate, Robert Poer, in the same barony.[67] Poer's seisin was seemingly reversed after Walter de Lacy's succession in 1189, but Meath was in the Lord John's hands again between 1192 and 1195. The younger Hugh's tenure in Ratoath may also have been interrupted during this period, and it was only in December 1198 that he received confirmation for his sub-tenancies in Meath from the Lord John.[68]

In Meath, Hugh's ability to exercise lordship was constrained by the existing tenurial framework and competition with Angevin royal agents. We have seen that he may not have held outside of Ireland at all, but any operation in Normandy may only have exposed Hugh to the theme pervading northern French romance literature: 'of the hopes and dreams of the *juvenes*, of the young adventurer who gains the love of a rich heiress by his valour, and thus succeeds in establishing a great lordship far from his own people and founding a powerful dynasty'.[69] Love may have been a lower priority outside the literary paradigm, but a good marriage was certainly one way for younger sons to break the shackles of inheritance and emerge from the shadows of elder siblings.

Just such a match was achieved by Hugh de Lacy in 1194×99, by his marriage to Lescelina, daughter of Bertram III de Verdun (†1192). Bertram was lord of Alton, in Staffordshire, and a *curialis* of the Lord John, by whom he had been granted a substantial stake centred at Dundalk (Co. Louth), in Airgialla (anglicised Uriel).[70] In free marriage with Lescelina, and by agreement with

Saxons came'). John had been designated Lord of Ireland by Henry II at the Council of Oxford in 1177.

65 Arlene Hogan, *The priory of Llanthony Prima and Secunda in Ireland, 1172–1541: lands, patronage and politics* (Dublin, 2008).

66 *Ir. cartul. Llanthony*, 78–81, 213, 286.

67 See Robert's grants to St Thomas's Abbey, Dublin (*Reg. St Thomas*, 224, 254, 270, 273), in response to which Hugh II de Lacy confirmed to the same abbey his father's grant of rights in Ratoath and Dunshaughlin: appendix I, no. 5. See also, M. T. Flanagan, 'Poer, Robert (†1178?)', in *ODNB*.

68 Veach, *Lordship*, 83–6.

69 Duby, 'Youth in aristocratic society', 121.

70 Brendan Smith, *Colonisation and conquest in medieval Ireland: the English in Louth, 1170–1330* (Cambridge, 1999), 31–2. Bertram de Verdun was made seneschal of Ireland following John's return to England, and had custody of Hugh I de Lacy's castle of Drogheda after the latter's death in 1186: Mark Hagger, *The fortunes of a Norman family: the de Verduns in England, Ireland and Wales, 1066–1316* (Dublin 2001), 48–9.

her brother, Thomas, Hugh received half of the settled de Verdun lordship in Uriel, with the exception of Dundalk and its hinterland.[71] The union offered little in immediate material terms, reserving to Thomas the principal strategic and economic hubs of the de Verdun lordship.[72] The real value for Hugh lay in the further clause prescribing that whatever he or Thomas would afterwards conquer in the 'land of war' (*terra guerre*) was to be equally apportioned between them as they had divided the 'land of peace' (*terra pacis*).

Walter de Lacy's pledge to uphold the terms of the marriage agreement, along with 'friends on both sides', would seem to classify it as a family strategy. In general, heads of noble families were reluctant to allow younger sons to marry for fear that lateral branches would overrun the central patriline.[73] It was dangerous to give any cadet a biological head start, and yet Walter de Lacy appears to have been instrumental in negotiating Hugh's marriage before securing his own. In line with the model of family as a 'corporate unit',[74] Walter may only have had in mind the advancement of the de Lacy brand. The de Verduns' links with north-west England would be useful in securing trade and communication between Walter's port of Drogheda and Chester,[75] while their intimacy with the Lord John would help to smoothen relations following Walter's resumption of lordship in Meath.[76] No less likely is that, in furthering his brother's ambitions, Walter was addressing the danger of having a frustrated cadet tethered in his own lordship. It was distance, not intimacy, which characterised many of the most successful sibling relationships in the medieval period, and 'different roads' remained the most popular direction for aristocratic brothers.[77] In negotiating his own brother's marriage and backing his subsequent efforts at conquest, Walter may have been motivated as much by the need for sibling space as concern for the 'family' interest.

❖

71 Appendix I, no. 4.

72 Thomas retained the fortress at Castletown Mount, with the expanding borough of Dundalk, as well as the harbour on the Castletown river: Paul Gosling, 'From Dún Delca to Dundalk: the topography and archaeology of a medieval frontier town, A.D. 1187–1700', *JLAS* 22 (1991), 223–353; A. J. Otway-Ruthven, 'The partition of the de Verdon lands in Ireland in 1332', *PRIA* C 66 (1967–8), 401–55, at 403–4.

73 Green, *Aristocracy*, 335–6.

74 Sylvia Federico, 'Shifting horizons of expectation: the late medieval family (preface to section)', in Davis, Müller and Rees Jones (eds), *Love, marriage and family ties*, 121–8, at 123–4.

75 See below, 59.

76 Thomas de Verdun had promised to do everything in his power, whether by giving money or other means, to secure the Lord John's consent for the marriage: appendix I, no. 4.

77 Joel Rosenthal, *Patriarchy and families of privilege* (Philadelphia, PA, 1991), 111; Howard, 'We are broderen', 140–1.

In medieval representations of the *rota Fortunae* the hand of the goddess is the motive cause, beginning and directing the spinning of her wheel, orchestrating the lives of others.[78] Today we accept a more sophisticated view of causation, but might it still be possible to point to circumstances which, in lieu of fate, set the younger Hugh de Lacy's career on a particular course? Confinement to Ireland left Hugh with little option but to adopt the prerequisite characteristics of a freebooting colonist. 'Ambition may have been the motor of conquest', writes Peter Crooks, 'but it would not have taken [the incomers] far had it not been backed up by a certain flintiness of character, great tenacity, and a willingness to use violence and withstand fierce reprisals'.[79] These traits pervade Hugh's early career and are presented by Veach as part of a wider strategy to maintain the de Lacys' dominance in Ireland, whereby 'Walter pursued their advancement through official channels, attending the king, sitting on commissions and serving as royal representative, while Hugh and William used the blunt (if effective) method of martial conquest'.[80] If his limited means initially caused Hugh to play the part of the warlike cadet, however, the quasi-regal image he would fashion subsequent to his creation as earl of Ulster implies that he would have preferred the role of metropolitan magnate to that of frontier warrior.

Hugh's early consignment to the political periphery was a direct result of his brother's reluctance to part with the choicest parts of his inheritance, a miserly disposition contrasting with Walter's later commemoration as 'the bountifullest Englishman for horses, cloaths, mony and goold that ever came before his tyme into this kingdome [of Ireland]'.[81] Walter was also constrained after 1200 by the terms of his marriage to Margery, daughter of William de Braose, by which he agreed not to act in such a way towards his lands in Normandy or England that could diminish his own children's inheritance.[82] There is little early evidence of acrimony among the de Lacys, and Walter even appears to have taken steps to augment his younger brother's personal authority after the Lord John's intrusion, empowering Hugh to confirm to the canons of Llanthony 'all reasonable donations' made to them by his father and brother in England, Wales and Ireland.[83] Nevertheless, the possibility remains that the fissure manifesting in their fraternity after 1210 could have widened along pre-existing fault lines, perhaps sourced to the uneven distribution of their father's lands.

78 John Marenbon (ed.), *Routledge history of philosophy, vol. 3: medieval philosophy* (London, 2003), 476.

79 Peter Crooks, 'Divide and rule: factionalism as royal policy in the lordship of Ireland, 1171–1265', *Peritia* 19 (2005), 263–307, at 263.

80 Veach, *Lordship*, 265.

81 *AClon.*, 1241.

82 *Rot. oblatis*, 81; *Rot. chart.*, 80; *Pipe roll 3 John*, 87; Frame, 'Aristocracies', 145.

83 Appendix I, no. 2.

The adventurous spirit of *juvenes* was a much-coveted and exploited commodity in the Irish colony. Hugh's acquisitions in the de Verdun lordship were hugely significant, augmenting his seigneurial income with new rents and revenues and allowing him to recruit his own personal following from among the de Verdun affinity.[84] Meanwhile, Hugh's brother-in-law, Thomas, gained an adjunct in conquest and helped to secure the most important components of his frontier lordship. Another example of this kind of expansionist strategy, taking advantage of youth as the 'spearhead of feudal aggression',[85] is the grant by William de Burgh to Hugh de Lacy of ten cantreds in Connacht (1189×99).[86] The seizure of territory was one thing, but effective conquest entailed the extension of settlement to a manageable degree, in consideration of the requirements of defence. Men like William de Burgh and Thomas de Verdun were prepared to grant away large portions of their nominal claims to those willing to help shoulder the burden of conquest, in the knowledge that, for aristocratic cadets like Hugh de Lacy, the *terra guerre* was also the land of opportunity.

Crucially, it was Hugh's maturity as a man 'with little to lose and much to gain' which brought him to the attention of the English crown.[87] Instances of royally sponsored factionalism are present from the very nascence of the Irish colony, but it was under King John (1199–1216) that inter-baronial conflict was especially cultivated as a controlling mechanism.[88] In dealing with wayward or recalcitrant subjects, John's *modus operandi* was to set them up against men of 'secondary importance'.[89] When someone was required to rein in the lord of Ulster, John de Courcy, Hugh de Lacy fitted the brief superbly.[90] If anything controlled the wheel of aristocratic fortune it was 'the policies, interests and whims of kings, or those governing in their name'.[91] Hugh had perhaps proved himself useful during the continental campaign of 1199, when he witnessed a royal charter at Rouen.[92] Turning to his astonishing rise to prominence between 1201 and 1205, we find that one of the most significant consequences of Hugh's modest standing was that it rendered him malleable in royal hands.

84 See below, ch. 2.

85 Duby, 'Youth in aristocratic society', 115.

86 *Gorm. reg.*, 143–4. This amplified an earlier grant of six cantreds made to de Lacy by the Lord John: below, 28.

87 Crooks, 'Divide and rule', 281.

88 Ibid., 263–85.

89 Painter, *King John*, 24.

90 See ch. 1.

91 Bothwell, *Falling from grace*, 6.

92 *Gorm. reg.*, 163.

2

Rise

The making of an earl, 1201–05

On 29 May 1205 some of the greatest among the Angevin clergy and nobility gathered at Winchester cathedral to celebrate the feast of Whitsun (Pentecost). This was not only a religious festival but a *coronatio*, an occasion on which the king was liturgically elevated and his majesty displayed by the public wearing of his crown. The cruciform cathedral space became a realm in microcosm, where social standing depended on one's nearness or distance from the *rex coronatus*. After the ecclesiastical dignitaries, the spaces closest to the king during the solemn procession into the church, or at the banquet table following the conclusion of the ceremony, were reserved for the first rank of nobility – the earls.[1] This small elite welcomed its newest member on Whitsunday when, in a public ceremony apart from the royal *coronatio*, King John tied a sword around Hugh de Lacy's waist, symbolising his investiture as earl of Ulster.[2]

With the sole exception of William Marshal (†1219), earl of Pembroke and lord of Leinster, Hugh now notionally outranked every other member of the settler community in Ireland, including his elder brother, Walter. Earls did not wear crowns, but *dignitas* could still be conveyed in other ways. An unmistakable ostentation is detected in one of Hugh's earliest comital charters, 'given by our own hand at Rathbeggan (bar. Ratoath, Co. Meath) on the thirteenth of January in the second year of our earldom (1207)'.[3] Those close to the earl could also lay claim to the honour bound up in his comital title. Around 1270, almost three decades after Hugh's death, his second wife was still styling herself 'Emelina de Lacy, countess of Ulster' in charters to her chantry chapel in Wiltshire. Emelina had since remarried to a grandson of Henry II, but for her

1 H. G. Richardson, 'The coronation in medieval England', *Traditio* 16 (1960), 111–202, at 134–5; Martin Biddle, 'Seasonal festivals and residence: Winchester, Westminster and Gloucester in the tenth to twelfth centuries', *ANS* 8, 51–63.

2 *Rot. chart.*, 151a; *CDI*, i, no. 263. Just three other earldoms were created or re-created by King John: Hereford, for Henry de Bohun (1199); Pembroke, re-created for William Marshal (1199); and Winchester, for Saer de Quincy (1207): Richard Mortimer, *Angevin England, 1154–1258* (Oxford, 1994), 79.

3 Appendix I, no. 12.

a connection to the comital title superseded even a link to Plantagenet royal blood.[4]

Some great men would never possess an earldom, but those created earls were almost always great men. There is no escaping the fact that, before 1205, Hugh de Lacy was not even chief in the Irish colony for wealth, land and influence. For this reason historians have struggled to unravel the 'complete mystery' of Hugh's promotion.[5] 'Perhaps the king could not resist the temptation to annoy everyone to some extent', suggested Painter, defaulting to the position that whatever seems inexplicable in John's troubled reign can be attributed to caprice.[6] Others have looked to the man whom de Lacy displaced in Ulster, John de Courcy, who is usually stated to have made an enemy of the crown by assuming 'the rule and belligerent independence of an autonomous Irish king'.[7] According to this paradigm, having wrested Ulster from de Courcy's control through military conquest, Hugh de Lacy 'got his reward' for services rendered to the crown in the form of a comital title.[8]

Whatever the underlying cause, John de Courcy's demise brings us little closer to understanding why Hugh de Lacy received a comital title along with the lordship of Ulster. An explanation for this especial favour must take into account the Irish colony's place within a wider political setting. Royal policy towards Ulster was conditioned by King John's preoccupation with war against Capetian France and the intricacies of Angevin diplomacy in the Irish Sea zone. At the same time, it was a particular set of political circumstances which conspired in Hugh de Lacy's favour in May 1205. As plans for a continental expedition crumbled, the king was dealt the additional blow of betrayal by one of his closest supporters, William Marshal, lord of Leinster, whose subsequent disgrace coincided precisely with Hugh de Lacy's elevation. It is in the Marshal's duplicity, and an ill-fated royal scheme to alter the balance of baronial power in Ireland, that we find the most convincing context for Hugh de Lacy's sudden ascent on Fortune's wheel.

4 Magdalen College, Oxford, MSS Wanborough, 6a, 19, 20a, 22, 23, 24, 25, 31a, 33, 36a, 48a, 56a, 57a, 58a, 59a, 66. I am grateful to Prof. David Crouch, University of Hull, for making me aware of this collection. The fourteenth-century *Book of Lacock* describes Emelina's second husband, Stephen Longespée, as *Com[es] Ulton[ie]*: *Annals and antiquities of Lacock Abbey, in the county of Wiltshire*, ed. W. L. Bowles and J. G. Nichols (London, 1835), appendix 1, ii.

5 Painter, *King John*, 47.

6 Ibid.

7 F. X. Martin, in *NHI*, ii, 134.

8 Orpen, *Normans*, 206.

The grant of Ulster

In his late twelfth-century 'Life of St Patrick', Jocelin of Furness gave the striking epithet, *princeps Ulidiae*, to the patron of his work, John de Courcy.[9] Along with the fact that John minted his own coins, the hagiographer's description has been seen as evidence that, in the aftermath of his spectacular conquest of Ulaid in 1177, de Courcy sought to position himself as direct successor to the kingdom's Irish rulers.[10] There is little doubt that John's was a uniquely unencumbered brand of lordship. In Orpen's words, he 'exercised *jura regalia* even more completely than the great palatine lords of Leinster and Meath; he had a virtually unlimited jurisdiction, appointed his own feudal officers, created barons, and parcelled out the greater part of the territory among them'.[11] According to the received narrative, this was too much for the English crown to swallow: 'the king used Hugh de Lacy to get rid of [de Courcy]', wrote James Lydon, 'rewarding his service with the earldom of Ulster'.[12] What this theory overlooks, however, is that when the opportunity arose for the crown to tighten its grip on Ulster in re-granting the lordship to Hugh de Lacy, the chance was either missed or declined.

Composed in the first decades of the thirteenth century, the legal treatise *De legibus et consuetudinibus Angliae* was in little doubt about the importance of earls: 'for kings associate such persons with themselves in governing the people of God, investing them with great honour, power and name when they gird them with swords'.[13] By the time Hugh de Lacy was belted by King John, however, the only certain advantage associated with an earldom was the personal honour conveyed by the comital title itself. The primary responsibilities of the Anglo-Saxon earl had been administrative and military, involving his officiation in the court of the shire and command of its militia, as well as the general maintenance of justice and public order. In return, the earl enjoyed the revenue from those estates annexed to his office as well as the profits of justice, including the third penny from the pleas of the shire. Even before the Norman Conquest, the administrative function of the earl was becoming less pronounced. He had always been surpassed in importance in the shire court by the bishops, but now found his provincial brief subsumed by sheriffs as executors

9 John Colgan, *Acta triadis thaumaturgae* (Louvain, 1647), 64. For de Courcy's use of hagiography for the purposes of self-promotion, see M. T. Flanagan, 'Jocelin of Furness and the cult of St Patrick in twelfth-century Ulster', in Clare Downham (ed.), *Jocelin of Furness: proceedings from the 2011 conference* (Donington, 2013), 45–66, and below, 32–3, 52.

10 J. F. Lydon, *The making of Ireland: from ancient times to the present* (London, 1998), 70.

11 Orpen, *Normans*, 159.

12 Lydon, *Making of Ireland*, 70.

13 Henry de Bracton, *De legibus et consuetudinibus Angliae*, ed. G. E. Woodbine, trans. S. E. Thorne (4 vols, Cambridge, MA, 1968–77), ii, 32.

of local administration. The earl's status as foremost power in his earldom was uncertain by the twelfth century, as the comital title began to be conferred on barons without a significant territorial interest in the territory to which their title was attached.[14]

Under the Angevin kings, the theory that all secular authority was held in the king's hand meant that liberties and franchises had to be specially delegated, and so the privileges once associated with comital rank ceased to be automatic.[15] Earls could still be powerful men, but influence was no longer guaranteed by the possession of honorific rank. While the earl of Chester presided over his *comitatus* in relative freedom, the pipe roll from 1130 could be examined 'without learning that there was an earl of Buckingham'.[16] With the 'imperial drift' of the earldom into Wales and Ireland, there is no sense of a constitutional template being rolled out to outlying components of the Angevin realm.[17] An earl's rights depended on his individual circumstances, and in itself the formation of an earldom based on the territorial lordship of Ulster can tell us little about how Hugh de Lacy's power compared with John de Courcy's, or why he was endowed with the comital title. A first step to the demystification of Hugh's elevation, therefore, must be a consideration of the range of liberties delegated to him by the king, which were arguably greater than those enjoyed by any other colonist.

By the royal charter of 29 May 1205, Hugh was to have Ulster 'as well, freely, quietly and fully as John de Courcy held and possessed it', with the sole reservation of *ordinatione crocearum*.[18] Some ambiguity surrounds what exactly was being held back for the crown. The 'crosses' – that is, jurisdiction in church land – had been exempted in several charters issued by the Lord John between 1185 and 1199.[19] Seeking evidence for the erosion of baronial rights in the thirteenth-century colony, A. J. Otway-Ruthven connected this jurisdiction (*crociae*) with the reservation in Hugh de Lacy's charter. This is a misreading of *ordinatione crocearum*, however, which more accurately alludes to the royal right of assent to the appointment of freely elected episcopal or archiepiscopal

14 For the evolution of the comital office, see F. M. Stenton, *The first century of English feudalism, 1066–1166* (2nd edn, Oxford, 1961), 229–31; Robert Bartlett, *England under the Norman and Angevin kings, 1075–1225* (Oxford, 2000), 208–9.

15 Susan Reynolds, *Fiefs and vassals: the medieval evidence reinterpreted* (Oxford, 1994), 360.

16 Stenton, *First century*, 231.

17 David Crouch, 'Earls in Wales and Ireland', in idem and Hugh Doherty (eds), *The earl in medieval Britain* (forthcoming for Cambridge University Press).

18 *Rot. chart.*, 151a; *CDI*, i, no. 263.

19 M. T. Flanagan, 'Defining lordships in Angevin Ireland: William Marshal and the king's justiciar', in Martin Aurell and Frédéric Boutoulle (eds), *Les seigneuries dans l'espace Plantagenêt, c. 1150–1250* (Bordeaux, 2009), 41–59, at 53–4.

officials.[20] The confusion may arise from an earlier royal letter to the barons of Ireland, issued on 2 May, informing them that Ulster had been given to Hugh de Lacy with the reservation of *crociis de terra illa* – 'the crosses of that land'.[21] We should not automatically take this to mean the same thing as *ordinatio crocearum*. Rather, it appears that King John initially took Ulster's cross lands into his hand, but amended his position so that only the right of royal assent was claimed. The broad implication is that Hugh de Lacy enjoyed the same freedoms over *crociae* as John de Courcy, who certainly exercised direct lordship in church land, having delegated criminal jurisdictions to the clergy of Down (1202×05).[22]

The second important feature of de Lacy's charter is its unusually favourable requirement of military service. Hugh was to provide one knight from each of his earldom's (eleven) cantreds, setting an extraordinarily low quota in comparison with the lordships of Leinster (one hundred knights) and Meath (fifty).[23] The financial burden presented by scutage, the monetary payment made in lieu of personal military service, was also mitigated. Scutage was levied with increasing regularity in England but instances in Ireland are more difficult to reconstruct owing to the absence of financial records. Nevertheless, while money-service is not explicitly alluded to until 1238, there is some evidence pointing to its much earlier use.[24] In England exemptions from scutage were frequently offered as an incentive towards greater loyalty.[25] This was impractical in Ireland, where the monopolisation of land by a small number of settlers meant that tenants-in-chief had to pay their dues if feudal assessment was to be at all lucrative. At the end of the thirteenth century £200 was raised from scutage in Leinster and £100 in Meath, while a paltry £6 was collected from Ulster.[26] This striking disparity may well have had its roots in the *servicium* defined in Hugh de Lacy's charter, which, whether rendered in men or money, set Ulster apart from Ireland's other great franchises.

Hugh de Lacy's usurpation of John de Courcy has been seen as an example

20 A. J. Otway-Ruthven, 'Anglo-Irish shire government in the thirteenth century', *IHS* 5, no. 17 (1946), 1–28, at 7; eadem, *Med. Ire.*, 182. The right of assent was by now the crown's only certain jurisdiction in the area of episcopal election: Uta-Renate Blumenthal, *The investiture controversy: church and monarchy from the ninth to the twelfth century* (Philadelphia, PA, 1988), 142–59.

21 *RLP*, 54a.

22 Gearóid Mac Niocaill, 'Cartae Dunenses', *Seanchas Ard Mhacha* 5 (1970), 418–24, at 421, no. 7.

23 A. J. Otway-Ruthven, 'Knight service in Ireland', *JRSAI* 89 (1959), 1–15, at 1. For the correspondence of cantreds with native Irish administrative units, see Paul MacCotter, 'Functions of the cantred in Medieval Ireland', *Peritia* 19 (2005), 308–32.

24 Otway-Ruthven, 'Knight service', 4.

25 T. K. Keefe, *Feudal assessments and the political community under Henry II and his sons* (Berkeley, CA, 1983), 20–40.

26 Otway-Ruthven, 'Knight service', 5, 11–13.

of the 'significant leitmotiv of the period': royally sponsored factionalism.[27] But if anything, de Lacy's earldom was even more loosely bound to the crown than his predecessor's lordship had been. If de Lacy's harassment of de Courcy was endorsed by King John, the decisive motivating factor cannot therefore have been the lord of Ulster's seigneurial independence. Projecting back to the beginning of the thirteenth century, moreover, we find that the evidence for royal complicity in the early skirmishes over Ulster is not altogether conclusive.

The Imprisonment of John de Courcy, 1201

The first visible rift between Hugh de Lacy and John de Courcy played out against a background of dynastic wrangling in Connacht, following on from the usurpation of its king, Ruaidrí Ua Conchobair, by his son, Conchobar Máenmaige, in 1185. Opportunistic Anglo-Norman mercenaries jostled to take advantage of the political tumult, touting their services to rival Irish dynasts. In 1189 Ruaidrí's brother, Cathal Crobderg ('Redhand') Ua Conchobair, won the kingship. An uneasy peace endured for ten years before Cathal Crobderg was himself expelled by his great-nephew, Cathal Carrach ('The scabby') Ua Conchobair, in alliance with William de Burgh (†c.1206), the foremost Anglo-Norman power in north Munster.[28] Cathal Crobderg's first attempt to regain the kingship failed after his allies, the northern kings of Tír Eógain (Tyrone) and Fir Manach (Fermanagh), refused to take the field against de Burgh, only to be routed by Cathal Carrach's army on their retreat towards Ulster.[29] It was only then, in 1201, that Cathal Crobderg solicited Anglo-Norman aid for an expedition to recover the kingship, entering into a 'league of amity' with John de Courcy and Hugh de Lacy.[30]

This was a chance for de Courcy to avenge the heavy defeat inflicted on him in 1188 by Conchobar Máenmaige, when he had been forced to flee from Connacht 'without a whit of triumph'.[31] Hugh de Lacy's motivation is more difficult to ascertain. He had a familial connection to Connacht's ruling house through his father's second 'marriage', to a daughter of Ruaidrí Ua Conchobair,[32] but this cannot explain why one Ua Chonchobair dynast was favoured over another. Indeed, it was only recently that Cathal Crobderg had raided into

27 Crooks, 'Divide and rule', 268.
28 For the progress of the dynastic war, see Helen Perros, 'Crossing the Shannon frontier: Connacht and the Anglo-Normans, 1170–1224', in Barry, Frame and Simms (eds), *Colony and frontier*, 117–39, at 123–30.
29 *ALC*, 1201.
30 *AFM*, 1200 [*recte* 1201].
31 *AU*, 1188.
32 See above, 14.

Walter de Lacy's lordship of Meath, but Hugh's readiness to overlook this indiscretion is but an early manifestation of what will become a recurrent motif, namely the placement of personal ambition before the fraternal bond.[33] Another possibility is that Hugh was acting as a vassal of the lord of Ulster. Before taking de Courcy prisoner in 1201, de Lacy had offered sanctuary in one of his castles, for which he was John's 'man' (*homo*); the fortress is unidentified in Howden's chronicle, but may have been situated in north Louth, where Hugh's lands marched with de Courcy's.[34] Most likely is that de Lacy was attempting to make good on an existing territorial claim in Connacht. At some point between 1189 and 1199, Hugh had been granted six cantreds in modern Sligo and Roscommon by the Lord John, as count of Mortain.[35] This gift was negated by John's subsequent award of the whole of Connacht to William de Burgh.[36] In what would appear to be a compensatory gesture, de Burgh then granted de Lacy ten northern cantreds, comprising roughly one-third of the province.[37] Hugh's intrusion in the Connacht succession against William's ally, Cathal Carrach, was an ungracious response to de Burgh's magnanimity.

The expedition of 1201, mounted at no small expense to the participants, can only be described as an unmitigated disaster. Landing at the mouth of the river Erne (Co. Donegal), the allies proceeded southwards 'in pursuit of the cows and people of the Connachtmen', until they reached the monastic settlement at Kilmacduagh (Co. Galway). Nearby, in a forest clearing, they were ambushed and routed by Cathal Carrach's men. Sixty knights, *vel amplius*, were killed in the mêlée, while de Courcy narrowly escaped with his life after being struck by a stone and thrown from his horse. Many more were slaughtered during a demoralising, week-long transport eastwards across Loch Ree, towards Meath.[38] Of eight 'battalions' which had marched into Connacht, just two returned.[39] Amity dissolved into enmity as de Courcy and de Lacy sought recompense for

[33] *ALC*, 1199, 1200.

[34] *Chron. Houedene*, iv, 176, and below, 64–5.

[35] *Rot. chart*, 139b; *CDI*, i, no. 241. These were 'Trichonthes' (Three Tuaths); 'Moylupatirlele' (Moylurg); 'Moyhee' (Tireragh on the Moy); 'Corhin' (Corran); 'Scleflunede' (Slieve Lugha); and 'Luine' (Luigne): see MacCotter, *Medieval Ireland*, 131–50. Tireragh, Corran, Slieve Lugha and Luigne would be granted to Hugh de Lacy by Richard, son of William de Burgh, c.1235: see below, 190.

[36] *Rot. chart.*, 218b.

[37] *Gorm. reg.*, 143–4. In addition to the six cantreds previously awarded by the Lord John, de Burgh's grant included Carbury-Drumcliff, two cantreds of Tirawley, and Erris. The definitive *terminus ante quem* is provided by de Burgh's death c.1206.

[38] *ALC*, 1201; *AClon.*, 1200 [*recte* 1201]; *MCB*, 1201; A. M. Freeman, 'The annals in Cotton MS Titus A. XXV', *Rev. Celt.* 41 (1924), 301–30; 42 (1925), 281–305; 43 (1926), 358–84; 44 (1927), 336–61, *s.a.* 1201; *AFM*, 1199 [*recte* 1201]; *AU*, 1201.

[39] *AU*, 1201.

their heavy losses. 'As soon as the foreigners arrived in Meath', we are told, 'they arrested Cathal Crobderg as a pledge for [the payment of] wages'.[40]

We are now confronted with what Orpen called a 'mutilation' in the record.[41] According to the annals of Loch Cé, 'John was taken to Ath-cliath [Dublin] until he gave pledges from himself that he would obey the king of the Saxons'.[42] At first glance, the prisoner would appear to be John de Courcy. However, Orpen has shown that the personal name *Eoin* was interlined at a later date, and so Cathal Crobderg is more likely to have been the subject of the entry.[43] This still leaves us to contend with other notices alluding to de Courcy's capture by the de Lacys in the same year, and to King John's connivance in the act.[44] Of these, perhaps the most intriguing is found in the contemporary chronicle of Roger of Howden, who claims that Walter de Lacy had attempted to 'treacherously' seize de Courcy, only for Hugh de Lacy to offer John refuge in one of his castles. Then, having accepted safe conduct into the fortress, de Courcy was taken prisoner by Hugh 'for the purpose of delivering him up to the king of England, who had long wished to hold him'.[45] De Courcy's release was only secured after retaliatory attacks by his partisans on the de Lacys' lands, 'with fire, sword and famine'.[46]

A private motive for de Courcy's incarceration cannot be ruled out. The payment of a ransom could have helped to offset the losses incurred by Hugh in the Connacht campaign, the calamitous outcome of which he perhaps blamed on his senior partner. Underlying tensions between the pair may also have surfaced as a result of the intersection of their respective ambits in north Louth.[47] Even so, de Courcy's imprisonment could still have been sanctioned or encouraged by the crown. The confiscation of de Courcy's English manor of Middleton

40 *ALC*, 1201.

41 Orpen, *Normans*, 226.

42 *ALC*, 1201.

43 Ibid., i, 222n; Orpen, *Normans*, 226.

44 *ALC*, i, 222–3 (citing the so-called Dublin annals of Inisfallen); *MCB*, 1200 [*recte* 1201]. For the possible utilisation of *Mac Carthaig's book* (*MCB*), a fifteenth-century compilation, in the construction of the Munster-focused Dublin annals of Inisfallen, in the eighteenth century, see Meidhbhín Ní Úrdail, 'Some observations on the "Dublin annals of Inisfallen"', *Ériu* 57 (2007), 134–53.

45 *Chron. Houedene*, iv, 176.

46 Ibid. The annals of Clonmacnoise (*Mageoghagan's book*) may conflate the separate imprisonments of Cathal Crobderg and John de Courcy, noting that Cathal was held captive at Hugh de Lacy's castle of Nobber (*caput* of bar. Morgallion): *AClon.*, 1200 [*recte* 1201]. The principal source for Conell Mageoghagan's compilation of 1627 was the earlier compilation by Maoilín Ó Maoil Chonaire (1423), hereditary historian of the Uí Chonchobair, itself drawn from the 'Clonmacnoise chronicle' breaking off c.1227: D. P. McCarthy, *The Irish annals: their genesis, evolution and history* (Dublin, 2008), 287–93; Katharine Simms, *Medieval Gaelic sources* (Dublin, 2009), 287–93.

47 See below, 64–5.

Cheney, in 1201, certainly points to some degree of royal displeasure.[48] It is still a leap, however, to suggest that the crown's goal at this early stage was regime change in Ulster. If Roger of Howden is to be believed, the king was already plotting de Courcy's replacement. Judged by Gillingham as the most important contemporary historian of the North Channel region, Roger may have accompanied Henry II to Ireland in 1172, and he appears to have derived some of his information on Ulster affairs from contacts close to John de Courcy.[49] In 1201, however, the chronicler was resident in his Yorkshire parish and no longer as close to the beating heart of Angevin government as he had been during the reign of Henry II.[50] There is no doubt that the lord of Ulster had been a source of inconvenience for the future King John as an agent of Richard I in Ireland, but Howden's statement, that the king 'long wished' to seize de Courcy, may represent the use of old or imagined information in relating a current event.[51] The Irish annals, admittedly even further removed from the English court, state the purpose of de Courcy's imprisonment to have been merely the extraction of promises of better behaviour.[52]

Pax regis, 1202–03

If Hugh de Lacy had acted on behalf of the crown in arresting John de Courcy, it did not appear to improve his standing in the Irish colony, where he continued to cut a distinctly peripheral figure. No further action against John de Courcy is attested in 1202, and Hugh's only certain act in this year was the construction of a castle at Dún Ocalla, above Loch Ree, the natural frontier between Meath and Connacht.[53] It was the land north of the Shannon, rather than east of the Bann, which continued to hold his attention. Meanwhile, if Hugh had held land in

48 *Pipe roll 3 John*, 187; *5 John*, 186.

49 John Gillingham, 'The travels of Roger of Howden and his views of the Irish, Scots and Welsh', in *ANS* 20, 151–70.

50 A. A. M. Duncan, 'Roger of Howden and Scotland, 1187–1201', in Barbara Crawford (ed.), *Church, chronicle and learning in medieval and early Renaissance Scotland: essays presented to Donald Watt on the occasion of the completion of the publication of Bower's Scotichronicon* (Edinburgh, 1998), 135–59, at 148–50.

51 John had replaced de Courcy as justiciar of Ireland with one of his curial favourites, Peter Pipard, in 1191. In 1194, during the Lord John's rebellion, Pipard was arrested by de Courcy and his co-justiciar, Walter de Lacy: Seán Duffy, 'John and Ireland: the origins of England's Irish problem' in S. D. Church (ed.) *King John: new interpretations* (Woodbridge, 1999), 221–45, at 237; Veach, *Lordship*, 86. In 1199 the king asked the justiciar, Meiler fitz Henry, to inquire whether Henry Tyrel had sided with John de Courcy and W[alter] de Lacy in targeting his adherents in Ireland: Duffy, 'John and Ireland', 86; *CDI*, i, no. 90.

52 *ALC*, i, 222–3 (citing the Dublin annals of Inisfallen); *MCB*, 1200 [*recte* 1201].

53 *MCB*, 1202.

the duchy of Normandy, he did so only until February 1203, when the honor of Le Pin was granted to William de Braose.[54] This appears to have been part of a strategy encouraged by the king for the more efficient defence of Normandy, whereby the de Lacy estates in the duchy were managed by de Braose, while Walter de Lacy stewarded his father-in-law's Irish honor of Limerick.[55]

One enticing scenario is that the crown sought to offset the loss of Hugh's Norman honor by encouraging him in an assault on the lordship of Ulster. *Mac Carthaigh's book* records a battle between de Courcy and Hugh de Lacy at Downpatrick (Co. Down) in 1203, 'in which John was captured and his people slaughtered, so that he had to surrender his lordship and his castles to Hugh'.[56] In July 1202, and again in September 1203, de Courcy was granted safe conduct in coming to England to negotiate peace with the king.[57] On this basis, it has been argued that the crown was now acting in concert with Hugh de Lacy as part of a strategy to undermine the lord of Ulster by both military and political means.[58]

The entry in *Mac Carthaigh's book* placing the battle of Downpatrick in 1203, however, is actually behind by one year.[59] This means that Hugh de Lacy's first direct assault on the lordship of Ulster occurred in 1204, *after* John de Courcy's two summonses to court. While de Courcy appears to have been in breach of the *pax regis* by 1202, the crown was addressing its grievances through diplomatic channels alone. Moreover, there were others in the Angevin colony being subjected to harsher treatment; not least of these was William de Burgh, who was disseised of his Irish lands in 1203 for warring in Connacht against Cathal Crobderg, whose kingship was now endorsed by the crown.[60] It becomes difficult to interpret two safe conducts, separated by more than a year, and the temporary confiscation of an English manor, as proof that the king was already intent on cutting down the lord of Ulster. Whatever had aroused royal antipathy towards de Courcy did not yet warrant more serious action. The most likely source of the king's discomfort was de Courcy's lordship strategy in Ulster, which had come into competition with royal efforts to influence the character of the Irish episcopate.

In the entirety of his reign, King John attempted to influence just seven episcopal appointments in Ireland. This figure may have been significantly

54 *Rot. Norm.*, 74, and above, 15.

55 See Veach, *Lordship*, 111–13.

56 *MCB*, 1203. See also, *AFM*, 1203; *ALC*, 1203.

57 *RLP*, 15b, 34b.

58 Veach, *Lordship*, 116.

59 The same set of annals places Hugh de Lacy's comital creation in 1204 ('Hugh de Lacy an earl and justiciar from the king of England in Ireland'): *MCB*, 1204.

60 *ALC*, 1202, 1203; *Rot. lib.*, 67; *RLP*, 39–41b.

higher had his first effort been rewarded with greater success.[61] In 1201, after the death of Tommaltach (Thomas), archbishop of Armagh, the king sought to have his own man – the Oxford graduate, Humphrey of Tickhill – elected to the archiepiscopal office. Instead, the suffragans of Armagh promoted the candidacy of the abbot of Bangor, Echdonn Mac Gilla Uidir (Eugenius).[62] As John tried in vain to resolve the dispute in his favour, his frustrations were compounded by a similar manifestation of clerical independence in Normandy, where the installation of royally sponsored candidates to the cathedral churches of Lisieux (1200) and Sées (1201) met with stiff resistance.[63]

If the 'Anglicisation' of the Irish episcopate was promoted by local Anglo-Norman lords,[64] John de Courcy appears to have acted exceptionally. Perhaps in compensation for an absence of secular support in consolidating his conquest of Ulaid, de Courcy had forged close links with local churchmen.[65] In 1205, recounting the election and consecration of Mac Gilla Uidir, Pope Innocent III mentioned *ipsius terre principes* among the secular supporters of the appointment.[66] If, as seems likely, John de Courcy was one of these *principes*, his endorsement of Eugenius's candidacy can only have harmed his relationship with the crown.[67]

Armagh was not the only Irish diocese in which the king's right of assent was being circumvented. In 1202 the bishop of Down, Echmílid mac Máel Martain (Malachias III), took advantage of the papal legate John of Salerno's presence in Ireland in order to resign his office. Bypassing the usual formalities attached to the nomination and election of a successor, the legate parachuted in Ralph, abbot of Melrose in Scotland, to fill the vacancy.[68] In doing so, he may have held in mind the advice of the papal *curia* concerning the ongoing dispute in Armagh: that in the event of a judgement against Eugenius, a new candidate should be found who was of neither English nor Irish nation.[69] John de Courcy had no influence over the selection of Malachias's successor at Down, but he appears to have established some rapport with the legate. John of Salerno was

61 Armagh (1201), Cashel (1206), Limerick (1207), Waterford (1210), Cork (1214) and Killaloe (1216): J. A. Watt, *The church and the two nations in medieval Ireland* (Cambridge, 1970), 55–6; W. L. Warren, 'Church and state in Angevin Ireland', *Peritia* 13 (1999), 259–75.

62 Watt, *Two nations*, 57–9, 226–30; Aubrey Gwynn, 'Armagh and Louth in the twelfth and thirteenth centuries', *Seanchas Ard Mhacha* 2 (1955), 17–37, at 28–30.

63 *RLP*, 16b, 28a, 29a, 29b; *CDI*, i, nos 168, 176–8; Ralph Turner, *King John* (London, 1994), 152–3.

64 Watt, *Two nations*, 55.

65 See below, 78.

66 *Pont. Hib.*, i, no. 52.

67 Flanagan, 'De Courcy', 176.

68 *NHI*, ix, 280; James Leslie and Henry Swanzy, *Biographical succession lists of the clergy of the diocese of Down* (Enniskillen, 1936), 1.

69 *Pont. Hib.*, i, no. 52 (22 February 1202 to 23 February 1203); Watt, *Two nations*, 229.

probably at Downpatrick on 9 June 1202, where he confirmed grants made by John de Courcy, *nobilis vir*, to the monastic community at Nendrum, and participated in the liturgy surrounding the translation of the bodies of saints Patrick, Brigid and Colum Cille.[70]

The cordial welcome extended to John of Salerno was one strand of de Courcy's wider initiative to ingratiate himself with the papacy. A rubric of a letter sent by Innocent III to the lord of Ulster in 1200, replicated in kind to the king of the Isles and to the prior and monks of St Patrick at Down, mentions *donatione denarii sancti Petri*.[71] The reference to 'Peter's Pence' in an Irish context is intriguing because the collection of this annual payment had been one of the conditions by which Pope Adrian IV had reportedly conceded Ireland to Henry II in 1155.[72] Marie Therese Flanagan has plausibly suggested that, in offering to collect this payment, John de Courcy was entering into a relationship of vassalage with the papacy.[73] A precedent may be found in Scandinavia, where 'it was fairly common for secular lords ... to obtain the protection of the Roman church for themselves and their lands by paying a regular tax of this kind'.[74]

King John may not have been unduly troubled by de Courcy's courtship of Innocent III, as his own relationship with the pope was at this stage still relatively cordial in 1201.[75] However, it is in the obstruction of royal policy in regard to the Armagh vacancy that we may find the clearest indication of what may have caused de Courcy to breach the king's peace.

Crown vs. de Courcy, 1204–05

John de Courcy's grip on Ulster only really began to loosen in 1204. At some point in this year he was defeated by Hugh de Lacy and the 'foreigners of Meath' at Downpatrick and expelled temporarily from his lands.[76] Meanwhile, Walter de Lacy was enlisted by the crown to bring legal pressure to bear against the lord of Ulster. On 31 August, along with the justiciar of Ireland, Walter

70 Flanagan, 'De Courcy', 155–6; eadem, 'Jocelin of Furness and the cult of St Patrick', 50–6.

71 *Pont. Hib.*, i, no. 46.

72 Ibid., no. 4; Flanagan, 'De Courcy', 174n; Barbara Crawford, 'Peter's Pence in Scotland', in G. W. S. Barrow (ed.), *The Scottish tradition: essays in honour of Ronald Gordon Cant* (Edinburgh, 1974), 14–23, at 15. For evidence surrounding the authenticity of Pope Adrian's bull *Laudabiliter*, see Watt, *Two nations*, 35–9; A. J. Duggan, 'The power of documents: the curious case of *Laudabiliter*', in Brenda Bolton and Christine Meek (eds), *Aspects of power and authority in the Middle Ages*, *International Medieval Research* 14 (Turnhout, 2007), 251–76.

73 Flanagan, 'De Courcy', 174.

74 Crawford, 'Peter's Pence', 18.

75 Turner, *King John*, 154.

76 *AU*, 1204; *AFM*, 1203 [*recte* 1204]; *ALC*, 1203 [*recte* 1204].

was instructed to cause de Courcy to come to the king's service, as he 'had sworn and given hostages to do'.[77] A council of barons in Ireland was to set a time limit, in default of which de Courcy's lands would be considered forfeit and eight cantreds of Ulster would be given to Walter and Hugh de Lacy. A failure to comply with these terms is clear from the subsequent grant of eight unspecified Ulster cantreds to the de Lacy brothers on 13 November, the same day on which the king renewed the grant he had first made as count of Mortain to Hugh de Lacy, of six cantreds in Connacht.[78] Hugh had already been awarded an unspecified fee in Ireland, to the value of sixty marks conditional on good service, on 1 September.[79]

It is difficult by this stage to see the de Lacys as anything other than agents of the crown, harvesting the first fruits of their labour. This said, Hugh de Lacy was still some distance from becoming sole lord of Ulster, let alone an earl. Only eight of Ulster's eleven cantreds were to be conferred on the de Lacys in the event of de Courcy's default, with the rest to be delivered to the crown along with a 'reasonable aid', that is, a significant money payment. Moreover, as the senior brother, it was Walter de Lacy who may have claimed the lion's share of the designated portion. Hugh's additional gifts from the crown begin to take on the appearance of conciliatory gestures, designed to placate the beneficiary over the full position in Ulster that his victory at Downpatrick had perhaps aimed to secure. Tellingly, Hugh was only to be granted his sixty-mark fee once he had handed over hostages or other securities to the justiciar of Ireland, and it was to remain in his possession for only as long as he served the king faithfully. If Hugh was by now a royal weapon, he was being deployed with care.

Crucially, it appears that the legal forfeiture of Ulster was not actually carried to its conclusion. On 21 October John de de Courcy had been granted safe conduct in coming to negotiate with the king.[80] He may not have been able to do so given the precariousness of his position, but something interrupted the process of disseisin first initiated in August. A marginal note reveals that the mandates from 13 November were cancelled because one of the royal agents dispatched across the Irish Sea, Ralph of Cirencester, brought the effecting documents back with him to England, where they were torn at Woolwich, the manor of the English justiciar, Geoffrey fitz Peter.[81] It may also have been at this point that de Courcy's English estate of Middleton Cheney was returned

77 *RLP*, 45a; *CDI*, i, no. 224.

78 *Rot. chart.*, 137b, 139b; *CDI*, i, nos 240–1.

79 *RLP*, 45b; *CDI*, i, no. 227.

80 *RLP*, 47a; CDI, i, no. 234.

81 *Rot. chart.*, 137b, 139b; *RLP*, 48a; *CDI*, i, nos 237–41. For Ralph of Cirencester, a royal clerk, see S. D. Church, *The household knights of King John* (Cambridge, 1999), 21, 65.

for his maintenance (*ad se sustentandum*).[82] From a share of eight cantreds in Ulster and six of his own in Connacht, Hugh de Lacy now had only a sixty-mark fee to show for his efforts.

The threat of disseisin was commonly employed as a means of exerting political control, but only in a minority of cases did intimidation lead to permanent forfeiture.[83] In the harassment of John de Courcy, what the king may have sought was not the lord of Ulster's destruction, but his compliance. In identifying which aspect of royal policy de Courcy was to submit to, our focus is attracted to the 'guttering candle'[84] of Plantagenet dominion in Normandy. Most of the principal magnates in Ireland had served the king at home or abroad since the resumption of the war with Capetian France in 1202. William Marshal was one of the king's busiest lieutenants in Normandy, and continued to act as royal envoy to Philip II after the duchy's desertion by the king in December 1203.[85] William de Braose joined the king abroad in July 1202 and was given custody of John's ill-starred nephew, Arthur of Brittany.[86] Walter de Lacy was part of a group tasked with organising incidental aid from the Irish colony in February 1204.[87] John de Courcy, meanwhile, had played no visible part in the defence of the king's continental inheritance, and it may be that the prospect of disseisin or usurpation was being used to coax him into fulfilling his vassalic obligations. This may be the implication of the royal letter addressed to the barons of Ulster on 1 September, the day after Walter de Lacy was authorised to bring legal proceedings against de Courcy, urging them to cause their lord to come into the king's service, as they had sworn oaths to do, or else risk their own lands and hostages.[88]

With Hugh de Lacy prowling on the borders of his lordship, de Courcy was understandably unwilling to leave Ulster unattended. The crown was no doubt aware of this dilemma – indeed, it may have contributed to it by encouraging de Lacy's assault on Downpatrick – and so it is tempting to suggest that an unrealistic demand for personal service was being imposed on de Courcy in order to justify his disseisin, although the subsequent hesitation to enforce this judgement remains a perplexing detail. Moreover, de Lacy's incursion into Ulster may not have occurred until after the initiation of legal proceedings

82 *RLC*, i, 33b.

83 Otway-Ruthven, *Med. Ire.*, 182.

84 Warren, *King John*, 90.

85 Crouch, *William Marshal*, 82–3.

86 Painter, *King John*, 28; F. M. Powicke, *The loss of Normandy, 1189–1204: studies in the history of the Angevin Empire* (3rd edn, Manchester, 1999), 319–22.

87 *Rot. chart.*, 133–4; *CDI*, nos 199–201.

88 *RLP*, 45a; *CDI*, i, no. 224. For the list of the hostages given for de Courcy in 1203, see *RLP*, 55b.

against his adversary in August, and so de Courcy may not have been initially impeded from meeting his feudal commitments.

The obvious caveat is that, with Normandy already abandoned, there was no pressing need for magnates and their retinues to attend the king abroad at the time John de Courcy was being pressed for service.[89] However, there were ways to meet the crown's need in a domestic setting. The contraction of his hegemony was viewed by King John as a temporary, if considerable, setback. All possible streams of revenue were exploited in the replenishment of the Angevin war chest, with significant amounts of money being diverted from Ireland to the king's treasuries in England and Poitou.[90] On the same day that he made his thinly veiled threat against the fees and hostages of the barons of Ulster, 1 September 1204, John directed general letters to his faithful subjects in Ireland, thanking them for the aid and good service which they had already given him, and inviting them provide a further aid to the justiciar 'without delay'.[91] In light of this clear connection between incidental financial aid and *servicium*, a plausible interpretation of John de Courcy's prosecution is that it was designed to procure from him a money payment in lieu of military service.

It was not only Ireland's secular lords whom the king was pressing for funds. In early 1204 John had encouraged the clergy in Ireland to be as generous as their English counterparts in providing for him in his hour of need, through an aid to be explained to them by Walter de Lacy and other royal agents.[92] With the Armagh election dispute still ongoing, the king reassured the province's suffragans that any help they could give him in his 'pressing necessity' would not afterwards be taken as a precedent.[93] On the same day, 1 February, probably with his coffers in mind, the king informed the clergy and laity of Armagh that Ralph Petit (*alias* Parvus), archdeacon of Meath, was to be recognised as archbishop and given counsel, aid and obedience.[94] In the royal nomination of Petit, whose family was closely affiliated with the de Lacys in Meath, we may find a link to Hugh de Lacy's incursions into Ulster.[95] Certainly, Hugh would have been more willing to press the case of the crown's favoured candidate than John de Courcy, who appears to have upheld his endorsement of Archbishop Eugenius.

89 Powicke, *Loss of Normandy*, 160–9.

90 *RLC*, i, 10a, 12a, 34b, 36a; *CDI*, i, nos 231–2, 262, 267.

91 *RLP*, 45b; *CDI*, i, no. 228.

92 *Rot. chart.*, 133b; *CDI*, i, no. 201.

93 *Rot. chart.*, 133b; *CDI*, i, no. 198.

94 *Rot. chart.*, 133b; *CDI*, i, no. 200.

95 Ralph Petit's brother, William, was Walter de Lacy's constable in Meath and was entrusted along with his lord with the collection of incidental aid in 1204: *Rot. chart.*, 133b; *CDI*, i, no. 201.

Regime change in Ulster

The documents which would have sanctioned John de Courcy's forfeiture and replacement by the de Lacys were quite literally torn up. There are several possible explanations for the king's hesitation. Ralph Petit's candidacy for the archiepiscopal office would seem to have been withdrawn by February 1205, when Archbishop Eugenius presided over a clerical assembly convened in the Petit holding of Mullingar in the lordship of Meath.[96] Recognition as primate may have eased the pressure on Eugenius's secular supporters and diminished some of the appeal of the de Lacys as alternative lords of Ulster. Another possibility is that de Courcy complied with the demand for personal or material service. William de Burgh had already redeemed himself in the eyes of the crown in this way,[97] but there is nothing to show that the lord of Ulster followed suit.

Perhaps the most likely cause of the king's volte-face was de Courcy's residual influence in the Irish Sea zone. Marriage to the sister of the king of Man, Rögnvaldr Guðrøðarson, c.1180, had provided him with access to the kind of military resources which could derail attempts to effect permanent regime change in north-east Ireland.[98] The Ulster–Manx alliance also threatened to undermine plans for the recovery of Normandy. With the English Channel now a frontier with a hostile realm, the development of a naval capability was vital to maintain contact with the king's remaining continental possessions and to defend the coast of England.[99] The crown had around fifty galleys at its disposal in 1204, with five stationed in Irish ports, and considerable sums were spent on new vessels to supplement the royal fleet.[100] Equal energy was expended in appropriating the ships of allies on the 'Celtic fringe', including the future earl of Atholl, Thomas of Galloway, who was promised half of any plunder he could win from the king's enemies in return for engaging his *galiotis* in service to the crown.[101]

To this sea-going client base was added Rögnvaldr, king of Man, when on 8 February King John's 'beloved kinsman' was placed under royal protection.[102]

96 Watt, *Two nations*, 229.

97 Having served the king abroad in late 1203, de Burgh's lands (except Connacht) were restored to him by a royal mandate of 29 April 1204: *Rot. lib.* 67; *RLP*, 39–41b.

98 R. A. McDonald, *Manx kingship in its Irish Sea setting, 1187–1229: King Rögnvaldr and the Crovan dynasty, 1187–1229* (Dublin, 2007), 126–8; idem, 'Dealing death from Man: Manx sea power in and around the Irish Sea, 1079–1265', in Seán Duffy (ed.), *The world of the galloglass: kings, warlords and warriors in Ireland and Scotland, 1200–1600* (Dublin, 2007), 45–76; *NHI*, ii, 135.

99 For an overview of Angevin naval policy and capability, see N. A. M. Rodger, *The safeguard of the sea: a naval history of Britain, 660–1649* (London, 1997), 50–60.

100 *Pipe roll 7 John*, xiii–xv; *RLC*, i, 33.

101 *RLP*, 51.

102 Rymer, *Foedera*, i, pt. 1, fo. 91.

It has been proposed that John intended Rögnvaldr's detachment from his brother-in-law in Ulster;[103] the English king had already undermined one maritime compact by offering his illegitimate daughter, Joan, in marriage to the Welsh prince of Gwynedd, Llywelyn ap Iorwerth, thereby trumping the union already agreed between Llywelyn and the daughter of the king of Man.[104] However, this daughter was the widow of Llywelyn's uncle, Rhodri ap Owain, and her proposed marriage to the prince of Gwynedd had been blocked by the church on grounds of consanguinity.[105] If King John was opportunistic in his offer of an alternative (as was Llywelyn in accepting it), he cannot be accused of acting deviously in this instance.

The 'detachment' theory also ignores a significant correlation found in the chancery record. On the same day as the king of Man was taken under royal protection, 8 February, the safe conduct first given to John de Courcy in October was extended to last until a fortnight after Easter in 1205, strongly implying that Rögnvaldr was seeking assurances over his brother-in-law's security amid his own negotiations with the crown.[106] King John's primary concern at this stage was not the dismemberment of the Manx–Ulster alliance, but rather Rögnvaldr's integration into the Angevin ambit. The intention may have been to requisition the Manx fleet for the continental expedition being planned for early summer. Alternatively, Rögnvaldr may have been employed to defend the English coastline from French attack, just as his brother, Óláfr II, would be commissioned by Henry III in 1235 to guard against a Scottish threat.[107]

If de Courcy's legal forfeiture was now diplomatically problematic, it does not follow automatically that the king would be displeased if his demise were to be effected by some other means. A clue as to the crown's amended strategy may be found in the annulment of Hugh de Lacy's grant for his six Connacht cantreds. This may not be so much a sign of royal displeasure as an indication that a greater prize was now within Hugh's grasp. What may have been unofficially communicated to de Lacy was that, should he manage to wrest Ulster from John de Courcy's control through military conquest, he would have the whole lordship for himself, in place of the fragmentary portions of Ulster and Connacht envisaged by the 13 November provisions. The crown could publicly disassociate itself from Hugh's 'private' war, ensuring that neither de

103 Veach, *Lordship*, 118.

104 J. E. Lloyd, *A history of Wales from the earliest times to the Edwardian conquest* (3rd edn, 2 vols, London, 1939), ii, 617.

105 *Cal. papal letters, 1198–1304*, 8, 13, 19. See, however, Huw Pryce, *Native law and the church in medieval Wales* (Oxford, 1993), 83–5, where it is suggested that Llywelyn may have exploited canon law in order to cause his marriage to Rhodri's widow to be annulled, having been offered a more attractive match by King John.

106 *RLP*, 50a.

107 Rymer, *Foedera*, i, pt. 1, fo. 218.

Courcy's downfall nor Rögnvaldr's participation in reprisals against de Lacy would jeopardise long-term Manx co-operation with wider Angevin strategic objectives.[108]

The best, if curiously underused source for subsequent events is the *ex parte* statement of John de Courcy to the papal *curia* detailing his usurpation at the hands of Hugh de Lacy. According to the letter of Innocent III from July 1205, ordering an investigation into the legality of de Lacy's actions,[109] Hugh had unexpectedly invaded Ulster with a large army, in league with some of de Courcy's own men. De Courcy and a small band of followers held out against the interlopers for some time, but he was eventually defeated and taken prisoner. Seeing that de Courcy was in danger of being put to death, some local churchmen secured an agreement whereby John would be released after renouncing all of his Irish lands, along with rights to future restitution, and handing over to Hugh de Lacy all his fortresses and homage, as well as all authentic confirmations or deeds obtained from the apostolic see and others. Further, as corroborated by annalistic sources, de Courcy promised to go to the Holy Land as a crusader and never to return to Ireland.[110]

De Lacy then insisted on a further condition, that he would not allow de Courcy to leave unless the archbishop of Armagh, and some suffragan bishops who were with him at the time, pronounced anathema on whoever should infringe or limit those conditions. De Lacy swore in haste (or immediately) that as soon as de Courcy handed over to him his fortresses, castles and authentic documents he would be released immediately along with two of his *nepotes* (nephews or kinsmen) being held in chains; that Hugh would disinherit no one who had been granted a fief by de Courcy; and that he would permit John to take away his arms and chattels. De Courcy then swore that he would leave all that he possessed in Ireland, adding another oath to the effect that, unless Hugh faithfully observed his promise, he would in no way be bound by his oath and would have the right to injure his captor as best he could.

The appeal to Innocent III was made on the grounds that Hugh had not fulfilled his side of the agreement: de Courcy's *nepotes* were still held captive; no attempt had been made to restore his arms and chattels; and his oaths had been extorted through fear of death. De Courcy therefore sought absolution from his crusading vow and took refuge with his allies west of the river Bann in the

108 Rögnvaldr would be awarded 30 marcates of English lands 'for his homage and service' on 28 April 1206: *RLC*, i, 68, and below, 93.

109 *Pont. Hib.*, i, no. 64.

110 *ALC*, 1204 [*recte* 1205] ('John de Curci was taken prisoner, and released after being crossed to go to Jerusalem'); *Chron. Mann*, 26 ('Hugh de Lacy came with his army to Ulster and fought against John de Courcy, whom he seized and put in chains before subjecting Ulster. Afterwards John de Courcy was allowed to go free').

native kingdom of Tír Eógain.[111] Recognising his usurper as a *deus ex machina* contrived by the Angevin court, de Courcy lobbied for the support of the apostolic see but wasted no ink or vellum in appealing to his secular overlord, King John.

Household favourite

Hugh de Lacy's subjection of Ulster cannot be precisely dated, but it probably took place before he was extended safe conduct to court on 23 March, to last until Michaelmas (29 September 1205).[112] He had arrived in England by the end of April, when he first appears as a witness in chancery enrolments.[113] The crown initially sought to turn de Lacy's success to its own constitutional advantage. By 2 May, he was granted Ulster as John de Courcy had held it 'on the year or day on which the same Hugh defeated and captured the same John in the field', thus fixing his seigneurial autonomy at the level of his precursor. In reserving Ulster's *crociae* to the crown, however, the king was encroaching on one of the freedoms exercised by de Courcy by claiming jurisdiction in church land.[114] The initial endowment of Ulster did little to elevate Hugh's standing in comparison with other tenants-in-chief. He witnessed five royal charters before 2 May, achieving a position of third in the attesting sequence.[115] While superficially impressive, none of these enrolments list more than seven witnesses, while those whom de Lacy 'outranked' were mostly members of the royal household.[116] A more accurate perception of how Hugh fitted into the aristocratic strata is achieved in consideration of the names appearing before his, such as that of William de Braose, who was accorded precedence over de Lacy in a further two testing clauses on 3 May, subsequent to the grant of Ulster.[117]

A very different picture is presented by the amended charter issued to de

111 *AU*, 1205; *AFM*, 1204 [*recte* 1205].
112 *RLP*, 51b; *CDI*, i, no. 256.
113 *Rot. chart.*, 148.
114 Crossed lands were 'held immediately from the crown, and were therefore exempt from the jurisdiction of the liberty, forming enclaves of land in which the royal administration had full force': Otway-Ruthven, 'Anglo-Irish shire government', 7.
115 *Rot. chart.*, 148. Caution must be exercised when making inferences from royal charters or their witnesses. 'There are distortions both in the chronology and the types of charter that survive, and the witnesses to such charters, though presumably high in royal favour, were by no means the only or necessarily the greatest of the servants of the court': Nicholas Vincent, 'The court of Henry II', in Christopher Harper-Bill and Nicholas Vincent (eds), *Henry II: new interpretations* (Woodbridge, 2007), 278–335, at 299.
116 With the exception of Warin fitz Gerold, one of the most prominent barons never to be awarded a comital title: Painter, *King John*, 22.
117 *Rot. chart.*, 148.

Lacy on 29 May, by which the terms of Hugh's tenure had been adjusted to include the 'crosses', in return for a negligible *servicium*. More significantly, in Ulster's metamorphosis from liberty to earldom, de Lacy gained admission to the select band of magnates in possession of a comital title. An explanation for this dramatic improvement in his circumstances must take into account the worsening position of the king, according to whose will the fortunes of his subjects ebbed and flowed.

May 1205 saw the disintegration of royal plans for the speedy recovery of Normandy. Having organised England against the threat of a Capetian-sponsored invasion at the beginning of the year, John had used the remaining contents of his war chest in amassing a vast expeditionary force to strike for the continent in early June.[118] In what has been labelled more tragedy than fiasco, the royal fleet, bristling with men and arms, failed to leave English shores.[119] John could do nothing without his baronage, who, worn out by perpetual demands for money and foreign service, flatly refused to follow the king abroad.[120]

As baronial resistance stiffened, the king had become increasingly reliant on a small number of household officials and intimates.[121] Hugh de Lacy found himself drafted into this group as a recent beneficiary of royal patronage. On 2 May he was retained in royal service, and the Irish justiciar was instructed to defend Hugh's newly acquired territories as if they were the king's.[122] De Lacy was itinerant with the royal court at Windsor and London in the early part of May, and at Dorchester at the end of June.[123] In the interim, he appears to have been employed in an administrative capacity. On 22 May the king instructed his treasurer and chamberlains to pay twenty-four marks to Hugh's messenger. The payment had already been ordered twice, but owing to negligence had not been handed over.[124] Only under extraordinary circumstances would the king resort to dispensing wages to those in his service, so it seems more likely that Hugh had been charged with a mission outside the court.[125] The sum was ultimately to be delivered to John's 'business manager',[126] Reginald Cornhill, sheriff of Kent.

118 Contemporary chronicles describe the mustering of 1500 ships and 14,000 sailors at Portsmouth: *The historical works of Gervase of Canterbury*, ed. William Stubbs, Rolls Series (2 vols, London, 1879–90), ii, 98; Ralph of Coggeshall, *Chronicon Anglicanum*, ed. Joseph Stevenson (London, 1875), 152–3. While the main fleet was intended for Normandy, a smaller force was being prepared at Dartmouth, the convenient point of egress to Poitou: *Pipe roll 7 John*, xviii–xx, xxxiv; Warren, *King John*, 112.

119 *Pipe roll 7 John*, xii.

120 Warren, *King John*, 110.

121 Turner, *King John*, 129.

122 *RLP*, 54a; *CDI*, i, no. 260.

123 *Rot. chart.*, 148–56.

124 *RLC*, i, 34a.

125 For the rewards of royal service, see Church, *Household knights*, 74–100.

126 Painter, *King John*, 137.

Its exact purpose is not known, but the repeated demand for its completion is at least indicative of an increasingly burdened administration.

A shortage of willing supporters forced the king to widen his friendship circle. Once regarded by John as his 'worst enemy among the English barons',[127] the pliancy of Earl Ranulf of Chester earned recognition of his claim to Richmondshire and the cancellation of long-standing debts.[128] Ranulf was frequently with the royal court in the first half of 1205, and he would enjoy a cordial relationship with the crown for the rest of John's reign. Between 30 April and 23 July just seven witnesses are listed in the charter rolls with greater frequency than Hugh de Lacy, aside from the royal steward, Peter de Stokes.[129] As with Earl Ranulf, might de Lacy's utility during a period of crisis have commended him to the crown? This may be so, but a comital title would seem to be an entirely disproportionate reward. Other forces were at work, chief among them the king's discovery of another vassal's duplicity.

William Marshal's division of loyalty

Once 'beyond reproach',[130] by spring 1205 the reputation of William Marshal as a man of honour was in danger of impeachment. The continental war had placed those holding estates on each side of the English Channel in a tight bind. Philip II demanded that all landholders in the duchy of Normandy should perform exclusive liege homage to him or face permanent forfeiture. If they did so, they would no longer be regarded as vassals of King John, and risked losing their English property. While some found a way around this obstacle by dividing their lands among family members, the earl of Pembroke formulated an altogether more creative solution.

In May 1204, exploiting his capacity as Angevin ambassador, the Marshal persuaded Philip Augustus to delay the confiscation of his Norman estates by one year. Meanwhile, King John made efforts to mitigate his supporter's potential losses by granting William custody of Goodrich castle (Herefordshire) and permitting him to annex Cilgerran into his earldom of Pembroke.[131] In Ireland, every effort was made to accommodate William's interests in competition with those of the

127 Ibid., 29.

128 *RLP*, 51a; *RLC*, i, 30a, 60b.

129 *Rot. chart.*, 148–56. These were Geoffrey fitz Peter, earl of Essex, and William, earl of Salisbury (twenty-five appearances, respectively); Ranulf, earl of Chester (twenty-four); Roger, constable of Chester (twenty-one); Saer de Quincy (eighteen); Hubert Walter, archbishop of Canterbury (fifteen); Robert fitz Roger, sheriff of Northumberland (thirteen). Hugh de Lacy appears twelve times.

130 Powicke, *Loss of Normandy*, 294.

131 *Rot. chart.*, 124a; *RLC*, i, 4b; Crouch, *William Marshal*, 84.

royal justiciar and Marshal tenant, Meiler fitz Henry.[132] In 1204, following the death of Gerald fitz Maurice, holder of Uí Failge in the lordship of Leinster, fitz Henry took the fee into his own possession, falsely claiming that he had been instructed to do so by royal writ.[133] Uí Failge's strategic location, bridging Meiler's lands in Leinster with his cantred of Cenél Fiachach (Ardnurcher) in Meath, very much implies that he was acting in his own self-interest.[134] King John took the Marshal's side in the dispute, recognising Gerald fitz Maurice's heir and property as *de feodo ipsius comitis*.[135] If in later years the Marshal would clash with the crown over encroachment on his jurisdictions in Leinster,[136] in this instance the king was willing to ignore his own right to prerogative wardship.[137] The recognition of the Marshal's claim in Uí Failge was seemingly part of a wider programme to placate the earl over the impending confiscation of his Norman lands.

In spring 1205 the king demonstrated further graciousness by granting the Marshal permission to swear fealty to Philip II. Instead, dramatically overstepping the bounds of his remit, William performed 'liege homage' to Philip for his estates on the French side of the sea. In effect, he divided his loyalty between the two kings, becoming Philip's vassal in Normandy and John's man in England.[138] It may be that William was more guilty of 'over-optimism'[139] than 'intentional deception',[140] but he must have known that his oath would be regarded as an act of treachery by King John. Despite all of the king's indulgences, the Marshal had pursued a personal agenda and was now unable to fight for John without compromising his vassalic obligations to Philip II. If one of the king's staunchest supporters had acted in this way, what chance had John in persuading the dissenting barons to fall into line?

The Marshal's breach with the crown may not have been as serious as his near-contemporary biography would have us believe.[141] Some punitive

132 Meiler was a child of an illegitimate son of Henry I and one of the first Anglo-Norman interlopers in Ireland, where he was enfeoffed in Leinster by Strongbow: see M. T. Flanagan, 'Fitz Henry, Meiler (†1220)', in *ODNB*.

133 Flanagan, 'Defining lordships', 44–6.

134 In 1184 Hugh I de Lacy granted Meiler the cantred of Ardnurcher (Horseleap, Co. Westmeath) along with his niece in marriage: *Deeds of the Normans*, ll. 3136–9; *Song of Dermot*, ll. 3138–41; *Expug. Hib.*, 194–5.

135 *RLP*, 38a; *CDI*, i, no. 195.

136 See below, 94–8.

137 In theory, the crown had the right of wardship to any land held by a tenant-in-chief during a minority: Paul Brand, *The making of the common law* (London, 1992), 449.

138 *HWM*, iii, 148. The constitutional implications of the oath are obscure, owing to its rarity: Warren, *King John*, 113; Crouch, *William Marshal*, 86; Sidney Painter, *William Marshal: knight-errant, baron and regent of England* (Baltimore, MD, 1933), 139.

139 Crouch, *William Marshal*, 87.

140 Painter, *William Marshal*, 141.

141 The biography is the only source noting a stand-off between the Marshal's supporters and the king's *bachelers* at Portsmouth: *HWM*, ii, ll. 13175–248.

measures were taken, including the delivery of his son, William, as a hostage and the withdrawal of some privileges.[142] However, as attested by his continued presence in the chancery record, the Marshal was not completely disgraced. In their approach to discipline, the Angevin kings of England were altogether more calculating than their Norman predecessors, targeting a subject's status or peace of mind as often as their lands or person.[143] King John's response to the Marshal's disloyalty may have been no less cerebral. Word of the contentious oath had not reached the English court by 9 May, when the king instructed Meiler fitz Henry to uphold the rights of John Marshal, William's nephew and steward in Leinster.[144] The Marshal was reportedly afforded a 'frosty' reception by King John upon his return from France,[145] so his position was probably discovered shortly before his reappearance in the chancery record on 1 June.[146] This brings back into view the creation of the earldom of Ulster, effected just three days earlier on Whitsunday 29 May.

One plausible theory is that, still smarting from his vassal's deception, King John was seeking to counterbalance the Marshal's influence in Ireland by elevating one of his peers in the Irish colony to the rank of earl. The idea of a 'politic transfusion of dignity'[147] is convincing, but why was Hugh de Lacy, by any standards still one of the most junior members of the colonial nobility, selected as this comital counterpoint? Care had to be taken so as not to create one over-mighty subject in order to punish another. For this reason the prize of an earldom may have been withheld from William de Braose, who was present at court at the same time as Hugh de Lacy. De Braose was already in possession of a large assemblage of estates in England and the Welsh March in addition to his Irish honor of Limerick. His relationship with the king has been characterised as one 'of mutual usefulness rather than affection',[148] and John had already taken steps to contain his power within acceptable limits. Part of this royal strategy involved offsetting de Braose's power with that of the brothers, William and Hubert de Burgh, his respective territorial rivals in Ireland and Wales. William de Burgh's own unruliness had already resulted in Limerick's transference into de Braose's hands. Then, in spring of 1205, Hubert de Burgh was captured by the French at Chinon in the Loire valley.[149] The de Burgh check having been rendered ineffective, May 1205 was an especially

142 *HWM*, ii, ll. 13271–3; Crouch, *William Marshal*, 91.

143 Crouch, *William Marshal*, 89–90.

144 *RLP*, 42a; *CDI*, i, no. 216.

145 *HWM*, ii, ll. 13052–3.

146 *Rot. chart.*, 153a.

147 Crouch, 'The earl in Wales and Ireland'.

148 Warren, *King John*, 107.

149 Painter, *King John*, 44–5.

inopportune moment to provide de Braose with the additional windfall of a comital title.

Walter de Lacy was also overlooked, despite the fact that the proximity of his midlands lordship to that of William Marshal recommended it as the ideal counterweight. Indeed, one theory surrounding Hugh I de Lacy's grant of Meath in 1172 holds that Henry II had intended the beneficiary to offset Strongbow's influence in Leinster.[150] As in the case of Walter's father-in-law, William de Broase, the king may have feared that the grant of an earldom would cause the lord of Meath's influence to exceed tolerable bounds. No such difficulty would be encountered in the promotion of Walter's younger brother, whose confinement to the Irish colony would ensure that the seigneurial balance of power in England remained unaffected. Hugh had acted in the crown's interest in displacing John de Courcy, and his efficacy amid the frantic build-up to the continental expedition must have further counted in his favour. At the very least, the king must have been confident that a sense of gratitude would cause him to remain compliant with the royal will.

The Winchester *coronatio*

In commenting on Hugh de Lacy's comital promotion, historians have universally overlooked the significance of its timing and location. Whitsunday was one of the principal religious festivals at which the king was liturgically elevated, and Winchester one of the royal residences where the crown was traditionally worn.[151] There is no direct evidence that a royal *coronatio* took place on this occasion, but care should be taken before concluding, *ex silentio*, that the king was as reticent to wear his crown as his father, Henry II, had been.[152] The *Festkrönung* was especially exploited by John's predecessors and successors in times of political crisis as a public way to reaffirm their sovereignty. Stephen's Christmas crown-wearing in 1141 was intended to communicate the recovery of his regality following his imprisonment at the hands of the Empress Matilda. The liturgy from that occasion was regurgitated in 1194 to mark the recommencement of Richard I's personal rule, subsequent to his release from captivity in Germany.[153] In 1265, according to the chronicle of Thomas Wykes, Henry III chose to wear his crown at Westminster for the feast of St Edward's translation,

[150] For a critique of this theory, see Colin Veach, 'Henry II's grant of Meath to Hugh de Lacy in 1172: a reassessment', *Ríocht na Mídhe: records of the Meath Archaeological and Historical Society* 18 (2007), 67–94, at 79–86.

[151] Biddle, 'Seasonal festivals and residence'.

[152] Bartlett, *England*, 128–9.

[153] George Garnett, *Conquered England: kingship, succession and tenure, 1066–1166* (Oxford, 2007), 250.

shortly after his victory against the Montfortian faction at Evesham, 'as if he had obtained the regal majesty which he had recently been without'.[154]

King John had every reason to exploit the theatre and didactic function of the royal *coronatio* in 1205. A crown-wearing would mark the beginning of what was expected to be a lengthy continental campaign, while publicly underlining John's regality as increasingly cacophonous dissenting voices threatened the viability of the royal expedition. There may not have been a ceremony of such solemn splendour as those alluded to above from the reigns of Stephen or Richard I, which were little less than second ordinations;[155] but even an understated affair could have drawn parallels with John's own coronation 'proper' on Ascension day in 1199, the anniversary of which (27 May) so often fell close to Whitsunday, and rarely so close as in 1205.[156]

The Whitsun feast had particular symbolic resonance as the commemoration of Pentecost, when the apostles had been equipped with paracletic power to go among the gentiles, contending with demons and darkness. The analogy is unlikely to have been lost on John as he prepared to dispatch his vassals beyond the sea to battle the Capetian enemy. In 1242, during one of his pilgrimages to the shrine of the Virgin Mary at Walsingham, Henry III timed his call to arms for his proposed expedition to Poitou with the vigil of the feast of the Annunciation.[157] But it was the particular suitability of Pentecost to the idea of commencement which would later recommend it as the setting for the Feast of the Swans, that 'superb piece of royal theatre'[158] orchestrated by Edward I on 22 May 1306, at Westminster, to boost baronial morale and secure fresh recruits for an impending Scottish campaign.[159]

[154] *Ann. mon.*, iv, 177, cited in Björn Weiler, 'Symbolism and politics in the reign of Henry III', in Michael Prestwich, Richard Britnell and Robin Frame (eds), *Thirteenth century England IX: proceedings of the Durham conference, 2001* (Woodbridge, 2003), 15–41, at 23.

[155] Garnett, *Conquered England*, 250n.

[156] The king celebrated Whitsunday at Winchester on four occasions during his reign (1205, 1208, 1214, 1215), whereas he observed Christmas there just once (1206), and was never at Winchester for Easter Sunday: 'Itinerary of King John', *RLP*, l–lxxiv. It should be pointed out that John's regnal years began, unusually, on the date of the moveable feast of the Ascension, rather than the original coronation date (27 May). An article exploring John's exploitation of the symbolism of the Pentecost feast in times of particular crisis is currently in process.

[157] Nicholas Vincent, 'King Henry III and the blessed Virgin Mary', in R. N. Swanson (ed.), *The church and Mary: papers read at the 2001 summer meeting and the 2002 winter meeting of the Ecclesiastical History Society* (Woodbridge, 2004), 126–46, at 134.

[158] Peter Cross, 'Knighthood, heraldry and social exclusion in Edwardian England', in idem and Maurice Keen (eds), *Heraldry, pageantry and social display in medieval England* (Woodbridge, 2002), 39–68, at 50.

[159] Close to 300 young barons assembled at Westminster to be knighted on the same day as the future Edward II, taking vows against the king's enemies on a platter of decorated swans: Matthew Strickland, 'Treason, feud and the growth of state violence: Edward I and the 'war of the earl of Carrick', 1306–7', in Chris Given-Wilson, Ann Kettle and Len Scales (eds), *War, government*

An extra significance was given to the Whitsunday ceremonial by the cult of St Swithun, looking on from his reliquary behind the high altar in Winchester cathedral, whose saintly skill-set was of especial interest for those about to undertake a short but tricky Channel crossing.[160] The ninth-century bishop of Winchester is today associated with the legend whereby rain on his feast day (15 July) is thought to herald another forty days of summer showers. The origin of this tradition is obscure,[161] but a popular belief concerning the saint's influence over the weather may already have been established by the thirteenth century, when Giraldus Cambrensis inserted Swithun in a Life of St David. Within, an angel appears to David and instructs him to send Swithun across the sea, promising to 'supply him both with wind as well as with a means of transportation'.[162] In tenth-century *Vitae* of Swithun it is the saint himself who is able to ensure speedy journeys for those invoking his name, such as the slave-girl invisibly conveyed 'in a split second' (*in pungentis ictu*) from her place of captivity in Winchester town to the sanctuary in the old minster.[163]

A royal crown-wearing was also an occasion for the dispensation of privilege, providing the setting in which baronial status could be controlled and the king's favour displayed. The distribution of coronation services was a royal prerogative, but conditional on status. If the king wished one of his vassals to perform a specific role in the ceremony, the candidate had to possess the rank apposite to the service. The privileges of bearing liturgical objects or symbols of state at the head of the royal procession, for example, were exclusively reserved for those of comital rank.[164]

Hugh de Lacy's promotion qualified him to undertake a privileged part in the crown-wearing ceremony. A parallel can be drawn with William Marshal's own promotion in 1199, on the same day as the king's ordination, when John rewarded the men instrumental in securing his accession to the throne – the Marshal and Geoffrey fitz Peter – by belting them as earls of Pembroke and Essex.[165] The Marshal had borne the royal sceptre at the head of the royal

and aristocracy in the British Isles, c. 1150–1500: essays presented to Michael Prestwich (Woodbridge, 2008), 84–113, at 104–8.

[160] Michael Lapidge, *The cult of St Swithun: Winchester studies 4.ii: the Anglo-Saxon minsters of Winchester* (Oxford, 2003), 34–5.

[161] Ibid., 48–9, where it is noted that the feast of St Swithun's deposition (2 July) coincides with the feasts of Processus and Martinianus, with whom similar prognostic traditions had become associated ('during the central Middle Ages, if not earlier').

[162] Ibid., 148–9 (*ego ei tam ventum quam vehiculum ministrabo*).

[163] The miracle is related both in Lantfred's *Translatio et miracula S. Swithuni* and Wulfstan's *Narratio metrica de S. Swithuno*: ibid., 303–5, 497–503.

[164] Richardson, 'The coronation in medieval England', 129–34.

[165] Roger of Howden states incorrectly that Marshal was created earl of Striguil: *Chron. Houedene*, iv, 20–1; Crouch, *William Marshal*, 86.

procession during Richard I's coronation in 1189.[166] Comital status appears to have enabled him to perform a more honorific service a decade later, serving the king's table girded with the sword symbolic of his rank.[167] Returning to 1205, the *Histoire* implies that the Marshal had already presented himself at court by 29 May.[168] If, as seems quite likely, John was liturgically elevated on Whitsunday, an apt way to remind the assembled crowd (and William Marshal himself) that men and women were broken and made at the king's discretion would have been to replace the earl of Pembroke in the crown-wearing ritual with the freshly belted *comes Ultonie*.[169]

❖

After Whitsunday, the royal court made its way from Winchester to the south coast, where King John inspected his forces at Portsmouth on a daily basis (between 5 and 9 June).[170] Hugh de Lacy was still part of the royal coterie 'all ready and willing to go with the king over sea'.[171] On 6 June the lands of the 'most dear and estimable' earl of Ulster were taken under the king's protection, and he was retained in royal service.[172] Three days later, de Lacy was granted a prest of 100 Irish marks against what he was expected to spend in foreign service.[173] Meanwhile, William Marshal headed a group in opposition to the continental expedition. On 15 June, unable to persuade his barons to put to sea, the king was left with no option but to call off the whole enterprise, much to the chagrin of the army.[174] The frustrations of the rank and file were shared by the king, who immediately levied an enormous tax from the baronage for having dared to defy him.[175]

166 *Chron. Houedene*, iii, 9. Howden's description was adapted from a mid-twelfth-century directory: Richardson, 'The coronation in medieval England', 181–5.

167 *Chron. Houedene*, iv, 90 (*ipsi illa die servierunt ad mensam regis accincti gladiis*).

168 The king's accusation of treachery took place before the royal entourage arrived at Porchester (31 May): *HWM*, ii, ll. 13060–96; Kate Norgate, *John Lackland* (London, 1902), 107.

169 In 1239, representing another instance of royal discipline by exclusion, Henry III denied Simon de Montfort access to the churching of the queen: Weiler, 'Symbolism and politics', 20. The archbishop of York refused to attend Richard I's *coronatio* in 1194 after being prohibited from carrying the cross at the head of the procession: *Chron. Houedene*, iii, 246–8.

170 Norgate, *John Lackland*, 107.

171 Coggeshall, *Chronicon Anglicanum*, 154.

172 *RLC*, i, 37a; *CDI*, i, no. 265.

173 *Documents illustrative of English history in the thirteenth and fourteenth centuries, selected from the records of the Queeen's remembrancer of the exchequer*, ed. Henry Cole (London, 1844), 271.

174 Coggeshall, *Chronicon Anglicanum*, 153.

175 Norgate, *John Lackland*, 112.

De Lacy is last attested at court on 23 June.[176] The transformation in his fortunes since his initial summons, exactly four months earlier, is scarcely believable. Hugh had arrived in England as a second-rank subject. He departed, not only as Ulster's liberally enfranchised lord, but in possession of Ireland's first earldom. As such, he was intended to play a more conspicuous role in Irish affairs as co-adjutor to the king's representative in Ireland. On 30 June the king instructed Meiler fitz Henry to have 'undoubted trust concerning those things which [Hugh] will tell you on our behalf, about our affairs which concern our own advantage and the peace of the land'.[177]

The factors identified by Robin Frame as permitting aristocratic cadets to achieve success in Angevin Ireland were fourfold, namely the creation of sub-tenures, an advantageous marriage, military conquest and royal patronage.[178] Sub-enfeoffment in Meath and marriage to Lescelina de Verdun had placed Hugh de Lacy on the landholding ladder. The lordship of Ulster had been won in the crucible of battle. How high a noble could ascend, however, was dictated by the 'parsimonious policy' of the crown.[179] Some magnates were difficult to ignore, but Hugh de Lacy's achievements before 1205 hardly cried out for recognition. He had ingratiated himself with the king by usurping John de Courcy, and earned further commendation for his loyalty at a time of particular crisis. Nevertheless, the reality may be that the creation of the earldom of Ulster owed less to the actions of Hugh de Lacy than to those of the double-dealing William Marshal. Hugh's deployment as a counterpoint to the lord of Leinster would only prove workable for as long as the earl of Ulster's interests harmonised with royal policy. By the time the king next had cause to take action against William Marshal in Ireland, however, de Lacy would be an opponent, not an agent, of the crown.

[176] *Rot. chart.*, 158a.
[177] *RLC*, i, 40a; *CDI*, i, no. 268.
[178] Frame, 'Aristocracies', 145.
[179] Bartlett, *England*, 208.

3

Ascendancy

Lordship in Ulster, 1205–10

According to the Manx chronicle, it was only the timely intervention of Walter de Lacy and the barons of Meath which prevented the nascent earldom of Ulster from meeting with an early disaster:

> In the year 1205 John de Courcy regained his strength and collected a very large force; he took Reginald (Rögnvaldr), king of the Isles, with him to Ulster with about one hundred ships. On landing at the port of Strangford he showed little enthusiasm to besiege the castle of Rath (Dundrum, co. Down). A large army under the command of Walter de Lacy took them by surprise and routed them completely.[1]

One of the most serious threats faced by new lords was the 'hovering presence' of the men they had replaced.[2] If, on this occasion, de Courcy was forced to abandon his bid for restoration 'without obtaining power',[3] but while he remained at large under the protection of Manx and Irish allies he would continue to represent an alternative focus of fidelity for the barons of Ulster. Royal endorsement could only go so far in recommending Hugh de Lacy to his new tenants, many of whom had arrayed against him during the conflict of 1204–05. The earl may well have been conscious of the warning from history provided by his English *consanguineus*, Ibert II de Lacy, who assumed control of the honor of Pontefract in 1135 after tenants loyal to Ibert's father, Robert, took advantage of the death of King Henry I to murder the lord imposed on them by the crown.[4] Many of Ulster's churchmen also had strong ties to the previous regime, having either been transplanted to Ulster by de Courcy or having benefited from his energetic patronage. The quality of de Lacy's dominical lordship may have been especially impaired by the sentence of

1 *Chron. Mann.*, 26, *s.a.*, 1206.

2 David Crouch, 'Strategies of lordship in Angevin England and the career of William Marshal', in Christopher Harper-Bill and Ruth Harvey (eds), *The ideals and practice of medieval knighthood II: papers from the third Strawberry Hill conference* (Woodbridge, 1988), 1–25, at 6.

3 *ALC*, 1205.

4 *Chronicles of the reigns of Stephen, Henry II and Richard I*, ed. Richard Howlett, Rolls Series (4 volumes, London, 1884–9), iii, 140; Wightman, *Lacy family*, 68–73.

excommunication likely to have been pronounced against him by the primate of Ireland and partisan of John de Courcy, Archbishop Eugenius of Armagh.[5]

In his study of William Marshal's lordship in England and Ireland, David Crouch outlined two broad types of strategy utilised by lords consolidating themselves in new acquisitions. By a process of *assimilation*, the incomer sought to win the allegiance of those under his sway by lavishing patronage on tenants and churchmen, appropriating feelings of loyalty by adopting names or symbols associated with the previous dynasty. In contrast, through policies of *colonisation*, lords ripped up the tenurial and spiritual fabric of their lordship, replacing the existing aristocratic elite with their own supporters, and throwing up new religious houses filled with clerical staff sympathetic to the founder. The latter strategy appealed most to lords whose positions were especially precarious. For this reason, it was favoured by William Marshal in Ireland, whose status as an absentee *curialis* had not endeared him initially to the battle-hardened frontiersmen of Leinster, and whose eventual renovation of his Irish lordship involved its division among his entourage and outfitting with new abbeys.[6]

Bearing in mind the looming spectre of John de Courcy's regime, perhaps the most surprising aspect of Hugh de Lacy's lordship strategy after 1205 is that it did not intrude more on Ulster's social and religious life. True, Hugh's family and friends in Meath and Uriel were endowed with portions of his new acquisition, and as a blunt measure of socio-political interaction, it is their names which appear most regularly in Hugh's comital *acta* in the period 1205–10. But, remarkably, there was no wholesale uprooting of John de Courcy's followers, nor any perceivable attempt to establish new colonies of canons and monks as counterpoints to those installed by the previous regime. Instead, de Lacy appears to have turned to propaganda and the power of self-promotion in order to cast himself, *pro Anglicis et Hibernicis*, as the authentic successor to John de Courcy and as Ulster's legitimate lord.

Legitimising lordship: the language of power

Charters and the comital image

'Almost always', proposes Bruce Mazlish, 'leadership will be defined in opposition to that of prior leadership'.[7] Accepting that lordship is also a 'creative act',[8] Hugh de Lacy's first pressing task was to present a brand of lordship more

5 *Pont. Hib.*, i, no. 64, and below, 81–2.

6 Crouch, 'Strategies of lordship'.

7 Bruce Mazlish, 'Leader and led, individual and group', in idem (ed.), *The leader, the led and the psyche: essays in psychohistory* (Hanover, NH, 1990), 249–66, at 255.

8 Ibid., 252.

appealing than that of his precursor. He could hardly mythologise his conquest, for John de Courcy had already done so, blunting Irish opposition by appropriating the cults of local saints and casting himself as hero of Merlin Silvester's supposed prophecy, that 'a white knight, astride a white horse, and bearing a device of birds on his shield, will be the first to enter Ulaid and overrun it with hostile intent'.[9] One of the devices best suited to self-promotion was the written word, and the revised *Vita Patricii* commissioned by John de Courcy had lauded its patron as Ulster's *princeps* and 'a most special admirer and venerator of St Patrick'.[10] No such effort to sponsor hagiographical material is known to have been made by Hugh de Lacy, although some mileage could perhaps have been made from the 'discovery' of the parents and brother of St Brendan (of Clonfert) at Walter de Lacy's English manor of Ludlow (Shropshire), c.1200.[11] Instead, it was through his comital *acta* that the earl made one of his most assertive legitimising claims.

Hugh's early charters had called attention to his pedigree as son of the conqueror of Meath, and his was arguably a more distinguished descent than de Courcy's, despite some recent revisions to the latter's familial origins.[12] But, if a good name was useful for those making their way in the world, it commanded respect only by proxy, and Hugh could now distinguish himself in other ways than the invocation of illustrious forebears.[13] What set de Lacy apart from his peers and *antecessores* was his social rank, and it is no surprise to find that the opening protocol in each of his charters after 1205, with the exception of those issued in exile (1211–21), identifies the grantor as 'earl of Ulster' (*comes Ultonie*).

An earl's style was not always accompanied by a territorial label, as in the case of Earl David of Huntingdon (†1219), whose addresses underlined his connections to the Scottish crown in preference to his tenure 'of Huntingdon'. Keith Stringer has argued that the absence of the geographical designation reflects the weakness of David's position in England and the honorific character

9 *Expug. Hib.*, 174–5. Giraldus preferred to leave a full account of de Courcy's conquest 'to be unfolded more fully by his own historians': ibid., 176–7, 180–1.

10 Helen Birkett, *The saints' lives of Jocelin of Furness: hagiography, patronage and ecclesiastical patronage* (York, 2010), 141–71. For evidence that de Courcy may have already been familiar with Patrick before his involvement in Ireland, as a result of the saint's established popularity in Normandy and England, see Flanagan, 'Jocelin of Furness', 47–9.

11 Robert Bartlett, 'Cults of Irish, Scottish and Welsh saints in twelfth-century England', in Smith (ed.), *Britain and Ireland*, 67–86, at 77. For other 'discoveries' of saints' remains in twelfth-century Ireland, prior to the *inventio* of Patrick, Brigid and Colum Cille, orchestrated by John de Courcy, see Flanagan, 'Jocelin of Furness', 52–3.

12 Duffy, 'First Ulster plantation', 5–8; Flanders, *De Courcy*, 43–69, 154–5.

13 Just seven of Hugh's post-1205 charters feature *pro anima* clauses, and in none of these are his mother and father mentioned by name: appendix I, nos 9, 11, 16–17, 19, 25, 29.

of his comital title.[14] Conversely, the consistent employment of the territorial style in Hugh de Lacy's charters could represent the donor's claim to real power in the localities comprising his *comitatus*. Around 1195 Earl Ranulf III of Chester was described as *princeps* in the poem, *De laude Cestrie*, composed by Lucian, a monk of St Werburgh's at Chester,[15] with the ostensible intention of presenting Ranulf as master of a 'distinct people' and a 'self-conscious realm'.[16] It is tempting to view Hugh de Lacy's employment of territorial style as a response to the assertion of strong local lordship implied by John de Courcy's own designation by Jocelin of Furness as *princeps* of Ulster. Tempting, although perhaps unsatisfactory, as it seems that the style was also used by earls with a restricted array of powers.[17]

The loss of de Lacy's original *acta* denies us recourse to external features of his charters which could have provided visual cues to the earl's prestige.[18] The comital title would certainly have been replicated in the legends from Hugh's seals, but what effect de Lacy's promotion had on his chosen iconography remains unclear. Seal designs were becoming more idiosyncratic at the beginning of the thirteenth century, introducing more of the recognisable insignia of aristocracy, whether military accoutrements, heraldic elements or hunting imagery. The downside to novelty was that it broke with tradition, and incoming lords might claim greater legitimacy by eschewing current fashions and displaying continuity with the iconography of their predecessors. In 1188, after his succession to the duchy of Brittany was engineered by Henry II in order to offset Capetian influence, Earl Ranulf III of Chester issued a new seal which was notably retrograde in appearance, inspired by those of his Breton precursors.[19]

Turning to the internal features of Hugh's charters, we find that their *clausulae*

14 K. J. Stringer, 'The charters of David, earl of Huntingdon and lord of Garioch: a study in Anglo-Scottish diplomatic', in idem (ed.), *Essays on the nobility of medieval Scotland* (Edinburgh, 1985), 72–101, at 80.

15 *Extracts from the MS liber Luciani de laude Cestrie written about the year 1195 and now in the Bodleian Library, Oxford*, ed. M. V. Taylor, *The Record Society of Lancashire and Cheshire* 64 (1912), 61.

16 David Crouch, 'The administration of the Norman earldom', in A. T. Thacker (ed.), *The earldom of Chester and its charters: a tribute to Geoffrey Barraclough*, *Journal of the Chester Archaeological Society* 71 (1991), 69–96, at 71–2.

17 Stringer, 'Huntingdon charters', 80.

18 A note in Ware's copy of de Lacy's charter to Geoffrey Faber (1190×1205) states that the original instrument was attached *cum effigie equitis armati*, the equestrian seal featuring the mounted figure: appendix I, no. 1. Matthew Paris described the arms of Hugh I de Lacy as green with a gold border, and Walter de Lacy's as gold with a red band: *Chron. maj.*, vi, 474. Walter's two seals respectively featured a mounted knight and winged creature on the obverse, with his heraldic device on the reverse: Veach, *Lordship*, 263, 277n.

19 T. A. Heslop, 'The seals of the twelfth-century earls of Chester', in Thacker (ed.), *Chester and its charters*, 179–97. See also, Patterson (ed.), *Gloucester charters*, 30.

were manipulated in such a way so as to underline his social standing. The boldest statement of power was made by the imitation of protocols normally unique to the royal writ. Particularly striking is the use of the plural of majesty innovated under King Richard I by his chancellor, William Longchamp.[20] Each of Hugh's charter-texts from the period 1205–10 features the *pluralis maiestatis*, a clear break from earlier *acta* in which the singular is invariably employed.[21] By way of comparison, no charter of the earls and countesses of Gloucester (to 1217), and just three authentic charters issued by the Anglo-Norman earls of Chester (to 1237) – out of 469 – employ the plural style.[22]

The injunctive clause in two of de Lacy's earliest comital charters contains the specific formula, *quare volumus et firmiter precipimus* ('wherefore we wish and firmly order').[23] This mandatory statement, in the singular (*quare volo*, etc.), was one of the formulae appropriated from royal charters by the greater nobility in the twelfth century, but which had largely disappeared from English baronial *acta* by c.1200.[24] Its longer survival in Scotland has been attributed by Stringer to the greater autonomy of the baronage in the kingdom of Scots, where 'rights still depended more or less closely upon the actual *voluntas* of the lord'.[25] The perpetuation of the formula in Hugh de Lacy's comital *acta*, amplified with the plural style, could constitute either an example of deliberate anachronism on the earl's part, with the intention to transmit a sense of importance still associated with the formula, or a statement that those under de Lacy's sway in Ulster were subject to his will.[26]

A similar assertion may be found in the treatment of warranty, which represented a commitment on the part of the grantor to prove their right to property in the event of legal challenge, or to provide an exchange for property lost in default of that duty. In England, explicit warranty clauses are increasingly common from the beginning of the thirteenth century.[27] But in only three of Hugh de Lacy's charters, all from the second comital period (1227–42), is there a clear undertaking of warranty.[28] As with the *quare volo* formula, the divergent practice in de Lacy's *acta* is mirrored in a Scottish context. The explanation may lie in the lesser degree of independence available to barons in England, where

20 Ralph Turner, 'Longchamp, William de (†1197)', in *ODNB*.

21 Appendix I, nos 8–15.

22 *Charters of the Anglo-Norman earls of Chester*, nos 390, 412, 469. John Hudson, 'Diplomatic and legal aspects of the charters', in Thacker (ed.), *Chester and its charters*, 153–78, at 161.

23 Appendix I, nos 12–13, as well as one post–1227 charter (no. 19).

24 *Transcripts of charters relating to the Gilbertine houses of Sixle, Ormsby, Catley, Ballington and Alvingham*, ed. F. M. Stenton, *Lincoln Record Society Publications* 52 (Horncastle, 1922), xxxiii.

25 Stringer, 'Huntingdon charters', 87.

26 For the earlier employment of the singular form (*quare volo precipio*), see appendix I, nos 3, 6.

27 *Gilbertine charters*, ed. Stenton, xxix

28 Appendix I, nos 19, 29–30.

a lord's decision to grant lands or privileges was more likely to be subjected to legal challenge in the royal courts.[29] If warranty implied weak lordship, then its exclusion from Hugh de Lacy's early comital charters could itself have been an insinuation of power.

Despite their unfortunate redaction by later editors, the rights and geographical features listed in appurtenance clauses of Anglo-Norman charters, accompanied by 'stock adverbial phrases' (*bene et in pace*, etc.),[30] were much more than diplomatic flourishes. Given the general trend towards scribal precision, it is unlikely that any kind of jurisdiction or proprietorial right would be carelessly included in baronial charters without direction.[31] Lists of appurtenances in Hugh de Lacy's comital charters, concerning property where he enjoyed the rights apposite to chief tenancy (Ulster and Uriel), are generally more extensive than those found in his charters relating to Meath, where Hugh held by sub-tenancy. One charter from January 1207, granting the Ulster cantred of Dufferin (Co. Down) to Roger Pipard, included rights to fisheries (*piscatura*), an appurtenance not found in any of de Lacy's pre-comital acts.[32] It is not that the conditions of Hugh's sub-tenure were especially constricting; after all, his charter for Ratoath and Morgallion awarded rights to fisheries along with other liberal jurisdictions.[33] The crucial factor is how a word like *piscaria* might have manifested materially in the landscape. Fisheries, deer parks or rabbit warrens were coveted adjuncts to lordship, and their accompanying physical structures were potent symbols of seigneurial control.[34] In parting with such lucrative franchises, the grantor not only won the gratitude of the beneficiary, but demonstrated to all that he held the keys to wealth and power in his hand.

If de Lacy could afford to be more generous to his supporters after 1205, this is not to say that he was careless in dispensing privilege. The earl may have delegated fishing rights to Roger Pipard in Dufferin, but he also took care to exempt 'the pleas belonging to our sword' (criminal jurisdictions, with the profits of justice), as well as the revenue from the cantred's rabbit warrens.[35] The phrasing of the reservation is significant. The tying of a sword around an earl's waist symbolised the delegation of the crown's right to discipline and punish,[36]

[29] Stringer, 'Huntingdon charters', 91.

[30] M. T. Flanagan (ed.), *Irish royal charters: texts and contexts* (Oxford, 2005), 30.

[31] *Gilbertine charters*, ed. Stenton, xxii, xxxii.

[32] Appendix I, no. 12.

[33] *Gorm. reg.*, 142, 190.

[34] Margaret Murphy and Kieran O'Conor, 'Castles and Deer parks in Anglo-Norman Ireland', *Eolas: Journal of the American Society of Irish Medieval Studies* 1 (2006), 53–70.

[35] The Anglo-Normans introduced rabbit-farming to Ireland: ibid., 58, citing Fergus Kelly, *Early Irish farming* (Dublin, 1997), 13. In 1211–12, as seneschal of Ulster, Roger Pipard accounted for £10 from the sale of 2000 rabbit skins: *Pipe roll Ire. 1211–12*, 54–5.

[36] Crouch, 'Administration of the Norman earldom', 72.

and imagery of the *gladius* was normally only used by kings and their immediate social inferiors. In Hugh de Lacy's case, the earl's *voluntas* could be enforced by a comital sword which was both broad and far-reaching.

It is usually accepted that one of King John's achievements in Ireland was the extension of royal authority through the transference of powers from the courts of the liberties to those of the crown.[37] However, if Kenneth Nicholls was correct to identify a 'swift decline in seigneurial jurisdictions'[38] into the thirteenth century, the encroachment on private franchises was far from a uniform process. We have seen that Hugh de Lacy was awarded essentially the same assemblage of jurisdictions in 1205 which John de Courcy had enjoyed. There was no amendment to Hugh's position such as those made in the revised royal charters issued for Meath and Leinster, in 1208, which reserved the 'crosses' to the king along with jurisdiction in error and the four pleas of the crown: arson, rape, forestall and treasure-trove.[39] Of these four, only arson and (possibly) forestall were offences punishable by death.[40] Jurisdiction over the major crimes continued to be delegated in Ireland, as it had been in Hugh de Lacy's charter for Ratoath and Morgallion, c.1190, which ceded to him 'judgement of fire and water, battle and gallows'.[41] If the crown was successful in infringing on private franchises in Meath and Leinster, in Ulster the earl continued to wield the power of life and death over his tenants. Between 1224 and 1235, three decades after royal and papal prohibitions of the judicial ordeals, Hugh was able to grant his castle of Carlingford to his daughter Matilda, *cum judicio ignis et aque, duelle et furcarum*.[42]

A final impression of importance is conveyed by the concluding protocol in de Lacy's early comital charters. Place/date clauses are extremely rare before the late thirteenth century: out of two hundred deeds examined by Stenton relating

37 Orpen, *Normans*, 259.

38 K. W. Nicholls, 'Anglo-French Ireland and after', *Peritia* 1 (1982), 370–403, at 372. In 1204 the justiciar in Ireland was authorised to issue several writs of the royal chancery, and in 1207 a royal mandate instructed that no one was to answer for their tenements or on the pleas of the crown except before the king or the justiciar: *RLP*, 47b, 76b.

39 *Rot. chart.*, 176a, 178a.

40 F. W. Maitland and Frederick Pollock, *The history of English law* (2nd edn, 2 vols, Cambridge, 1923), ii, 492; N. D. Hurnard, 'The Anglo-Norman franchises', *EHR* 64, no. 252 (1949), 289–327, at 306–7, 321.

41 *Gorm. reg.*, 142, 190.

42 Appendix I, no. 20. Henry III forbade the use of the ordeals in 1219, in response to the judgement of the Fourth Lateran council (1215): *Pat. rolls, 1216–32*, 186; Robert Bartlett, *Trial by fire and water: the medieval judicial ordeal* (Oxford, 1986), chs 4–5. The ordeals of fire and water were applied to a range of crimes (e.g. heresy, theft and sexual offences) as well as 'civil' cases concerning property or status, while trial by combat was reserved for more serious offences: Bartlett, *Trial by fire and water*, 24–5, 106–10. The select delegation of these formulae to predominantly high-status grantees implies the conveyance of actual jurisdiction: Nicholls, 'Anglo-French Ireland and after', 377.

to Gilbertine religious houses, only three later examples provide an exact date of issue, while no such clauses are found in the *acta* of Earl David of Huntingdon.[43] Against this wider trend, five of Hugh de Lacy's charters from his first comital period are precisely dated.[44] All five reference his earldom in preference to the Incarnation or regnal year, implying that the concluding diplomatic owed more to the assertion of status than meticulous record-keeping. The exclusion of place/date clauses in Hugh's post-restoration charters, meanwhile, underlines the fact that it was immediately following his acquisition of Ulster, and in response to political insecurity, that he found it most necessary to call attention to his *comitatus*.

The construction of identity

The obvious exploitation of the *carta* as promotional tool begs the question of where Hugh de Lacy derived his acute awareness of trends in the written record. In 1309×10 it was found that the earl 'had a chancery of his own',[45] but he is unlikely to have had any kind of sophisticated record-producing office which might normally be understand by the term 'chancery'. At this time even established earldoms had only small secretariats, relying on scribes supplied by local religious communities.[46] After 1227 the earl's clerk was Michael Waletun (*nostrum clericum*), who witnessed de Lacy's charter to the church of St Patrick at Down.[47] In the first comital period (1205–10), when the self-conscious construction of charter diplomatic is most obvious, the earl had at least two other notaries among his clerical staff. William the clerk appears as final attestor in three comital instruments from the period 1205–10, and is presumably synonymous with the William (*clericus*) de Kermerdin (Carmarthen), listed as final witness in another.[48] Between 1217 and 1227, during Hugh de Lacy's exile, one Michael Grossus (*alias* le Gros) granted his land of 'Maynthone' to the priory of Llanthony along with his body, if by chance it should happen that he should die in England, as Michael's father had 'first discussed with Thomas

43 *Gilbertine charters*, ed. Stenton, xxxii; Stringer, 'Huntingdon charters', 94.

44 Appendix I, nos 11–15.

45 *Cal. Carew* MSS, vi, 450.

46 Clanchy, *From memory to written record*, 58; Patterson (ed.), *Gloucester charters*, 25–30; M. T. J. Webber, 'The scribes and handwriting of the original charters', in Thacker (ed.), *Chester and its charters*, 137–51, at 146–7.

47 Appendix I, no. 25.

48 Ibid., nos 9, 11–13. For appearances of Baldwin de Kermerdin, see ibid., nos 1, 3, 5. The Augustinian priory at Carmarthen was probably affiliated to Llanthony Prima (Gwent), a de Lacy foundation: David Knowles and R. N. Hadcock, *Medieval religious houses: England and Wales* (London, 1971), 139, 152–3.

of Turtisbury (Tutbury, Staffordshire?), clerk of the lord Hugh de Lacy, earl of Ulster'.[49] The earl's clerks were not only responsible for record production, but appear also to have been empowered as comital delegates, giving or withholding dominical consent for the actions of de Lacy's tenants.

The stylisation of the earl's charters may well have been achieved in consultation with the records of others. In the secretariats of other earls and countesses, elements of royal charter protocol were copied from instruments received from the English chancery.[50] It is also noteworthy that John de Courcy had resigned *scripta autentica* to Hugh de Lacy along with his castles and fortifications,[51] and at least one unusual formula occurs in acts of both men. In 1192×93 de Courcy dedicated a grant to the canons of St Patrick at Down for the souls of those 'who have died and who may die in my service' (*qui mortui sunt et morientur in servicio meo*).[52] Not later than 1210, with a slight re-ordering of syntax and inflected with the majesterial plural, the distinctive commemoration was repeated by Hugh de Lacy in his charter to St Andrews cathedral priory (*qui in nostro servicio mortui sunt vel morientur in servicio nostro*).[53] The grant to St Andrews was a novel endowment, and so the repetition of the *qui mortui* formula would seem to point either to some overlap in notary staff or to the use of de Courcy's confiscated *scripta* as diplomatic templates.

Intriguingly, several of the most remarkable features of de Lacy's comital style are paralleled in charters of the earls of Chester. While relatively few of the Chester *acta* feature the majesterial plural, the earls' clerks were still 'among the most pre-eminent imitators of English royal chancery style', and distinguishing characteristics of their charters are the frequent employment of the territorial style and place/date clauses.[54] Most notably, just after a charter of Hugh de Lacy referred to *placitis ad nostrum gladium pertinentibus*, cases reserved to the comital court of Ranulf III of Chester began to be described by the earl as 'pleas of the sword'.[55]

The establishment of some kind of symbiotic relationship between the Chester and Ulster secretariats is perhaps less fanciful than it may seem at first. John de Courcy's connections with the region are by now well established,[56]

49 *Ir. cartul. Llanthony*, 96–7 ('Maythone' is unidentified). The charter was witnessed by Luke de Netterville, archbishop of Armagh (1217–27): *NHI*, ix, 274. Michael Grossus (as Michale de Gros) witnessed a comital charter from 1227×41, in favour of the burgesses of Nobber (bar. Morgallion): appendix I, no. 21.

50 Patterson (ed.), *Gloucester charters*, 29; Hudson, 'Diplomatic and legal aspects', 177–8.

51 *Pont. Hib.*, 134–5, no. 64.

52 *CPR, 1367–70*, 177; Mac Niocaill, 'Cartae Dunenses', 421, no. 8.

53 Appendix I, no. 9.

54 Hudson, 'Diplomatic and legal aspects', 155–6, 176–8, at 177.

55 Crouch, 'Administration of the Norman earldom', 72.

56 Duffy, 'First Ulster plantation', 15–17.

and it is not impossible that some of the monks brought from the abbey of St Werburgh to staff de Courcy's Benedictine foundation at Down, c.1183, had previously served the Chester *curia* and were thereafter enlisted to draft instruments of Hugh de Lacy.[57] The de Lacys also had their own links to Chester, and both Hugh I and Walter de Lacy held land respectively from earls Hugh and Ranulf III in England.[58] Veach has noted the thriving business between the ports of Chester and Drogheda, and in one charter of Walter de Lacy, granting trading concessions to the citizens of Chester, Earl Ranulf is described as the lord of Meath's *consanguineus*.[59] This apparent familial bond helps to explain the political support lent by Ranulf to Hugh following the latter's return from crusade in the early 1220s.[60] It is also conceivable that it led to some transmission of propagandistic technique between the comital secretariats in Chester and Ulster.

Symbols of power: hostings and hostages

The language framing the earl of Ulster's charters was clearly intended to inspire deference to his dignity. Those most likely to appreciate the results, however, were fellow members of the settler elite to whom the intricacies of charter diplomatic were most familiar.[61] It is not that Hugh's comital promotion made no impact on the native Irish: the author of the northern chronicle later incorporated into *Mac Carthaigh's book* took note of his creation as 'an earl and justiciar from the king of England in Ireland'.[62] But the social markers of the 'Foreigners' meant less to other native commentators who continued to identify the earl of Ulster and his siblings as 'sons of Hugo [I]'.[63] For the earl to impress his legitimacy on an Irish audience he would require different parlances of power from the written instrument, but with similar overtones of regal authority.

In 1206 the earl and his confederates from Meath and Leinster devastated the ecclesiastical *civitas* of Armagh for ten successive days and nights. Turning

57 In his charter granting ten carucates of land to St Werburgh's, in 1183, de Courcy stipulated that the new cathedral chapter at Down should be free from dependency on the Chester abbey: *The chartulary or register of the abbey of St Werburgh, Chester*, ed. James Tait (2 vols, Manchester, 1920–3), ii, 471–2. However, a late twelfth-century calendar of St Werburgh's listed the translation to Down of the bodies of SS Patrick, Columba and Brigid, implying ongoing contact with the Ulster community: Flanagan, 'De Courcy', 175.

58 Veach, *Lordship*, 193.

59 Ibid.

60 See below, 136, 141–5.

61 For the Latin charter in the European tradition, as adopted by Irish kings in the twelfth and early thirteenth centuries, see Flanagan, *Irish royal charters*.

62 *MCB*, 1204 [*recte* 1205].

63 *ALC*, 1205, 1208; *AFM*, 1206, 1207.

south-west into Monaghan, Hugh then burned Tedavnet, Kilmore and Clones, before striking northwards into the kingdom of Tír Eógain (Tyrone). There, he attacked Tullaghoge, royal headquarters of the king of Cenél nEógain, Áed Méith Ua Néill, penetrating as far north as Ciannachta (bar. Keenaght, Co. Londonderry) in Tír Conaill. This campaign was followed in early 1207 by another assault on Armagh around the feast of St Brigid (1 February), ferocious enough to prompt Archbishop Eugenius to cross to the court of King John to 'succour the churches of Ireland and to accuse the Foreigners'.[64]

The Anglo-Norman interlopers in Ireland clearly sought direction as to what their actions would communicate to the native polities they encountered. But, while John de Courcy had found inspiration in the book of prophecies by Colum Cille, which he kept 'as a kind of mirror for his own deeds',[65] Hugh de Lacy could develop cultural comprehension in consultation with members of his own family. Bearing in mind his connection to the Connacht dynasty of Uí Conchobair, it may be more than happenstance that de Lacy's chosen route through central Ulster in 1206 echoed the one taken by Ruaidrí Ua Conchobair forty years previously, in 1166, as part of his circuit of the north marking Ruaidrí's inauguration as high-king.[66] It would also seem credible that, in his rehearsal of Ua Conchobair's itinerary, de Lacy was announcing his own arrival as a major power in the north, conjuring up any sense of deference still associated with the defunct office of *ard-rí* (high-king). Of the ministerial functions of Irish kingship, it was the capacity to act as war-leader which, 'in the popular mind, most required to be tested'.[67] A parallel can be drawn between de Lacy's marauding campaigns of 1206–07 and the *crech ríg* ('royal prey') undertaken by recently inaugurated Irish kings to demonstrate their military prowess and suitability for kingship.[68]

The power of symbolism was also deployed by de Lacy in his efforts to extract hostages from Áed Méith Ua Néill at Tullahogue, inauguration site of the kings of Cenél nEógain.[69] The use of human sureties as symbols of political submission was a common feature of Anglo-Norman and native Irish society, but the

64 MCB, 1206, 1207; *AU*, 1207 [*recte* 1206]; *AFM*, 1206; *ALC*, 1206. Eugenius had arrived in England by 19 July 1207, when the king sent him to execute episcopal office in the vacant see of Exeter, and in Worcester: *RLC*, i, 88a; *CDI*, i, no. 331; *English episcopal acta, XI: Exeter, 1046–1184*, ed. Frank Barlow (Oxford, 1996), xlvi. Eugenius does not appear in the Worcester records.

65 *Expug. Hib.*, 176–7.

66 MCB, 1166; Seosamh Ó Dufaigh, 'Medieval Monaghan: the evidence of place-names', *Clogher Record* 16, no. 3 (1999), 7–28, at 14.

67 Eoin MacNeill, *Celtic Ireland* (2nd edn, Dublin, 1981), 122.

68 Pádraig Ó Riain, 'The "crech ríg" or "royal prey"', Éigse 15 (1973), 24–30.

69 AU, 1207 [recte 1206]; AFM, 1206; Elizabeth Fitzpatrick, *Royal inauguration in Gaelic Ireland, c. 1100–1600: a cultural landscape study* (Woodbridge, 2004), 139–56.

keeping of hostages was especially resonant in an Irish context. As exemplified in the wisdom-text, *Cert cech ríg co réil* ('The tribute of every king is clearly due'), probably composed for an eleventh-century predecessor of Áed Méith Ua Néill, the collection of hostages was nothing less than an obligation of kingship:

> Take hostages from all × so that you may be a keen prince,
> and be able to chastise × on every business about which you go.
> Make not peace without a hostage × wherever your power extends;
> chief king of the peoples × let your sentence not be false.
> Though the people be leal × let there be strife against even a shadow
> until their hostages × be in your own hands.[70]

Few treatments of medieval hostageship omit the enticing prescription in the Irish legal treatise, *Din techtugad* ('Of the appropriation of land'), that 'he is not a king who does not have hostages in fetters'.[71] Certain gradations of surety were over-qualified to be held in chains, however. Until the eleventh century two principal types of hostage are referred to in Irish sources. The *gíall* was associated with 'base-clientship' and agreements in which the hostage-giver admitted the superior status of the recipient. An *aitire*, meanwhile, was a man or woman of high social standing, and carried no such implications of subordination. Thus, while *géill* could be shackled, *aitiri* should not be.[72]

It has been suggested that societal upheaval caused these distinctions in typology to fade, leading to the interchangeable use of *géill* and *aitiri* in written sources.[73] By the mid-twelfth century another term appears most frequently in the annals – *braighdi* – which, in its evolution from *brága* ('neck/throat'), carried with it definite connotations of physical restraint, reflecting the growing trend towards the mistreatment of political hostages in the later twelfth century, as inferred from the more frequent instances of execution or mutilation in the annals.[74] Strikingly, the sole use of *aitiri* in the annals of Ulster in the period 1120–1220, during which time their content (with that of the annals of Loch Cé) is drawn from an Armagh/Derry chronicle, comes from the entry

70 *Cert cech ríg co réil*, ed. and trans. Tadhg O'Donoghue, in Osborn Bergin and Carl Marstrander (eds), *Miscellany presented to Kuno Meyer* (Halle, 1912), 258–77; *NHI*, i, 895–6.

71 D. A. Binchy, *Corpus iuris Hibernici* (6 vols, Dublin, 1978), i, 219; Adam Kosto, *Hostages in the Middle Ages* (Oxford, 2012), 38–9. For hostages as symbols of submission, see Katharine Simms, *From kings to warlords: the changing political structure of Gaelic Ireland in the later Middle Ages* (Woodbridge, 1987), 96–116.

72 Robin Chapman Stacey, *The road to judgement: from custom to court in medieval Ireland and Wales* (Philadelphia, PA, 1994), 109–11.

73 As a result of the consolidation of petty kingdoms into larger confederations, and the numbers of independent polities reduced, 'the boundary between "free" and "unfree" became substantially more difficult to determine, as degrees and types of "unfreedom" multiplied': ibid., 111.

74 T. F. O'Rahilly, 'Some instances of vowel shortening in Modern Irish', *Ériu* 13 (1942), 128–34, at 129–30; Kosto, *Hostages*, 49–53.

concerning Hugh de Lacy's campaign in Tír Eógain, during which he 'took not the pledges nor hostages (*géill na eidire*) of Aedh Ua Neill'.[75] In the particular use of *aitiri*, against the lexical trend, the annalist may have been attempting to convey a special meaning still associated with the term. The political context argues against the possibility that de Lacy did not wish the extraction of hostages from the king of Cenél nEógain to connote the latter's subordination. Perhaps what the entry is expressing, however, relates to the other traditional characteristic of the *aitire*; that, in addition to hostages of a usual kind (*géill*), de Lacy had demanded sureties from Áed Méith Ua Néill of the highest social status – most likely sons, or brothers of the king – as appropriate for his own, self-perceived special dignity.

Denied recognition as overlord of Tír Eógain, some of the cultural currency de Lacy failed to extract from Áed Ua Néill in the form of human sureties, he afterwards sought to secure in plunder. The taking of a cattle-tribute (*bóruma*), usually by force, was a regular feature of the early reigns of incoming Irish lords,[76] and it was perhaps as much *crech ríg* as *chevauchée* which proceeded under the earl of Ulster into Tír Conaill and seized the cows of Ciannachta 'to a countless number'.[77]

Frontiers: extent and expansion

In 1205 Hugh de Lacy was granted Ulster as 'entirely' as John de Courcy had held it,[78] that is, the eleven cantreds comprising the colonised and uncolonised portions of the ancient fifth of Ireland.[79] Cantreds were contemporary administrative units, but are of little assistance as accurate indicators of lordship. These sometimes mirrored the extents of pre-Anglo-Norman rural deaneries, but only in a minority of cases.[80] Grants of cantredal clusters also failed purposefully to distinguish between settled areas (which might attract a beneficiary to a particular location) and those territories beyond the militarised frontier (which might be granted as a stimulus for conquest, or for defensive reasons). Essentially, actual political boundaries in Angevin Ireland cut through the cantredal system.

A more precise definition of the area controlled by Hugh de Lacy depends on the extent of John de Courcy's conquest. At its height this was coterminous with

75 *AU*, 1207 [*recte* 1206].
76 Eoin MacNeill, *Phases of Irish history* (Dublin, 1920), 238; Ó Riain, '*Crech ríg*', 24–5.
77 *AU*, 1207 [*recte* 1206].
78 *Rot. chart.*, 151a; *CDI*, i, no. 263.
79 For the cantreds of Ulster, see MacCotter, *Medieval Ireland*, 228–35.
80 Ibid., 273.

the native kingdom of Ulaid, east of the Bann and Newry rivers, comprising the eastern part of Co. Down and the southern portion of Co. Antrim, with outposts at Coleraine (Co. Londonderry) and in west Co. Down. Across the Bann to the west lay the semi-independent Irish polities of Uí Echach Cobo and Uí Thuirtri, as well as the powerful northern Uí Néill kingdoms of Cenél nEógain and Cenél Conaill. To the south and south-west lay Airgialla (anglicised Uriel), under the kingship of Murchad Ua Cerbaill (†1189) and overlordship of Cenél nEógain.

There are risks in attempting to frame the lordship of Ulster in terms of modern county boundaries or contemporaneous political units. Claiming that John de Courcy was 'conscious of the Irish ancestry of the principality he ruled',[81] McNeill cites a charter of de Courcy to the priory of St Andrew in the Ards, a cell of Lonlay in Normandy, in which he granted the tithes of all his lordship *ab aqua de Darnart usque in aquam de Carlingford*, 'traditional definitions of the limits of the Ulaid kingdom'.[82] This first boundary is the Ravel Water (*Fregbail*) in Co. Antrim, which appears frequently in Irish sources as the northerly limit of the Dál nAraidhe polity (of which *Darnart* is a corrupt Anglicisation).[83] But the southern boundary of Ulaid was more fluid, at one point in time stopping short of Carlingford Lough, at another stretching as far south as the river Boyne.[84] Of which tradition was John de Courcy most conscious? In addressing this question we come closer to knowing what constituted the earldom of Ulster after 1205, and identifying what territories Hugh de Lacy held in Uriel prior to his comital promotion.

In 1549 the 'county of Ulster' extended from north Antrim to Dundalk (Co. Louth), and the last documentary reference to the Cooley peninsula forming part of Co. Down comes from as late as 1603.[85] Carlingford was administered as part of Uriel in 1211–12,[86] but in the later thirteenth century it would be accounted for as one of the ports of Ulster along with Coleraine, Carrickfergus, Strangford and Dundalk.[87] There appeared to be no uncertainty on King John's part when, in 1212, he granted one knight's fee near Carlingford, 'in the part of Ulster near the sea', to the king of Man.[88]

Modern scholars have been surprisingly reluctant to place Carlingford in the earldom of Ulster, but with little justification. The first references to Anglo-Norman activity in north Louth come from the 1170s,[89] and by 1180 John

81 McNeill, *Anglo-Norman Ulster*, 15.
82 *Mon. Ang.*, vi, pt 2, 1123; McNeill, *Anglo-Norman Ulster*, 16.
83 Reeves, *Eccl. ant.*, 334–5; Orpen, 'The earldom of Ulster (ii)', 51–2.
84 F. J. Byrne, *Irish kings and high-kings* (London, 1973), 68, 107–8, 113.
85 *Cal. Carew MSS*, i, 223–4; iv, 450–1.
86 *Pipe roll Ire. 1211–12*, 53–69.
87 *CDI*, ii, no. 1902.
88 *Rot. chart.*, 186b; *CDI*, i, no. 428.
89 *AU*, 1176, 1178; *MCB*, 1176, 1178.

de Courcy was able to count '*Equen*, in Louth' as part of his conquest.[90] In a later charter from 1185×89, however, de Courcy stated the southern limit of his lordship to be *aquam de Carlingford* (Carlingford Lough).[91] This territorial contraction might have had something to do with the machinations of the Lord John, who made a grant to Peter Pipard of four burgages at Drogheda, and four more at Carlingford, with fishing rights, c.1189.[92] If Pipard's grant encroached on de Courcy's Ulster, it did so only temporarily. In 1193 de Courcy was able to grant the revenue from a ferry crossing at Carlingford to the church of St Patrick at Down.[93] A year later Peter Pipard was arrested by Walter de Lacy and John de Courcy, as co-justiciars of Richard I.[94] Around the same time, the Lord John's vill of Louth 'was plundered and burned, together with its castle, by Niall Mac Mathgamna and John de Courcy'.[95] We might detect both a degree of retribution in the act and confirmation that de Courcy's influence once again spread into Uriel.

The situation is confused by Hugh de Lacy's charter to his daughter, Matilda, 1227×35, in which he granted his 'castle of Carlingford with all its rights and appurtenances with all the land which [he] had with her mother in Cooley and Uriel'.[96] It has been assumed that Hugh had acquired Carlingford through his marriage to Lescelina de Verdun (1194×99).[97] This reading is problematic, as the mountains cutting the Cooley peninsula in two represented a considerable natural obstacle to expansion south from Ulster, or east from Dundalk. There is no evidence that Carlingford or north Cooley was ever part of the de Verdun lordship.[98] If Hugh de Lacy made gains there before 1205, he must have done so in division of the 'land of war' beyond the frontier of de Verdun settlement.[99] Again, there is nothing to show that he did so. A more plausible limit of Hugh's conquest is offered by the location of his fortress at Raskeagh, near the Armagh/Louth border, complete with its large bailey, a feature often indicative of 'military preparedness' and a nearby frontier.[100]

90 A. J. Otway-Ruthven (ed.), 'Dower charter of John de Courcy's wife', *UJA*, 3rd ser., 12 (1949), 77–81; Edmund Curtis, 'Two unpublished charters of John de Courcy, *princeps Ulidiae*', *Belfast Natural History and Philosophical Society Procedings* (1928), 2–10.

91 *Mon. Ang.*, vi, pt 2, 1123.

92 *Ormond deeds*, i, 364, no. 863 (1).

93 *CPR, 1367–70*, 177; Mac Niocaill, 'Cartae Dunenses', 421, no. 8.

94 M. T. Flanagan, *Irish society, Anglo-Norman settlers, Angevin kingship: interactions in Ireland in the late twelfth century* (Oxford, 1989), 282.

95 MCB, 1196.

96 Appendix I, no. 20.

97 Paul Gosling, *Carlingford town: an antiquarian's guide* (Newry, 1992), 3.

98 Hagger, *De Verduns*, 55.

99 Appendix I, no. 4.

100 Gosling, 'From Dún Delca to Dundalk', 253. For Raskeagh's attribution to Hugh de Lacy, see Smith, *Colonisation and conquest*, 45.

South-east of Raskeagh, around the bay from Dundalk, lies Ballymascanlan, granted by Hugh de Lacy to the Cistercian abbey of Mellifont no later than 1205.[101] From the landmarks alluded to in the charter-text, it seems that Hugh granted the monks a sizeable wedge of territory stretching from Dundalk Bay to the Armagh/Louth border, and from his motte at Raskeagh as far as the Cooley mountains.[102] The purpose of such an all-encompassing gift, 'combining piety with prudence',[103] may have been the establishment of an ecclesiastical buffer zone beyond the militarised frontier running from Raskeagh to Castletown/Dundalk. In his study of Welsh marcher lordships, Brock Holden has noted the reputation of the Cistercians for pastoral farming and their experience in refining challenging topography.[104] Mac Íomhair pictures the monks dispatched from Mellifont to Ballymascanlan 'felling timber, bringing land under cultivation, and attracting settlers to the sparsely-populated country'.[105]

Significantly, north Cooley boasts no examples of Anglo-Norman mottes contemporaneous to that erected at Raskeagh.[106] This could be seen as evidence that the area was quickly pacified by Anglo-Norman colonists.[107] The impression left by Hugh de Lacy's charter to Mellifont, however, is that the territory between Raskeagh and Carlingford was still contested before 1205. The attribution of settlement at Carlingford to de Lacy's direction is shown to be without foundation.[108] Instead, Hugh was only able to grant it to his daughter, 'with' (*cum*) his estates in Uriel, because of his acquisition of Ulster.

In de Lacy's marauding raids into central provincial Ulster, undertaken in 1206–07, we may perceive an attempt to extend the limits of Anglo-Norman settlement in another direction, at the expense of his Irish opponents west of the Bann. In 1207 the earl's second descent on Armagh, around the feast of St Brigid (1 February), was parenthesised by the drafting of two comital charters.[109] The first, issued on 13 January, granted the Ulster cantred of Dufferin (Co. Down) to Roger Pipard.[110] The other, issued on 2 March to the Meath and Staffordshire tenant, Hugh Hose, appears to have represented a grant of territory

101 Appendix I, no. 7.

102 Diarmuid Mac Íomhair, 'The lordship of Ballymascanlan', *JLAS* 17, no. 2 (1970), 79–83.

103 Ibid., 80.

104 Brock Holden, *Lords of the central marches: English aristocracy and frontier society, 1087–1265* (Oxford, 2008), 83.

105 Mac Íomhair, 'Lordship of Ballymascanlan', 80.

106 Otway-Ruthven, 'Partition', 407; Hagger, *De Verduns*, 55.

107 Smith, *Colonisation and conquest*, 45.

108 For an example of the unsubstantiated identification of Hugh de Lacy as the builder of Carlingford castle, see T. E. McNeill, *Castles in Ireland: feudal power in a Gaelic world* (London, 1997), 40.

109 MCB, 1207.

110 Appendix I, no. 12.

in north Monaghan: specifically, in the land of Uí Méith Macha ravaged by the earl's army in 1206–07.[111]

The grant to Hose is demarcated within the charter-text as *in Omcht Maygas et Schagh Clogh cum quatuor feodis militum pertinenciis in circuitu*. Some of these defining words, phonetic renderings of Irish place names, can be reconstructed to reveal simple meanings if not exact geographical locations: 'Schagh' resembles *sceagh*, or *skeagh*, meaning 'the hawthorns'; 'Clogh' is close to *cloch*, the Irish for 'stone' or 'rock', sometimes denoting a monument or fortification.[112] The ordering of words in the donative clause may indicate a general region, 'Omcht', in which 'Maygas' and 'Schagh Clogh', with four knights' fees, were situated. Alternatively, the placement of the conjunction allows that 'Maygas', *in* 'Omcht', may have been geographically distinct from 'Schagh Clogh', with the knights' fees being appurtenant only to the latter.

The charter's issue at Galtrim, *caput* of Hugh Hose's barony of Deece, initially points to a location in Meath, a conclusion apparently supported by the attestation of tenants of that lordship. However, whereas into the thirteenth century it was common for parties to the physical act of conveyance to meet close to the piece of land subject to gift, the charter testifying to the terms of that grant could be issued anywhere.[113] This has a double implication: firstly, a place/date clause alone, which records only where the written instrument was created, cannot reveal the location of the intended gift; secondly, witnesses may have a connection to the district in which a charter was issued, but not to the lands outlined in its donative clause. The point is well made by the earl of Ulster's charter to Roger Pipard, drafted at Hugh's manor of Rathbeggan in Meath, but granting the Ulster cantred of Dufferin. The witness list to that charter features the same group of barons – Walter, Robert and William de Lacy, Richard de Tuit and William le Petit – who would attest the grant to Hugh Hose, drafted two months later.

If the charter's place of issue is ultimately unhelpful, the date of creation implies a connection with Hugh de Lacy's expeditions into central Ulster. One of the earl's targets in 1206 was Tullaghogue (Tullyhogue, Co. Tyrone), the fortified inauguration site and seat of the kings of Cenél nEógain. Situated just a few miles south of Tullaghogue, on the outskirts of Dungannon (Co. Tyrone), the village and townland of Moygashel (deriving from *maigh gcaisil* – 'the plain of the stone ring-fort') provides an intriguing linguistic parallel to the 'Maygas' of Hugh de Lacy's charter.[114] Unable to extract hostages from Áed Ua Néill

111 Ibid., no. 13. See also, Daniel J. F. Brown, 'Select document: a charter of Hugh II de Lacy, earl of Ulster, to Hugh Hose', *IHS* 38, no. 151 (2013), 492–510.

112 Patrick McKay (ed.), *A dictionary of Ulster place-names* (Antrim, 1999), 150, 154–5.

113 *Gilbertine charters*, ed. Stenton, xvii.

114 McKay (ed.), *Dictionary of Ulster place-names*, 113.

at Tullaghogue, could the earl have intended to strike a blow to the influence of the king of Tír Eógain by installing an Anglo-Norman vassal on his very doorstep?

If we are to equate 'Maygas' with Moygashel, a plausible interpretation of 'Omcht' is that it represents a corruption of Uí Méith (Macha), a territory in Airgialla (Uriel) which, in the early twelfth century, spanned most of the modern baronies of Monaghan, Trough and Cremorne (Co. Monaghan), but whose influence had once extended north of the river Blackwater into Tyrone, perhaps even reaching as far as Moygashel.[115] Following this identification, a possible site for 'Schagh' is the townland of Skeagh, in the barony of Monaghan and parish of Drumsnat (Druim Sneachta), centrally placed between the parishes of Clones, Kilmore and Tedavnet laid waste by the forces of Hugh de Lacy in 1206.[116] Just south-east of Skeagh is the townland of Mullanacross, where St Molua reputedly founded the monastery associated with the early literary codex, *Cín Dromma Snechta* (*The book of Drumsnat*), in the sixth century.[117] In the derivation Mullanacross, from *mullach na croise*, perhaps meaning 'the hilltop of the cross',[118] we have an allusion to a potentially stone-built monument, or its relic, to which the 'Clogh' of the charter to Hugh Hose – seemingly appended to 'Schagh' – could refer.[119] An alternative origin for 'Schagh' is found in the townlands of North and South Tirnaskea (Tír na Sceach), close to Tedavnet, most certainly one of the constituent churches of Uí Méith Macha. Tedavnet was also of some early importance as the monastic site associated with the sixth-century virgin saint, Damnat (Dympna),[120] and was visited by Ruaidrí Ua Conchobair in 1166 as part of his northern campaign.[121]

The use of native polities as geographical indicators was not unusual in contemporary land grants. 'In identifying parts of what was for them a new

[115] Ó Dufaigh, 'Medieval Monaghan', 7–28. 'Liskenane', granted by Hugh de Lacy to Geoffrey Sancmelle on 6 June 1207, is possibly Liskenna, a Mac Cionaoith (McKenna) stronghold in Trough barony: appendix I, no. 14; Ó Dufaigh, 'Medieval Monaghan', 23–6; A. L. Brindley (ed.), *Archaeological inventory of county Monaghan* (Dublin, 1986), 69.

[116] Late twelfth-century scholiastic notes to the *Félire Óengusso* place Drumsnat in Farney (*Fernmaig*), just beyond the western boundary of Uí Méith as it had been at its height in the early part of the ninth century: *Félire Óengusso ('the martyrology of Óengus')*, ed. and trans. Whitley Stokes, Henry Bradshaw Society 29 (London, 1905), 180; Ó Dufaigh, 'Medieval Monaghan', 13.

[117] Brindley (ed.), *Archaeological inventory of county Monaghan*, 86; Bearnárd Ó Dubhthaigh, 'A contribution to the history of Drumsnat', *Clogher Record* 6, no. 1 (1966), 71–103.

[118] eDIL (Electronic dictionary of the Irish language), letters M, col. 201; C, col. 548 (http://www.dil.ie).

[119] A cross noted by the national sites and monuments database as having stood on the edge of the ancient cemetery site at Mullanacross, is not included in the archaeological inventory: SMR, no. MO013–002001- (http://www.archaeology.ie/smrmapviewer/mapviewer.aspx).

[120] Padraig Ó Riain, *A dictionary of Irish saints* (Dublin, 2011), 256–7.

[121] Ó Dufaigh, 'Medieval Monaghan', 14.

territory but not an empty one', notes Brendan Smith, 'the English used the names of the most recent Irish occupants'.[122] Annalistic references to Uí Méith Macha disappear from the 1180s, reflecting the absorption of the kingdom by the ascendant Meic Mathgamna. Clearly though, even contemporaries struggled to keep up with the shifting political landscape. In 1184 the king of Airgialla, Murchad Ua Cerbaill, with his Anglo-Norman ally Hugh I de Lacy, attacked what the annals describe as north Farney ('tuaisceart Fearnmuighi'), a rather vague allusion to the Meic Mathgamna acquisition in what had been Uí Méith Macha.[123] By the beginning of the thirteenth century the assimilation of the latter polity may still have been incomplete. At least in Trough barony, shown by Seosamh Ó Dufaigh to be the ancestral home of the Uí Méith, neither the Uí Néill in Tír Eógain nor the Meic Mathgamna based in Farney were able to make significant inroads.[124] That said, even if Uí Néill influence did not extend south of the Blackwater by the thirteenth century, it seems scarcely possible that Moygashel, situated in such close proximity to Tullaghogue, had not been subsumed by Cénel nEógain.[125] A subsequent reference to Moygashel constituting part of Uí Méith Macha would seem to be hopelessly anachronistic, but Anglo-Norman charters were little concerned with giving due deference to the achievements of Irish polities, especially those whose accomplishments impinged upon the ambitions of the incomers.

As a caveat to the candidacy of Uí Méith Macha, Drumsnat and Tedavnet, it could be argued that northern Monaghan was not technically Hugh de Lacy's to grant, having been confirmed to Peter Pipard by the Lord John c.1189, as part of Peter's conquest in Uriel.[126] In reality, the Pipard settlement seems to have been confined to Fir Rois; the barony of Ardee in Louth; and the half-cantred of Mudorne, corresponding to the barony of Farney in Monaghan.[127] Soon after the construction of a castle at Donaghmoyne, in 1193, probably delineating the northern limit of this colonised portion, the Pipard lands in Ireland passed to Peter's brother, Roger, related to Hugh II and Walter de Lacy through his marriage to Alice, a daughter of Hugh I de Lacy.[128] This marital union and an aspiration to secure territory beyond the Donaghmoyne Pass, a strategic access point into the north of Ireland, may help to explain the route followed by de

122 Smith, *Colonisation and conquest*, 34.

123 MCB, 1184; Ó Dufaigh, 'Medieval Monaghan', 17.

124 Ó Dufaigh, 'Medieval Monaghan', 17–26.

125 Pressure on Uí Méith in the eleventh century led to their establishment of another branch, Uí Méith Mara, in what is now Omeath in the Cooley peninsula (Co. Louth): L. P. Murray, 'Omeath', *JLAS* 3, no. 3 (1914), 213–31.

126 *Ormond deeds*, i, 364–6, no. 863 (1), (4); Otway-Ruthven, 'Partition', 402–3; MacCotter, *Medieval Ireland*, 235–45. The areas in brackets refer to whole cantreds, not the allotted portions.

127 Otway-Ruthven, 'Partition', 403; MacCotter, *Medieval Ireland*, 238.

128 ALC, 1193; Smith, *Colonisation and conquest*, 37, 41, 46.

Lacy in 1206, which took the earl and his men through several constituent parts of the original Pipard grant, namely Armagh, Tedavnet, Kilmore and Clones.[129] It seems plausible that Roger Pipard had turned to his brother-in-law, the earl of Ulster, for help in realising his territorial claims. A further inference is that the grant of Dufferin in Ulster, made to Pipard by Hugh de Lacy in January 1207, and witnessed by three members of the Hose family – James, William and Hubert – was a reciprocal gift for the land in Monaghan granted by sub-tenure to Hugh Hose two months later.

The Pipard claim in north Monaghan becomes more a guide than an obstacle to the location of Hugh Hose's grant. If Roger Pipard aimed to attract coadjutants to the business of conquest by giving away portions of his unsettled stake to an ally, it made strategic sense to abdicate territorial rights in the region north of Farney and the Pipard manor of Donaghmoyne, into the ancient heartland of the Uí Méith. Such a strategy, if it was envisaged, was ultimately unsuccessful. Hugh de Lacy's aspirations of breaking the Uí Néill stranglehold in central Ulster came to very little, and there is no evidence that Hugh Hose or other of the earl's vassals were able to gain a foothold in north Monaghan. De Lacy had been unable to obtain, in the form of hostages, the symbols of submission from Áed Méith Ua Néill at Tullaghoge which might have legitimised any claim to supremacy in the north.[130] Ulster, in its provincial sense, would remain divided between Gael and Gall.

Tenancy and affinity

Continuity of tenure

Before his acquisition of land in the de Verdun lordship (1194×99), Hugh de Lacy had been confined to his sub-tenancies in the baronies of Ratoath and Morgallion, in which the existing settlement pattern had not allowed for an extensive programme of patronage. Marriage granted de Lacy access to a new circle of tenants settled in the de Verdun *terra pacis*, as well as the chance to attract his own supporters with stakes in the *terra guerre*, although most of those willing to accept the risks of frontier lordship were probably other ambitious cadets, with few other territorial interests within the Irish colony and even fewer outwith.[131] The procurement of a comital title afforded an even greater

129 E. P. Shirley, *The history of the county of Monaghan* (London, 1879), 15.

130 *AU*, 1207 [*recte* 1206]; *AFM*, 1206.

131 Elias de Say had followed Hugh I de Lacy to Ireland, but it was a de Say cadet whom Hugh II installed in Louth before 1202, at Stephenstown: appendix I, no. I; Wightman, *Lacy family*, 135–7, and below, 82, 84–5.

opportunity for de Lacy to reward existing supporters with land and office, as well as to cultivate vassals of a higher calibre. His first problem, however, was how to deal with the tenants of his superseded opponent.

The obvious tactic adopted by incoming lords was to clear the board of a rival's friends in order to make room for their own. Crouch observed that, in the ongoing tussle between the Senlis and Canmore claimants to the earldom of Huntingdon (or Northampton), 'whenever the seesaw of fortune favoured one side against the other, there would be a new colonisation of one side's followers, and a clear-out of those of the other side'.[132] Much blood had been spilt during the war for Ulster, and it would be unsurprising if Hugh de Lacy's strategy conformed with the Huntingdon model. John de Courcy's submission to de Lacy in 1204 had been conditional on the latter's promise that he would in no way disinherit anyone who had been granted a fief by de Courcy.[133] But the renunciation of these terms left de Lacy free to act in regard to the barons of Ulster as he saw fit.

On the basis that they had provided hostages to the crown in 1204, McNeill estimated that the loyalty of de Courcy's seigneurial household 'resulted in their disappearance'.[134] This interpretation is directly contradicted by the accusations of treachery levelled by de Courcy against his own inner circle, as recounted in the letter of Pope Innocent III from July 1205:

> When [de Courcy] was rejoicing in tranquil security and placed no small trust in those of his household and servants, the noble man Hugh de Lacy, with the counsel of those in whom [John] trusted, intruded into his land with a large army and waged war against him, with John's men rebelling/defecting against him in the conflict.[135]

At the mercy of a capricious king, the hostages provided by de Courcy's men in 1203 seem more like motives for their relatives' defection than evidence for their displacement.[136] According to the fourteenth-century annals compiled by John de Pembridge, head of the Dominicans in Ireland (1331–43), once Hugh de Lacy had gained an advantage in the war, he dealt out rough justice to those who had broken the code of aristocratic honour by abandoning their lord, lining his own pockets in the process:

> then Hugh de Lacy, earl, repaid and gave gold and silver to all the traitors to John de Courcy, greater [or] lesser, but at once hanged all the said traitors and took all their property, and so Hugh de Lacy was lord over all Ulster.[137]

132 Crouch, 'Strategies of lordship', 8.

133 *Pont. Hib.*, i, no. 64.

134 McNeill, *Anglo-Norman Ulster*, 63–4.

135 *Pont. Hib.*, i, no. 64.

136 *RLP*, 55b.

137 *Chartul. St Mary's, Dublin*, ii, 308–9. For Pembridge's annals, based on an earlier Cistercian chronicle maintained in Dublin, see Bernadette Williams, 'The Dominican annals of Dublin', in

An embellished version of this account is found in the sixteenth-century *Book of Howth*, which describes how de Lacy expelled the deserters, only for them to be forced to port at Cork 'by chance of weather and lack of skilful men'. Being brought before the earl, Hugh 'took from them their treasure, and after hung [sic] them in chains till they consumed all away'.[138] This extra tantalising detail is compromised by the interests of the work's patron, Christopher St Lawrence, baron of Howth, who claimed ancestry from one of de Courcy's (presumably faithful) vassals, Tristram Amaury St Lawrence. As a result, the *Book* is eager to portray de Courcy as the heroic victim of betrayal, induced by 'evil, false, feigned and envious tales' devised by Hugh de Lacy.[139] It is also conditioned by Howth's disillusionment with Elizabethan policy towards Ireland, with de Courcy's downfall being presented as an allegory, foreshadowing the mistreatment of the Anglo-Irish nobility by 'new men' imported from England.[140]

The execution of defectors by Hugh de Lacy would have been a stark reminder to the remaining tenant community about the consequences of disloyalty, while generating a pool of wealth to be distributed among the earl's own followers. But some of John de Courcy's most prominent vassals appear alive and well in Hugh de Lacy's earldom. De Lacy's grant of Dufferin to Roger Pipard, drafted at one of Hugh's estates in Meath in January 1207, was attested by one Richard fitz Robert. There would be little reason to suspect this to be the eponymous seneschal of John de Courcy, were it not for the fact that he is bracketed in the witness list by two other de Courcy associates, Walter Logan and Reginald Hacket.[141] Robert Savage and 'H.' Passelewe, witnesses and beneficiaries in later comital charters, can also be connected to de Courcy tenants.[142]

With least to fear from Hugh de Lacy were those landed families with existing connections to their new overlord. Seán Duffy showed that Richard

Medieval Dublin II: proceedings of the Friends of Medieval Dublin symposium, 2000, ed. Seán Duffy (Dublin, 2001), 142–68, at 153–68.

138 *Cal. Carew MSS*, vi, 111–12.

139 Ibid., 111.

140 Valerie McGowan-Doyle, *The book of Howth: Elizabethan conquest and the old English* (Cork, 2011), 12–14, 55–8.

141 For appearances of Richard fitz Robert, Walter de Logan and William Hacket (presumed relative of Reginald Hacket) in de Courcy's charters, see Mac Niocaill, 'Cartae Dunenses', 419–21, nos 1, 4–8; *Mon. Ang.*, vi, pt 2, 1123; Reeves, *Eccl. ant.*, 190. Ballywalter (Co. Antrim) was 'Walter de Logan's town' in 1306: Reeves, *Eccl. ant.*, 67. Walter de Logan was with Hugh de Lacy against King John in 1210: *RLC*, i, 147a; *CDI*, i, no. 476.

142 For attestations in de Lacy's *acta*, see appendix I, nos 22, 29. For the earl's grant to Robert Savage, of the tuath of 'Kineltweuthel' in 'Dalrod' (Dál Riata, north Antrim), probably dating from the second comital period (1227–42), see appendix II, no. v, and below, 173. For appearances in John de Courcy's charters, see Mac Niocaill, 'Cartae Dunenses', nos 1, 5, 7; *Mon. Ang.*, vi, pt 2, 1123. William Hacket and William Savage had both supplied hostages for de Courcy in 1203: *RLP*, 55b.

Talbot, lord of Ballyhalbert (*Talbetona* or *Talbotyston* in the fourteenth century) in the Ards (Co. Down),[143] was probably drawn to John de Courcy's conquest from Yorkshire[144]. Talbots were also closely affiliated with the de Lacys in England. During the civil war of King Stephen's reign, Geoffrey Talbot and Gilbert de Lacy (head of the Herefordshire de Lacys and grandfather of Hugh II), described as Geoffrey's *cognatus*, raided Bath on behalf of the empress Matilda.[145] In 1156 one Richard Talbot held the Herefordshire manor of Linton with Hugh de Longchamp, another de Lacy associate.[146] This is unlikely to have been the same Ulster tenant of John de Courcy, but an established familial link in an English context may explain the adherence of the Talbots to Hugh de Lacy after 1205.[147]

There was no systemic displacement of Ulster tenants after 1205. Nevertheless, the obligations of lordship required Hugh de Lacy to give shares in his new lordship to the men who had helped win it for him. Some de Courcy tenants must either have had their lands confiscated and reassigned or their conditions of tenure adjusted. Lack of evidence precludes a comprehensive survey of landholding changes, but there may have been more comital grants of the kind made to Roger Pipard, which placed an intermediate authority between Hugh de Lacy and those who had held directly from John de Courcy in Dufferin.[148] The earl's brother-in-law also assumed mesne lordship over other de Lacy tenants installed in the locality such as the de Mandevilles, drawn from Hugh's estates in Uriel.[149] The intrusion of new men was always unpopular with existing communities, and the subscription of former de Courcy vassals to the grant of Dufferin may have been a legitimising tactic on the earl's part, mitigating any offence caused by the reorganisation of the cantred's tenurial structure.

143 H. C. Lawlor, 'Mote and mote-and-bailey castles in de Courcy's principality of Ulster (i)', *UJA*, 3rd ser., 1 (1938), 155–64; (ii), 2 (1939), 46–54, at (i), 159; Reeves, *Eccl. ant.*, 20, 56.

144 Duffy, 'First Ulster plantation', 20–1.

145 *Gesta Stephani*, ed. K. R. Potter and R. H. C. Davis (2nd edn, Oxford, 1976), 58–9.

146 G.E.C., *Peerage*, xii, 607.

147 Robert Talbot witnessed in appendix I, no. 24. He was disseised in 1210 and 1224 for his part in Hugh de Lacy's rebellions: *RLC*, i, 223a, 226a, 241a; ii, 32a; *RLP*, 191; *CDI*, i, nos 626, 643, 663, 707, 1263.

148 Including Elias of Chester at Rathgorman; Richard de Dundonald at Dundonald; and William Copeland around Donaghadee: Duffy, 'First Ulster plantation', 16–17, 19–20.

149 Brendan Smith, 'Tenure and locality in north Leinster in the early thirteenth century', in Barry, Frame and Simms (eds) *Colony and frontier*, 29–40, at 34–5; Lawlor, 'Mote and mote-and-bailey castles (i)', 161.

Comital affinity

The group of vassals comprising the earl's household, to whom the business of lordship was delegated, cannot be satisfactorily reconstructed. We know some of John de Courcy's officials because, in an imitation of royal practice, they appear in his charters along with their titles.[150] Curiously, given Hugh de Lacy's otherwise assiduous simulation of regal protocol, no such affectation is found in his own charters aside from the single designation of a clerk. This is not to say that the earl had no steward, constable, chamberlain, forester or lesser officials attached to him 'for the purpose of creating the mode of life desired by the noble master'.[151] Rather, the absence of household officers in witness lists may be a natural consequence of the peripatetic nature of de Lacy's lordship, as evidenced by the high proportion of comital charters issued outside Ulster in the period 1205–10.[152] In peaceable or nucleated honors a lord's officers could be constantly attendant on him, giving him counsel and fulfilling the domestic remit of their posts. On the other hand, the administration of scattered or vulnerable lands might require dominical representatives to be exactly where the lord was not. Whereas Adam de Audley held the constableship of all Hugh de Lacy's conquests in Uriel and Ulster prior to 1210, his name is nowhere to be found in the earl's charters.[153]

The Staffordshire manor of Audley was held from the de Verduns, and in 1187 Adam de Audley had rendered the account for the honor of Chester on behalf of Bertram de Verdun.[154] He probably followed Bertram to Ireland, where his experience as an administrator may have recommended him for an influential position in Hugh de Lacy's *mesnie*.[155] In frontier areas a lord's survival could depend on the capabilities of his constable, whose remit included command of the army and responsibility for the maintenance and improvement of fortresses. In the northern English honors of Mowbray and Chester the constable took precedence over the steward as the foremost household official.[156]

150 McNeill, *Anglo-Norman Ulster*, 63; Mac Niocaill, 'Cartae Dunenses', 418–24, nos 1–2, 4–8 (Richard fitz Robert, seneschal; Roger de Courcy of Chester, constable; Adam, chamberlain).

151 Kate Mertes, *The English noble household, 1250–1600: good governance and politic rule* (Oxford, 1988), 5.

152 Appendix I, nos 11–13, 15.

153 *CCHR, 1226–57*, 36–7; *CDI*, i, no. 1505. Adam held in Ulster at 'Rinles' (Killard, near Audleystown, Co. Down), and in Uriel at 'Kien' (Kane, Co. Louth): appendix II, no. vii.

154 *The great roll of the pipe for the thirty-third year of the reign of King Henry II, A.D. 1186–7*, ed. J. H. Round, Pipe Roll Society (London, 1915); *CDI*, i, no. 82.

155 After his death, c.1211, Adam's lands were confirmed to his brother Henry (†1246), a witness to two comital charters in 1207: *Pipe roll Ire. 1211–12*, 54–5; appendix I, nos 12–13, II, no. vii; Robin Frame, 'King Henry III and the shaping of a peripheral lordship', in idem, *Ireland and Britain*, 31–58, at 44n.

156 Green, *Aristocracy*, 209.

A similar development could have taken place in Ulster. Intriguingly, Roger of Chester had acted as John de Courcy's steward before becoming his constable, and his priority in some later witness lists may imply an improvement, rather than diminution, of his status.[157]

One benefit of comital rank was that it allowed Hugh de Lacy to attract higher-status tenants. The negative corollary was that, the greater the man, the more likely it was that he was a significant landholder in his own right. In the same year as he was granted a stake in central Ulster by Hugh de Lacy, 1207, Hugh Hose purchased his familial manor of Penkridge in Staffordshire.[158] This supplemented the estates he already held from the crown near Dublin, and his barony of Deece in the lordship of Meath.[159] In isolation, Hose's eclectic interests appear to typify the kinds of interweaving tenurial relationships which bound magnates together in the Irish colony. In the proper political context, however, his attraction as a comital vassal may more accurately represent a case of divided loyalty, a factor already contributing to the erosion of honorial power in England and which now threatened to undermine aristocratic ties across the Irish Sea.[160]

In June 1210, in an effort to spare their lord from royal sanction, a group of Walter de Lacy's vassals, including Hugh Hose, attended King John at Dublin, where they consented to the punishment of Hugh de Lacy.[161] In the face of multiple allegiance, Hose had little choice but to act in the interest of one overlord to the direct detriment of another. In a legal sense, he cannot be said to have acted improperly: in the event of double vassalage, obligations of liegeance were owed, either to the lord from whom the largest fief was held, or with whom there was the earliest formal bond, criteria both fulfilled by Walter de Lacy. Neither was Hose obliged to object to the earl's punishment if it was the will of the king, to whom obedience was to be rendered before any other.[162] Nevertheless, his actions at least remind us that bonds of tenure were no guarantee of enduring loyalty. The point is further underlined by the case of Roger Pipard, granted a whole cantred of Ulster by Hugh de Lacy in 1207, but who is unlikely to have made much effort to prevent his brother-in-law's

157 Mac Niocaill, 'Cartae Dunenses', 419–21, nos 1–8.

158 *Rot. oblatis*., 403; *CDI*, i, no. 368.

159 Hose had also been granted 'Dervach' (Durrow, Co. Offaly) and 'Kenel' (Kells, Co. Meath) by Walter de Lacy: BL, Add. MS 4821, fo 142.

160 For the debate over the cohesiveness of the English honor in the thirteenth century, and the effect of multiple tenure, see D. A. Carpenter, 'The second century of English feudalism', *Past & Present* 168 (2000), 30–71; Crouch, *Nobility*, 280–92.

161 See below, 109–10.

162 Reynolds, *Fiefs and vassals*, 371. F. L. Ganshof, *Feudalism* (New York, 1961), 104.

subsequent ejection from his earldom, after which he appears in the Irish pipe roll for 1211/12 as the crown's steward for Ulster and Uriel.[163]

Equally problematic, in light of Hugh de Lacy's denunciation by his brother in 1210, is the use of kinship as an indicator of lasting affinity. As explored in the next chapter, the de Lacy brothers continued to provide reciprocal political support subsequent to Hugh's comital promotion, but their fraternal bond appears to have been more fragile than intimated by the earl's charters, in which Walter is the most frequent attestor in the period 1205–10.[164] Hugh was not the only de Lacy sibling to encounter difficulties with the familial 'head'. In 1206, two years after losing his Norman estates at Lassy and Campeaux, Gilbert de Lacy presented himself against Walter on account of a plea of trespass in Ireland, but the latter 'did not come or excuse himself'.[165] Gilbert appears to have enjoyed a less fraught relationship with Hugh de Lacy, from whom he was awarded benefices in the Cooley peninsula prior to their grant to the priory of St Andrews (1205×10).[166]

Records of loyalty

Although ruinous for the earl of Ulster, King John's expedition to Ireland, in 1210, allows us a greater insight into de Lacy's circle of influence. The English chancery rolls have preserved the names of those men entrusted by Hugh with the defence of his earldom against royal forces, for which they were distrained, imprisoned or financially penalised. It is these lesser figures, often absent from witness lists, whose loyalties were seemingly less changeable than the earl's more eminent associates.[167]

Veach's statement that Hugh de Lacy 'shared some of Walter's household personnel' is made on the basis that two of the lord of Meath's intimates are also among the most frequent attestors to Hugh's *acta*. Walter's constable in Meath, William le Petit, witnessed several of the earl of Ulster's charters before 1210,[168] as did Richard de Tuit.[169] It must always be borne in mind that the chance

[163] *Pipe roll Ire. 1211–12*, 52–69. Walter de Lacy's inner circle were seemingly no more loyal, with William le Petit acting as royal steward for Meath after 1210: ibid., 21–47.
[164] See appendix I, nos 9, 11?, 12–13.
[165] *Curia regis rolls of the reigns of Richard I and John, preserved in the Public Record Office* (7 vols, London, 1922–35), iv, 195; CDI, i, no. 299.
[166] Appendix II, no. iii.
[167] For the usefulness of witness-lists, see Dauvit Broun, 'The presence of witnesses and the writing of charters', idem (ed.), *The reality behind charter diplomatic in Anglo-Norman Britain* (Glasgow, 2011), 235–90.
[168] Appendix I, nos 6, 11–13.
[169] Ibid., nos 5–6, 9, 11–13.

survival of charter-texts can lead to distortions in the evidence. Moreover, while charters can demonstrate a certain amount of personal interaction, they are not necessarily helpful in establishing the depth of emotional bonds existing between grantees, beneficiaries and attestors. Both William le Petit and Richard de Tuit were part of the embassy denouncing Hugh de Lacy to King John, and their prior charter attestations should be attributed to their prominence within the tenant community in Meath, where the majority of Hugh's surviving instruments were drafted, rather than some overlapping of seigneurial households.

It was from the lower branches of the colonial nobility from which the earl recruited most of his supporters, and three of the envoys to King John in June 1210 (Richard Tuit, Richard de Feipo and Hugh Hose) had familial cadets who were punished by the crown for their adherence to the earl of Ulster. John de Feipo was imprisoned until February 1215. Matthew de Tuit was disseised of his fee of *Typermesan* (Kilmessan, co. Meath) and probably followed Hugh de Lacy to Occitania, being dispatched to negotiate with the English crown in 1216. Having escaped from royal custody in 1213, Hubert Hose would also join his lord on the Albigensian crusade.[170]

In submitting to the king in 1210, Walter de Lacy placed his younger brother's estates in Meath at the crown's discretion, as well as 'the lands and castles of his brother Walter's vassals who have gone with the aforesaid Hugh'.[171] Among this group was the family of Sancmelle (possibly from *sang-mêlé*, 'mixed-blood'), whose representatives, Walter, Godfrey and Robert, were captured by royal forces at Carrickfergus, *caput* of the earldom of Ulster, in July.[172] Walter Sancmelle appears to have held from Hugh de Lacy at Cenél Enda (Co. Westmeath), while Godfrey Sancmelle may have been the 'Geofrey Samell' to whom the earl granted the 'seargeantship of Liskenane' (possibly Liskenna, Co. Monaghan) on 6 June 1207.[173] Several members of the family would fight for Hugh again during his rebellion of 1223–24.[174]

The trail of evidence also turns up partisans of the earl whose Irish activities are obscure, but whose families were active in or around the de Lacys' English estates. Peter de Dunstanville was fined for having been against the king in 1210.[175] He was presumably related to the Dunstanville lords of Shifnal, north

170 *RLP*, 128b, 150a, 194a; *CDI*, i, nos 453, 535, 623, 719; *Pipe roll 14 John*, 157–8; below, 127.

171 See below, 109–10.

172 *RLC*, i, 140b, 197b; *RLP*, 134a; *CDI*, i, nos 495; 551; 553.

173 Appendix I, no. 14; Reeves, *Eccl. ant.*, 58. A seargeantship 'would seem to indicate a sergeant's fee (that in question is defined as five ploughlands) as distinct from that of a knight': K. W. Nicholls, 'Abstracts of Mandeville deeds', *Anal. Hib.* 32 (1985), 1–26, at 3. Those holding by serjeanty tenure often provided some personal service to their lord in lieu of military service: see Bartlett, *England*, 217.

174 See below, 150, 156n, 157–8.

175 *RLP*, 129a; *CDI*, i, no. 539.

of the de Lacy castle of Bridgnorth in Shropshire.[176] Robert Weldebof was fined thirty marks and a hunting dog for his release in 1214, and restored to his Ulster fee of 'Edereskel' (near Comber, Co. Down) two years later.[177] His family (*alias* Walbieffe) can be traced to Breconshire in Wales, bordered to the east by the de Lacy heartland in Herefordshire and Monmouthshire.[178] One of the settlements controlled by the Walbieffes near Brecon was Lanhamlach, from which we might infer that another of the defenders of Carrickfergus in 1210, Stephen de Lanhamelach, was a member or a vassal of the family.[179]

Perhaps the most striking aspect of the earl of Ulster's affinity is its extension to men with links to the branch of the de Lacy family centred on the English honor of Pontefract. Richard de Alta Ripa escaped from royal custody with Hubert Hose in 1213.[180] His family (*alias* de Hautrive, de Hautrey or Dautrey) had interests in Berkshire and Sussex but can also be traced to the manor of Hapton in Lancashire, which in the thirteenth century comprised part of the lordship of Clitheroe belonging to the Pontefract de Lacys.[181] At Pontefract, in September 1213, the king ordered one Eudo de Stapleton, captured in Ireland in 1210, to be released to Richard de Alta Ripa.[182] The de Stapleton family derived their toponym from a settlement situated four miles south-east of Pontefract.[183] The participation of these men in the defence of Ulster is given extra significance in the following chapter, which argues for Hugh de Lacy's complicity in a plot against King John being fermented by the earl's English kinsmen. The implication of the Scottish crown in the same conspiracy calls our attention to another of de Lacy's partisans captured in 1210, Michael fitz Roger, who would eventually be released from royal custody by petition of the king of Scots.[184]

176 A. T. Gaydon (ed.), *A history of the county of Shropshire, vol. 2* (London, 1973), 80–3.
177 *RLP*, 125b; *CDI*, i, no. 522.
178 H. C. Lawlor, 'The vassals of the earls of Ulster (ii)', UJA, 3rd ser., 4 (1941), 23–7, at 23–4; *Liber feodorum, the book of fees commonly called testa de Nevill reformed from the earliest MSS by the deputy keeper of the records* (3 vols, London, 1920), ii, 800, 806, 813.
179 Lawlor, 'Vassals of the earls of Ulster (ii)', 23–4.
180 *Pipe roll 14 John*, 157–8; *CDI*, i, no. 453.
181 William Farrer, *History of the county of Lancaster, vol.* 6 (London, 1911), 507–12.
182 *RLP*, 104b; *CDI*, i, no. 486.
183 *Early Yorkshire charters: being a collection of documents anterior to the thirteenth century made from the public records, monastic chartularies, Roger Dodsworth's manuscripts and other available sources*, ed. William Farrer (3 vols, Edinburgh, 1914–16), iii, §25.
184 *RLC*, i, 151b; *CDI*, i, no. 487.

The earl and the church

A spiritual deficit?

The relative ease with which John de Courcy had consolidated his conquest of Ulaid after 1177 was partly achieved through his promotion of Irish saints and the cultivation of good relations with local churchmen. Ensuring that 'military domination was quickly followed by spiritual domination',[185] few strategies recommended themselves more to incoming lords than the foundation of new religious houses, and de Courcy had also introduced several monasteries to Ulster affiliated with his familial lands in England. Benedictines from St Werburgh's, Chester, provided a new chapter for the cathedral church at Downpatrick. The same order provided communities at Nendrum and St Andrew in the Ards (Black Abbey), respectively cells of St Bees (Cumberland) and Stogursey (Somerset). Cistercians were introduced from Cumbria to staff the abbeys of Inch and *Iugum Dei* (Grey Abbey), while the Augustinians were represented at Toberglory, near Downpatrick, a cell of St Mary's, Carlisle.[186] At Carrickfergus, Premonstratensian canons were introduced from the Scottish abbey of Dryburgh, to serve the spiritual needs of de Courcy's seigneurial *caput* from their monasteries at St Mary's Abbey (Woodburn) and Dieux la Croisse (White Abbey).[187]

Hugh de Lacy's early treatment of the church in Ulster stands in stark contrast with his predecessor's ingratiating piety. Seemingly willing to eschew the obvious benefits of sponsorship, no new spiritual centres were founded by the earl in 1205–10, nor can a single grant to a church or churchman in Ulster be credited to him. The only known ecclesiastical beneficiary of de Lacy's patronage in this period was the abbey of St Thomas, Dublin, where his father and mother were buried, to which Hugh granted the church of Dundalk, with appurtenances, oblations and the obventions of the castlery of Dundalk.[188] De Lacy had hardly been an enthusiastic patron of the church prior to his acquisition of Ulster, but this had owed more to the realities of lordship than to some areligious sentiment. Even before its award to Hugh I de Lacy, in 1172, the Irish over-kingdom of Mide, with Brega, was already densely populated by *viri religiosi*, and the subsequent placement of Anglo-Norman manors at existing monastic centres was as much a space-saving endeavour as it was a political

[185] Holden, *Lords of the central marches*, 82.

[186] See Duffy, 'First Ulster plantation', 5–10; Flanagan, 'De Courcy', 165–70.

[187] Miriam Clyne, 'The founders and patrons of Premonstratensian houses in Ireland', in Janet Burton and Karen Stöber (eds), *The regular canons in the medieval British Isles* (Turnhout, 2011), 145–72, at 148–54.

[188] Appendix I, 11.

strategy.[189] By the time Hugh II was politically active in Meath, more land in the liberty had been alienated to the religious houses associated with the settler community.[190] His early charters were mainly confirmations or renewals of anterior grants, and no novel endowments were forthcoming once the Lord John's intrusive patronage in Ratoath had been overcome.[191]

De Lacy had not been alone in exhibiting such parsimonious piety. As the first waves of Anglo-Norman conquest had subsided and land became less available, so too the impetus for religious sponsorship had begun to recede. Even in the registers of Llanthony, one of the institutions most favoured by the barons of Meath, records of new endowments in Ireland diminish conspicuously at the end of the twelfth century.[192] As new frontiers opened up, however, the pulse of patronage quickened again, and it is no surprise that the earliest evidence for a novel pious donation of Hugh II de Lacy's comes from the period subsequent to his marriage, when he granted Ballymascanlan, in the contested portion of Uriel, to Mellifont Abbey (1194×1205).[193]

In Ulster, de Lacy may again have been confronted with an excess of sacred space. The bishop of Down cannot have been far from the mark when, in 1269, he claimed that his diocese contained 'more priests and religious than in any other part of equal dimensions in Ireland'.[194] This state of affairs owed much to the zealous patronage of John de Courcy, who had boosted the reforming programme within the diocese of Ulaid, and subsumed the secular power base of his Dál Fiatach precursors, by creating a kind of ecclesiastical sub-lordship around Downpatrick, supported through the lavish bestowal of tithes from John's animals and hunting, revenues from several of his ferry crossings, as well as proceeds of justice in ecclesiastical land.[195] At the end of a protracted struggle for Ulster, and having to manage a frontier lordship in Uriel in addition to his estates in Meath, it would be little wonder if Hugh de Lacy was initially reluctant to add to the material advancement of the church at the expense of his comital demesne and revenue.[196] This said, de Lacy's coffers cannot have

[189] Byrne, *Irish kings and high-kings*, 269; M. T. Flanagan, 'Anglo-Norman change and continuity: the castle of Telach Cail in Delbna', *IHS* 28, no. 112 (1993), 385–9; Edel Bhreathnach, 'Authority and supremacy in Tara and its hinterland, c. 950–1200', *Discovery Programme Reports* 5 (Dublin, 1999), 1–25, at 15–17.

[190] Murphy and Potterton (eds), *Dublin region*, 81–4.

[191] Appendix I, nos 1–3, 5–6.

[192] Hogan, *Llanthony*, 70.

[193] Appendix I, no. 7.

[194] *CDI*, i, no. 2551.

[195] Mac Niocaill, 'Cartae Dunenses', 419–21, nos 1–8; Flanagan, 'De Courcy', 155–70; Ann Hamlin, 'The early church in county Down to the twelfth century', in Lindsay Proudfoot (ed.), *Down history and society: interdisciplinary essays on the history of an Irish county* (Dublin, 1997), 47–70.

[196] A similar privation may have caused William Marshal to wait two decades after his acquisition

been much more depleted in 1205 than upon his restoration to Ulster in 1227, after which we shall see him introduce the Franciscans and Hospitallers into the earldom and lobby for the construction of a new Cistercian abbey.

The function of monastic communities as buttresses of secular lordship could render them vulnerable to the political opponents of their patron. In 1204, betraying some feelings of insecurity as John de Courcy's fortunes waned, the monks of Black Abbey in the Ards sought protection and confirmation for their property from the papal *curia*.[197] However, if there is no evidence that Hugh de Lacy supplemented the privileges of his rival's foundations after 1205, neither is there anything to show that he treated them roughly. We have seen that prior links with de Lacy or his *socii* had prompted the defection of some of John de Courcy's followers, and the same connections may also have safeguarded Ulster's regular clergy.

The installation of the canons of Prémontré at Carrickfergus, by 1183, has stood out as unusual among the foundations orchestrated under John de Courcy because their filiation, Dryburgh Abbey, was located in a region of Scotland with no obvious historical links with north-east Ireland.[198] Duffy unravelled this particular mystery in noting Dryburgh's foundation by the de Moreville lords of Lauderdale and Cunningham, whose close ties with north-west England placed them within John de Courcy's sphere of operation.[199] The political landscape of the Irish Sea zone was redrawn in 1186 on the death of William de Moreville, however, after which his impressive assemblage of property came to be controlled by his brother-in-law, Roland, lord of Galloway.[200] Inconveniently for John de Courcy, the creation of the de Moreville-Galloway hegemony placed Dryburgh under the patronage of the dynastic competitors of Duncan mac Gillebrigte, lord of Carrick, who was at that time allied with the lord of Ulster. Roger of Howden relates a battle between de Courcy and the petty kings (*reguli*) of Ireland in 1197:

> of which he put some to flight, slew others, and subjugated their territories; of which he gave a substantial part to Duncan, son of Gilbert, son of Fergus [of Galloway], who,

of Leinster in 1189 before adding to the religious infrastructure of his Irish lordship: Crouch, 'Strategies of lordship', 19–25.

[197] *Pont. Hib.*, i, nos 59–60.

[198] J. R. S. Phillips, 'The Anglo-Norman nobility', in J. F. Lydon (ed.), *The English in medieval Ireland* (Dublin, 1984), 101. For the Premonstratensians at Carrickfergus, see Clyne, 'The founders and patrons of Premonstratensian houses', 151–4; *Med. relig. houses*, 204; I. B. Cowan and D. E. Easson, *Medieval religious houses: Scotland* (2nd edn, London, 1976), 100–1; T. E. McNeill, 'The Premonstratensian houses of Carrickfergus, White Abbey and Woodburn', *Peritia* 2 (1983), 265–6.

[199] Duffy, 'First Ulster Plantation', 10–11.

[200] Keith Stringer, 'The early lords of Lauderdale, Dryburgh Abbey and St Andrew's priory at Northampton', in idem (ed.), *Nobility of medieval Scotland*, 44–71.

> at the time that the said John was about to engage with the Irish, came to assist him in Ireland with not a small number of troops.[201]

Before 1203, no doubt adding to de Courcy's discomfiture, Roland's son, Alan, married a daughter or sister of Roger de Lacy, constable of Chester and *consanguineus* of de Courcy's competitor, Hugh II de Lacy.[202]

The installation of Premonstratensians in Ulster may have been initiated under John de Courcy, but in light of Dryburgh's situation within Alan of Galloway's hegemony, as well as Alan's connections with the Pontefract de Lacys, the white canons at Carrickfergus may not have been overly alarmed by Hugh de Lacy's assumption of lordship in 1205. Nor may the earl have been automatically disposed against them, or the communities at Nendrum and Grey Abbey, whose parent houses in Cumberland (St Bees and Holm Cultram) benefited from the generosity of Alan of Galloway and his forebears.[203] Significantly, Hugh de Lacy's own Cestrian connections could have helped to smoothen relations with the Benedictines serving in the cathedral priory at Downpatrick, affiliated with the Chester abbey of St Werburgh, if not with Ralph, the Cistercian bishop of Down (1202–12) and titular abbot of the Downpatrick community.[204]

De Lacy and Armagh

Rather than an indication of hostility, the negative evidence for religious patronage under Hugh de Lacy in the period 1205–10 may actually demonstrate the earl's comfort with the spiritual *status quo*. However, in contrast to de Lacy's apparently cordial relations with the clergy in colonised Ulster, Hugh's interactions with the primatial church of Armagh, situated *inter Hibernicos*, were characterised by antagonism and mutual intimidation from the beginning.[205]

It was proposed in the previous chapter that John de Courcy was one of the *principes* who had supported the election of Archbishop Eugenius in 1201,[206] and Eugenius may have had opportunity to repay the favour in the face of Hugh de Lacy's incursions. In July 1205 he was appointed as head of the papal judges

201 *Chron. Houedene*, iv, 25.

202 R. D. Oram, *The lordship of Galloway* (Edinburgh, 2000), 112–13.

203 *The register of the priory of St Bees*, ed. James Wilson (Durham, 1915), 71–2; *The register and records of Holm Cultram*, ed. Grainger Francis and W. G. Collingwood, *Cumberland and Westmorland Antiquarian and Archaeological Society Record Series* 7 (1929), 48–56.

204 *NHI*, ix, 280; Leslie and Swanzy, *Clergy of Down*, 1.

205 The heads of the largest ecclesiastical centres like Armagh controlled huge amounts of wealth and resources: Katharine Simms, 'Frontiers in the Irish church: regional and cultural', in Barry, Frame and Simms (eds) *Colony and frontier*, 177–200, at 188–9.

206 See above, 32.

delegate tasked by Pope Innocent III with investigating the waging of unjust war by de Lacy against John de Courcy. If the commission found that Hugh had acted wrongfully, they were to instruct him to return whatever he had taken in such a violent manner. If these instructions were unheeded, Eugenius and his colleagues were to compel Hugh to comply, provided the case against him be proved, by the imposition of a personal excommunication and an interdict on his lands.[207] As the pope was writing, he was probably unaware that de Lacy had already been invested as earl of Ulster by King John. Nevertheless, Eugenius's partisanship makes it highly likely that he fulfilled his papal commission to the letter.

In England instances of excommunication were becoming rarer by the thirteenth century, in the face of more stringent canonical regulation.[208] In Ireland, however, the 'holy man's curse' remained the weapon of choice for ecclesiastics.[209] One did not offend the primatial church lightly. Giraldus relates how, in 1185, the tenant of Hugh I de Lacy, Hugh Tyrel, took away a cooking pot from Armagh as spoil during a raid on the *civitas*, 'cursed by the maledictions of all the clergy', only for his lodgings and part of the vill of Louth, to which he had retired, to be consumed by fire. Finding that the stolen item had escaped the flames, Tyrel repented and returned the pot to Armagh.[210] It remains unclear, however, just how seriously the prospect of ecclesiastical censure was taken by native Irish and settler elites. In 1202 a knight of Hugh II de Lacy, one 'H.' de Say, failed to relinquish land he had intruded upon belonging to St Mary's Abbey in Louth, despite a threat of anathema delivered by none other than the papal legate in Ireland, John of Salerno.[211] In the fourteenth century Archbishop Milo Sweteman of Armagh (1361–80) bemoaned the ineffectiveness of excommunication at constraining the excesses of the king of Oirthir, Malachias Ua hAnnluain (O'Hanlon), against the church of Armagh.[212] Nevertheless, Sweteman's complaint makes clear that it was only after Ua hAnnluain and his *malefactores* obtained absolution from repeated sentences of excommunication, by swearing oaths and making promises of good behaviour, that they returned to their evildoing. 'Excommunication was not able to quash O'Hanlon's violence', notes Gundacker, 'but neither was the sanction rendered

207 *Pont. Hib.*, i, no. 64.

208 R. H. Helmholz, 'Excommunication in twelfth-century England', *Journal of Law and Religion* 11, no. 1 (1994–5), 235–53; F. D. Logan, *Excommunication and the secular arm in medieval England: a study in legal procedure from the thirteenth to the sixteenth century* (Toronto, 1968), 13–22.

209 Helmholz, 'Excommunication', 238.

210 Giraldus Cambrensis, *The history and topography of Ireland*, ed. J. J. O'Meara (Mountrath and Harmondsworth, 1982), 89–91; Smith, *Colonisation and conquest*, 57.

211 *Pont. Hib.*, i, no. 63; *Cal. papal letters, 1198–1304*, 22.

212 *The register of Milo Sweteman, archbishop of Armagh, 1361–1380*, ed. Brendan Smith (Dublin, 1996), no. 133.

irrelevant in the face of that violence'.[213] Over a century earlier, that Hugh de Lacy perceived anathema to be a limiting factor on noble behaviour seems clear from his prior insistence that John de Courcy's submission to him be upheld by the threat of ecclesiastical censure.[214]

Although chiefly a spiritual punishment, part of the effectiveness of excommunication was its potential to unravel social ties and undermine the exercise of power. Uncertainty surrounded the anathematised authority's right to collect rents or debts,[215] and in the late twelfth century Hugo of Pisa's *Summa* urged the vassals of an excommunicate lord to withdraw from his company, refraining from aiding or defending him.[216] The accompanying withdrawal of clerical services from an excommunicate's land could also prove problematic. Invoking divine intervention, the judicial ordeals, which still presided over a wide range of crimes in the Irish liberties, were overseen and officiated by the church. A treatise of Bishop Gilbertus of Limerick (1106–38) stated the obligations of priests to include the blessing of bread and water used in the ordeals, while the judicial 'hot iron' was to be consecrated by a bishop.[217] Secular lordship could not function without the co-operation of local churchmen, and any censure applied to de Lacy by Eugenius could have gravely undercut Hugh's capacity to discipline and punish, a crucial prerogative in frontier conditions.

Aside from any de Courcy partisanship, Eugenius may have feared that the new secular master of Ulster would seek to emulate his father, Hugh I de Lacy, who in 1184 had supported the attempts of the king of Airgialla, Murchad Ua Cerbaill, to topple Archbishop Thomas (Tommaltach Ua Conchobair) of Armagh and replace him with the bishop of Louth/Airgialla, Máel Ísu Ua Cerbaill.[218] This scheme had failed, but Thomas's death in 1201 provided the de Lacys with an ideal opportunity to install one of their own *natio* in the primatial office. The first election conducted during the ensuing vacancy, convened at Drogheda in the lordship of Walter de Lacy, identified three potential candidates, of which two (Simon Rochfort, bishop of Meath, and Ralph Petit, archdeacon of Meath) were closely affiliated with the de Lacys.[219] However, Eugenius's election seems to have been recognised as legitimate by the English

[213] Jay Gundacker, 'Absolutions and acts of disobedience: excommunication and society in fourteenth-century Armagh', *Traditio* 64 (2009), 183–212, at 203.
[214] *Pont. Hib.*, i, no. 64.
[215] Gundacker, 'Absolutions and disobedience', 197.
[216] Elizabeth Vodola, *Excommunication in the Middle Ages* (London, 1986), 67–9, 219–20.
[217] M. T. Flanagan, *The transformation of the Irish church in the twelfth century* (Woodbridge, 2010), 66–8.
[218] Smith, *Colonisation and conquest*, 26.
[219] *Pont. Hib.*, i, no. 52; Watt, *Two nations*, 226–7.

of his province by 1205, when he presided over a clerical assembly at Mullingar, the chief manor of William le Petit in the lordship of Meath.[220]

The motive force for Eugenius's animosity towards Hugh de Lacy was probably the issue of proprietary rights. In late August 1206, at Clisson in Brittany, King John received two Irish monks from Mellifont Abbey, who offered three hundred marks of silver and three marks of gold on behalf of the archbishop of Armagh to have certain lands and liberties found before Hamo de Valognes, justiciar of Ireland (1196–99), to belong to Armagh. The current justiciar, Meiler fitz Henry, was ordered to act in the matter according to the king's advantage, and further instructions were issued to Hugh de Lacy to adhere to the decision.[221] We have no record of the earlier judgement under Hamo de Valognes, but we might infer from the mandate to de Lacy that the lands in dispute lay within the earl's ambit.

Further traction is gained in consideration of a letter of Pope Innocent III, issued on the same day as the response to John de Courcy's complaint, 1 July 1205, indicating that the canons of St Mary's Abbey in Louth had appealed to John of Salerno when he was papal legate to Ireland (1202) concerning land which they claimed had been granted to them by the king of Airgialla before the arrival of the English, and which they had held in peace for a long time. Then, acting on foot of a grant by Hugh de Lacy, and ignoring the admonitions of the legate, the aforementioned 'H.' de Say had illegally occupied the land, claiming his right to do so in respect of a law introduced by the English to the effect that grants made to religious houses by the Irish were not valid in competition with the rights of the colonists. The pope appointed papal judges delegate to hear the case in Ireland, notwithstanding any such law which was contrary to natural justice or any written law.[222]

As suggested by Otway-Ruthven, it would seem that the land in question was 'in that part of the parish of Louth which is in the barony of Upper Dundalk, where Stephenstown was originally Stephenstown de Say, and where the canons of Louth still held Rossmakay at the dissolution'.[223] Significantly, it was during the justiciarship of Hamo de Valognes that St Mary's appears to have come under the jurisdiction of Armagh, which could have provided the impetus for Archbishop Thomas to make an appeal to the justiciar concerning land that had been alienated from the abbey before coming under the supervision

[220] *Reg. St Thomas*, 348–9.

[221] *RLP*, 67a, 72b. Following Sweetman (*CDI*, i, no. 335), the mission has been wrongly placed in 1207: Brendan Smith, 'The Armagh-Clogher dispute and the "Mellifont conspiracy": diocesan politics and monastic reform in early thirteenth-century Ireland', *Seanchas Ard Mhacha* 14 (1991), 26–38, at 31. King John was at Clisson between 30 August and 2 September 1206: 'Itinerary of King John', *RLP*, l–lxxiv.

[222] *Pont. Hib.*, i, no. 63; *Cal. papal letters, 1198–1304*, 22.

[223] Otway-Ruthven, 'Partition', 404.

of his diocese.[224] Thomas's death in 1201 may have provided de Say with the opportunity to exploit his grant from Hugh de Lacy, in turn prompting the canons of St Mary's to lobby the papal legate. By 1203 Archbishop Eugenius seems to have been residing at Louth, adding a further layer of significance to the contention.[225]

It is unlikely that the judges designated by the pope in 1205 found in favour of Armagh. The senior delegate, Felix Ua Ruanada, archbishop of Tuam, had been the prior of Saul (Co. Down).[226] But the other two papal appointees, Simon Rochfort, bishop of Meath, and the abbot of Kells, were both tied to the aristocratic community of which Hugh de Lacy and the de Says were still constituent members. It is not hard to imagine that, having exhausted every possible ecclesiastical judicial procedure by 1206, Eugenius sent representatives to King John, armed with silver and gold, pleading for intervention.

Alternatively, Eugenius's supplication may have been connected to encroachment by Hugh de Lacy in north Louth. The churches of Cooley had been granted to the diocese of Clogher under the diocesan structures devised at the synod of Ráith Breasail in 1111. For almost another century, however, they were subject to competing claims from the dioceses of Clogher and Armagh, as part of the disputed territory between Carlingford and the River Boyne, and it was only at the Mullingar assembly in 1205 that the quarrel was resolved in favour of Armagh.[227] In a charter from 1205×10, the churches of Cooley, with two others at Carlingford, were granted by Hugh de Lacy to the cathedral priory at St Andrews, in Scotland, 'as well and as fully as Gilbert de Lacy our brother possessed (*possedit*) the said benefices'.[228] In theory, the only way in which Gilbert could have had possession of these churches, as a secular lord, was to hold temporal rights of presentation to them. Given the propensity of the settlers to encroach on ecclesiastical land, however, it is not impossible that attempts were made to exploit the material property of local benefices as the archetypal *Eigenkirche*: 'a possession comprising not only the church building with its contents but its land, buildings, and stock, its tithes, dues, and offerings, and the appointment of its priest'.[229]

It has already been shown that Carlingford and its hinterland only came under Hugh de Lacy's control after his acquisition of Ulster. This raises the

224 Thomas Gogarty, 'St Mary's Abbey, Louth. With an account of the lives of St Mochta, Cristin, bishop of Louth and Donatus, prior of Louth', *JLAS* 4, no. 2 (1917), 169–89, at 169; Smith, 'The Armagh-Clogher dispute', 30.

225 *RLP*, 28a; *CDI*, i, no. 176; Gogarty, 'St Mary's Abbey', 169.

226 *NHI*, ix, 319.

227 Aubrey Gwynn, 'Armagh and Louth in the twelfth century', *Seanchas Ard Mhacha* 1 (1954), 1–11, at 1–6.

228 Appendix I, no. 9, II, no. iii, and below, 101.

229 Susan Woods, *The proprietary church in the medieval west* (Oxford, 2006), 1.

possibility that Gilbert de Lacy had assumed proprietorship of its benefices just prior to Eugenius's appeal to King John. The abbey of Mellifont, which provided the delegates to the king at Brittany, would certainly have been discomfited by any infringement of ecclesiastical property at Carlingford, so close to its daughter-house at Newry. As a caveat, if benefices in Cooley were subject to competing claims in 1206, the contention appears to have originated during the justiciarship of Hamo de Valognes (1196–99), when John de Courcy, the friend of Armagh, was lord of Ulster. The contraction of Ulster's territorial boundaries in the 1190s must be taken into account, however, and it may be that Armagh had been seeking confirmation of its rights in Cooley during a period of confusion. The initial aggressor against the archdiocese may indeed have been Peter Pipard, probably lord of Carlingford in 1189–92, who also came to blows with the bishop of Clogher over his violent seizure of church land at Donaghmoyne.[230]

❖

The precise judgement of Meiler fitz Henry concerning the rights of Armagh is unknown, but the subsequent persecution of the primatial church by Hugh de Lacy strongly implies that the decision was to the disadvantage of the (possibly) excommunicate earl. De Lacy's devastation of Armagh for ten consecutive days and nights in 1206, and a second attack in early 1207, prompted Archbishop Eugenius to make a personal accusation against his persecutors to King John. All of this must have bemused the annalist who had presented Hugh de Lacy's installation in Ulster as a break from the impious activities of John de Courcy, somewhat ungenerously assessed as the 'destroyer of the churches and territories of Ireland'.[231]

In a truer indicator of their different approaches towards the church in Ulster, while John de Courcy had enhanced the cult of Brigid by overseeing her translation (alongside Patrick and Colum Cille) at Downpatrick, Hugh de Lacy observed the occasion of the saint's feast in 1207 by launching an assault on Armagh, Ireland's ecclesiastical capital. De Lacy's own impending demise at the hands of the crown was perceived by the Irish as just punishment for this startling display of irreligiosity. 'Hugh Delacie the younger took the spoyles of Ardmach', state the Clonmacnoise annals for the year 1206, 'which was soone after revenged upon him by the Saints of Ireland'.[232]

230 Smith, *Colonisation and conquest*, 56.
231 *AU*, 1205.
232 *AClon.*, 1206.

4

Fall

The road to rebellion, 1205–10

If the waging of war was an expected aspect of governance under the Norman and Angevin kings, says Matthew Strickland, 'then much of this warfare was directed against rebellious vassals, often themselves leagued with the external enemies of the Anglo-Norman *regnum*'.[1] The nine weeks spent by King John in Ireland in 1210, during which he expelled the de Lacys from Ulster and Meath, remains a key set-piece in the relationship between crown and colony in the medieval period. Of the countless treatments of John's summer campaign, perhaps none has been more insightful into the king's motivations than the near-contemporary 'Barnwell' chronicle, which states the king's foremost concern to have been the suppression and punishment of the earl of Ulster:

> John, king of England, led an army over to Ireland, took many castles there and put to flight Hugh de Lacy who, with the greater part of Ireland occupied, was thought to be contemplating rebellion. With Ireland pacified and ordered according to his wishes, [the king] returned in peace.[2]

Having been elevated to comital rank by King John, the earl of Ulster's involvement in sedition appears on first glance to be ungrateful in the extreme. As Bothwell notes, 'one of the best ways to incense a king and bring about one's own quick, and often painful, demise was not only to betray the monarch's sacred trust – his realm – but to do so after the king had been foolish enough to show great favour'.[3] It was the withdrawal of royal esteem, however, which seems to have caused Hugh to bite the hand which had so recently nourished him with an earldom. William Marshal's swift restoration into the king's graces in 1205 removed the need for a counterbalance to his power in Ireland. The

1 Matthew Strickland, *War and chivalry: the conduct and perception of war in England and Normandy, 1066–1217* (Cambridge, 1996), 230.

2 *Memoriale fratris Walteri de Coventria*, ii, 202. The 'Barnwell' chronicle was composed and written at Peterborough (Cambridgeshire): Richard Kay, 'Walter of Coventry and the Barnwell chronicle', *Traditio* 54 (1999), 141–67. Walter of Coventry incorporated its well-informed and independent account (1202–25) into his own narrative at the end of the thirteenth century: Antonia Gransden, *Historical writing in England, c. 550–1307* (London, 1974), 339–45.

3 Bothwell, *Falling from grace*, 21.

subsequent exclusion of Hugh de Lacy's comital title in royal correspondence to the Irish colony implies that the king was actively ignoring or suppressing de Lacy's status as *comes Ultonie*.

It is the slight to his comital dignity which best explains Hugh's enthusiastic resistance to the royal faction during the baronial war of 1207–08, as well as his cultivation of links to opponents of the English crown outside Ireland. By 1209, with his kingdom already under interdict, King John found himself beset by conspirators, rebellious barons and hostile neighbours. In each of these expressions of opposition, we can identify at least one uniting factor in the person of the earl of Ulster. In Ireland, the de Lacy brothers were sheltering the fugitive William de Braose from the king's justice. Hugh can also be linked to an English plot involving his future patron on the Albigensian crusade, Simon V de Montfort. Finally, de Lacy's persuasive links to the king of Scots, William I (the Lion), illuminate both the Anglo-Scottish crisis of 1209 and the role of the French crown in pulling the strings of sedition from afar.

1210 – crime and punishment in King John's testimonial

The question of what merited the king's personal attention in Ireland has been answered in several different ways. For some the royal campaign was an emphatic response to the baronial crisis of 1207–08, when a consortium of leading magnates had come into conflict with the justiciar of Ireland, Meiler fitz Henry. With his authority at stake, the king's concern in 1210 was to bring his barons 'to book',[4] or 'to heel'.[5] Given that John made peace with the offending magnates in 1208, however, the prior unrest would appear insufficient to explain the king's sudden arousal to action two years later.[6] A different emphasis was provided by Lewis Warren, for whom a key objective of the royal campaign was the restoration of good relations with the Irish, as part of a 'comprehensive, well-planned and thoroughly researched scheme for the government of Ireland'.[7] This strand of Warren's thesis was called into question by Seán Duffy,

4 Duffy, 'John and Ireland', 240.

5 Duffy, 'Hugh de Lacy and the Albigensian crusade', 70.

6 For the course of the baronial war, see Flanagan, 'Defining lordships', 49–56.

7 W. L. Warren, 'King John and Ireland', in J. F. Lydon (ed.), *England and Ireland in the later Middle Ages: essays in honour of Jocelyn Otway-Ruthven* (Dublin, 1981), 26. See also, idem, 'John in Ireland, 1185', in John Bossy and Peter Jupp (eds), *Essays presented to Michael Roberts, sometime professor of modern history in the Queen's University of Belfast* (Belfast, 1976), 11–23; 'The historian as 'private eye'', in J. G. Barry (ed.), *Historical studies, IX* (Belfast, 1974), 1–18, at 17; 'Painter's King John – forty years on: an address to the Haskins Society conference, 1988', in *The Haskins Society Journal* 1 (1989), 1–9, at 3.

who pointed out that John was equally disdainful of the native kings in 1210 as he had been in 1185, on the occasion of his first Irish expedition.[8]

Others have been influenced by a remarkable letter published by the king soon after his return from Ireland, in which John attempted to justify his destruction of William de Braose, who had since fled to France, leaving his wife and eldest son imprisoned in Windsor castle.[9] According to the royal testimonial, the origin of the quarrel was William's steadfast refusal to address outstanding debts for his lordship of Limerick.[10] John's Irish expedition was brought about by the actions of Hugh and Walter de Lacy, and William Marshal, who had broken promises to expel de Braose from their company. 'We could not endure so great and so many transgressions of these men any longer', states the *querimonia*, 'and we gathered an army to deal with them in Ireland'.

On the face of it, the king's initial treatment of de Braose was consistent with that normally given to debtors. Those in arrears to the crown could expect to be subjected to distress (*districtio*), that is, following judgement, to have their moveable property confiscated until their debt was paid.[11] Just such a course of action is described as having taken place in the spring of 1208. After five years of non-payment, 'in line with the custom of our kingdom and by law of our exchequer', orders were given to seize de Braose's chattels in England, only for William to remove these 'so that they could not be found'. Instead, the king's bailiff in Wales was instructed to distrain de Braose by his Welsh property. Handing over three of his castles as security, de Braose agreed that all his lands would be forfeit should he miss the next deadline for payment.

Legal convention in the twelfth century held that the king could sequestrate temporarily lands for which debt was outstanding, but these should be restored after satisfaction had been made. All this changed under John, who frequently sought forfeiture of lands as a consequence of default.[12] Whether an abuse of the *lex scaccarii* or not, the threat of permanent confiscation made against de Braose was not unusual. Nevertheless, in the sequence of events above we have the first indication of financial law being used to clothe more sinister action. As Holden has noted, the idea that de Braose was able to conceal all his moveable

8 Duffy, 'John and Ireland', 240–2, at 240; idem, 'King John's expedition to Ireland, 1210: the evidence reconsidered', *IHS* 30, no. 117 (1996), 1–24.

9 The best version of the text, as recorded in the black book of the exchequer, has been transcribed by David Crouch: 'The complaint of King John against William de Briouze (*c.* September 1210)', in J. S. Loengard (ed.), *Magna Carta and the England of King John* (Woodbridge, 2010), 168–179 (translation of quoted passages is my own). For other printed versions, see Rymer, *Foedera*, i, pt. 1, fos 107–8 (Latin); *CDI*, i, no. 408 (English).

10 Totalling £2, 865 6*s*. 8*d*. in 1205/6: *Pipe roll 7 John*, 107.

11 Maitland and Pollock, *Hist. English law*, i, 353.

12 Ibid., 354; J. E. A. Jolliffe, *Angevin kingship* (2nd edn, London, 1963), 79–84.

property from the king's officers is outlandish,[13] and the suspicion must be that the 500 men raised by the bailiff of Wales was concerned less with seizing William's chattels than with harassing his family, dispatched soon after to the relative safety of Ireland.

John's handling of William de Braose went far beyond what might normally be expected in regard to creditors.[14] Instead, the punishments meted out to de Braose and his family were more appropriate for those guilty of serious criminal felony or treason. The final action aimed at William was his proclamation as an outlaw. This was the most potent sanction available to the crown, still reserved for the gravest of crimes and carrying with certain escheat or forfeiture the potential for mutilation or death.[15] De Braose had certainly acted criminally in his attack on Leominster, the location of a cell of Reading Abbey under royal protection, during which some of the king's men were killed or wounded.[16] However, there remains a peculiar emphasis on financial irregularity in John's complaint, and a reluctance to connect de Braose's violent contumacy with his final punishment of outlawry. Even before William's declaration as an outlaw his wife was compelled to make an outlandish fine of 40,000 marks for the *vita et membra* of her husband, herself and her family – in other words, to avoid the punishment of mutilation or execution normally reserved for traitors and rebels.[17]

For John Lloyd, the starvation of Matilda de Braose and her eldest son in royal custody represented 'the pitiless vengeance of the hardest heart in Christendom'.[18] The king was far from incapable of arbitrary cruelty, but it should be remembered that the same punishment had also been used against rebels by John's Angevin forebears.[19] Strange as it may seem, starvation may well have been a courtesy (where hanging or other forms of public execution

[13] Brock Holden, 'King John, the Braoses, and the Celtic fringe, 1207–1216', *Albion* 33 (2001), 1–23, at 8.

[14] For a synthesis of the evidence pointing away from a financial motive for de Braose's destruction, see ibid., 8–9.

[15] Maitland and Pollock, *Hist. English law*, ii, 467n, 580–1.

[16] While the king was in Ireland, John's complaint alleged that de Braose 'did what evil he could to us' (*nobis malum fecit quod potuit*), burning down a mill and three cottages (*bordellos*).

[17] Strickland, *War and chivalry*, 240–57.

[18] Lloyd, *History of Wales*, ii, 632. In the chronicle of Roger of Wendover, Matilda's fate is attributed to her refusal to hand over hostages to the king on the basis that John had 'basely murdered his nephew, Arthur, whom he ought to have taken care of honourably': *Flores hist.*, ii, 48–9; *Roger of Wendover's Flowers of history, comprising the history of England from the descent of the Saxons to A.D. 1231 formerly ascribed to Matthew Paris*, trans. J. A. Giles (2 vols, London, 1849), ii, 247–8. For the suspicious disappearance of the king's nephew, Arthur of Brittany, in 1203, see Powicke, *Loss of Normandy*, 309–26. While William de Braose may have had unique knowledge of Arthur's fate, Wendover's account of de Braose's downfall is unfavourably critiqued in Warren, *King John*, 11–14.

[19] Strickland, *War and chivalry*, 256.

were not), acknowledging the deference due to the noble body.[20] As a penalty for her husband's debts, the treatment of Matilda de Braose was harsh in the extreme; in the context of treason, it was in keeping with the laws and standards of the time. Indictment for treason was also extended to those aiding or consenting to it.[21] As a woman Matilda could not be outlawed, but she could be 'waived' (set outside the protection of the law) and therefore condemned without judicial process.[22] As for the younger William de Braose, a school of thought held that the son of a traitor, stained by the father's guilt, should not only face disinheritance but be put to death.[23]

The reason why accusations of treason were not made clear in the king's testimonial may lie in the nature of the offence and the procedure for its conviction. The crown was the injured party in cases of treason, and it was unbefitting for the king to act as both victim and judge. Traitorous barons were considered worthy of the sternest of penalties, but only after judgment and conviction by peers. Delegation to *iudicium parium* could result in exoneration, however, a possibility the king may have been unwilling to countenance in this instance. Due process also took time: by right, an earl should be granted one month to respond to a summons to trial and a baron up to three weeks, presenting a problem if the threat of rebellion was imminent.[24]

This brings the purpose of the king's *querimonia* into focus. That John went to the trouble of justifying his actions at all testifies to the fact that the aristocratic community was alarmed by some aspect of de Braose's treatment.[25] The barons' problem cannot have been with the punishment of a traitor, for all such were deserving of their fate. Issue may have been taken with the arbitrary enforcement of punishment *sine judicio*, however, which set a very dangerous precedent.[26] The king could not openly expose de Braose's participation in treason because he had acted contrary to the laws governing its prosecution. Instead, it appears that John made every effort to connect William's punishment with debt, an offence which could have been dealt with summarily by the king or his justices.

20 Ibid.

21 J. G. Bellamy, *The law of treason in England in the later Middle Ages* (Cambridge, 1970), 7.

22 Bracton, *De legibus et consuetudinibus Angliae*, ii, 353–4.

23 Bellamy, *Law of treason*, 9.

24 Maitland and Pollock, *Hist. English law*, i, 410.–11; Bellamy, *Law of treason*, 8.

25 As seems clear from the letter's address ('let it be made known to all of you what offence caused William de Braose to flee from our land') and sealing clause ('so that the truth about these things might be established, we and our earls and barons subscribed below have attached our seals to this letter as witnesses to its truth'). See also, Crouch, 'Complaint of King John', 168.

26 Clause 39 in Magna Carta (1215) stated that 'no free man shall be arrested, or imprisoned, or disseised, or outlawed, or exiled, or in any way destroyed, nor will we go against him, nor will we send against him, save by the lawful judgement of his peers or by the law of the land': David Carpenter, *Magna Carta* (London, 2015), 63–4.

The association of William de Braose with sedition, deliberately obfuscated by the king's *querimonia*, must call the actions of William's *socii* in Ireland into question.[27] The intriguing indictment of Hugh de Lacy, as presented by the 'Barnwell' annalist (above), is given weight by another inconsistency between crime and punishment in the king's *querimonia*. William Marshal was accused of sheltering William de Braose from the king's justice along with the de Lacy brothers, yet he escaped serious sanction in 1210. The disparity cannot be explained by resistance to the royal army, for Walter de Lacy offered none. Neither can the Marshal's excuse – that de Braose was his friend and lord (*mis amis e mis sire*) – have held much weight with the king.[28] What set the de Lacys apart from the Marshal was the stain of *suspected* treason, for which forfeiture and exile were the order of the day. The emphasis is important because, although both Walter and Hugh de Lacy forfeited their lands in 1210, it is by no means certain that the brothers were equal partners in rebellion. While some persuasive evidence exists connecting the earl of Ulster with domestic and external enemies of the crown, there is much less to indict the lord of Meath. Restored to royal favour soon after the baronial crisis of 1207–08, Walter de Lacy's motive for contemplating treason is difficult to establish. The same cannot be said for Hugh de Lacy, whose grievance with the crown first manifested in the months immediately following his investment with the earldom of Ulster.

Estrangement and dissension, 1205–08

The first chapter argued that the creation of the earldom of Ulster was borne of crisis, being more an act of reprisal against William Marshal than a recognition of Hugh de Lacy's merits. What had been conceived by the king in haste was repented of almost as swiftly. John had been reconciled to the delay of his continental expedition by summer 1205. Performing the most abrupt of *volte-faces*, he then received the Marshal back into his favour, reverting 'to his former habit of displaying friendliness in [William's] company, as if he bore no grudge against him or was angry with him'.[29] With the earl of Pembroke's brief disgrace at an end, there was no longer any pressing need for a counterbalance to his power in Ireland. However, Hugh de Lacy's promotion – publicly enacted

27 'The *querimonia* was an exercise in legal justification': Colin Veach, 'King John and royal control in Ireland: why William de Briouze had to be destroyed', *EHR* 129, no. 540 (2014), 1051–78, at 1071.

28 *HWM*, ii, line 14305; iii, 158. The Marshal may have held from William de Braose at Speen, in Berkshire: Painter, *William Marshal*, 162.

29 *HWM*, ii, lines 13263–70; Crouch, *William Marshal*, 99–100.

and ratified by royal charter – could not be easily undone. John's extraordinary solution appears to have been to pretend that he had never tied the comital sword around Hugh's waist.

Between 29 May 1205 and his departure from court at the end of July, riding high in royal estimation, de Lacy appears as 'earl of Ulster' in the chancery rolls.[30] From that point on Hugh's comital title is conspicuously absent, not to feature in the royal records again until after his restoration by Henry III in 1227.[31] In the same way as the honorific title was used by de Lacy to assert himself as Ulster's legitimate lord, its exclusion from royal mandates may well have been an equally deliberate editorial choice on the part of the king, not to mention a source of considerable embarrassment to de Lacy, whose promotion may have been regarded by some of his peers as undeserved. We find an echo of this policy in the reign of Henry III, when the recognition or withholding of royal titles in correspondence with Irish kings reflected the rise and fall of those men in royal favour.[32] It may have been the subtraction of substance from his comital style, therefore, and a sense that he had something to prove, which caused de Lacy to be so proactive in advertising his status through the language of his own *acta*.

Meanwhile, adding injury to insult, the royal hand was being extended to de Lacy's political opponents. Facing terminal reversal in his war with Philip Augustus, John was in no position to refuse the substantial monetary gift offered to him by the monks of Mellifont in August 1206, seemingly to advance the interests of the archbishop of Armagh against those of Hugh de Lacy. Preoccupation with the French war also dictated the ongoing courtship of the king of Man, despite the part played by Rögnvaldr in John de Courcy's unsuccessful bid for restoration in Ulster.[33]

By the time tensions among the settler community combusted into full-scale warfare in 1207, Hugh de Lacy's hegemonic rights and aristocratic dignity were already being undermined by the crown. This goes some way to explaining the apparent relish with which Hugh took up arms against the justiciar of Ireland, Meiler fitz Henry, whose efforts at self-aggrandisement had set him at loggerheads with his peers. In late 1206 the justiciar's son, Meiler the younger, seized William de Braose's honor of Limerick, then in the charge of Walter de Lacy.[34] Despite de Braose's mounting debt for Limerick, the young Meiler's assault does not appear to have been orchestrated by the crown. In early 1207 the justiciar was instructed to return what had been taken from de Braose (men, lands,

30 *RLC*, i, 36a, 40a; *Rot. chart.*, 158a; *Documents illustrative of English history*, ed. Cole, 271.

31 *CCHR, 1226–57*, 36–7; *CDI*, i, no. 1505.

32 Frame, 'England and Ireland', 23.

33 See above, 37–9, 50.

34 *AClon.*, 1205 [*recte* 1206]; *AFM*, 1205 [*recte* 1206].

chattels and arms), 'as William has served the king well'.[35] However, the same mandate prescribed that the city of Limerick should be retained for the use of the crown, John plainly judging that more could be done to his advantage with the strategic settlement in the hands of his administrator.

In 1204, the contention between fitz Henry and William Marshal over the latter's fee of Uí Failge (Co. Offaly) had taken on extra meaning because of Meiler's dual status as Marshal tenant and royal representative.[36] Now, the retention of Limerick placed in jeopardy Meiler's cantred of Cenél Fiachach (Ardnurcher/Horseleap, Co. Westmeath), which he held from Walter de Lacy. Under 1207 the annals of the Four Masters report that 'the sons of Hugo de Lacy and the English of Meath marched to the castle of Athnurcher [*alias* Ardnurcher] and continued to besiege it for five weeks, when it was surrendered to them, as was also the territory of Fircal; and Meyler was banished from the country'.[37] As 'Fircal' (*Fir Cell*, Co. Offaly) does not appear to have been included in the original grant of Cenél Fiachach, it has been suggested that the locality could have been occupied by the justiciar to the detriment of Walter de Lacy.[38] Hugh de Lacy's lands may also have been targeted. In the aftermath of Ardnurcher's capture Meiler was forced 'to abandon and forsake all the cantred of Kinaleagh from Burr (Birr, Co. Offaly) to Killare'.[39] In the north of 'Kinaleagh' (Kinalea, Co. Westmeath), near the hill of Uisnech, was Cenél Enda, probably the 'Knelene' granted to Hugh de Lacy along with Ratoath and Morgallion, c.1190.[40]

In 'banishing' Meiler, Walter de Lacy did little more than exercise his prerogative as fitz Henry's overlord in Meath. Even so, King John was unwilling to allow the representative of regnal lordship to suffer the indignity of treatment as a recalcitrant tenant, and Walter was summoned to England in April to answer for 'injuries and trespasses' committed against the justiciar.[41] Around the same time, having been blocked from doing so on several occasions by the king, William Marshal crossed to Ireland, where he drafted the dissenting baronial faction into his own running dispute with the justiciar over Uí Failge.[42] The

35 *RLC*, i, 77b; *CDI*, i, no. 310.

36 See above, 43.

37 *AFM*, 1207. See also *AClon.*, 1207; *ALC*, 1207 (where Walter and Hugh de Lacy are named as the instigators of the assault). On 13 January 1207 the de Lacys were at Rathbeggan, in Meath; around 1 February Hugh was harassing the *civitas* of Armagh; on 2 March Walter witnessed his brother's grant to Hugh Hose at Galtrim, in Meath: appendix I, nos 12–13; *MCB*, 1207. Assuming that the attack on Ardnurcher continued for five weeks, as reported in the annals, the siege must have commenced after this last date.

38 Flanagan, 'Defining lordships', 51; Orpen, *Normans*, 237.

39 *AClon.*, 1207.

40 Hogan, *Onomasticon*, 219; Veach, 'A question of timing', 177n.

41 *RLC*, i, 81a; *CDI*, i, nos 324–5.

42 *HWM*, ii, lines 13355–77; Crouch, *William Marshal*, 101–2.

king must now have begun to appreciate the folly of his treatment of Hugh de Lacy, so recently groomed as co-adjutor to Meiler fitz Henry and foil to the lord of Leinster, now agitating against the justiciar and among those magnates 'well satisfied' by the Marshal's appearance in Ireland.[43]

On 23 May John registered his astonishment at the intention of the barons of Leinster and Meath (including Walter and Hugh de Lacy) to submit the justiciar to legal judgement over Uí Failge without royal consent.[44] In supporting the Marshal's *iura* the de Lacys were striking a further blow for magnate power, but we may wonder to what extent Meiler's actions over Uí Failge had provoked the genuine outrage of his peers. After all, the initial challenge to the Marshal's interests had not prevented the de Lacys from acting as agents of the crown in 1204–05, and it was not until the brothers' own positions were threatened that they appear to have been much concerned with the abuse of vicarious royal authority in Leinster.

If Uí Failge was an issue through which a multitude of baronial frustrations were expressed, the corollary is that the dissenting parties could be bought off at differing cost to the crown. The concerns of Walter de Lacy and William Marshal were particular, centring on rights to property, and could be addressed through a process of negotiation. Hugh de Lacy's grievances were more ephemeral in nature, rooted in the withdrawal of royal favour and injuries to his comital dignity. While in the first months of 1207 we find the lords of Meath and Ulster working together to further each other's interests, it is in the same year that their pursuit of different political agendas began to place significant stress on the de Lacy fraternity. A fundamental difference between the two men, and one which dictated their respective handling by the king, was that Walter could be controlled through the distraint of lands or revocation of custodies in England, while Hugh's exclusive operation in Ireland made him less susceptible to normative forms of discipline.

Ludlow castle had already been removed from Walter's custody on 5 March,[45] and the prospect of more serious sanction left him with little option but to comply with his recall to court, where he had arrived by the middle of July.[46] It seems that the elder brother's political nous was not initially of much benefit to the younger. Walter's journey to England coincided with that of the archbishop of Armagh, who presented a personal complaint to King John concerning the recent assaults on his archiepiscopal seat that had been orchestrated by Hugh de Lacy.[47] In an evident acknowledgement of Eugenius's archiepiscopal status, John

43 *HWM*, ii, line 13436.
44 *RLP*, 72a; *CDI*, i, no. 329.
45 *RLP*, 69b–70a; *RLC*, i, 79–80.
46 *Rot. chart.*, 167b; *CDI*, i, no. 330.
47 *AU*, 1207.

dispatched the complainant to execute episcopal office in the vacant bishoprics of Exeter and Worcester.[48] Just six days previously, on 13 July, custody of Ludlow had been granted to William de Braose, restoring it to Walter de Lacy's indirect control.[49] The lord of Meath's recuperation in royal graces does not appear to have affected his brother's status, and the king's conciliatory treatment of Archbishop Eugenius may help to explain Hugh's ongoing attachment to the dissenting colonial faction.

In Ireland, partisans of the Marshal continued to carry out reprisals against Meiler, and it was at the justiciar's request that William was recalled to England in September.[50] Thereafter the king pursued a twofold strategy to isolate the lord of Leinster. The first strand of the royal scheme involved the appeasement of Walter de Lacy, culminating in a grant of the cantred of Ardmayle (Co. Tipperary).[51] The second strand, enacted at a summit on the Irish situation convened at Woodstock in November, saw the king win over some of the Marshal's inner circle through the lavish bestowal of royal patronage.[52] The justiciar was dispatched back to Ireland at the end of 1207 with instructions to recall those whom the Marshal had left behind to defend his lands.[53] As Meiler made the crossing he must have believed that the task of restoring royal authority to Leinster would be a relatively simple one. But there was still one leading magnate in Ireland with the means and motive to complicate matters.

As soon as the Marshal had departed for England, members of Meiler's faction had descended on Leinster, burning barns and granges at New Ross (Co. Wexford) in the Marshal's demesne, and killing a score of its defenders.[54] Several of fitz Henry's men were captured in retaliation, but any confidence the Leinster barons may have had in their ability to withstand further assaults was undermined by the justiciar's return from court, armed with letters demanding their immediate recall to England.[55] Caught between allegiance to their immediate overlord and the crown, the barons' defiant response is colourfully described by the Marshal's biographer:

> Then they deliberated and decided unanimously, as was their duty, to send Jordan [de Sauqueville] to the earl of Ulster, entreating him to come and help the Marshal, for he

48 *RLC*, i, 88a; *CDI*, i, no. 331; *English episcopal acta, XI*, ed. Barlow, xlvi.

49 *RLP*, 74a.

50 *HWM*, ii, lines 13553–4.

51 *RLC*, i, 98a; *CDI*, i, no. 363. Ardmayle does not seem to have been subject to royal grant before 1207: C. A. Empey, 'The settlement of the kingdom of Limerick', in Lydon (ed.), *England and Ireland in the later Middle Ages*, 1–25, at 1, 3, 10, 16.

52 *Rot. chart.*, 171–4; *CDI*, i, nos 339–61; Crouch, *William Marshal*, 106.

53 *HWM*, ii, lines 13627–76.

54 Ibid., lines 13565–73; Crouch, *William Marshal*, 109.

55 *HWM*, ii, lines 13679–92.

> had very great need of it. Jordan went immediately and the earl came in very splendid array, with sixty-five knights, well armed and riding chargers, and two hundred soldiers under arms, brave men, courageous and renowned for their deeds. He also brought one thousand foot soldiers, who all had it in their hearts to strike fine blows and perform well, who all knew how to handle their arms. I have no wish to give an account of all their deeds, of which there were many fine ones, for that would look like boasting. There was no arrogance or pride in them, but the fact is that what Meiler sought to do to [the Marshal's] lands was done to him by the earl's men.[56]

The glowing portrayal of the earl of Ulster here is curious because, at the time of the *History*'s compilation in 1224×26, the younger William Marshal had recently commanded a royal army against Hugh in Ireland.[57] The explanation may lie in the identity of the biography's chief informant, John of Earley, who was one of the elder Marshal's deputies whom de Lacy saved from destruction in 1208.[58]

If the estimation of the earl's military capability may be hyperbolic, the *History* does not appear to have overestimated the success of Hugh's intervention: 'another great war broke out between Hugo de Lacy and Meyler', state the annals of the Four Masters, 'and the result was that nearly all Meyler's people were ruined'.[59] Further detail on the target of de Lacy's assaults is provided by the Clonmacnoise annals, which record 'contention and strife between Meyler and Hugh Delacie, that between the said parties the land of Foherties was wasted, preyed, and destroyed'.[60] This was probably Forth (Co. Carlow), adjoining Meiler's holdings in Laigis (Leix).[61]

De Lacy had earned the appreciation of the Leinster barons, but his intervention on their behalf now threatened to undermine his elder brother's rapprochement with the king. The news coming from Ireland was little short of humiliating for the crown. Meiler had been 'overwhelmed and taken', and compelled to hand over hostages to the Marshal's men.[62] At Hugh de Lacy's hands, the justiciar – and, by extension, the king – had suffered a dreadful defeat. John's reaction was predictably rash. News of Meiler's capture reached court during Lent, which began on 20 February in 1208.[63] On that day the mariners of Wales were ordered to prepare to pass the king's forces into Ireland[64]

56 Ibid., lines 13763–85. Jordan de Sauqueville held Holywood and Ardglass (Co. Down) from Hugh de Lacy in 1210: *CDI*, i, nos 404, 775; H. C. Lawlor, 'Mote and mote-and-bailey castles (ii)', 54.

57 See below, 156–60.

58 *HWM*, iii, 4, 23–5.

59 *AFM*, 1207 [*recte* 1208]

60 *AClon.*, 1207 [*recte* 1208].

61 Hogan, *Onomasticon*, 430.

62 *HWM*, ii, lines 13871–88.

63 Ibid., lines 13867–70.

64 *RLP*, 79a; *CDI*, i, no. 374.

and the Marshal's confederates in Ireland were again summoned to England on pain of forfeiture.[65] The king's fit of pique appears to have been eased by the Marshal's careful and deferential conduct at court, and plans for an Irish expedition were shelved. Instead, John came to an understanding with the Marshal, ordering Uí Failge's return and declaring that no more action should be taken against him.[66] On 28 March a new royal charter was issued for Leinster, allowing custody of fees in wardship to the Marshal but reserving some novel jurisdictions to the crown.[67]

At the same time, the goodwill extended to Walter de Lacy during the winter of 1207/8 evaporated. Despite his absence from Ireland at the height of the baronial crisis, Walter was compelled into negotiating a new peace concerning his Irish possessions, *in eadem forma* as that agreed with William Marshal.[68] On 24 April Walter received his own modified charter for Meath.[69] Like the Marshal, he was to receive custody of fees in wardship and surrendered the four pleas of the crown; rights in cases where justice had not properly been served in the liberty court; and jurisdiction in cross lands. An extra clause not included in the charter for Leinster, however, prescribed that the king's writs would now run in Meath. These revised terms were supposedly granted *ad petitionem Walteri*, but it seems unlikely that the lord of Meath specified more restrictive conditions than those offered to his counterpart in Leinster and which so radically undercut his independence. Perhaps more likely is that the erosion of Walter's franchisal power owed much to the actions of his younger brother in forcing the king into an embarrassing reversal of royal policy over Leinster.

1208 – justiciar or hostage?

The immediate repercussions of the inter-baronial conflict have been obscured by a dubious tradition holding that Meiler was replaced as justiciar by Hugh de Lacy. A first objection to Orpen's suggestion, that de Lacy was 'probably chief governor for a few months from the autumn of 1208',[70] can be made on chronological grounds. Meiler's last appearance as justiciar in the chancery rolls is from 19 June 1208.[71] His eventual successor, John de Grey, bishop of Norwich, had certainly arrived in Ireland by 28 November, when he drafted a charter at the

65 *RLP*, 79a; *RLC*, i, 103a; *CDI*, i, no. 374.
66 *RLC*, i, 105a; *RLP*, 80b; *CDI*, i, nos 375, 378; Flanagan, 'Defining lordships', 52–3.
67 *Rot. chart.*, 176a; *CDI*, i, no. 381.
68 *RLC*, i, 106b; *CDI*, i, no. 376.
69 *Rot. chart.*, 178; *CDI*, i, no. 382.
70 Orpen, *Normans*, xlii.
71 *RLP*, 84b.

abbey of Ossory (Jerpoint, Co. Kilkenny).[72] Flanagan suspected that de Grey was actually appointed earlier in the year, noticing that his attestations of royal charters cease abruptly on 20 July.[73] This leaves a very narrow window in which de Lacy could have occupied the justiciarship.

Uncertainty may also surround Orpen's authorities, the (Dublin) annals of Inisfallen and the eighteenth-century antiquary Walter Harris (†1761). Published in 1764, Harris's posthumous edition of Ware's *Antiquities of Ireland* wrongly lists Hugh de Lacy (with the specious title 'lord of Meath') as justiciar on two other occasions (1189–91 and 1203–05).[74] Meibhbhín Ní Úrdail has noted resemblances between the eighteenth-century (Dublin) annals of Inisfallen and *Mac Carthaig's book* (MCB), a fifteenth-century compilation, which could point to the latter's incorporation in the former.[75] However, there are several *lacunae* in MCB for which other sources must have been consulted during the compilation of the Dublin annals. This process probably began in 1765, the year after the publication of Harris's work, leaving open the intriguing possibility that the antiquarian's faulty record of Hugh de Lacy's appointment was added to the Dublin annals to fill the gap in MCB for the year 1208.

Given Hugh de Lacy's part in the crown's humiliation over Uí Failge, it seems almost absurd that he should have been granted the custody of Ireland, even as an interim solution. In fact, other evidence could show that the king attempted to hold de Lacy to account for his contumacy. On 9 April 1208, amid ongoing negotiations with Walter de Lacy prior to the re-granting of Meath, the king instructed Robert de Vieuxpont to 'hold Hugh de Lacy, hostage of Walter de Lacy, without iron[s], insofar as he may be safely kept in custody'.[76] Veach has argued against this having been Hugh, earl of Ulster, on the grounds that *comites* were not usually kept as hostages, and the absence of a comital title in the royal edict.[77] However, as we have seen, Hugh's rank no longer held much weight with the king, and the exclusion of his comital style is entirely consistent with royal policy stretching back to 1205.[78] An alternative candidate is the son of Robert de Lacy, younger son of Hugh I, listed among the 'hostages of Ireland' in 1207.[79] No connection to Robert is specified in the mandate to Robert de Vieuxpont, however, against the usual chancery practice of denoting a hostage's filial relationship. This may imply that de Vieuxpont's charge was of a higher

[72] *English episcopal acta, VI: Norwich, 1070–1214*, ed. Christopher Harper-Bill (Oxford, 1990), no. 370.

[73] Flanagan, 'Defining lordships', 54n.

[74] James Ware, *Antiquities of Ireland*, ed. Walter Harris (Dublin, 1764), 102.

[75] Ní Úrdail, 'Some observations on the 'Dublin annals of Inisfallen'', 148–53.

[76] *RLC*, i, 110a.

[77] Veach, 'Nobility and crown', 167n.

[78] For Hugh's three appearances in the English rolls between 1205 and 1208, see *RLP*, 67a, 72.

[79] *RLP*, 72.

status than normally expected of a surety, as does the deferential instruction that he be held *extra ferrum*.

The taking of hostages was an integral component of King John's 'machinery of intimidation',[80] and an intriguing episode in the Marshal's biography reveals how willing the king was to confound expectations surrounding hostageship, and the social standing of hostages, to make a political point. Normally, aristocratic *obsides* were the sons or brothers of influential men, whose custody would not unduly affect the functioning of the political community. During his Irish expedition in 1210, however, John demanded several of William Marshal's most intimate supporters as sureties – Geoffrey fitz Robert, Jordan de Sauqueville, Thomas of Sandford, John of Earley and Walter Purcel – all important landholders in their own right. Ignoring the Marshal's offer to supply the sons of his 'worthy vavasors' instead, John remained resolute in his demand, stating that 'he wished to have no hostages in the matter except those he had informed [William] of'. Once he had secured permission from his vassals to designate them as hostages, the Marshal reluctantly complied.[81]

Four of these five hostages had conspired with Hugh de Lacy to bring about Meiler fitz Henry's defeat two years previously,[82] implying that the king was pursuing a vendetta against the men responsible for his justiciar's chastening in 1208.[83] A similar vengeful compulsion could conceivably have led the king to demand the earl of Ulster as a hostage in 1208, but exactly how Robert de Vieuxpont could have taken de Lacy into custody remains unclear, unless Hugh voluntarily committed himself to royal officers. This seems unlikely in the extreme, but to dismiss outright the earl's candidacy as an *obses* would be to ignore one of the pervading themes of King John's reign, namely the stretching of the apparatus of power beyond expected limits, especially in areas furthest from royal supervision, such as Ulster, where the adaptation of controlling mechanisms was most necessary. Moreover, the indignity of acting as a hostage would certainly help to contextualise Hugh's concurrent efforts to associate himself with political opponents of the crown across the North Channel, in Scotland.

80 Bartlett, *England*, 48–51, at 50.

81 *HWM*, ii, lines 14319–69. In 1174 Henry II took twenty-one high-status hostages from King William of Scotland; these, however, were to be allowed to designate a son or relative in place of themselves once certain castles had been handed over to the English: *Anglo-Scottish relations: some selected documents*, ed. E. L. G. Stones (2nd edn, Oxford, 1970), 6–8; Bartlett, *England*, 49.

82 With the exception of Thomas of Sandford: *HWM*, ii, lines 13464–509.

83 The Marshal's castle of Dunamase (Co. Laois), conceded to the crown in 1210, had been surrendered by Meiler fitz Henry in 1208: ibid., lines 14123–32; iii, 157.

Enemy of the crown

Preserved in the register of St Andrews cathedral priory is a copy of a charter of Hugh II de Lacy, as earl of Ulster, granting to the church of St Andrew *in Scocia*, and to the canons serving there, the churches of Rooskey, Carlingford and of Cooley (Co. Louth) in Ireland.[84] The charter-text contains no dating clause, but the confirmation of de Lacy's gift by King Henry III, on 27 September 1237, has led historians to ascribe a coeval date of issue to the original endowment.[85] In fact, recent prosopographical analysis of the witnesses to de Lacy's grant has revised the date of issue to the first comital period (1205–10), at least twenty-seven years before the charter's ratification by Henry III.[86]

An explanation for this considerable temporal disparity might be found in the terms of the Anglo-Scottish Treaty of York, concluded on 25 September 1237, five days before the royal confirmation of de Lacy's grant.[87] The three days of negotiations at York, presided over by the papal legate, Otto, revolved around the humiliating terms that had been imposed by King John on his counterpart, William I of Scotland (†1214), in the Treaty of Norham (1209).[88] By the terms of that earlier concord – as rehearsed in a recently discovered letter of King John[89] – William agreed that his son, the future Alexander II, would do homage to John for the kingdom of Scots upon his succession, and granted the English king the right to negotiate the marriages of his daughters, a 'privilege' for which William was to pay some 15,000 marks. Despite the reservation to William of his (purely nominal) claims in the three northern counties of Northumberland,

84 Appendix I, no. 9, and above, 85. For a full exploration of the charter's significance, see Daniel J. F. Brown, 'Power and patronage across the North Channel: Hugh de Lacy, St Andrews and the Anglo-Scottish crisis of 1209', *Scot. Hist. Rev.* 94, no. 1 (2015), 1–23. Whether St Andrews made good on its claim to Irish benefices is unclear. Carlingford is not found under any Irish diocese in the papal taxation of 1302, but appears in Armagh diocese from 1375: *CDI*, v, no. 693; *Register of Milo Sweteman*, ed. Smith, 139. Professor Dauvit Broun (University of Glasgow) kindly pointed out to me that the priory's rights would have been surrendered after the 1314 Parliament of Cambuskenneth, which made it unlawful to hold simultaneously from the kings of Scotland and England.

85 See, for example, Veach, *Lordship*, 140.

86 Brown, 'Power and patronage', 2–5. *Ante quem* from the death of Richard de Tuit, in 1211: *ALC*, 1211; *AClon.*, 1210 [*recte* 1211]; *Chartul. St Mary's, Dublin*, ii, 312. The composition of the testing clause is strikingly similar to those in two other comital *acta* from 1207, while all three instruments were drafted by the same clerk, William, whose name is not found in any post–1227 charters: appendix I, nos 9, 12–13.

87 *Anglo-Scottish relations*, ed. Stones, 38–54.

88 A. A. M. Duncan, *Scotland: the making of the kingdom* (2nd edn, Edinburgh, 1996), 533–4, and below, 106, 166, 195.

89 Carpenter, *Magna Carta*, appendix I (found by Carpenter in an early fourteenth-century cartulary of St Augustine's Abbey, Canterbury). For the terms of the treaty, not all of which were recounted in King John's letter, see ibid., 238–41, updating the synthesis of documentary evidence provided in Duncan, *Scotland*, 241–9.

Westmoreland and Cumberland, the Melrose chronicle's estimation of Norham as 'against the interests of the Scots'[90] hardly does justice to the abject quality of the subjection.

In 1237 King Alexander II set aside any lingering misgivings over the Norham provisions in return for land in the northern counties.[91] Another of the York sub-clauses concerned the mutual restoration of sensitive documents relevant to the negotiations at Norham, prescribing that, 'if, in those writings or instruments, there are found any points not touching the present business which concern the interests of either king, these points ought to be set out afresh in letters/charters of each king'.[92] Five days after the conclusion of the York negotiations, Henry III confirmed the rights of St Andrews priory to churches in Ireland. It seems plausible to infer from this chronology that the priory's earlier charter from Hugh de Lacy represented one of the contentious points discovered in the material relating to the Norham negotiations in 1209, and that the confirmation of its terms by the English king represented a concession to the 'interests' of the Scots.[93]

The aggrandisement of the cathedral priory at St Andrews has been seen as vital to the efforts of the Canmore kings of Scots to have the see recognised as an archdiocese, and to undermine the claims over the Scottish church made by the English province of York.[94] The installation of royal *familiares* in the bishopric, meanwhile, had led to the functioning of the episcopal *curia* at St Andrews as something like an ecclesiastical arm of secular government.[95] In 1189, following the resolution of a lengthy succession dispute at St Andrews, King William I appointed his cousin and former chancellor, Roger de Beaumont, son of the earl of Leicester, to the see.[96] In 1202 Roger was succeeded by another former royal chancellor, William Malveisin, who was translated from Glasgow.[97]

90 *The chronicle of Melrose Abbey: a stratigraphic edition. Volume 1: introduction and facsimile edition*, ed. Dauvit Broun and Julian Harrison (Woodbridge, 2007), 131.

91 *Anglo-Scottish relations*, ed. Stones, 38–54.

92 Ibid., 48–9 (*debent predicta capitula per utrisque regis literas innovari*). For the restoration of 'obligaciouns, intrumentz et autres muniments' as part of the Anglo-Scottish Treaty of Northampton (1328), see ibid., 335–7.

93 All but one of the witnesses to Henry's confirmation also attested the York treaty.

94 Brown, 'Power and patronage', 11; A. D. M. Barrell, *Medieval Scotland* (Cambridge, 2000), 42–7; A. A. M. Duncan, *The kingship of the Scots, 842–1292: succession and independence* (Edinburgh, 2002), 82–98; idem, *Scotland*, 257–77; idem, 'The foundation of St Andrews cathedral priory', *Scot. Hist. Rev.* 84, no. 217 (2005), 1–37.

95 Duncan, *Kingship*, 86.

96 John Dowden, *The bishops of Scotland*, ed. J. M. Thomson (Glasgow, 1912), 10–12; Duncan, *Scotland*, 270–4. Roger was the king's cousin through William's mother, Ada, sister of the earl of Leicester.

97 Dowden, *Bishops of Scotland*, 12–14; D. E. R. Watt, *A biographical dictionary of Scottish graduates to A.D. 1410* (Oxford, 1977), 374–9.

In light of St Andrews' importance to the Canmore kings, could Hugh de Lacy's endowment of its cathedral priory be evidence of the earl's attraction into William I's ambit? Such an affiliation can be seen to have served the strategic interests of the king of Scots, the integrity of whose realm was partly influenced by the activities of Gaelic Irish and Anglo-Norman power-players across the North Channel. John de Courcy's conquest of Ulaid had initially played into the hands of the Scottish crown, serving to check the influence of Cenél nEógain, from whom the Mac William pretenders to the Scottish throne may have recruited support.[98] Of greater concern for the king of Scots was John de Courcy's political alliance with Duncan of Carrick, whose autonomy frustrated the efforts of the crown to extend its influence west of the river Nith. In the same year (1197) as de Courcy granted his ally a 'substantial' stake in Ulster, King William made a clear attempt to limit Duncan's expansionist ambitions by establishing a royal outpost at Ayr, just north of the earl of Carrick's seat at Turnberry.[99]

Alan of Galloway was far more receptive to Scottish royal influence than his cousin and territorial rival, Duncan of Carrick, as evidenced by the willingness with which Alan undertook his duties as constable of Scotland.[100] The integration of Alan's lordship into the Scottish milieu was as much pursued in the ecclesiastical sphere as it was in the secular. Whithorn, Galloway's bishopric, had remained separate from the Scottish ecclesiastical province, and effectively subject to York, even after Galloway's status as a dependency of the English crown was terminated by the Quitclaim of Canterbury (1189).[101] In 1209 the English appointee to Whithorn was replaced by Alan of Galloway's chamberlain, Walter.[102] It may be more than coincidence that, around the same time that the constable of Scotland installed his own man at Whithorn, to the benefit of the *Scoticana ecclesia*, a grant was made by Alan's relative, Hugh de

98 Stringer, 'Periphery and core', 87–8; Alasdair Ross, 'Moray, Ulster and the Mac Williams', in Duffy (ed.), *The world of the galloglass*, 24–44, at 36–8. De Courcy's brother-in-law, the king of Man, was also being deployed by William I as policeman in the Hebredian zone: McDonald, *Manx kingship*, 108–10, and below, 146–7.

99 *Chron. Houedene*, iv, 25; Barrell, *Medieval Scotland*, 88–9.

100 For political developments in the Galloway region subsequent to the rebellion of 1174, see Oram, *Galloway*, 87–112, 191–218.

101 Brown, 'Power and patronage', 12–13; R. D. Oram, 'In obedience and reverence: Whithorn and York, *ca*. 1128–*ca*. 1250', *The Innes Review* 42 (1991), 83–100; *Scotia pontificia: papal letters to Scotland before the pontificate of Innocent III*, ed. Robert Somerville (Oxford, 1982), nos 80, 156. King Richard I probably influenced the appointment of Bishop John in 1189: Oram, 'Whithorn and York', 92–3.

102 Gordon Donaldson, 'The bishops and priors of Whithorn', *TDGNHAS*, 3rd ser., 27 (1948–9), 135; Brown, 'Power and patronage', 13.

Lacy, to another church intimately connected to the king of Scots' ecclesiastical programme.[103]

If not via Galloway, the earl of Ulster could have come into contact with the Scottish court through the fitz Alans, hereditary stewards of Scotland, whose English relative, William II fitz Alan, had married an unnamed daughter of Hugh I de Lacy in 1175.[104] The fitz Alans' stock had fallen at the Scottish court by 1201, however, as a result of a marriage alliance with Duncan of Carrick,[105] and a more likely intermediary between earl of Ulster and king of Scots was the bishop of St Andrews, William Malveisin (†1238). Little is known about William's early career before his arrival at the Scottish court as a royal clerk in the mid 1180s, but in 1212 he was granted leave by King William to visit his relatives in France (*Galliae*).[106] It has been claimed that the bishop was the same *Willelmus Malusvicinus* who witnessed several continental charters of King Henry II alongside Hugh I de Lacy in the 1170s.[107] In actual fact, this witness was more likely to have been a nephew of Odo, count of Brittany.[108] An alternative theory concerning the bishop's lineage may still lead back to the earl of Ulster, however. William's episcopal entourage included several men whose names can be linked to the lower Seine valley, raising the possibility that the bishop belonged to the family of Mauvoisin with interests in the same region of France, and whose representative, Robert II Mauvoisin, would fight alongside Hugh de Lacy on the Albigensian crusade.[109]

At the end of May 1209 the bishop of St Andrews was dispatched by William I at the head of an embassy to King John, as part of negotiations surrounding the king of Scots' long-standing claims in the northern counties.[110] According

103 It is the political import of St Andrews and its pretensions to metropolitan status which might have recommended it for patronage by Hugh de Lacy, in preference to other religious houses closer to the king of Scots' heart, such as his personal foundation at Arbroath (where he would be buried).

104 R. W. Eyton, *Antiquities of Shropshire* (12 vols, London, 1854–60), vii, 220–50; Brown, 'Power and patronage', 13–14. In 1210 Hugh II de Lacy entrusted his sons to the care of Alwyn, earl of Lennox and a close associate of the fitz Alans: below, 113.

105 Oram, *Galloway*, 132–3.

106 *Scotichronicon*, iv, 534; Watt, *Scottish graduates*, 374.

107 M. A. Pollock, 'Rebels of the West, 1209–1216', *Cambrian Medieval Celtic Studies* 50 (2005), 1–30, at 21 (where William's co-attestor is said to be Hugh II de Lacy, only born c. 1170); *Recueil des actes de Henri II*, ii, 84–5, 90, 92–5; *The cartae antiquae rolls, 11–20, printed from the original manuscripts in the Public Record Office*, ed. James Conway Davies, Pipe Roll Society (London, 1960), 91; *CDI*, i, no. 50.

108 Watt, *Scottish graduates*, 374.

109 Ibid.; M. A. Pollock, *Scotland, England and France after the loss of Normandy, 1204–1296: 'auld amitie'* (Woodbridge, 2015), 36–40; below, 119n, 125, 128.

110 *Annals of the reigns of Malcolm and William, kings of Scotland*, ed. A. C. Lawrie (Glasgow, 1910), 361; *RLP*, 91a; Duncan, *Scotland*, 224–6; D. D. R. Owen, *William the lion: kingship and culture, 1143–1214* (East Linton, 1997), 13–17

to Bower's *Scotichronicon*, after delivering their message to the English king, the envoys were surprised to find John 'more displeased than they had believed and much provoked by their answers, thundering out threats against the kings of Scotland and their country'. Bishop Malveisin and his fellow emissaries related the unexpected development to King William at Forfar, 'and threw not just the king but the whole kingdom into a considerable panic'. Sensibly, as King John made preparations for an assault on the Scots, William fell back on diplomacy and agreement was reached between the two kings at Norham (Northumberland) by 7 August.[111]

Of several theories advanced to explain this sudden flaring of tension,[112] the least problematic is alluded to in the annals of Margam, which allege that the king of Scots had 'entered into an alliance with [King John's] enemies'.[113] John's most intractable enemy was King Philip of France, and it may have been news of an expected Franco-Scottish marriage alliance which arrived at the English king's court on 28 May 1209, in the care of one Fulcher, 'a secret messenger from overseas parts'.[114] Just such a revelation might help to rationalise John's violent reaction to the Scots' delegation, dispatched from Stirling just four days earlier and led by a Frenchman in the person of the bishop of St Andrews.

It is Bishop Malveisin's capacity as envoy in 1209 which brings back into focus Hugh de Lacy's charter to St Andrews. Bower makes clear that the Scottish embassy was acting on a 'plan' worked out by King William's advisers at Stirling. The strategy cannot have involved military grandstanding, but the Scots may well have sought to exploit King John's insecurities in the ecclesiastical sphere. England had been placed under papal interdict in 1208 following John's refusal to recognise Stephen Langton's appointment as archbishop of Canterbury.[115] This was the ideal opportunity to revive St Andrews' hopes of metropolitan status, and it is surely significant that Langton's father, Henry, found refuge at St Andrews priory in the wake of the interdict.[116] There is no direct evidence that the Scots were still actively lobbying for St Andrews'

111 *Scotichronicon*, iv, 448–51.

112 Examined in A. A. M. Duncan, 'John, king of England and the kings of Scots', in Church (ed.), *King John: new interpretations*, 247–71, at 255–9.

113 *Early sources*, ed. Anderson, ii, 373.

114 *Rot. Lib.*, 118; Duncan, 'John, king of England', 260–1.

115 Warren, *King John*, 159–73; Turner, *King John*, 155–73.

116 *Gervase of Canterbury*, ii, lxiii. Wendover connected King John's fury at the Scots in 1209 with the harbouring of ecclesiastical refugees: *Flores hist.*, ii, 50. The Dunstable annals claim that the bishops of Rochester and Salisbury travelled to Scotland in 1207–8, but *cum regis Angliae gratia*: *Ann. mon.*, iii, 31. Stephen Langton would absolve Hugh de Lacy from excommunication in 1224, while his brother, Walter Langton, was Hugh's fellow crusader in Occitania: ibid., 91–2; Nicholas Vincent, 'England and the Albigensian crusade', in Björn Weiler and Ifor Rowlands (eds), *England and Europe in the reign of Henry III, 1216–1272* (Aldershot and Burlington, 2002), 67–97, at 73, and below, 119, 131n, 160, 164.

elevation, though William Malveisin had an ideal opportunity to broach the issue during a mission to Rome in 1207.[117] In any case, the important consideration for the Scots would be to demonstrate a willingness to exploit John's vulnerability in order to secure concessions over the northern counties. If St Andrews was to be used as a bargaining chip, an appropriate exhibition of its growing prestige would certainly have been the presentation of a document in which the see was granted rights to churches in King John's lordship of Ireland.

Although *prima facie* a conveyance of minor Irish benefices, the confirmation of Hugh's charter to St Andrews in 1237, just subsequent to the conclusion of the Treaty of York, hints at its political import. Even if it was used by the Scots in a show of strength in 1209, de Lacy's gift was hardly a treasonous act in itself. However, it could point to friendship between the earl of Ulster and king of Scots at a time when King John was probably made aware of Franco-Scottish intrigue. De Lacy's patronage could have been especially damning if his fidelity was already under scrutiny. At some point in 1209, Philip Augustus of France composed a letter to an 'I' or 'J' *de Latiaco*, discussing an offer made by the addressee to undermine King John by friends and attacks in England, and by 'friends and the defence of castles in Ireland'.[118] Once he had received confirmation that the plot was being enacted, Philip promised that he would take advice about certain lands held by the letter's recipient in England. Despite some extremely problematic attempts to identify either Hugh or Walter de Lacy as the intended recipient of the letter,[119] a more satisfactory candidate is John de Lacy (future earl of Lincoln), son of Roger, constable of Chester and head of the Pontefract de Lacys (†1211).[120]

This is not to exculpate Hugh de Lacy, except to say that he might only have played a supporting role in the conspiracy, rather than a leading one. Pointing to collusion between the Herefordshire and Pontefract de Lacys are the Dunstable annals for 1210, which describe a plot to set Simon de Montfort

117 Watt, *Scottish graduates*, 378–9.

118 *Recueil des actes de Philippe Auguste roi de France publié sous la direction de* M. *Charles Samaran membre de l'institut, tome III, années du règne XXVIII à XXXVI*, ed. M. J. Monicat and M. J. Boussard (3 vols, Paris, 1916–66), iii, 161–2, no. 1079 (*de guerra facienda in Anglia cum Johanne rege Anglie per amicos et imprisios quos ibidem vos dicit habere, et in Hibernia similiter per amicos et deffensionem castellorum*).

119 See, for eample, Veach, *Lordship*, 139; Duffy, 'Hugh de Lacy and the Albigensian crusade', 71; Duncan, 'John, king of England', 259, where (relying on a copyist's mistake in rendering the recipient's initial) Hugh II is identified as the most likely of the two brothers, being the 'bolder opponent' of the king. This is despite the absence of a comital title in the letter's opening address and the fact that Hugh had no English lands to be restored.

120 As first suggested in Painter, *King John*, 253–5. John de Lacy's conspiratorial credentials have been challenged on the basis of his apparent minority in 1209, as well as his father's loyalty to the crown, factors both undermined in Brown, 'Power and patronage', 18–20.

on the throne of England.[121] As lord of Montfort l'Amoury (Île-de-France), Simon was already occupied as leader of the Albigensian crusade, but he had ample cause to welcome the destruction of the man who had confiscated his Leicestershire inheritance in 1207.[122] King John was also actively promoting the cause of his brother-in-law, Raimond VI, count of Toulouse, the principal opponent of the crusade.[123] It was to Simon's entourage that Hugh de Lacy would ultimately flee after his expulsion from Ulster in 1210, and de Montfort appears to have maintained contact with the earl of Ulster's English *consanguinei*. An instrument of Simon's from early 1210 detailed expenses incurred by his son Amaury – previously thought not to have visited England[124] – on a trip undertaken at the beginning of 1209 to 'Syreborne'.[125] This is possibly Shireburn (*alias* Sherburn) near Clitheroe (Lancashire), where the Pontefract de Lacys held from the archbishop of York.[126] Colin Veach has uncovered further possible evidence of the earl of Ulster's complicity in a French/Montfortian plot, noting that the man entrusted with the king of France's conspiratorial letter in 1209, Roger des Essarts, would later be one of Hugh's fellow crusaders in Occitania.[127]

William de Braose, named by the 'Barnwell' chronicle as Hugh de Lacy's associate in sedition,[128] had his own links with the de Montforts through his daughter's marriage to Simon's uncle, Robert de Breteuil (†1204), earl of Leicester. It is this link which may bring de Braose's destruction by King John into sharpest relief. Whatever had first aroused John's antipathy, until the middle of 1208 the king displayed the usual traits of royal displeasure, withdrawing privilege and withholding patronage. William had lost custody of Glamorgan in February 1207, but there is nothing else at this stage to substantiate Holden's accusation of a 'tide of royal harassment'.[129] In July 1207, when de Braose was given charge of Ludlow, he was still being described by the king as *dilectus* et *fidelis*.[130]

The decision to ruin de Braose was only made in spring 1208, and thereafter pursued with single-minded ferocity. One possibility is that William's involvement in the Irish baronial war had counted against him. The annals of Worcester, *sub anno* 1208, claim that de Braose was suspected of complicity

121 *Ann. mon.*, iii, 33–4.
122 *RLP*, 68b.
123 Vincent, 'England and the Albigensian crusade'.
124 Crouch, *Image of aristocracy*, 71.
125 Auguste Molinier, 'Catalogue des actes de Simon et d'Amauri de Montfort', *Bibliothèque de l'École des Chartes* 34 (1873), no. 37.
126 Wightman, *Lacy family*, 30.
127 Veach, 'King and magnate', 200.
128 *Memoriale fratris Walteri de Coventria*, ii, 202.
129 Holden, 'King John, the Braoses and the Celtic fringe', 10.
130 *RLP*, 74a.

in the actions of his tenant in Ireland, Geoffrey de Marisco, who had captured the city of Limerick *et alia plura castella*. Having ignored a summons to court, de Braose then strengthened his castles in Wales and prepared for a fight.[131] Undermining the testimony of the Worcester annals, the trial for Geoffrey de Marisco's misdeeds began at Dublin in November 1207, when de Braose was in attendance at the king's Woodstock council, and there is no hint in the royal records that William was linked to the crimes of which Geoffrey de Marisco was accused and exonerated.[132] If, however, de Braose's tenants had played some part in Meiler fitz Henry's defeat, it would help to explain why, on the same day that Walter de Lacy came to peace touching his Irish possessions (19 May 1208), an order was given for the younger William de Braose to be delivered to Walter at Ludlow as surety for his father's good behaviour.[133] Even so, the swift release of the hostage implies that factors outside Ireland lay behind de Braose's subsequent harassment.[134] Another of William's sons, Giles, bishop of Hereford, fled to Normandy in the wake of the papal interdict pronounced in March 1208.[135] The prospect of an ecclesiastical exile in league with Philip Augustus could have been enough for King John to commence his programme of persecution.

The asylum granted to the de Braoses in Ireland, by the de Lacys and William Marshal, can only have antagonised the king further. But it was only during the Anglo-Scottish negotiations in 1209 that the scale of opposition to John's rule became apparent, with news of Franco-Scottish intrigue providing a further indictment of de Braose's enduring links with the *regnum Francorum*. It has been suggested that 'no evidence' exists to connect the Scots with the strand of sedition being organised in northern England, with the tacit support of Philip Augustus.[136] An understanding of William I's contact with the French court as strictly bilateral, however, would overlook the king of Scots' own relationship to Simon de Montfort, a nephew of the king's cousin Roger, bishop of St Andrews until 1202.[137] It would also ignore William's friendship with Hugh de Lacy – a probable subscriber to the conspiracy – as evidenced by Hugh's patronage of St Andrews and revealed during the Norham negotiations.

131 *Ann. mon.*, iv, 396 (Worcester annals). De Marisco held from de Braose in the honor of Limerick: Empey, 'The settlement of Limerick', 11–12.

132 *RLP*, 77a; *CDI*, i, no. 351; Flanagan, 'Defining lordships', 52.

133 *RLP*, 80b.

134 The younger William participated in the burning of Leominster later in the year: Crouch, 'King John's complaint'; *CDI*, i, no. 408.

135 *Ann. mon.*, i, 29 (Margam annals).

136 Duncan, 'John, king of England', 258–9.

137 Dowden, *Bishops of Scotland*, 10–11. It was possibly through the association of the Beaumonts and Mauvoisins in France which led to William Malveisin's entry into Scottish service: Pollock, *Scotland, England and France*, 37.

The flight of the earl

One by one, King John moved to deal with the sources of his anxiety, leading armed expeditions into several corners of the British Isles. A show of strength was enough to force the Scots into a humiliating submission at Norham – by which 'all ills' moved between the two kingdoms were to cease[138] – causing John's opponents to look elsewhere for support. Llywelyn ap Iorwerth, the dominant power in north Wales, had provided men for John's Scottish campaign in 1209, but their relationship broke down soon after.[139] Llywelyn was probably one of the 'number of the Welsh who were in league with William de Braose and Hugh de Lacy', and who now moved 'to attack the frontiers of England'.[140] The Welsh princes were subdued by a military force under the justiciar of England, Geoffrey fitz Peter, and rendered homage to the king at Woodstock.[141] Meanwhile John isolated the malcontents among the English baronage by extracting oaths of fealty from all his free tenants, even 'from boys who were twelve years old throughout the whole kingdom'.[142]

In the summer of 1210 John turned his attention to Ireland, the last refuge for those fermenting rebellion against the crown.[143] The first intriguing aspect of the campaign is Walter de Lacy's response to the threat of punitive action. On 28 June 1210, barely a week after the royal army landed at Crook, in Waterford, a group of Walter's barons met the king at Dublin and delivered the following message, recorded by royal clerks but omitted from the printed volumes of the *Red book of the exchequer*:

> Firstly, [Walter] greeted the lord king as his liege-lord from whom he holds everything that he holds and he asks his mercy to relax the anger which he has against him so that he can come before him, for on no account does he wish to plead against him, and he places all his castles and all his lands in the hand of the lord king that he may do his will with them as his lord, either by taking from them what he wishes or by pardoning

[138] Carpenter, *Magna Carta*, appendix I (*et omnia mala inter nos mota cessabunt in perpetuum per hac conventionem*).

[139] Warren, *King John*, 197–8; Lloyd, *History of Wales*, i, 631–2. Llywelyn was married to John's illegitimate daughter, Joan.

[140] *Memoriale fratris Walteri de Coventria*, ii, 202. In 1212 Llywelyn allied himself with Philip Augustus, raising the possibility that the French king had supported the Welsh uprising of three years previously: R. F. Treharne, 'The Franco-Welsh treaty of alliance in 1212', *Bulletin of the Board of Celtic Studies* 18, no. 1 (1958), 60–75. For the later alliance between Llewelyn and Hugh de Lacy in 1223, see below, 143–5, 171.

[141] *Ann. mon.*, iii, 32 (Dunstable annals); *Flores hist.*, ii, 51.

[142] *Flores hist.*, ii, 51; *Flowers of history*, ii, 249.

[143] The best account of John's campaign is still to be found in Orpen, *Normans*, 248–61. Owing to the absence of chancery enrolments in this period, the royal praestita rolls are the main source of information for the king's itinerary: *Rot. lib.*, 177–228; *CDI*, i, nos 403–9. For the logistics, see S. D. Church, 'The 1210 campaign in Ireland: evidence for a military revolution?', *ANS* 20, 45–57.

> the same Walter as he wishes. [The ambassadors] then added that [Walter] consented to some punishment for his brother, Hugh de Lacy, through whom Walter himself, the aforesaid ambassadors and his other vassals have suffered great injury. Concerning the lands of Hugh de Lacy and the castles which he holds from the aforesaid Walter de Lacy, it will be done according to the will of the lord king and according to his counsel and it will be done in like manner concerning the lands and castles of his brother Walter's vassals who have gone with the aforesaid Hugh. [Walter] will make amends for all the excesses done against his own vassals or against his neighbours, the lord king's vassals, by the counsel of the lord king.[144]

Had Walter and his ambassadors really 'suffered' at his brother's hands, or was his profession of innocence merely a belated attempt to deflect the king's anger? It is difficult to accept that Walter had no case to answer. In one late thirteenth-century Welsh chronicle he is described as a *rebellis*, who had resigned all his garrisons and lands to the king in order to preserve his life and members.[145] This said, Walter's relatively swift recall from exile in 1213 might imply that he had played a lesser role in treason.[146] As for the 'great injury' inflicted on him by his brother, there is some evidence suggesting that Hugh was agitating beyond the bounds of his earldom in the months before the king's descent on Ireland. The earl was at Dublin on 8 March, where he informed his bailiffs that he was taking the canons and property of St Thomas under his protection, ordering that no molestation or crime was to be inflicted on them.[147] During his revolt of 1223–24 Hugh would source arms and supplies from sympathisers in and around Dublin, and the 1210 mandate could imply that de Lacy was mustering a force in the city's vicinity from which the canons of St Thomas were seeking special protection.[148] Even so, there is nothing to show that Hugh had impinged upon the lordship of Meath.

Alternatively, Walter might justifiably have resented his younger brother's actions during the baronial crisis of 1207–08, when Hugh's intervention on behalf of the Leinster barons may have led to the erosion of Walter's franchisal power in the re-granting of Meath. Whether he was personally guilty of treason or not, Walter's willingness to point the finger of blame at his brother must say something about the fragility of their fraternity. From 1210 onwards, to speak of the 'de Lacys' as one political force – as most modern commentators are still

[144] TNA, E 164/2 (King's remembrancer, *Red book of the exchequer*), fo 180b; *CDI*, i, no. 402.

[145] *Annales Cambriae*, ed. John Williams ab Ithel, Rolls Series (London, 1860), 67n (where Hugh de Lacy is described as a *vir perversus*). For the chronicle, from BL, MS Cotton Domitian, A. 1, see *Annales Cambriae*, trans. Paul Martin Remfry (Shrewsbury, 2007), 27–34, 111.

[146] *RLC*, i, 134b; *RLP*, 99b.

[147] Appendix I, no. 15.

[148] The canons of St Thomas would provide Hugh with wine and horses during his Irish revolt of 1223–4: see below, 150–1.

content to do – is to ignore the profound effect of King John's arrival in Ireland on the brothers' association.

After Walter de Lacy's submission the king proceeded to take several of Meath's most important settlements into his hands, including Walter's seat of power at Trim and the *capita* of Hugh's baronies, Ratoath and Nobber.[149] John arrived at Dundalk by 8 July, where 400 of the earl of Ulster's *servientes* defected to the king.[150] Having lost what must have been a sizeable portion of his army, Hugh retreated north towards his power base in Ulster, burning his castles in Uriel 'before the king's eyes'.[151] Meanwhile, John had received the submission of the king of Connacht, Cathal Crobderg, whose forces joined the expeditionary force as it progressed north in pursuit of the earl.[152] Much has been made of the conciliatory attitude shown by the English king towards the native Irish during his summer expedition, contributing to Warren's extravagant assessment of John as 'the most successful high-king Ireland had ever seen'.[153] But, if appeasement ensured that the king's campaign proceeded without impediment, it can hardly have been a long-term objective given that John would leave his lordship of Ireland having aggravated not only the king of Connacht, but also Áed Méith Ua Néill, king of Tír Eógain.[154] John had no desire to be Ireland's *ard rí*, but he had few qualms about manipulating the Irish kings for his own ends.

The swift occupation of Ulster owed much to the king's foresight in bringing John de Courcy with him to Ireland.[155] It was probably de Courcy's local knowledge which led the army to forgo the usual land route north from Carlingford, with its defensible mountain and forest passes. Instead, Carlingford Lough was bridged with a string of pontoons, enabling the army to take an easier course through eastern Lecale (Co. Down), circumnavigating and

149 Orpen, *Normans*, 249–51. It was presumably around this time that John granted the barony of Ratoath to Philip of Worcester: *Gorm. reg.*, 179–80; Orpen, *Normans*, 250.
150 *Rot. lib.*, 194; Orpen, *Normans*, 251.
151 *AFM*, iii, 164, citing the 'Dublin annals of Inisfallen'.
152 *AClon.*, 1208/9 [*recte* 1210].
153 Warren, 'King John and Ireland', 39. See also, idem, *King John*, 196; Otway-Ruthven, *Med. Ire.*, 81. John had also received the submission of the king of Thomond, Donnchad Cairprech Ua Briain: *MCB*, 1210; Duffy, 'King John's expedition to Ireland', 5.
154 Duffy, 'King John's expedition to Ireland', 1–24, at 21; idem, 'John and Ireland', 241. Áed Ua Néill met John at Carrickfergus in July, but refused to hand over hostages or acknowledge him as overlord: *AFM*, 1209 [*recte* 1210]; *AClon.*, 1208/9 [*recte* 1210]; *AI*, 1210; *Histoire des ducs de Normandie et des rois d'Angleterre*, ed. Francisque Michel (Paris, 1840), 112–14. Cathal Crobderg's refusal to bring his son to a conference with the English king led John to apprehend several of Cathal's entourage as hostages: *ALC*, 1210, 1211. For the 'government backlash' against Ua Néill and Ua Conchobair after 1210, see Duffy, 'John and Ireland', 241–2.
155 See below, 158–9.

isolating de Lacy's fortress at Dundrum.[156] Having captured this castle, the army then progressed to Ardglass, held by Jordan de Sauqueville, the same Marshal satellite who had entreated Hugh de Lacy to aid the tenants of Leinster against Meiler fitz Henry in 1208. After seizing the earldom's ecclesiastical centre, Downpatrick, the king then proceeded to Carrickfergus, de Lacy's secular seat, where the earl and his remaining forces were waiting.[157]

A withering assessment of Carrickfergus's defence is given in the Marshal's biography:[158] 'They behaved like cowards, given the fact that they were not unprepared and the castle was strongly built and well garrisoned; but out of fear, and giving into threats, the traitors surrendered.'[159] Had the earl's men really put up such a 'poor show of defence'?[160] Carrickfergus castle is described as 'very strong' in the account of the siege preserved in the *Histoire des ducs de Normandie*, based on eyewitness testimony.[161] The Marshal's biographer, however, fails to mention that Hugh de Lacy had already taken flight from the fortress by the time it was surrendered to the king. In Bower's *Scotichronicon*, it was only after the town of Carrickfergus had been attacked 'relentlessly', and the castle's garrison had been 'abandoned by their *princeps*', that the defenders 'opened the castle gates and surrendered it and themselves to the king'.[162]

Compiled in the fifteenth century, the section in Bower's chronicle covering the years 1209–12 was based on a narrative (source 'S') drawn from good information, 'almost certainly from somebody who was close to the scene and familiar with the events and people involved'.[163] It has even been proposed that 'S' was originally compiled at St Andrews in the early thirteenth century; moreover, in light of the accurate description of the Anglo-Scottish crisis of 1209, a likely author was the bishop of St Andrews himself, William Malveisin.[164] Hugh de Lacy sought refuge at St Andrews after his flight from Ireland, and

[156] 'Dublin annals of Inisfallen', cited in Orpen, *Normans*, 251–2. It was perhaps John de Courcy who advised the king to bring bridge-making materials (*pontes*) with him to Ireland: *Pipe roll 13 John*, 39.

[157] Orpen, *Normans*, 252.

[158] The Marshal travelled with the king to Ireland, as presumably did John of Earley, the chief source of information for the biography: *HWM*, ii, lines 14179–256.

[159] Ibid., lines 14271–8.

[160] Ibid., line 14280.

[161] *Histoire des ducs de Normandie*, 112. The author was in the retinue of Baldwin de Béthune, a participant in the summer campaign: Duffy, 'King John's expedition to Ireland', 6–9; Church, *Household knights*, 19, 35. Even without the middle curtain, added by 1224, or the outer ward and imposing gatehouse of Hugh de Lacy's later design (see below, 170–1), the fortress at Carrickfergus, situated on a peninsula next to the harbour, already boasted the stone-built polygonal enclosure and large keep of John de Courcy's construction: McNeill, *Anglo-Norman Ulster*, 9–12; T. E. McNeill, *Carrickfergus castle* (Belfast, 1981), 19–27.

[162] *Scotichronicon*, iv, 460–1.

[163] Ibid., xix–xxv, at xxiii–iv.

[164] Ibid., xxiv.

Bower's account of Ulster's subjection by the king could contain information personally related to Malveisin by the earl himself. The chronicle's provenance gives credence to some of its unique episodes, such as the earl's pursuit of 'some of the king's army, knights and others, who had incautiously entered his territory by boat'.[165] At the same time, much of the detail in the *Scotichronicon* tallies with other sources, such as the statement that, in his retreat from Dundalk, Hugh 'burned the greater part of the land he occupied to prevent it providing protection for the enemy'.[166]

The chronicle is also valuable for the reconstruction of the earl's itinerary subsequent to his flight from Ulster. Aside from de Lacy and his sons, those who took ship from Carrickfergus included Matilda de Braose; her eldest son, William the younger, with his wife and sons; and another of Matilda's sons, Reginald.[167] Hugh's wife, meanwhile, was left behind at Carrickfergus 'because her husband detested her'.[168] The fugitives made their way via the Isle of Man to Galloway,[169] where Matilda and the younger William de Braose were captured by the earl of Carrick and conveyed back to Ireland by Duncan's former overlord in Ulster, John de Courcy, whom King John had dispatched to receive the prisoners.[170] Hugh de Lacy managed to escape along with Reginald de Braose. Leaving his sons in the care of Alwyn, earl of Lennox (†1217),[171] he travelled on to St Andrews, seeking refuge with the community he had so recently endowed with Irish benefices.[172]

❖

'Within a framework of arbitrary, monarchical government', writes Strickland, 'baronial rebellion formed one of the principal means both of expressing political discontent and of seeking the redress of grievances'.[173] But even

165 Ibid., 460–1. The royal army was at Carrickfergus between 19 and 28 July: *Rot. lib.*, 196–208; *CDI*, i, nos 404–7; Orpen, *Normans*, 253–4.

166 See above, 111.

167 Rymer, *Foedera*, i, pt. 1, ff 107–8.

168 *Scotichronicon*, iv, 462–3.

169 *Histoire des ducs de Normandie*, 113; *Early sources*, ed. Anderson, ii, 378–81.

170 Rymer, *Foedera*, i, pt. 1, ff 107–8.

171 *Scotichronicon*, iv, 460–1; Pollock, 'Rebels of the West', 25. Either Alwyn or his father commissioned a poem commemorating their family's descent from a king of Munster: Pollock, 'Rebels of the West', 19–20. For a possible connection between Lennox and Cenél Conaill, dynastic rivals of Cenél nEógain, Hugh de Lacy's principal Irish rivals, see Seán Duffy, 'The prehistory of the galloglass', in idem (ed.), *The world of the galloglass*, 1–23, at 11.

172 *Scotichronicon*, iv, 460–1, and above, 101–2.

173 Matthew Strickland, 'Against the Lord's anointed: aspects of warfare and baronial rebellion in England and Normandy, 1075–1265', in John Hudson and George Garnett (eds), *Law and government in medieval England and Normandy* (Cambridge, 1994), 56–79, at 56.

disenchanted noblemen did not lightly entertain thoughts of revolt against a king who 'could command an effective siege train, professional engineers and seasoned mercenary troops'.[174]

The chances of success for rebels were slim, and the price of failure was steep. The events of 1209–10 demonstrate just how far diplomatic tendrils could reach beyond Ulster, as Hugh de Lacy negotiated sedition with confederates in England, Wales, Scotland and France. However, the earl seems to have seriously overestimated his ability to resist royal justice. 'Unless in receipt of substantial aid from external allies', notes Strickland elsewhere, 'the forces of baronial rebels were almost always at a financial, logistical and military disadvantage'.[175] De Lacy was left virtually alone to carry the fight to the crown, while his allies were of little use in deflecting the king's anger. Hugh's own brother had offered him up as a scapegoat, while a new era of Anglo-Scottish co-operation, ushered in by the Treaty of Norham, made his connections with the court of William I count for very little. According to the *Scotichronicon:*

> being fearful lest at some stage he might fall into the hands of the king of England because of the treaty of friendship between the king of Scotland and king John, [Hugh] took ship and went abroad. Just shortly after his departure certain knights sent as spies to seek out the said Hugh reached St Andrews. But when they did not find him, they returned whence they had come cheated of their hopes.[176]

It was only by the skin of his teeth that de Lacy evaded capture in 1210, and the gruesome fate which would befall Matilda and William II de Braose. He had his life, but mere existence was not worth much for a noble without land or power, and Hugh was left with little option but to follow the well-trodden path taken by other unsuccessful rebels against the English crown: to the continent, and the crusading life.

174 Strickland, *War and chivalry*, 231.
175 Ibid.
176 *Scotichronicon*, iv, 461.

5

Exile

Between two kingdoms, 1210–27

In March 1208 Pope Innocent III had called a crusade against the dualist 'Cathar' heretics and their sympathisers among the southern French nobility.[1] The trigger for the 'Albigensian crusade' was the murder of the papal legate, Pierre de Castelnau, a crime thought to have been carried out by supporters of the count of Toulouse, Raymond VI de Saint-Gilles (†1222). Over the next few years, an army of *crucesignati* under the leadership of Simon de Montfort occupied much of Languedoc, and at the Fourth Lateran council (November 1215) Raymond's lands and titles were officially conferred on the chief crusader.[2] The count's protestations to the council are described by one of his partisans, the anonymous continuator of the Occitan *canso* begun by William de Tudela:

> Tossed among the waves, I can find no shore; I do not know which way to turn, by land or sea. Nor can I think it was ever supposed that I should go begging my bread through the world! Everyone will be rightly amazed to see the count of Toulouse prey to all dangers, with no town or burgh of my own to which I can withdraw.[3]

[1] While 'Albigensians' (*Albigenses*) featured in western European chronicles, 'Cathar' may not have been used by contemporaries. A variety of terms were used by the people of Languedoc to refer to the heretics of their villages, of which *bons omes* ('good men') or *bonas femnas* ('good women') were among the most popular: Mark Pegg, *The corruption of angels: the great inquisition of 1245–46* (Princeton, NJ, 2001), 15–20; Daniel Power, 'Who went on the Albigensian crusade?', *EHR* 128, no. 524 (2013), 1047–85, at 1070–5. There are no references to the Albigensian crusade in the Irish annals: Katherine Hurlock, 'The crusades to 1291 in the annals of medieval Ireland', *IHS* 37, no. 148 (2012), 517–35, at 530–1.

[2] Unless otherwise stated, references to the course of the crusade are taken from Robert Wolff and Harry Hazard (eds), *A history of the crusades, II: the later crusades* (Philadelphia, PA, 1962), 277–324; Jonathan Sumption, *The Albigensian crusade* (London, 1978).

[3] *Song of the Cathar wars*, 81, §151. William was a priest from Navarre in the retinue of Baldwin, estranged brother of Raymond VI. His portion of the *Song* covers events up until 1213, when it was taken up by an anonymous continuator hostile to the crusaders. He wrote for a southern audience but was broadly in favour of the crusade, although sometimes critical of its methods: Elaine Graham-Leigh, *The southern French nobility and the Albigensian crusade* (Woodbridge, 2005), 18–29.

Whether dramatised or not,[4] Raymond's appeal expresses something of what it meant to be an exile. The landless man was cut off from the fount of power, while separation from the trappings of nobility brought with it a new sense of vulnerability. Not only was the count 'prey to all dangers', but he could question whether it was proper that his son, 'nobly born, of good family and better lineage than anyone can describe … go wandering through the dangers of the world like some wicked thief?'[5] Displacement from one's base occasioned a profound emotional response and an adverse psychological effect. 'A man who loses his land suffers deeply', pronounces the *Song's* continuator elsewhere, or in one French translation of the Occitan, *a le coeur douloureusement serré* – he 'is grievously wounded in the heart'.[6] But while one man descended on Fortune's wheel, another was raised up. One of those to benefit from Raymond's difficulties was another political exile, Hugh de Lacy, who joined the crusade in 1211 and was rewarded with lands in the county of Toulouse.

The political wilderness could be a bleak and desolate place, as it was for Anselm, archbishop of Canterbury (†1109), described by the continuator of Pseudo-Ingulf as 'dragging out a weary existence in exile beyond the sea'.[7] And we can only imagine the anguish suffered by William de Braose over the fate of his family before his own death, near Paris, barely a year after his flight from King John.[8] But the experience of de Braose's partner in rebellion, Hugh de Lacy, reminds us that banishment need not have been a wholly negative experience. The structure of exile has been defined as 'an uprooting from native soil and translation from the centre to the periphery, from organised space invested with meaning to a boundary where the conditions of experience are problematic'.[9] In swapping Ireland for Occitania, however, Hugh de Lacy was transplanted to a space where his fellow crusaders shared the same language and values.[10] Neither was his experience one of gloomy isolation, with the charter evidence showing that a core of vassals followed their lord into exile.

4 The *Song's* description compares favourably with other eyewitness accounts of the council: Stephen Kuttner and Antonio Garcia y Garcia, 'A new eyewitness to the Fourth Lateran council (1215)', *Traditio* 20 (1964), 115–78.

5 *Song of the Cathar wars*, 80, §150.

6 Ibid., 73, §143; *La chanson de la croisade Albigeoise, tome II: le poème de l'auteur anonyme (I*[re] *partie)*, ed. and trans. Eugène Martin-Chabot (Paris, 1957), 44–5.

7 *Ingulf's chronicle of the abbey of Croyland with the continuation of Peter of Blois*, trans. H. T. Riley (London, 1854), 229.

8 See below, 119.

9 Robert Edwards, 'Exile, self, and society', in María-Inés Lagos-Pope (ed.), *Exile in literature* (Bucknell, PA, 1988), 15–32, at 16–17.

10 Contingents of the army were drawn from regions such as Picardy and Burgundy, but the majority of the principal participants came from Normandy and the Île-de-France: Power, 'Who went on the Albigensian crusade?', 1058–60. For de Montfort's affinity, see Christine Keck, 'L'entourage de Simon de Montfort pendant la croisade Albigeoise et l'établissement territorial des

An idea central to some medieval accounts of banishment is that the shedding of the 'self' might allow for the creation of a new identity.[11] For de Lacy, exile at least meant abandoning any pretensions to comital rank, and his continental charters are stripped of the quasi-regal lexicon found in earlier comital *acta*. The *Song*, in which de Lacy is a key protagonist, may lump him in with the 'French' crusading elite, but this is hardly more anachronistic than his recent description as an 'Englishman' on crusade.[12] One of de Lacy's continental charters from 1217, dated in reference to 'Philip [as] king of France', hints that Hugh's allegiance was now with the *regnum Francorum*.[13] Significantly, in the factional conflict at the court of Henry III in the 1220s, he was courted by the 'alien' party, while his brother, Walter, sided with the 'native' barons. Perhaps Hugh was shrewd enough not to hold any identity or allegiance too closely: at the same time as he was referencing Philip Augustus in one of his charters, negotiations were being conducted concerning a return to the Angevin realm.[14]

De Lacy's return to the British Isles in 1221 illustrates perfectly the observation that 'an attempted return to grace … was not meant for the impatient, or the faint of heart'.[15] Along Hugh's arduous road towards recovery, he would once again find himself at war with the English crown. The eventual resuscitation of Hugh's fortunes is testament to his belligerence and a striking adaptive quality. His return to Ireland was marked by a more nuanced diplomacy, and it was only an alliance with his former enemy, Áed Méith Ua Néill, which saved de Lacy from destruction by royal forces in 1224. In the end, however, it was the confluence of favourable political conditions – luck, in other words – which would pave the way for Hugh's reinstatement as earl of Ulster.

De Lacy and the Albigensian crusade, 1211–21

Taking the cross

In tracing de Lacy's first movements in exile, an immediate task is the separation of fact from fiction. A story preserved in Pembridge's annals,[16] repeated in the sixteenth century in Grace's annals and the *Book of Howth*,[17] alleged that

crucesignati', in *La croisade Albigeoise: actes du colloque du Centre d'Études Cathares, Carcassonne, Octobre 2002, sous la présidence de Michel Roquebert* (Balma, 2004), 235–43.

11 Edwards, 'Exile, self and society', 20–1.

12 Vincent, 'England and the Albigensian crusade', 73.

13 Appendix I, no. 18.

14 *Pat. rolls, 1216–25*, 34.

15 Bothwell, *Falling from grace*, 209.

16 *Chartul. St Mary's, Dublin*, ii, 311.

17 *Annales Hiberniae*, 24; *Cal. Carew MSS*, vi, 121–2.

Walter and Hugh de Lacy fled initially to the Norman abbey of St Taurin d'Évreux (dép. Eure), where they lived and worked among the monks. At last discovering the identity of his guests, the abbot of St Taurin lobbied successfully for the restoration of the brothers' lands and titles.

While much of the content is clearly spurious, proven de Lacy connections to St Taurin have led historians to allow the tale's essential truth, and picture the brothers reuniting in Normandy.[18] It is not that the story lacks tantalising detail,[19] and its credibility is further enhanced by the historic importance of St Taurin (and its superior abbey at Fécamp) to the Norman families of others implicated in the intrigue of 1209–10, Simon V de Montfort and Bishop Malveisin of St Andrews.[20] The genre must be kept in mind, however. Central to the earliest incarnation of the tale, in Pembridge's annals, is the de Lacy brothers' anonymity and subsequent revelation as noblemen. This is a device in common with other fictional or pseudo-historical anecdotes from the high Middle Ages, where high-born protagonists are compelled to conceal their identity, only for their inherent noble characteristics – speech, dress or manner – to give the game away. The classic example concerns Richard I's return from the Third crusade disguised as a peasant, and the coronation ring which exposed the king, leading to his capture and ransom.[21]

Another feature of contemporary literature was the association of sin and the punishment of exile, based on the biblical example of Adam and Eve, driven from Eden to work in the dust.[22] The same theme of penitent labour shines through in the de Lacy tradition, with the brothers taking on various base tasks in the latrines or gardens of St Taurin. Presentation in annalistic form offers a facade of credibility, but the story owes more to a literary than a historical genre. Its integrity is further compromised by the quality of the brothers' relationship, which after Walter's scapegoating of his younger sibling, strongly argues against a reunion in exile. On the balance of probability, St Taurin hosted one of the brothers, or none at all.

The second difficulty we encounter is pinpointing exactly when Hugh de

18 Veach, *Lordship*, 144; Orpen, *Normans*, 254. Hugh I de Lacy had granted to the abbey the churches and tithes of Fore (Co. Meath): M. P. Sheehy, 'Cairteacha Meán-Aoiseacha do Mhainistir Fhobhair (XII–XIII Céad)', *Seanchas Ard Mhacha* 4 (1960), 171–5; *Calendar of documents preserved in France*, ed. Round, nos 302, 314–15.

19 Such as the (unidentified) cell of St Taurin, said to have been founded by Hugh de Lacy in Ulster: *Chartul. St Mary's, Dublin*, ii, 311.

20 Pollock, *Scotland, England and France*, 41–2.

21 Timothy Reuter, 'Nobles and others: the social and cultural expression of power relations in the Middle Ages', in A. J. Duggan (ed.), *Nobles and nobility in medieval Europe: concepts, origins, transformations* (Rochester, NY, 2000), 85–100, at 94–5. According to the annals of Waverley, William de Braose fled to France in 1210 disguised as a beggar (*quasi mendicus clandestine transfretavit*): *Ann. mon.*, ii, 265.

22 Edwards, 'Exile, self and society', 19.

Lacy took the cross. William de Tudela implausibly places him among Simon de Montfort's entourage at the capture of Carcassonne from Raymond-Roger Trencavel (viscount of Béziers/Albi, Carcassone/the Razès) in 1209, a year before Hugh's banishment from Ireland.[23] The author's patron, Baldwin, brother of Raymond of Toulouse, would not go over to the crusaders until March 1211, and so William's notice may more accurately reflect the composition of de Montfort's inner circle at the time of Baldwin's defection.[24] Strikingly, 'Uges de Lasis' appears in Tudela's list immediately after one Roger des Essarts, the same Norman intermediary who had liaised between Philip Augustus and a member of the de Lacy family in 1209.[25]

Equally enticing as a de Lacy reunion at St Taurin is the prospect that Hugh re-joined his co-conspirator, William de Braose, at the Capetian court. It may even have been de Lacy who first informed William of his family's fate at the hands of King John, but Hugh is unlikely to have remained in the Île-de-France long enough to witness the final effect of the news on de Braose, who died at Corbeil, near Paris, at the beginning of August in 1211, and was 'honourably buried' in the abbey of St Victor by another Angevin exile, Stephen Langton, archbishop of Canterbury.[26] Langton's officiation was required because the bishop of Paris, Peter de Nemours, had since departed for Languedoc with a contingent of eager recruits from the north. Most likely is that Hugh de Lacy and Walter Langton, Stephen's brother, were among this group of 'noble and powerful crusaders' who joined the army during Lent in 1211, and eagerly immersed themselves in 'Christ's business':[27] most immediately, in early May, by participating in the slaughter of around 300 heretics and knights who had defied the soldiers of God at Lavaur (dép. Tarn).[28]

The arrival of new reinforcements throughout the summer of 1211 was required to revive the work of the crusaders, which 'at that time had reached a low ebb'.[29] Raymond of Toulouse was organising a counter-offensive with the

[23] *Song of the Cathar wars*, 27–8, §36.

[24] See Tudela's statement that 'if I had been there with them and seen and met them and travelled with them in the land they conquered, this book would be the richer, I promise you, and the song much better': ibid., 28, §36.

[25] Roger des Essarts was killed defending Le Pujol, near Toulouse, in 1213: *Hist. Albigensis*, 198.

[26] *Ann. mon.*, i, 31 (Margam annals); v, 40; *Chron. maj.*, ii, 532. Langton spent most of his time in exile at Pontigny, but he had longstanding links to Paris, were he had spent some time in the 1180s as a master of theology: Christopher Holdsworth, 'Langton, Stephen (c.1150–1228)', in *ODNB*.

[27] *Hist. Albigensis*, 110, §113.

[28] Ibid., 110–18, §§ 213–30, at 110, §213. Alternatively, bearing in mind de Lacy's connection to William Malveisin, Hugh might have joined the army later in the year along with the 'hundred chosen French knights' recruited by de Montfort's lieutenant, and the bishop of St Andews's presumed relative, Robert Mauvoisin: ibid., 71n, 143, §286.

[29] Ibid., 143, §286.

help of Savari de Mauléon, King John's feared seneschal of Poitou, who supplemented the southern forces with cavalry from the Périgord.[30] At this moment of crisis de Montfort convened a meeting of his advisers at Carcassonne, at which Hugh de Lacy played a pivotal role. The accepted wisdom was that the smaller crusading force should hold out at either of the strongest points in their conquest, Carcassonne or Fanjeaux, until relief arrived or Raymond's mercenaries disbanded. This strategy would concede both territory and initiative to the southerners, however, and a more daring course of action was proposed by Hugh de Lacy, who knew only too well from the defence of Carrickfergus that castle walls were no guarantee of safety:

> Trust me, there is only one thing to do. If you shut yourself up in Carcassonne and they go after you, they will lay siege and keep you there, trapped. Go to Fanjeaux and it will be just the same. Wherever you go, they will track you down, and you will be defeated and disgraced till the end of the world. Believe me, you should go to the weakest castle you possess, wait for them to come up and then, once you have reinforcements, attack, and I am certain you will defeat them.[31]

By adopting Hugh's advice and entrenching themselves at Castelnaudary, a salient *castrum* (fortified settlement) south-east of Toulouse, the crusaders forced Raymond into a choice: either to bypass the outpost and press on to Carcassonne and the east, stretching his supply line in the process, or risk meeting the crusaders in open battle.[32] The plan worked to perfection; pinning the southerners down at Castelnaudary, a contingent of crusaders defeated Raymond's ally, the count of Foix, at the nearby village of Saint-Martin-la-Lande. Demoralised, Raymond raised his siege of Castelnaudary on the next night.[33]

At the earlier Carcassonne council, de Montfort had promised to reward de Lacy for his sagacity, no matter how events should pan out.[34] Simon was true to his word, and in the subsequent distribution of the crusader conquests Hugh was given Castelnaudary, the focus of his innovative defensive strategy.

[30] For Angevin involvement in the crusade, see Vincent, 'England and the Albigensian crusade'; Claire Taylor, 'Pope Innocent III, John of England and the Albigensian crusade (1209–16)', in J. C. Moore (ed.), *Pope Innocent III and his world* (Aldershot, 1999), 205–28.

[31] *Song of the Cathar wars*, 50, §91. De Lacy gives the same speech in the late thirteenth-century Occitan chronicle by 'L'Anonyme du Languedoc': *Recueil des historiens des Gaules et de la France, tome XIX*, ed. Michel-Jean-Joseph Bril and Léopold Delisle (Paris, 1880), 114–90, at 145. The principal difference is that Hugh, described as a *sage et valent homme*, proposes a stand at Fanjeaux (dép. Aude), a location he specifically warns against in the *Song*.

[32] L. W. Marvin, *The Occitan war: a military and political history of the Albigensian crusade, 1209–1218* (Cambridge, 2008), 118–19.

[33] *Song of the Cathar wars*, 49–55, §§ 87–106; *Hist. Albigensis*, 130–42, §§254–85.

[34] *Song of the Cathar wars*, 50, §91.

Moreover, any misgivings Hugh may have had at being accorded the 'weakest' fortress in de Montfort's collection were dispelled by the further award of two other notable *castra* in the Lauragais plain, Laurac (cant. Fanjeaux, dép. Aude) and Renneville (cant. Revel, dép. Haute-Garonne). These had been part of the assemblage of Aimery de Laurac of Montréal – 'the most powerful and noble man in the whole area except for the counts'[35] – before their confiscation by the crusaders in 1209, in exchange for other unfortified villages in the open country. Outraged by the diminishment of his fief and dignity, Aimery had subsequently defected to Count Raymond on two separate occasions and was executed at Lavaur in 1211, alongside his sister and lady of Lavaur, Girauda, 'a heretic of the worst sort'.[36]

During 1212, reinvigorated by their success at Castelnaudary, the crusaders occupied virtually the whole of Languedoc. The conquest had only been made possible by new waves of volunteers, however, and de Montfort's problem was how to hold on to his winnings once these 'forty-day pilgrims' returned home.[37] Simon's solution was to parcel out the principal settlements among trusted members of his permanent retinue, who could subdue their own locales while continuing to act as an ad hoc fighting force as and when required.[38] The new lords of Languedoc were not to be left to their own devices, however. The Statutes of Pamiers,[39] set out in December 1212, envisioned a south 'recast in a northern mould' by replacing the loose traditions of the Midi in regard to 'feudal' service with the more stringent customs of the Paris region.[40] The crusader-lords were obliged to provide Simon with the service of French knights, to the exclusion of *milites istius terrae*, 'whenever and wherever there is a war against his person'.[41] Leave would be granted to depart the theatre of war, but only for a period of time agreed by the chief crusader, upon pain of

35 *Hist. Albigensis*, 73, §135.

36 Ibid., 111, §215; *Song of the Cathar wars*, 41, §68; Malcolm Barber, *The Cathars: dualist heretics in Languedoc in the high Middle Ages* (Abingdon, 2014), 35–42, and below, 122–3, 125–6, 130.

37 Wolff and Hazard (eds), *Hist. crusades*, 294.

38 Keck, 'L'entourage de Simon de Montfort', 236–43.

39 An English translation is available in *Hist. Albigensis*, 321–9, based on Pierre-Clément Timbal, *Un conflit d'annexion au Moyen-Âge: l'application de la coutume de Paris au pays Albigeois* (Paris, 1950), 177–84.

40 Sumption, *Albigensian crusade*, 154. In the words of Peter des Vaux-de-Cernay, 'to promote both the observation of the Christian religion and the maintenance of peace and order in civil life … the count wished to impose a definite set of customs on his vassals and to set boundaries on their holdings of land, which it would be forbidden to transgress, so that his knights would be able to live honourably from sure and legitimate revenues whilst the ordinary people would be able to live under the protection of their lords unencumbered by immoderate exactions': *Hist. Albigensis*, 170, §362.

41 Nos 17, 18, 21–22.

forfeiture.[42] Permission was required to build or rebuild fortresses, and existing castles were to be surrendered if required for the waging of war.[43] To incentivise the resettlement of the towns and villages 'left empty through fear of the crusaders', administration was also tightly controlled.[44] The imposition of novel exactions was forbidden, as was the exceeding of existing *talliae*.[45]

Above all, Simon's barons were to be the local enforcers of religious orthodoxy, bound to proclaim, capture and pursue the enemies of God whenever the opportunity arose.[46] We might expect that Hugh de Lacy, whose relationship with the church in Ireland was arguably characterised by ambivalence, felt some discomfort in his new role of Christian warrior. Having exercised lordship in Ulster with virtually free reign, Hugh must also have found the limitations on his power unfamiliar, if not galling. Indeed, de Lacy's precursor at Laurac and Renneville, Aimery of Montréal, had refused an offer of assistance against the crusaders from King Peter II of Aragon which would have conceded the very principle of fortress 'rendability' which now constricted the new crusader-lords in the south.[47] Perhaps, though, now into his fifth decade, de Lacy was only too grateful to have merely re-joined the landed elite, albeit as a subordinate.

'Lord of the Lauragais'

Recounting the fall of Carcassonne to the crusaders in 1209, William of Tudela remarked on the reluctance of the northerners to settle in the lands they had conquered: 'The mountains are wild and the passes dangerous and none of them wanted to be killed in that country.'[48] It was not only topography with which the crusaders had to contend. The weak grip of counts of Toulouse or viscounts of Carcassonne on their more remote seigneurial centres had created an environment where corruption and violence could thrive.[49] 'The area had indeed long been exposed to plunder and rapine', wrote Peter des Vaux-de-Cernay

42 No. 19.

43 Nos 20, 23. For the custom of rendering castles to overlords in the kingdom of France, see Charles Coulson, 'Fortress-policy in Capetian tradition and Angevin practice: aspects of the conquest of Normandy by Philip II', in *ANS* 6, 13–39.

44 *Hist. Albigensis*, 61, §110.

45 Nos 8, 26, 31. These included the *guidagia* and *pedagia*, which provided for armed guards along thoroughfares, and 'frequently sold off by the higher nobility to castellans living along the route': Graham-Leigh, *Southern French nobility*, 97.

46 Nos 11, 37.

47 Barber, *The Cathars*, 36–7, 159.

48 *Song of the Cathar wars*, 27, §36.

49 Malcolm Barber, 'Catharism and the Occitan nobility: the lordships of Cabaret, Minerve and Termes', in Christopher Harper-Bill and Ruth Harvey (eds), *The ideals and practice of knighthood III: papers from the fourth Strawberry Hill conference* (Woodbridge, 1990), 1–19.

(Yvelines, Île-de-France), 'the powerful oppressed the powerless, the strong the weak'.[50] Peter was a supporter of the crusade, and his jaundiced assessment of Occitan society should be taken with caution.[51] Nevertheless, any crusaders who fell into the hands of hostile castellans or dispossessed *faidits* could expect the roughest of handling. In 1210 the men of Cabaret (Lastours), in the Black Mountains, patrolled the roads night and day, 'and whenever they came across any of our men either condemned them to a shameful death or ... most cruelly put out their eyes and cut off their noses and other members, and sent them back to the army'.[52] Those of higher status were afforded better treatment, but it was only after sixteen months in shackles that Bouchard de Marly, crusader-lord of Saissac, was given a bath, haircut, clothes and a palfrey by his captor, the lord of Cabaret.[53]

Dangerous though it was, the Midi was hardly any more hazardous than the Irish *terra guerre* in which Hugh de Lacy had forged his reputation, nor the passes of the Black Mountains any less safe than the Fews of Armagh. De Lacy's experience of frontier lordship marked him out as an ideal curator of conquered territory. His seigneurie was based around its two principal settlements in the Aude. The smaller of these, the hilltop village of Laurac (*alias* Laurac-le-Grand) had once been the capital of the Lauragais plain, and was one of the centres of the dualist heresy in the late twelfth century under its ruling family of de Laurac, headed by Sicard II (†1200) of Montréal, father of Aimery (†1211).[54] Ten kilometres to the north lay Castelnaudary (Occitan, *Castro novo d'Arri*), *caput* of Hugh's seigneurie and capital of the new *comté* of the Lauragais from 1477. Notwithstanding its proximity to the river Fresquel, the town appears not to have had its own internal supply of water during the

50 *Hist. Albigensis*, 170, §362. Writing his account of the crusade in the 1270s, William of Puylaurens described the region as rife with 'robbers and mercenaries, thieves, murderers, adulterers and manifest usurers': *The chronicle of William of Puylaurens: the Albigensian crusade and its aftermath*, ed. and trans. W. A. Sibly and M. D. Sibly (Rochester, NY, 2003), 8. References to Hugh de Lacy in some versions of William's *Chronica* have been attributed to seventeenth-century interpolations: *Chronique [de] Guillaume de Puylaurens: chronica magistri Guillelmi de Podio Laurentii*, ed. Jean Duvernoy (Paris, 1976), 18.

51 Peter (†1219) accompanied his uncle, the bishop of Carcassonne, to Languedoc, and was an eyewitness to most of the events he describes: *Hist. Albigensis*, ix–xxxii. In the fourteenth century Jean Froissart described the people of Languedoc as good and simple, knowing nothing of war (*bonnes gens et simples gens qui ne savoient que c'estoit de guerre*): *Oeuvres de Froissart, publiées avec les variantes des divers manuscrits*, ed. Kervyn de Lettenhove (Brussels, 1867–77), v (1346–56), 347.

52 *Hist. Albigensis*, 92, §173. This was only a reprisal for de Montfort's actions at Bram, near Castelnaudary, where he had blinded all of the defenders save one, allowed to keep one eye 'so that, as a demonstration of our contempt for our enemies, he could lead the others to Cabaret': ibid., 78–9.

53 *Song of the Cathar wars*, 39–40, §63.

54 Barber, *The Cathars*, 35–6, and below, 129. Another of the region's leading heresiarchs, Arnold Oth, was also from Laurac: *William of Puylaurens*, 25–6n.

siege of 1211, when sergeants made a daily trip of half a league to the river with the crusaders' horses. Despite its designation in the *Song* as the weak link in de Montfort's defences, Castelnaudary is elsewhere described as a 'notable *castrum*' by Peter des Vaux-de-Cernay, and was evidently of huge strategic significance, occupying an elevated site at the mid-point on the section of the Roman *Via Aquitania* connecting Toulouse and de Montfort's base at Carcassonne. It was comprised of two parts: the castle, at the highest point of the citadel, to the south-east, housing the lord and his retinue; and the lower suburb (*inferius burgum*) inhabited by the general populace.[55]

The château at Castelnaudary was one of those destroyed by the French crown in accordance with the Treaty of Paris/Meaux (1229),[56] but the outer defences of Hugh de Lacy's *castrum* – razed by Count Raymond prior to the siege of 1211 – may not have been very dissimilar to those described in Jean Froissart's account of the Black Prince's *chevauchée* through Languedoc, in 1355, when the town was only partially enclosed by walls (*elle n'estoit fermée*), made of earth in the local style (*fors de murs de terre selonch l'usage dou pays*).[57] Evidence for the size of the settlement is conflicting. Froissart described it as 'a very large town, and full of people and goods' (*une moult grosse ville et bon chastiel, et raemplie de gens et de biens*).[58] However, while the inner ward had been spacious enough to accommodate 500 knights and soldiers during the siege of 1211, the *castrum* was judged to be too cramped for the crowd assembling for the knighting of Simon de Montfort's son, Amaury, in 1213, when pavilions had to be erected outside the walls at a 'pleasant level place'.[59] Nevertheless, that Castelnaudary was chosen as the location for the ceremony at all must tell us something about the relationship between lord and chief crusader.

At some point before 1215 de Lacy also came to control Renneville, now a small village near Villefranche-de-Lauragais, twenty kilometres north-west of Castelnaudary, which Hugh conferred on the Hospitallers of Toulouse.[60] He

[55] *Hist. Albigensis*, 119–20, §233; 131–2, §§253–8. Today the town has no shortage of water, being a principal port on the Canal du Midi, constructed in the seventeenth century.

[56] Barber, *The Cathars*, 141–4.

[57] *Hist. Albigensis*, 119–20, §233; *Oeuvres de Froissart*, v, 346. Froissart was writing after the fact, but had access to good information as a courtier of Edward III's queen, Philippa of Hainault. Owing to a lack of good quality stone in the region, the walls (and castle) at Castelnaudary would probably have been built from a composite of earth, sand, straw, wood and stones: Peter Hoskins, *In the steps of the Black Prince: the road to Poitiers, 1355–6* (Woodbridge, 2013), 3, 55–60. The contemporary chronicle of Geoffrey le Baker notes that, along with the town and castle, the Black Prince destroyed the church of St Michel; Minorite and Carmelite convents; a hospital of St Antoine; and an Augustinian convent at nearby Mas-Saintes-Puelles: *Chronicon Galfridi le Baker de Swynebroke*, ed. E. M. Thompson (Oxford, 1889), 132; Hoskins, *Black Prince*, 59.

[58] *Oeuvres de Froissart*, v, 346.

[59] *Hist. Albigensis*, 132, §257; 196–7, §§429–30.

[60] Appendix I, no. 16.

is styled in the same grant as 'lord of the Lauragais' (*Lauragensis dominus*), an unprecedented title among the southern nobility and one which, if realised, would have seen de Lacy control a huge swathe of territory from Toulouse to Carcassonne, extending into the modern départements of Haute-Garonne, Aude and Tarn. Given that several other crusaders were also granted fiefs in the Lauragais, we may safely categorise the style as a reflexive affectation, based on Hugh's control of the historic capital of the Lauragais (Laurac), and in keeping with the kind of ostentation already seen in earlier comital *acta*. Perhaps some degree of displeasure among Hugh's neighbouring seigneurs led to the modification of his entitlement in later charters, where he appears only as lord of Laurac and Castelnaudary.[61]

A more realistic extent of de Lacy's lordship can be approximated using the places mentioned in his grants to the convent of Prouille (*alias* Prouilhe, Fanjeaux), founded c.1207 by St Dominic of Osma to shelter converted Cathar women, as a counterpoint to those communal houses established for the 'good women' in places such as Laurac and Montréal.[62] The eastern boundary stretched at least as far as the church of St Sernin at Villenouvette, between the Hospitaller commandery at Pexiora and the fortified village of Villepinte, where Hugh's lands marched with those of Alan de Roucy at Bram.[63] If, as appears likely, the eastern limit traced the course of the Fresquel, Hugh's territories would also have included the settlements at Saint-Martin-la-Lande and Lasbordes, the latter a perfect example of a *circulade*, a defensive design whereby buildings were organised in concentric circles around a central church or fortress.[64] To the west, de Lacy's stake extended to the communes of Payra-sur-l'Hers, including Agassens and Brésil, and Pech-Luna ('Moon-Hill'). Renneville, another twenty kilometres north-west, appears to have come under Hugh's sway as one of the possessions confiscated from Aimery of Montréal. The difficulty of controlling such an outlying settlement, detached from the main body of the seigneurie, recommended Renneville as an ideal subject of Hugh's grant to the Hospitallers of Toulouse, whose operation from the *munitio* (castle) would provide welcome protection for de Lacy's western flank. Laurac and its hinterland marked the southern boundary of the seigneurie, where it met Robert Mauvoisin's lands around Fanjeaux. The northern limit, meanwhile,

61 Ibid., nos 17–18.

62 Ibid.; *Cartulaire de Notre-Dame de Prouille*, ed. Jean Guiraud (2 vols, Paris, 1907), i, cccxxxii–iii. In 1355, when the Black Prince assumed membership of the community, Prouille had one hundred men and 140 women living in segregated cloisters: *Chronicon Galfridi le Baker*, 135; Hoskins, *Black Prince*, 86.

63 Appendix II, no. vi. Alan de Roucy was also lord of Thermes and Montréal: see below, 128, 135.

64 Jean-Paul Cazes, 'Un village castral de la plaine Lauragaise: Lasbordes (Aude)', *Archéologie du Midi Médiéval* 8–9 (1990), 3–25.

may not have extended much further than the Fresquel above Castelnaudary, into the foothills of the Black Mountains.[65]

De Lacy's *acta* attest to the agrarian diversity characteristic of the Lauragais, granting to the brothers and sisters at Prouille appurtenant rights of 'cultivated and uncultivated fields, forests, waters', as well as 'pastures, animals, dwellings, and wood to burn and to build dwellings'. Away from the fertile plain serviced by the rivers Fresquel and Tréboul, in the hills surrounding Laurac or on the southern slopes of the Montagne Noire, cereal crops and animal husbandry were less important than viticulture.[66] In 1211 Count Raymond's encampment in meadows beyond Castelnaudary's walls failed to prevent the defending crusaders from harvesting nearby vineyards, 'with their adversaries looking on and envying them'.[67] The custom of the Midi, whereby all male children had an equal share of the inheritance, contributed in no small part to the extremely fragmented nature of landholding in the Lauragais and the large numbers of shared plots and co-seigneuries typifying the region, simultaneously impoverishing and multiplying the local nobility.[68] In 1272, when the bailie of Castelnaudary was under French royal control, the *Liber reddituum serenissimi domini regis Francie* recorded almost 2000 fragments of *condomina*, of the kind granted by Hugh de Lacy to Prouille in 1217;[69] that is, the best plots of land appurtenant to churches or *castra*, which could not usually be purchased or acquired by those of lesser status.[70] The record also notes 493 vineyards (168 around Castelnaudary itself), 101 meadows, 368 gardens, 7 plots for growing animal fodder and 6 orchards.[71] If the pattern of splintered landholding acted as a leveller for the minor nobility, the overlord to whom they owed services and goods could grow rich from such an abundant land as the Lauragais:[72] of Hugh de Lacy's precursor at Laurac, Aimery of Montréal, William de Tudela claimed that 'there was not a richer knight in all the Toulousain nor the rest of the county, nor a more generous spender or of higher rank'.[73]

As participants in Simon de Montfort's 'unremitting war of movement',[74]

[65] For the extent of the royal bailie of Castelnaudary in the later thirteenth century, see Jean-Paul Cazes, 'Structures agraires et domaine comtal dans la bailie de Castelnaudary en 1272', *Annales du Midi* 99, no. 180 (1987), 453–77.

[66] Ibid., 455–63.

[67] *Hist. Albigensis*, 132, §258; *Song of the Cathar wars*, 51, §92.

[68] Pegg, *Corruption of angels*, 70.

[69] See below, 131.

[70] Cazes, 'Structures agraires et domaine comtal dans la bailie de Castelnaudary', 457; Monique Bourin, 'Peasant elites and village communities in the south of France, 1200–1350' in *Past & Present, suppl. 2* (2007), 105–6.

[71] Cazes, 'Structures agraires et domaine comtal dans la bailie de Castelnaudary', 457.

[72] For the rights and services claimed by the count of Toulouse in 1272, see ibid., 473–6.

[73] *Song of the Cathar wars*, 41, §66.

[74] Barber, *The Cathars*, 130.

the crusader-lords were not afforded the luxury of constant personal supervision of their new possessions. The delegation of administration and organisation to trusted retainers was therefore of paramount importance, and the witness clauses from de Lacy's charters may indicate some of those charged with the oversight of his lands, replacing the deputies (vicars or sub-vicars) employed by his southern precursors.[75] Several of these men were well used to the challenges posed by frontier lordship, having followed de Lacy into exile from Ireland. During Hugh II's Irish rebellion of 1223–24, Ralph Pedelowe would be tasked with buying arms and clothes from the Ostmen of Dublin, and the value of his service may be inferred from his later installation in the earldom of Ulster around Larne, close to de Lacy's seat at Carrickfergus.[76] Both Henry Wallensis (*alias* Walsh) and Henry fitz Leon had served de Lacy prior to 1210, and appear to have remained in Hugh's coterie after his restoration to Ulster in 1227.[77] Back in Ireland, in a charter which must date to 1213, John fitz Leon dedicated a grant relating to the church of Donaghmore (bar. Ratoath, Co. Meath) for the well-being of the soul of his lord, Hugh de Lacy (*pro salute anime domini mei*).[78] The distinction between the souls of the living (*pro salute anime*) and the dead (*pro anima*) implies that the dedication pertained to Hugh II de Lacy, lord of Ratoath until 1210, a striking testament to the kind of loyalty which, even in exile, the younger Hugh was able to inspire from among his former tenants in Meath. John's dedication to his 'living lord' was possibly also invested with a hope that his presumed relative, Henry fitz Leon, was still alive and well with de Lacy in southern France. In further testament to the durability of the bond between lord and vassal, another of the witnesses to Hugh de Lacy's grants in favour of Prouille was Hubert Hose, who had been arrested by King John's forces at Carrickfergus in 1210, only to escape from royal custody in 1213 and join his lord in Occitania by the next year.[79]

The other intriguing aspect of the witness lists are those toponyms (Belfort, Saint-Julien, Saint-Gauderic) associated with localities in the Aude.[80] The crusader occupation of Languedoc was no simple clash between 'northern'

75 Graham-Leigh, *Southern French nobility*, 135–6. The disappearance of witness-lists in northern France around this time represents 'a major shortcoming for reconstructing sociopolitical connections': Power, 'Who went on the Albigensian crusade?', 1054.

76 Appendix I, no. 26, II, no. iv, and below, 150.

77 Appendix I, nos 8, 22, 26–9. Walshestown is a townland in the parish of Saul (Co. Down): Reeves, *Eccl. ant.*, 39–40. The fitz Leons, taking their eponym from Leonisius de Bromiard, were tenants of Hugh II de Lacy in Ratoath, at Flenstown (par. Donaghmore, from 'Fitzleonstown'): appendix I, no. 6; *Reg. St Thomas*, 10–14, 20–25; Murphy and Potterton (eds), *Dublin region*, 82.

78 *Reg. St Thomas*, 282–3 (for the date of this grant I am grateful for the advice of Prof. M. T. Flanagan, Queen's University Belfast).

79 *Pipe roll 14 John*, 157–8; *CDI*, i, no. 453.

80 See Antoine Sabarthès, *Dictionnaire topographique du département de l'Aude comprenant les noms de lieux anciens et modernes* (Paris, 1912), 27, 387, 396–7.

and 'southern' values: much as membership of de Lacy's entourage in Ireland allowed cadets from middling families to achieve land and status, alliance with the new overlords of the Midi must have been attractive to those local members of the lesser nobility otherwise restricted by the prevailing attitudes concerning inheritance and landholding.

As well as from their own vassals, the lords of the Midi could draw political support from their neighbours. Another of the other witnesses to Hugh de Lacy's *acta*, Hugh de Campania (Champagne), was possibly an associate of the Champagnois crusader, Alan de Roucy, lord of nearby Bram and Montréal, whom the anonymous continuator of the *Song* portrays as speaking with the same dissenting voice as Hugh de Lacy during a conference of de Montfort's advisors in 1216.[81] Hugh's connection to Robert Mauvoisin, lord of Fanjeaux, has already been noted,[82] while the lord of Villesisicle, between Bram and Fanjeaux, was one William de l'Essart, a name perhaps associated with Roger des Essarts, Philip Augustus's messenger in 1209 and another of de Lacy's fellow crusaders.[83] The realities of warfare against an external enemy must have engendered among the crusader-lords the same kind of settler solidarity which characterised the early Anglo-Norman experience in Ireland, encouraged by cultural similitude and existing political or family ties, with co-operation replacing competition as the instinctive seigneurial mode.

For Angevin Ireland, the paucity of surviving evidence makes it difficult to access the layers of humanity living beneath the military-noble caste. This stands in stark contrast to Hugh's lands in the Midi, where it is possible to reconstruct more about the lives of those on the margins of society than those at its centre, thanks to the records of inquisitions conducted by the church in 1245–46, in which the people of Languedoc confessed their experiences of heretics and heresy.[84] While these mostly refer to the period subsequent to the crusaders' occupation, Dominican inquisitors teased out every encounter within living memory, and a few fascinating vignettes of life in Hugh de Lacy's seigneurie have been preserved.

When William de Tudela said accusingly of the southern nobility that they 'maintained the heretics in their castles and in their towers',[85] he might especially have had in mind the Lauragais, where the rituals of the *bons omes* had

[81] *Song of the Cathar wars*, 102–3, §§168–9. Described by Peter of Vaux-de-Cernay as a 'man of great probity', de Roucy took his name from the town near Reims, in Champagne. He was a vassal of Thibaut IV, count of Champagne, but also held from Philip Augustus, and died in defence of Montréal in 1221: *Hist. Albigensis*, 139–40, §279.

[82] See above, 104.

[83] *Cart. Prouille*, i, cccxxxiv.

[84] Toulouse, Bib. Mun., MS 609 (references to which, below, are taken from the transcript by the late French medievalist, Jean Duvernoy, accessed at www.jean.duvernoy.free.fr).

[85] *Song of the Cathar wars*, 18–19, §15.

been openly expressed before the arrival of the crusaders. At Laurac, in 1208, the leading heresiarch, Izarn de Castres, had disputed the essence of holiness in front of all the inhabitants.[86] A merchant, Raymond Arrufat, recalled seeing both Cathars and Waldensians in public at Castelnaudary, *ante adventum crucesignatorum*.[87] Many people, while not themselves *crezens*, sought blessings from the heretics or gave them succour, such as the resident of Villepinte who was urged by others to make a present of eels to the good men in his village.[88]

The effect of the crusade on the social and religious life of some individuals is difficult to gauge. In 1205 one girl, Crivessent Pelhicier, had gone to stay at Laurac with her grandmother and *socii sui heretices*, with whom she lived for five years.[89] This may well have been the very home established for the good women by Blanca, wife of Sicard II de Laurac and a Cathar *perfecta*.[90] However, whether Crivessent's stay was interrupted by the arrival of the crusaders, sworn to expunge heresy from their new seigneuries, or by some other circumstance, is impossible to say. Evidently some townspeople were prepared to renounce their beliefs under pressure from the church, although the doctrines of the Cathars retained their allure. William Auteri told his inquisitors that his mother and father, from Villepinte, had been reconciled *ad fidem catholicam* by the blessed Dominic (of Osma, founder of Prouille), in 1216.[91] Later, however, William's mother had returned to this *vomitum* and was burned (*combusta*).[92]

Those resisting conversion existed on the fringes of society, at once objects of deference and derision. On one occasion Raymond Arrufat had 'adored' the *bons omes* in the house of the lady Minha at Castelnaudary; at another time, he mocked his heretic half-sister by sending her three putrid fish.[93] Curiously, it does not appear that ordinary *crezens* were completely ostracised from their communities, although they might be physically separated. The Pamiers decrees compelled the crusaders to root out 'enemies of the faith' from their lands, but

86 Toulouse, Bib. Mun., MS 609, fo 198a; Pegg, *Corruption of angels*, 83.

87 Toulouse, Bib. Mun., MS 609, f. 250a. Another man saw Waldensians living openly at Castelnaudary, even reading and singing in church: ibid., fo 252b

88 Toulouse, Bib. Mun., MS 609, fo 177b; Pegg, *Corruption of angels*, 116.

89 Toulouse, Bib. Mun., MS 609, fo 85b; Pegg, *Corruption of angels*, 119.

90 Barber, *The Cathars*, 35.

91 Toulouse, Bib. Mun., MS 609, fo 251a.

92 Peter Symon saw his sister just once after she became a Waldensian, as she crossed the street in Castelnaudary in 1206; 'and he spoke to her and begged her to return to the catholic faith, but she did not wish to do so': Toulouse, Bib. Mun., MS 609, fo 252b.

93 Ibid., fo 250b (*tres pices salsos putridos pro derrisione*). Cathars abstained from meat out of fear that the deceased animal represented a reincarnated human being, but fish were sometimes exempted because they were thought to reproduce asexually. In the *melioramentum* ritual, interpreted by inquisitors as an act of 'adoration', a lay person bent on one knee and requested blessings from the *perfecti*: J. H. Arnold, *Inquisition and power: catharism and the confessing subject in medieval Languedoc* (Philadelphia, PA, 2001), ch. 4.

in reality this label seems only to have applied to those actively resisting the work of the church, and even ordained heretics (*perfecti*) were permitted to live outside town walls at an authorised location.[94]

The outgoing lord of Laurac and Renneville, Aimery of Montréal, was already dead by the time Hugh de Lacy took possession of his lands. Nevertheless, Aimery's surviving sisters had married into several other noble families in the region, and there was a genuine danger of such a powerful 'heretical network' becoming an alternative object of regard for the inhabitants of Hugh's *castra*, whose loyalties appear to have been somewhat mutable.[95] As the banner of Saint-Gilles approached Castelnaudary in 1211, for example, some inhabitants who had been guarding the outer defences for the crusader garrison 'climbed the walls, crossed over to the enemy, and abandoned the bourg'.[96] Yet, as he had in Ulster, it appears that de Lacy preferred policies of conciliation over rough colonisation. Some towns and villages under his sway were seemingly little affected by the incoming of a new overlord. Le Mas-Saintes-Puelles, just west of Castelnaudary, 'is not mentioned as a scene of conflict; no member of the leading families is recorded as having had a fighting part, nor are confiscations of property there known'.[97]

Nevertheless, it appears that some *crezens* left Le Mas during the war,[98] and one of the more peculiar testimonies from 1245–46 implies that at least one of the town's ruling elite was driven away. Around 1219 a lord of Le Mas, Bernard de Quiders, had interrupted a game of dice between some local men in the workshop of Peter Gauta by urinating on the tonsure of an acolyte, Peter-Raymond Prosat.[99] It is uncertain whether de Quiders was one of those dispossessed nobles who had returned to their former towns and villages in the Lauragais around the same time, buoyed by the death of Simon de Montfort and the resurgence of the house of Saint-Gilles.[100] It remains possible, however, that Bernard's vulgar display was not a reaction to the players' coarse language, as he himself rather implausibly claimed, but was instead related to a reassertion of seigneurial authority after an absence enforced by such churchmen as Peter-Raymond Prosat. That de Quiders was required to atone by wearing two yellow crosses, the distinguishing mark of the heretics, may suggest that the truer

[94] *Hist. Albigensis*, 323 (no. 15). An apparently contradictory statute (no. 11) forbade the crusaders knowingly to allow heretics to reside within their territories, upon pain of forfeiture.

[95] Barber, *The Cathars*, 34–8, at 35.

[96] *Hist. Albigensis*, 131, §256.

[97] W. L. Wakefield, 'Heretics and inquisitors: the case of Le Mas-Saintes-Puelles', *Catholic Historical Review* 69, no. 2 (1983), 209–226, at 214–15.

[98] Ibid., 215.

[99] Toulouse, Bib. Mun., MS 609, fo 3b, 18b; Wakefield, 'Heretics and inquisitors', 216; Pegg, *Corruption of angels*, 124–5.

[100] See below, 138.

version of events was presented by the sometime sodden cleric, who accused Bernard of having acted 'in opprobrium and vituperation of the whole catholic church'.[101]

Whether a broad policy of confiscation was implemented in Hugh de Lacy's lands is ultimately open to interpretation. De Lacy's grant of land at Agassens to Prouille, in late February 1217, included several plots formerly held by individuals whose names all appear in the Inquisitions of 1245–46 in connection with suspected heretical believers.[102] The form of these '*que fuerunt*' conveyances calls to mind the *Liber redituum* of 1272, which designated certain plots in the bailie of Castelnaudary in a similar manner (*item [dominus rex] habet I eminam terre qui fuit...*), seen by Cazes as evidence of comital appropriation of lands once owned by heretics.[103] Local men were evidently engaged as mercenaries by the crusader-lords, however, so it is perfectly possible that those named as former landholders in de Lacy's grant were not heretics, but had instead vacated their lands by virtue of their deaths in service to the crusade.[104]

There is little else from their own mouths to show that the good men and women of Hugh's territores were subjected to a punitive regime. One woman from Toulouse would later recall a visit to her heretic aunt near Castelnaudary, where she was 'instructed'.[105] This occurred in 1216, the same year in which one Peter Serni stayed for three days at Laurac, constructing a partition wall in the house of one *heretica*. Around the same time, Peter was also commissioned to build a new stone gateway for the town.[106] He and his six companions ate their meals, *de mandato communitatis eiusdem ville*, at the house of Izarn de Castres, the same heresiarch who had debated in the public square at Laurac eight years previously.[107] Clearly, the *bons omes* could still perform an important function within their communities. Mark Pegg has identified the house of de Castres

101 Toulouse, Bib. Mun., MS 609, fo 3b.

102 Appendix I, no 18. The Roger d'Orsans who had held at Agassens could have been the Raymond-Roger d'Orsans, *miles*, alleged in 1245–6 by several members of the community at Fanjeaux to have associated with prominent local heretics, but who denied any involvement with the Cathars in his own deposition, from 4 March 1246, even though he had seen the *bons omes* in public at Fanjeaux and Laurac thirty years previously (c.1216): Toulouse, Bib. Mun., MS 609, fos 152b, 154, 158, 164.

103 Cazes, 'Structures agraires et domaine comtal dans la bailie de Castelnaudary', 465.

104 See, for example, the capture of Lambert de Thury (de Montfort's marshal) and Walter Langton, in 1211, while riding near the land of the count of Foix 'with a large group of local men': *Hist. Albigensis*, 127–8, §248.

105 Toulouse, Bib. Mun., MS 609, fo 253b.

106 This was possibly the extant Saliège gate, framing Laurac's principal entrance, part of whose stonework may date to the early thirteenth century. I am grateful to Paul Duffy (Grassroots Archaeology) and Prof. Tadhg O'Keefe (University College Dublin) for their advice on this matter.

107 Toulouse, Bib. Mun., MS 609, fo 24b; Pegg, *Corruption of angels*, 120.

as a 'focal point, a safe domus, a separate space, where working men not from the village could eat and stay without disturbing the tempo of Laurac'.[108] The interaction between the heterodox and orthodox of Laurac and Castelnaudary, however, could only have continued with the permission of the overlord, Hugh de Lacy.

Offers of reconciliation, 1214–15

While Walter de Lacy was recalled from exile by King John in June 1213,[109] the first conciliatory approach to Hugh would not be made for at least another year. A royal letter issued to him on 22 April 1215 stated that Walter de Lacy had made a fine for Ulster; this being unpaid, and Hugh not causing it to be paid, even though the king had been in his vicinity for a long time, Ulster could only be turned to the crown's profit.[110] The context for this enigmatic communiqué is King John's vested interest in the course of the Albigensian crusade, and the baronial dissent engulfing the Angevin realm in 1215.

In 1196 Raymond VI married Joan, daughter of Henry II of England.[111] Once territorial competitors, the houses of Anjou and Toulouse became allied, and Raymond would find his brother-in-law, King John, a willing supporter in his struggle against Simon de Montfort.[112] Kinship aside, John was unwilling to allow de Montfort, claimant to the earldom of Leicester and possible pretender to the English throne, to gorge himself on land historically claimed by the dukes of Aquitaine. In early 1214, during his continental campaign, the English king came close to open warfare with the crusaders in the Agenais, having briefly occupied Simon's outpost at Marmande.[113]

It was around this time that the de Lacy brothers, now divided by allegiance, may have had a more plausible reunion than that alleged to have occurred at St Taurin d'Évreux. Walter de Lacy travelled in John's company as far as La Réole, near Marmande, and on 13 April he was tasked with purchasing horses for the king at Narbonne and Montpellier.[114] The errand took Walter far behind

108 Pegg, *Corruption of angels*, 120.

109 *RLC*, i, 134b; *RLP*, 99b. Walter's swift reconciliation supports the view that he had played a lesser role in the sedition of 1209–10.

110 *RLP*, 134a; *CDI*, i, no. 550.

111 The Plantagenets had previously helped to spread rumours of heresy in the Toulouse region: Vincent, 'England and the Albigensian crusade', 67–72.

112 Raymond spent Christmas in 1213 at John's court, and returned to the continent amply supplied, having possibly rendered homage to the English king for his lands: ibid., 75.

113 *Hist. Albigensis*, 228, §505; Vincent, 'England and the Albigensian crusade', 76. The Agenais had been under English control until 1196, when it formed part of Joan Plantagenet's dowry in her marriage to Raymond of Toulouse.

114 *RLP*, 113b; Veach, *Lordship*, 151. Since early 1214 Narbonne had been a base for a contingent

enemy lines, and Veach has suggested that John's true intention may have been to establish contact with his brother, Hugh.[115] The political context may hint at a different purpose for Walter's assignment. In April 1214 Raymond and his southern allies were converging on Narbonne to receive absolution from the papal legate, Peter of Benevento.[116] Walter's relationship to Hugh de Lacy may have predicated his choice as royal emissary, but any message entrusted to him was more likely intended for the southern leaders than for the crusaders.

The prospect of direct English intervention in the crusade was put paid to by the French victory at Bouvines in the summer of 1214, after which King John beat a hasty diplomatic retreat, offering Simon de Montfort 1000 marks for peace over the Agenais.[117] Thereafter the king played a double game. Renewed pledges to root out heresy were enough to immunise John's remaining continental territories from attack by the crusaders. But the king was still prepared to support his kinsmen in less visible ways. The count of Toulouse's son, the future Raymond VII, was at the English court in late 1214, and the case against Simon de Montfort at the Lateran council in the next year was presented by a group of English clerics, perhaps including the archbishop of Dublin, Henry of London.[118]

Aside from the letter noted above, there is no other evidence that Walter de Lacy had fined for his brother's lands.[119] In fact, while he was writing to Hugh de Lacy, the king was parcelling Ulster out among his Gallovidian and Manx vassals.[120] The support of these maritime lords was crucial in offsetting the threat posed by English baronial dissidents, and it is therefore unlikely that John would have risked offence by restoring Hugh de Lacy to Ulster. There was good reason to make an empty offer of reconciliation, however. John was still concerned with the plight of his kinsmen in the Midi, and with a French invasion of England looming, it would make strategic sense to weaken Simon de Montfort's position by enticing away a member of his inner circle. The approach to Hugh de Lacy was made at the height of the baronial crisis in England, as Walter de Lacy and other royalist magnates mobilised in support of the crown. The sorry state of the king's finances made a fine for Ulster particularly attractive, but it would not have been beyond John's capabilities to renege

of Aragonese horsemen to launch raids on the crusaders, perhaps resulting in a surplus of horses among the Narbonnais: Marvin, *Occitan war*, 200–1.

115 Veach, *Lordship*, 151.

116 Sumption, *Albigensian crusade*, 171–2.

117 *RLC*, i, 171.

118 Vincent, 'England and the Albigensian crusade', 77–8; Duffy, 'Hugh de Lacy and the Albigensian crusade', 80–1.

119 Walter did not reach an agreement touching his Irish lands until March 1215, and it seems unlikely that he would arrange his brother's restoration before securing his own: *RLP*, 131a; *CDI*, i, no. 541.

120 See below, 139–40.

on a promise of restoration after receiving payment.[121] In July 1215, ostensibly in response to John's overtures, Hugh dispatched one of his knights, Matthew de Tuit, to England.[122] Nothing came of the subsequent negotiations: perhaps de Lacy saw the king's offer for the hollow money-making ploy it probably was; or, he might simply have been reluctant to offer a palliative for the man who had cast him into exile.

It is testament to Hugh's powers of recovery after 1210 that he may now have considered a return to the British Isles as a step backwards. The year 1215 was the high-water mark for the crusaders, reflected by Simon de Montfort's recognition as count of Toulouse and duke of Narbonne at the Lateran council. Meanwhile, Hugh de Lacy was secure in his small but abundant seigneurie, and seemed prepared to end his days in Languedoc. The military orders were not actively engaged in the Albigensian crusade, but on the basis of the reception of the excommunicate Raymond VI as *confrater* of the knights of St John, in 1218, it has been argued that the Hospitallers sympathised with the plight of the southern nobility, with whom they had long-standing links.[123] However, in light of the order's ongoing drive to accumulate wealth and property, undertaken with increasing vigour from the beginning of the thirteenth century, pious donations from crusaders were far from unwelcome.[124] The lords of Laurac had been instrumental in the establishment of a commandery of Hospitallers at nearby Pexiora in the 1170s.[125] Displaying continuity with his Occitan precursors, and appeasing a group with valuable local knowledge and military capability, Hugh de Lacy became a *confrater* of the Hospitallers before 1215, granting his land at Renneville to their preceptory at Toulouse, and declaring his intention to assume their habit, 'if by chance it should happen that my body is overtaken by death'.[126]

[121] Warren, *King John*, 225, 232–3.

[122] *RLP*, 150a; *CDI*, i, no. 623 (safe conduct for Matthew de Tuit, 'knight of Hugh de Lacy', in coming to confer with the king concerning his lord's affairs).

[123] Dominic Selwood, *Knights of the cloister: Templars and Hospitallers in central-southern Occitania, c. 1100–c. 1300* (Woodbridge, 2002), 43–7, 115–42.

[124] Judith Bronstein, *The Hospitallers and the Holy Land: financing the Latin east, 1187–1274* (Woodbridge, 2005), 76–7.

[125] Ibid., 76. It may have been the wealthy commandery at Pexiora which, in 1355, avoided the rapine of the Black Prince's army by offering 10,000 gold florins: *Chronicon Galfridi le Baker*, 132; Hoskins, *Black Prince*, 60.

[126] Appendix I, no. 16 (*si forte contingeret quod corpus meum morte preoccuparetur*). The grant was acknowledged by Bernard de Capoulège, prior of the Hospitallers at Toulouse (1212–15): *Ordre de Malte: histoire du grand-prieuré de Toulouse*, ed. Antoine du Bourg (Toulouse, 1883), 24; Power, 'Who went on the Albigensian crusade', 1063n.

Reversals, 1216–21

The confidence with which the crusaders began 1216 was soon to dissipate. In April, while de Montfort was seeking confirmation of his new titles from Philip Augustus, the younger Raymond amassed an army of Provençals and invested Beaucaire, an important trading centre on the Rhône. As other *castra* went over to the Raymondines urgent messages were dispatched to Simon's barons scattered over Languedoc. Hugh de Lacy is named as one of those who 'rode fast and straight to Beaucaire, occupied the open fields, and drew up their ranks on the sands outside the town'.[127]

Siege and counter-siege continued for three months between June and August, with the crusader garrison holed up in the citadel; the southerners occupying the adjacent walled town; and Simon's men camped on lower ground below. Of several unsuccessful attacks mounted by the crusaders, de Lacy was involved in one of the bloodiest: 'many the helmets shattered and lances smashed', reports the *Song*, 'many the hands, arms, feet cut off, much the blood shed and brain-matter spilled'.[128] The losses sustained in this particular assault prompted de Montfort to seek the counsel of his advisors. Among these 'fifteen loyal friends' was Hugh de Lacy, who was seemingly forthcoming with his opinion. Urging de Montfort to put 'salt and pepper' to his plans, Hugh bemoaned the worsening conditions in the crusaders' camp:

> I have never seen a siege like this one: the besieged are happy, sheltered and at ease, they have good bread, fresh water, good beds and lodging, and Ginestet wine on tap, whereas we're out here exposed to every danger, with nothing to call our own but heat, sweat and dust, muddy watered wine and hard bread made without salt. We stand to arms all day and all night to defend our camp and we wait for them to raise their war cry again and renew their attack. If this hellish situation lasts any longer, we'll suffer worse torments than St Martial's fire!

Simon's acid reply was chastening: 'by God, sir Hugh', said the count, 'don't complain! You'd better not, for by the holy mass the priest blesses, you won't see Castelnaudary again, nor sir Alan [de Roucy] Montréal, until I've got Beaucaire back, rents, revenues, and all.'[129]

Our perception of this episode hinges on the authorship of the *Song*, which by this point was being continued by an anonymous partisan of Raymond

[127] *Song of the Cathar wars*, 89–90, §158.

[128] Ibid., 101, §167.

[129] Ibid., 102–3, §§ 168–9; *Recueil des historiens des Gaules*, 169–70. St Martial's fire was the gangrenous form of ergot poisoning, contracted from infected grains, especially rye: Plinio Prioreschi (ed.) *A history of medicine, vol. 6: Renaissance medicine* (Omaha, NE, 2007), 573.

VI.[130] From the detail provided we can be almost certain that the author was present at Beaucaire. From his vantage point in the town he would have been well placed to see the standards and heraldic insignia of those involved in the fighting. He might even have been able to monitor those going in and out of the chief crusader's tent, and so accurately describe the composition of de Montfort's colloquies. But the speeches he places in the mouths of the crusaders are inventions, projections of the prejudices of the southerners. If it suited Raymond's partisans to believe that 'force and wrongdoing triumph where law is helpless', we can hardly imagine the aphorism being voiced by Hugh de Lacy.[131] Nevertheless, some details about de Montfort's coterie – their territories and affiliations, for example – were plainly known to Raymond and his supporters, and it is likely that the Anonymous heard something of the rumblings of discontent coming from the crusaders' camp. We could well understand if Hugh de Lacy was reluctant to waste time and money far away from his Lauragais lands, although whether he was a spokesman for dissent, or presented his opinion so boldly, cannot be known.

The siege of Beaucaire was broken off in August 1216. As the tide turned against the crusaders in the Midi, a sea change had already taken place across the English Channel. Hugh de Lacy's old adversary, King John, was dead. On 18 November Henry III's minority council offered to restore Hugh's rights and liberties if he would come immediately to the crown's faith and service, granting him safe conduct to confer on the matter.[132] Walter de Lacy was an integral member of the regency council,[133] but we cannot automatically interpret the approach to his brother as a product of fraternal feeling. The proposition, made through the advice of Ranulf, earl of Chester, and William de Ferrers, earl of Derby (there is no explicit reference to Walter de Lacy), was just as pragmatic as that made by King John in the previous year. Prince Louis of France had landed in England in May 1216,[134] and numerous letters of the kind that was sent to Hugh de Lacy were being dispatched to baronial rebels and foreign powers, as the embattled regency sought to weaken Louis's cause and promote their own.[135]

It would indeed have been a coup for the regency to secure the support of someone like de Lacy, who was in the allegiance of Simon de Montfort, and

[130] The traditional view holds that the Anonymous was a middle-ranking man, perhaps a lawyer, in the service of the younger Raymond: Sumption, *Albigensian crusade*, 257. Other theories identify the author as one of the *Song's* protagonists, Guy de Cavalhon, an aristocratic troubadour; or a poet in the retinue of the count of Foix: Saverio Guida, 'L'autore della seconda parte della canso de la crotzada', *Cultura Neolatina* 63 (2003), 255–82; Graham-Leigh, *Southern French nobility*, 34–5.

[131] *Song of the Cathar wars*, 102, §169.

[132] *Pat. rolls, 1216–25*, 4.

[133] See Veach, *Lordship*, 168–72.

[134] D. A. Carpenter, *The minority of Henry III* (London, 1990), 13–27.

[135] Ibid., 22–3.

by extension, the French crown. Hugh's response to these latest overtures is unclear. A notice in the patent rolls from early 1217 stated that he was coming to the king's faith and peace (*venit ad fidem et pacem nostram*), and instructed the royal bailiffs not to impede his arrival.[136] There is nothing else to suggest that Hugh entered into serious negotiations. Nor, on the face of it, is there much evidence of a crisis of identity in his charter from 27 February 1217, and dated 'with Philip [as] king of France, Simon [as] count of Toulouse'.[137] We may perhaps see in the same grant, however, some further evidence of the battle-weariness observed by the Anonymous at Beaucaire. Notably, Hugh's charter was drawn up from his seigneurial *caput* at Castelnaudary while other of de Montfort's captains were busy investing the mountain fortress of Montgrenier (near Foix, dép. Ariège), in an arduous winter campaign described by Peter des Vaux-de-Cernay as less a siege than a martyrdom.[138]

In September the crusaders' fortunes receded still further when Toulouse was retaken and fortified against them. The ensuing eight-month siege was conducted with ever-dwindling resources and eclipsed even Beaucaire in terms of the hardships suffered by the attackers. Unable to ignore the obvious threat posed to his own lands by the defection of the region's principal settlement, Hugh de Lacy was among the first company to arrive at Toulouse,[139] while Simon himself reached the city at the beginning of October and immediately ordered his troops into an ill-conceived assault. Advancing over open ground, the attackers were decimated by salvos of missiles launched from the walls.[140] Perhaps picking out Hugh's banner in proximity to that of the chief crusader, the Anonymous – giving us the only eyewitness account of the mêlée – again imagines de Lacy's as the pragmatic voice of reason, delivering a stark assessment of the assault's progress: 'Count', said sir Hugh de Lacy, 'we are cut to pieces, we shall die here. Today will finish it, for I'm sure we have lost a third of our men. Let us withdraw, or they'll destroy us. Any more of this, and we're all dead men.'[141]

De Lacy is also used by the Anonymous at another point to express the sense of bewilderment beginning to overtake the crusaders, commenting despairingly

136 *Pat. rolls, 1216–25*, 34.

137 Appendix I, no. 18.

138 *Hist. Albigensis*, 264–5, §§588–90 (the siege of Montgrenier lasted from 6 February until 15 March).

139 *Song of the Cathar wars*, 123–6, §§ 184–5.

140 Marvin, *Occitan war*, 274–5.

141 *Song of the Cathar wars*, 133, §188. In the account of the Anonymous of Toulouse, Hugh's report is inflected with an even more critical tone ('my lord, so many casualties are going to be caused by your vengeance on that town; for many of your people are dead and I fear that at the end all will die, for I perceive that our enemies are in better shape'): *Recueil des historiens des Gaules*, 181.

that the defenders appeared to have even St Sernin (*alias* Saturnin) – the martyred third-century bishop of Toulouse – on their side.[142] Hugh's presence is noted at a conference of the Crusade leadership in early June, 1218,[143] and he was again at de Montfort's side when the defenders shattered the crusaders' giant siege-cat with a barrage of stones from their own engines. It did not escape the notice of the Anonymous that Hugh's hopes were absolutely interwoven with those of his patron. In response to Simon's prophetic boast that he would take Toulouse within a week, or die trying, de Lacy's plaintive cry was 'not so, please God!'[144]

Hugh's worst fears were realised on 25 June, when the chief crusader was struck and killed by a missile in front of the city walls. Simon's son, Amaury, was immediately elected as his successor, but there was little stomach among the rank and file to continue the fight, and Toulouse was abandoned in late July. Many crusaders now returned to their lands in the north, an option not available to someone like Hugh de Lacy, whose lordship to the east now lay exposed to the resurgent southerners. De Lacy was one of those who broke away from the main army at this point, joining a marauding band organised by the brothers, Foucaud and Jean de Berzy, for the desperate defence of their lands.[145] In spring 1219, while Amaury was besieging Marmande in the Agenais, the southerners led a force into the Lauragais, liberating several towns and villages from crusader occupation. At Baziège, close to Renneville, they met and defeated de Berzy and his confederates, and de Lacy may have been among the senior men captured and exchanged for the castellan of Marmande.[146]

The rest of Hugh's Occitan adventure can be told swiftly, not least because it is around this time that the two principal narratives of the crusade, the *Song* and *Historia Albigensis*, break off. One by one the crusader-lordships fell to the southerners, with Castelnaudary itself being taken in July 1220. We may imagine de Lacy with Amaury de Montfort and the remaining rump of crusaders during the eight-month counter-siege, the failure of which extinguished any hopes Hugh may have had of recovering his position in the Lauragais.[147] By late 1221, once again landless and probably close to penniless, de Lacy finally determined to revive his claims to his Irish earldom. In September Hugh was granted safe conduct to the English court.[148] Now, though, he would not be

[142] *Song of the Cathar wars*, 146–7, §194.
[143] Ibid., 164, §202.
[144] Ibid., 168, §204.
[145] *William of Puylaurens*, 63 and n.
[146] *Song of the Cathar wars*, 182–3, §210; *William of Puylaurens*, 63–4.
[147] William of Puylaurens wrongly places this event in the immediate aftermath of the siege of Toulouse, in 1218: *William of Puylaurens*, 63. Prince Louis of France took the cross in May 1219, but relinquished it again after only forty-five days: Sumption, *Albigensian crusade*, 203–4.
[148] *Pat. rolls, 1216–25*, 301; *CDI*, i, no. 1012.

dealing with a desperate regency, and it would take six more years of fighting to win back Ulster, swathes of which had already been meted out to other vassals of the crown.

The road to war, 1221–23

Ulster without an earl

The success of King John's expedition of 1210 was judged by F. X. Martin on the basis of the surviving Irish pipe roll from 1211–12, in which 'it can be seen that John's direct power, as witnessed by his ability to collect revenue, the touchstone of effective government, extended over a great part of the country'.[149] For the first time, Ulster was under the immediate control of the crown, its borders thrown open to royal officers. The pipe roll reveals an enlarged Dublin administration, but can it really be used as a marker of greater confidence or lasting efficiency? In 1220 the prior and monks of Downpatrick complained to the king that their churches were laid waste by war.[150] Ulster was clearly still a contested land, and the monks' protest reveals the crown's failure to fill the authoritarial void left by Hugh de Lacy.

After 1210 the royal demesne in Ulster (with Uriel) was accounted for by a steward, initially Hugh de Lacy's brother-in-law and sub-tenant in Dufferin, Roger Pipard.[151] Overarching policy was directed by the justiciar John de Grey, bishop of Norwich. Whatever de Grey's personal strengths as a tactician, and his early success in establishing Connacht as a protectorate of the crown, his plans to subdue the native polities in the north of Ireland met with stiff resistance, principally from the king of Cenél nEógain, Áed Ua Néill, whose rough handling in 1210 now appeared ill-advised.[152] Abortive attempts were made in 1211–12 to establish Anglo-Norman bases at Cáeluisce, on Lough Erne, and at Clones. In search of greater success the royal administration turned to external forces, and it may have been at the justiciar's behest that Thomas of Galloway plundered Derry and Inishowen with a fleet of seventy-six ships.[153]

After 1210 the maritime lords in the Irish Sea zone received generous grants from the English crown, spanning Ulster's entire coastline in their intended scope.[154] The southern approaches were guarded by the king of Man, who

149 *NHI*, ii, 144.
150 Reeves, *Eccl. ant.*, 229.
151 *Pipe roll Irc. 1211–12*, 53–69; *NHI*, ii, 143–6.
152 For the king of Connacht's submission in 1210, see *AClon.*, 1208/9 [*recte* 1210]; *ALC*, 1210.
153 *AU*, 1212; *ALC*, 1211, 1212; *AFM*, 1211.
154 Ronald Greeves, 'The Galloway lands in Ulster', *TDGNHAS*, 3rd ser., 36 (1957–58), 115–21; Oram, *Galloway*, 116–22.

held one knight's fee at Carlingford.[155] Duncan, earl of Carrick, was given fifty ploughlands around Larne (Co. Antrim), north of Carrickfergus.[156] Thomas, earl of Atholl, received three knights' fees in the north-west, with Ua Néill's part of Tír Eógain, excepting *Talachot* (probably Tullyhogue), and a portion allocated to Thomas's brother, Alan.[157] In reality, Thomas's influence was probably confined to the area surrounding Coleraine (Co. Londonderry), which he raided in 1214, erecting a castle with materials taken from the town's buildings and cemeteries.[158] By far the largest stake was reserved for Alan, lord of Galloway, whose 140 knights' fees covered the whole of the north-east between his brother's outpost at Coleraine and Duncan of Carrick's lands at Larne, with an additional two cantreds west of the Bann.[159]

Alan rendered homage to King John for his Ulster lands at Durham in February 1212, during Anglo-Scottish negotiations for a new treaty subsidiary to that agreed at Norham in 1209, and with the permission of William I of Scotland.[160] His installation in Ulster has been seen as mutually advantageous for the English and Scots: in competing with Áed Ua Néill's kingdom of Tír Eógain, Alan would help to neutralise the greatest threat to the Angevin colony in the north of Ireland; at the same time, he could mitigate any support being provided by Cenél nEógain for the Mac Williams, serial rebels in north-west Scotland and pretenders to the Scottish throne.[161]

The establishment of Gallovidian colonies in Ulster helps to contextualise the approaches made by the English crown to Hugh de Lacy in exile.[162] In 1215, during the English baronial crisis, both Alan and Thomas of Galloway remained (initially) faithful to their overlord in Ulster, King John.[163] Alan was at the king's side throughout the Runnymede negotiations in June, and received confirmation of his Ulster estates at the end of that month.[164] At the same time Alan's brother, Thomas, was issued with a charter for Coleraine and appointed custodian of Antrim castle.[165] The continued import of the Galloway region to King John makes it virtually unthinkable that he could have contemplated

155 *Rot. chart.*, 186b; *RLP*, 92b; *CDI*, i, no. 428.

156 *Rot. pat. Hib.*, ii, 364; *RLC*, i, 402b; *CDI*, i, no. 907.

157 *Rot. chart.*, 194; *CDI*, i, nos 468, 474.

158 *AU*, 1214; *ALC*, 1213 [*recte* 1214]. Thomas's stake was defined in 1215 as Kilsantan (Mount Sandel, Coleraine), with the castle at Coleraine ('Culrath') and twenty knights' fees in the surrounding hinterland: *Rot. chart.*, 210a; *CDI*, i, no. 565.

159 *RLP*, 98; *CDI*, i, no. 427.

160 *Johannis de Fordun chronica gentis Scotorum*, ed. W. F. Skene (2 vols, Edinburgh, 1871–2), i, 278; *Scotichronicon*, iv, 469; Stringer, 'Periphery and core', 85–6; Duncan, 'John, king of England', 263.

161 Stringer, 'Periphery and core', 85; Oram, *Galloway*, 116.

162 See above, 132–4.

163 Stringer, 'Periphery and core', 89.

164 *Rot. chart.*, 210a; *CDI*, i, no. 564; Stringer, 'Periphery and core', 89.

165 *Rot. chart.*, 210a; *RLP*, 146a; *CDI*, i, nos 565, 567.

Hugh de Lacy's restoration to Ulster at this point, giving credence to the interpretation of the royal communiqué dispatched to de Lacy in April as an empty offer.

It was only in late 1215, after the new king of Scots, Alexander II, threw in his lot with the English rebels, that the Gallovidian lords reconsidered their allegiance. Sensing an opportunity to enlarge his English hegemony, in 1216 Alan of Galloway aided Alexander in his occupation of Cumberland and Westmorland.[166] With much of Ulster now effectively in rebel hands, it is no surprise that in November Henry III's beleaguered minority council considered sanctioning Hugh de Lacy's restoration. Neither is it surprising that de Lacy's chief advocate was Ranulf of Chester, whose position in north-west England would be directly threatened by Gallovidian expansion.

Alexander II was reconciled with the English crown in 1217, but it would take two more years for relations to be normalised with the Gallovidians. Thomas, earl of Atholl, was granted peace over his Irish possessions on 19 June 1219.[167] In October Duncan of Carrick was restored to his Ulster estates of which he had been disseised for supporting rebellion.[168] Alan of Galloway was extended peace in 1220, receiving amended charters for his Ulster territories.[169] The delay in Alan's reconciliation has been attributed to a faction within Henry III's minority council lobbying for Hugh de Lacy's restoration. If, as has been suggested, this group was led by William Marshal, then the earl of Pembroke's death in 1219 may have removed the last obstacle to peace with Alan and his kinsmen.[170] In any case, by the time Hugh de Lacy was finally ready to renew his claims to Ulster, there was no longer any immediate strategic advantage to be had from his restoration. Moreover, the new figurehead of the minority council, Hubert de Burgh, was by no means sympathetic to Hugh's plight.

Return to the british isles

In 1221, according to the annals of Dunstable, 'Hugh de Lacy was exiled by the Albigensians and, [returning] to England, [petitioned] for restitution to his land in Ireland'.[171] This contemporary and well-informed chronicle is key to our understanding of Hugh's subsequent negotiations over Ulster, following his

166 See Stringer, 'Periphery and core', 89–90.
167 *RLC*, i, 392b; *CDI*, i, no. 879.
168 *RLC*, i, 402b; *CDI*, i, no. 907.
169 *RLC*, i, 415b, 420b; *CDI*, i, nos 936, 937, 942; Stringer, 'Periphery and core', 92.
170 Stringer, 'Periphery and core', 91–2; Oram, *Galloway*, 121.
171 *Ann. mon.*, iii, 75.

extension of safe conduct to the English court in September 1221.[172] Instead of an earldom, de Lacy was initially offered an annuity of 300 marks, 'because the king was sick/powerless' (*quia rex fuerat infirmus*).[173] The allusion to an enfeebled Henry III may imply that influential figures controlling the young king were opposed to de Lacy's restoration. Chief of these was the English justiciar, Hubert de Burgh, whose rise in royal favour had discomfited the men responsible for negotiating de Lacy's return, Earl Ranulf of Chester and Peter des Roches, bishop of Winchester.[174] As Henry III's guardian, Peter des Roches was in a unique position of influence, but by early 1221 Hubert de Burgh was taking steps to remove the king from the bishop's tutelage.[175] Curiously, at his most vulnerable moment, Peter chose to absent himself from court and undertake a pilgrimage to Santiago de Compostela in Spain. The departure of des Roches was viewed with suspicion by his enemies at court, and several of the bishop's affiliates were accused of plotting with the king of France during his absence.[176]

Bearing in mind Peter's later part in arranging Hugh de Lacy's return to the British Isles, it is not unthinkable that he made contact with the exiled earl during his journey abroad. The bishop's persuasive links to de Lacy's crusading companions make this even more likely. Peter's presumed relative from the Touraine, William des Roches (†1222), was the Capetian seneschal of Anjou and was present at the siege of Marmande in 1219.[177] We have seen that Hugh de Lacy was elsewhere in that year, raiding around the Lauragais in the company of the de Berzy brothers. In 1218, however, de Lacy had been at Toulouse with Gilbert des Roches, related by marriage to Amaury de Craon, William des Roches's son-in-law.[178] It is also notable that the bishop of Winchester controlled Simon de Montfort's English lands for a short period after his death in 1218.[179]

As part of his attempts to undermine Hubert de Burgh's power base at court, des Roches cultivated the support of the other principal cheerleader for Hugh de Lacy's restoration, Ranulf of Chester. Following his return from the Fifth

[172] From 1210 to 1242 the compilation of these annals was orchestrated by Richard de Morins, prior of Dunstable and sometime Angevin envoy to France. Richard was in London in 1223 to help resolve the issue of the bishop of London's jurisdiction over Westminster abbey, where he could have learned of Hugh de Lacy's return: Gransden, *Historical writing in England*, 332–6.

[173] *Ann. mon.*, iii, 75.

[174] *Pat. rolls*, 1216–25, 301.

[175] Carpenter, *Minority*, 239–43; Nicholas Vincent, *Peter des Roches: an alien in English politics, 1205–1238* (Cambridge, 1996), 195–8.

[176] *Ann. mon.*, iii, 68; Carpenter, *Minority*, 249–52; Vincent, *Peter des Roches*, 199–201. Des Roches had long been an extremely influential figure in Anglo-French diplomacy: Vincent, *Peter des Roches*, 203–4.

[177] *Song of the Cathar wars*, 187, §212; Vincent, *Peter des Roches*, 18–26.

[178] *Song of the Cathar wars*, 151, 160, 164, §§196, 200, 202; Vincent, *Peter des Roches*, 204.

[179] Vincent, *Peter des Roches*, 193.

crusade, in July 1220, Ranulf had become increasingly resentful of de Burgh's friendship with the new earl of Pembroke, William II Marshal.[180] A clue as to the volatility of the political climate is given by the 'Barnwell' annalist, who states that certain aliens were attempting to induce the earl of Chester into disturbing the kingdom.[181] A rift had opened between courtiers perceived as 'foreigners' – born in France or with significant links or interests there – and those described by the earl of Salisbury as *naturales homines Anglie*.[182] The situation of the de Lacy brothers on opposing sides of this divide must frame any discussion of their subsequent actions.

In 1222 Hugh appears to have attended the court of his advocate and *consanguineus*, the earl of Chester.[183] In that year Earl Ranulf agreed the marriage of his nephew, John *de Scotia*, to a daughter of the Welsh prince, Llywelyn ap Iorwerth. Hugh de Lacy's attestation in the accompanying (extant original) chirograph, as *comite Ulton*, is a clear signal of his revived comital pretensions.[184] Around the same time, another of Llywelyn's daughters, Gwenllian, was given in marriage to Hugh's half-brother, William de Lacy.[185] This joint alliance with the prince of Gwynedd, William II Marshal's chief antagonist in the Welsh march, posed a direct challenge to the earl of Pembroke, and by extension to Hubert de Burgh and his partisans. If Earl Ranulf was to undermine the Marshal's position, however, he would have to prevent William from exploiting his lordship of Leinster as a recruiting ground and economic prop for his activities across the Irish Sea.[186] With Walter de Lacy and other senior magnates in Ireland in alignment with the de Burgh–Marshal axis, one way to offset the Marshal's power, echoing King John's ill-starred policy of 1205, would be to effect Hugh de Lacy's restoration to the earldom of Ulster.

The prospect of confederacy with Llywelyn may have encouraged the minority council to reconsider de Lacy's demands, and directions for the restoration of Hugh's estates in the lordship of Meath were issued to Walter de Lacy on 23 June.[187] If the concession was intended to bring Hugh to the table, it

[180] Ranulf was probably one of the barons who moved to block the Marshal's marriage to Henry III's sister: ibid., 270–1.

[181] *Memoriale fratris Walteri de Coventria*, ii, 251; Carpenter, *Minority*, 271.

[182] Carpenter, *Minority*, 272–3.

[183] Henry de Audley, de Lacy's former tenant in Ulster and brother of his constable, Adam de Audley (†1211), had found service at the court of the earl of Chester after 1210: see R. F. Walker, 'Audley, Henry (†1246)', in *ODNB*.

[184] *Acts of Welsh rulers*, no. 252, 412–15; *Charters of the Anglo-Norman earls of Chester*, nos 411, 407–8. John, son of Earl David of Huntingdon, had been in the wardship of his cousin, Alexander II of Scotland, until March 1221, when his care was entrusted to Earl Ranulf: Keith Stringer, *Earl David of Huntingdon: a study in Anglo-Scottish history* (Edinburgh, 1985), 182–3.

[185] J. E. Lloyd, 'Who was Gwenllian de Lacy?', *Archaeologia Cambrensis* 19 (1919), 292–8.

[186] Lloyd, *History of Wales*, ii, 658–60.

[187] *RLC*, i, 501a.

failed to do so, and the government was left with no option but to prepare for war. Fearful of an assault on Ulster, Thomas of Galloway was ordered to give up custody of Antrim castle to the justiciar, who was better placed to defend the fortress and its environs than the absentee earl of Atholl.[188] Meanwhile, Earl Ranulf and Peter des Roches continued to advance Hugh de Lacy's interests at court, and in December, by agreement of the majority of the council, de Lacy was offered restoration to his marriage portion in Uriel.[189] Anticipating that Hugh might refuse any improved terms which still excluded Ulster, further security measures were taken in Ireland: tournaments were prohibited, and John Marshal, the earl of Pembroke's cousin, was dispatched to the colony at the crown's expense.[190] Concurrently, the anti-de Burgh faction was lobbying at the papal court for the curtailment of the young King Henry's minority.[191]

The overspill of tension came early in 1223, when Hugh de Lacy joined Llywelyn in an assault on William Marshal's lands in the Welsh march.[192] As Earl Ranulf moved to diffuse the situation, Marshal launched a counter-attack with an army amassed in Ireland and swiftly regained most of his possessions.[193] Llywelyn's rising had been temporarily subdued, but Hugh de Lacy's aggressive posturing inspired fresh deliberations over his own position. On 4 June a letter was issued to the Irish justiciar, Henry of London (archbishop of Dublin), informing him of a conference lately held at London to discuss Hugh de Lacy's demands. There, a proposal had been mooted whereby Hugh's lands and castles would be committed for five years to the earls of Chester, Salisbury and Gloucester, and Walter de Lacy, after which time they would be returned to the crown. However, the proposed custodians having being unwilling to accept these conditions, nothing further was done. The letter further warned that Hugh de Lacy was planning an invasion of Ireland and instructed the justiciar to supply and fortify the king's castles accordingly.[194]

Of the four intended curators of Hugh's lands, only Earl Ranulf was overtly an opponent to Hubert de Burgh. The earl of Salisbury, William Longespée, was de Burgh's firm ally,[195] as was Gilbert de Clare, earl of Gloucester, who would only later join a group of baronial dissidents.[196] The minority council was

188 Ibid., 505b; *CDI*, i, no. 1044.

189 *RLC*, i, 527b; *CDI*, i, nos 1073–4. These terms were to be conveyed to Hugh by his brother, Gilbert.

190 *CDI*, i, nos 1062–9.

191 Carpenter, *Minority*, 299–305.

192 Matthew Paris, *Historia Anglorum*, ed. Frederic Madden, Rolls Series (3 vols, London, 1866–9), iii, 82; Lloyd, *History of Wales*, ii, 661; Carpenter, *Minority*, 298.

193 Lloyd, *History of Wales*, ii, 661; Carpenter, *Minority*, 307–8.

194 *RLC*, i, 549b; *CDI*, i, no. 1110.

195 Carpenter, *Minority*, 272, 287.

196 Ibid., 49, 318–33. Gilbert was married to Marshal's sister, Isabella.

negotiating from a position of strength: with Llywelyn on the back foot in the Welsh march there was no pressing reason to capitulate to Hugh de Lacy, and the proposal to entrust his lands in the hands of three de Burgh partisans had only the semblance of a concession. The earl of Chester would be obviously discomforted by any agreement placing Ulster into the hands of the de Burgh–Marshal faction. Hubert and William were already bolstering their influence in Ireland by proxy, as evidenced by the appointment of John Marshal as custodian of Cork, Decies and Desmond, and Richard de Burgh as steward of Munster and constable of Limerick.[197] Indeed, by the time Hugh de Lacy's restoration was being discussed in early June, letters of excommunication had already been obtained against him from the papal *curia*.[198]

A final indictment of the custodial committee is provided by their subsequent actions during the summer of 1223. Walter de Lacy's manor of Ludlow was the setting for a summit around 10 July, at which William Marshal and Llywelyn failed to come to terms.[199] Thereafter Walter joined the earl of Gloucester and other magnates in a royal army, commanded by William Marshal and the earl of Salisbury, which marched against Llywelyn and Hugh de Lacy in late summer.[200] Llywelyn's swift defeat and submission rendered him unable to provide Hugh with any further meaningful assistance.[201] Moreover, the support of Earl Ranulf and Peter des Roches, which had been based on a strategy to topple the ascendant William Marshal in Wales, was now in doubt. To progress his claims to Ulster, de Lacy would have to turn to friends elsewhere.

'Beyond the sea'

In spring 1224 Queen Joan of Scotland wrote to her brother, the king of England, expressing regret at the harm being done to him by Hugh de Lacy. Reassuring King Henry that her husband, Alexander II, had forbidden any of his men from going to Ireland, Joan concluded her letter with a warning that the king of Norway was preparing an expedition in support of de Lacy.[202] The

197 *Pat. rolls, 1216–25*, 374–5; *CDI*, i, nos 1107, 1114, 1117.

198 In the same letter to Henry of London from 4 June, informing the justiciar of the London conference, the king intimated that he was sending Archbishop Henry letters of excommunication from the Pope, to be used against Hugh de Lacy and his accomplices, should they invade the king's land. These were to be used at the proper time, in advancement of the king's security and for Hugh's injury: *RLC*, i, 549b; *CDI*, i, no. 1110.

199 Carpenter, *Minority*, 308.

200 *Ann. mon.*, iii, 82; Carpenter, *Minority*, 308–9.

201 Llywelyn conceded any claims in Shropshire, while the Marshal received formal recognition of his own gains in south Wales, including custody of Cardigan and Carmarthen: Carpenter, *Minority*, 311–14; Lloyd, *History of Wales*, ii, 662–3.

202 *Royal and other historical letters illustrative of the reign of Henry III, from the originals in the Public*

queen's message is all the more perplexing because Anglo-Norwegian relations had seldom run so smoothly as in the first years of Hákon IV's reign (1217–63).[203] Direct Norwegian intervention in Ireland would be counter-intuitive in this context, but the possibility remains that, in his search for confederates, Hugh de Lacy had approached vassals of King Hákon with an existing interest in Irish affairs.

Just such a client was Jón Haraldsson, jarl of Orkney and earl of Caithness (1206–31). Among early Orcadian interlopers in Ireland were Jarl Sigurðr, killed at the battle of Clontarf in 1014, and his son, Þorfinnr, who was said to have carved out a 'large realm in Ireland'.[204] In the twelfth century Jarl Haraldr Maddaðarson (1139–1206) may have acted as secular protector to the monastery of St Comgall at Bangor (Co. Down), a role he is unlikely to have taken on without a territorial interest in the region.[205] A clue as to Haraldr's aspirations may be found in the Orcadian attack on 'Inis-Lachain' in 1170, possibly the *crannóg* of Loughan Island on the river Bann, just south of Coleraine (Co. Londonderry).[206] Any historic Orcadian hegemonic claim, to 'Inis-Lachain' or otherwise, may have caused Haraldr's successor, Jón Haraldsson, to cast a watchful eye towards Ulster.

Jarl Jón and Hugh de Lacy also possessed a shared enmity with Rögnvaldr, king of Man, who had renewed his vassalic relationship with the English crown in 1219, and was well placed to obstruct de Lacy's recovery of Ulster from his base at Carlingford.[207] We have seen that when Haraldr Maddaðarson occupied Caithness, c.1196, it was the jarl's cousin, the king of Man, whom William I of Scotland tasked with recovering the territory.[208] The Scottish crown had further cause to intrude in Orcadian affairs in 1222, when, at the instigation of Jarl Jón, a group of local men seized and murdered the bishop of Caithness.[209] Jón must

Record Office, ed. W. W. Shirley, Rolls Series (2 vols, London, 1862–6), i, 219–20; *CDI*, i, no. 1179.

203 Knut Helle, 'Anglo-Norwegian relations in the reign of Håkon Håkonsson (1217–63)', *Mediaeval Scandinavia* 1 (1968), 101–14.

204 *The Orkneyinga saga*, ed. A. B. Taylor (Edinburgh, 1938), 189; Patrick Topping, 'Harald Maddadson, earl of Orkney and Caithness, 1139–1206' in *Scot. Hist. Rev.* 62, no. 174 (1983), 105–20, at 112.

205 Barbara Crawford, 'Haraldr Maddaðarson, earl of Caithness and earl of Orkney (1133/4–1206)', in *ODNB*; Topping, 'Harald Maddadson', 109–10.

206 *AU*, 1170; Hogan, *Onomasticon*, 503. Killed in this raid was the king of Uí Méith, Diarmait Ua Ainbheith, whose additional role as 'leader of the horse-host of the king of Ailech', the polity centred on Inishowen, Co. Donegal, may appear to give credence to the placement of 'Inis-Lachain' in the north-west: *AU*, 1170; *AFM*, 1170. Since the destruction of the stronghold of Ailech in 1101, however, the designation 'king of Ailech' was used metonymically in its application to the ruler of the northern Uí Néill, and does not indicate an exact geographical location.

207 McDonald, *Manx kingship*, 142–3.

208 Ibid., 108–10. Rögnvaldr's grandfather had been married to a daughter of Jarl Hákon Pálsson of Orkney.

209 *Scottish annals from English chroniclers, 500–1286*, ed. A. O. Anderson (London, 1908), 337;

have feared that, in retribution, Alexander II would employ the same tactic as his father, William I, by sanctioning Manx intrusion in the region.

One way to mitigate this threat would be to disrupt Rögnvaldr's interests in the Irish Sea zone, but Jón may not have had to go as far as Ulster to achieve this goal. In 1223 Ólafr Guðrøðarson re-ignited the long-running feud with his brother, Rögnvaldr, by ambushing and mutilating his nephew in a raid on the Isle of Skye. The next summer, after Ólafr took a fleet of thirty-two ships to Man to contest the kingship, it was agreed that Rögnvaldr should retain both Man and his royal title, while his brother took over the outlying portions of the kingdom of the Isles.[210] R. A. McDonald has argued for Alexander II's connivance in Ólafr's attacks.[211] It was Ólafr's brother who was the historic ally of the Scottish crown, however, and Rögnvaldr's allies in the dynastic war of 1223–24 included Alan and Thomas of Galloway, both at that time closely aligned with the king of Scots.[212]

A more obvious choice of confederate for Ólafr was Alexander's rival in the Hebridean nexus, King Hákon IV of Norway, who continued to take umbrage with Rögnvaldr's refusal to recognise Norwegian suzerainty in Man and his enticement as an Angevin client. In late 1220 the minority council in England informed the justiciar of Ireland that Rögnvaldr's lands were under threat of Norwegian attack because he had rendered homage to Henry III.[213] The improvement in Anglo-Norwegian relations by 1223 mitigated against Hákon's direct intervention against Rögnvaldr, as it precluded any action on behalf of Hugh de Lacy in Ulster. However, the business could have been entrusted to someone like the jarl of Orkney, who was already firmly predisposed against the king of Man. In 1230, when Ólafr Guðrøðarson successfully lobbied King Hákon for support against Alan of Galloway in the Isles, it would be Jarl Jón who sheltered the Norwegian–Manx fleet and furnished Ólafr with one of his own longships, 'the Ox'.[214]

The kin-strife in Man played into Hugh de Lacy's hands, preventing Rögnvaldr and his Gallovidian allies from intervening in Ulster. Another factor worth considering is the bid for the kingship of Connacht made by Diarmait Ua Conchobair, half-brother of William *Gorm* de Lacy, in 1221, which was supported by a fleet from 'Insi-Gall' (the Hebrides), where Ólafr was gathering strength on the island of Lewis.[215] Bearing in mind Queen Joan's warning in

Duncan, *Scotland*, 528; James Gray, *Sutherland and Caithness in saga-time* (Edinburgh, 1922), 96–8.

210 McDonald, *Manx kingship*, 77–80.

211 Ibid., 152–3.

212 Stringer, 'Periphery and core', 94–5.

213 *RLC*, i, 439; *CDI*, i, no. 976.

214 Gray, *Sutherland and Caithness*, 98.

215 *ALC*, 1221, and below, 154.

1224, it may not be coincidental that in the previous year, as the strategic interests of the Orcadians, Hugh de Lacy and Ólafr Guðrøðarson converged, the jarl of Orkney was one of a group from 'west beyond the sea' who attended King Hákon's court at Bergen with 'letters concerning the needs of their lands'.[216]

One final facet of Orcadian affinity demands closer inspection. Through his (bigamous) marriage to a daughter of the earl of Ross, Máel Coluim Mac Heth, c.1168, Jarl Haraldr of Orkney had been drawn into rebellion against the king of Scots alongside the Mac Heths and Mac Williams.[217] Haraldr's connections to these kindreds add an extra dimension to the already convoluted politics of the region. We have seen that the distribution of Ulster territory among the Gallovidians after 1210 drove a wedge between the Mac Williams and their Irish protectors among Cenél nEógain. Here we have a proxy connection between Orkney and Tír Eógain, made all the more intriguing by the astute piece of diplomacy undertaken by Hugh de Lacy in advance of his return to Ireland, in securing the support of his formerly inveterate opponent, Áed Méith Ua Néill.[218]

The Irish rebellion of Hugh de Lacy, 1223–24

A '*sudden and secret arrival*'

Power in Angevin Ireland was most obviously invested in land, but opportunity could also present itself in appointment to ecclesiastical office, or to the secular administration. In some cases, multiple avenues of advancement might converge in one ambitious, or fortunate, individual. In 1213 one of King John's most talented *curiales*, Henry of London (†1228), was appointed archbishop of Dublin. At the same time the king sought to make the most of Henry's administrative aptitude by appointing him to the Irish justiciarship.[219] In 1223 the archbishop, whose formidable reputation earned him the nickname 'Scorchevillein' – 'flayer of serfs'[220] – faced the sternest test of his statesmanship

216 *Early sources*, ed. Anderson, ii, 455, 461.

217 Topping, 'Harald Maddadson', 112–15.

218 See below, 157–9.

219 Henry was justiciar for two terms (1213–15 and 1221–24) and was papal legate to Ireland in 1217–20. For his career, see Ralph Turner, *Men raised from dust: administrative service and upward mobility in Angevin England* (Philadelphia, PA, 1988); Margaret Murphy, 'Balancing the concerns of church and state: the archbishops of Dublin, 1181–1228', in Barry, Frame and Simms (eds) *Colony and frontier*, 41–56; Aubrey Gwynn, 'Henry of London, archbishop of Dublin: a study in Anglo-Norman statecraft', *Studies: an Irish quarterly review* 38 (1949), 297–306, 389–402.

220 Gwynn, 'Henry of London', 297.

when Hugh de Lacy landed in Ireland, raised a rebel army and marched on Dublin:

> Hugh de Lacy secretly passed over the sea [from Wales] to Ireland. And since Walter de Lacy, his brother, was lord of Meath, the said Hugh, having collected an army from the land of his brother, waged war in that part of Ireland which belonged to the king of England such that he reached almost as far as Dublin. And thus the archbishop of Dublin, who was then the king's justiciar in those parts, was constrained to buy a truce from him until the following summer because he was not prepared for the sudden and secret arrival of Hugh.[221]

What lay behind Henry's lukewarm response to rebellion?[222] A surprisingly well-informed source for Irish affairs, the annals of Dunstable appear to lay a charge of complacency at the justiciar's door. Having been instructed to ready the king's castles prior to Hugh de Lacy's clandestine appearance in Ireland,[223] it was perhaps in response to accusations of slothfulness that Henry would later write to the king, claiming to have placed 'a good and sufficient *familia*' in Ulster's fortresses, and to have spent significant sums of money in equipping men to guard the coastal areas.[224] What was not anticipated was an attack on the centre of colonial government itself. The royal administration in Ireland had been lax in its attitude towards the defence of Dublin: money set aside by the crown for this purpose, or gleaned from the murage tax of 1221, was spent on repairs instead of new walls or towers.[225] Archbishop Henry had been instrumental in the works at Dublin Castle, but nothing had been done to prepare the fortress against Hugh de Lacy's army. An inventory from c.1224 reveals little of defensive use beyond two mangonels, one crossbow (with wheel), one crossbow for the foot and 4500 bolts.[226] The city walls may also have been insufficiently redoubt. In 1225 the abbey of St Thomas, situated in Dublin's western suburb beyond the New Gate, was compensated for a fosse constructed on its lands.[227] We might imagine this earthen bank being hurriedly erected against

221 *Ann. mon.*, iii, 85.

222 For an expanded treatment of the following, see Daniel J. F. Brown, 'The citizens and archbishop of Dublin during Hugh de Lacy's Irish rebellion, 1223–4', in Seán Duffy (ed.), *Medieval Dublin XVII: proceedings of the Friends of Medieval Dublin symposium, 2015* (Four Courts Press, 2016). An earlier version of this study can be accessed at King's College London's 'Henry III fine rolls project' (www.finerollshenry3.org.uk), under 'Fine of the month' (December 2012).

223 *Pat. rolls, 1216–25*, 374–5, 378.

224 TNA, SC 1/60/125 (report of Henry, archbishop of Dublin, to King Henry III); Otway-Ruthven, *Med. Ire.*, 91.

225 J. F. Lydon, 'The defence of Dublin in the Middle Ages', in Seán Duffy (ed.), *Medieval Dublin IV: proceedings of the Friends of Medieval Dublin symposium, 2002* (Dublin, 2003), 63–79, at 65–7.

226 *CDI*, i, no. 1227; Lydon, 'Defence of Dublin', 69–70.

227 *CDI*, i, no. 1314.

Hugh de Lacy's forces, which had approached Dublin from Meath, north-west of the city.[228]

Henry's freedom of action as royal representative was also constrained by membership of the tenant community in Ireland. While allowing an individual to accumulate power through multiple channels, an ability to be at once a royal justiciar and landed magnate was an institutional weakness built into the Angevin administration. A catalyst for the baronial crisis of 1207–08 had been Meiler fitz Henry's abuse of the justiciarship for his own self-aggrandisement. Lessons from that conflict were not learned, however, and nothing was done to prevent subsequent justiciars from 'double-jobbing'. Around 1223 Henry of London granted to his nephew, John of London, the vill of 'Portmaclyueran' (perhaps Port, near Clonmore, Co. Louth), held by Henry from William Sancmelle, one of the rebels later captured by crown forces.[229] The implication seems to be that, at the time of Hugh de Lacy's revolt, the justiciar of Ireland was a Sancmelle tenant, a conflict of loyalty which caused Henry of London to relinquish his tenure at 'Portmaclyueran'.[230] As well as bonds of tenure, the justiciar may have shared blood ties with some of the rebels. Henry shared his family name, Blund, with relatives of William *Gorm* de Lacy, but what connection these may have had to the justiciar's line has yet to be established.[231]

Henry was further undermined by members of the Dublin mercantile and religious elites, who had been alienated by his overzealous prosecution of his secular and ecclesiastical jurisdictions.[232] An inquisition from late 1224 found that several individuals had aided Hugh de Lacy while his army was encamped outside the city walls. William Gallator had sold iron helmets to the rebels. Geoffrey de Lacy and John Forester, of Santry, bought arms and sent them to Hugh de Lacy, and 'related everything occurring in the city of Dublin to the same Hugh'. Adam Norensis, of the vill of the Ostmen (the settlement on the north bank of the Liffey), received money from Ralph Pedelowe (de Lacy's crusading associate) to buy arms and clothes. Canons of the abbey of St Thomas received two horses from one of de Lacy's men at *Kilrethe* (Kilruddery?, Co.

228 An unanswered question is to what extent de Lacy's confrontational strategy could have been influenced by Archbishop Henry's (possible) advocacy for the Count of Toulouse at the Fourth Lateran council in 1215: see above, 133.

229 *Gorm. reg.*, 150–2, 198; Eric St John Brooks, 'Archbishop Henry of London and his Irish connections', *JRSAI* 60 (1930), 1–22, at 11–14, and below. The Sancmelles had fought for Hugh de Lacy against King John in 1210: see above, 76.

230 In 1215 Henry took over Penkridge, the Staffordshire manor of another de Lacy affiliate, Hugh Hose: *Rot. chart.*, 218b; *CDI*, i, no. 652.

231 *Royal letters Hen. III*, i, 500–3; *CDI*, i, no.1203; Brooks, 'Henry of London', 1–10, and below, 158.

232 *Historic and municipal documents of Ireland, 1172–1320: from the archives of the city of Dublin*, ed. J. T. Gilbert, Rolls Series (London, 1870), 78–9; *CDI*, i, no. 1130; Murphy, 'Balancing the concerns of church and state', 50–2.

Wicklow), in exchange for one tun of wine with a cart and five horses. It was also found that one Thomas le Corner, with two other associates, 'received men of Hugh de Lacy and bought arms and other necessities in the city of Dublin to their work, against the prohibition of the lord justiciar, and conducted them to the wood outside the city by night'.[233] Thomas le Corner was no ordinary citizen, but a prominent wine merchant who would later serve as mayor of Dublin in 1231–32.[234] Evidently, Hugh de Lacy had links with a disaffected element within the urban elite: men who controlled Dublin's trade, commerce and public spaces; men who could keep a rebel army amply supplied, if they so wished.

William de Lacy and Bréifne

While Hugh de Lacy was marching against Dublin, his half-brother, William *Gorm*, was pursuing a personal agenda in Bréifne, the 'Rough Third' of the overlordship of Connacht comprising the modern counties of Cavan, Leitrim and Longford.[235] In 1223, after presumably taking part in Prince Llywelyn's revolt in Wales, the Annals of Loch Cé report that 'William de Laci came to Erinn, and constructed the crannog of Inis-Laodhachain; and the Connachtmen entered forcibly upon it, and let out on parole the people who were in it'.[236] The location of Inis-Laodhachain is illuminated by a letter of the king of Connacht, Cathal Crobderg, sent to the English court in spring 1224, requesting that lands occupied (*detinet*) by William de Lacy in Bréifne – defined as 'Ubriun', 'Conmacni' and 'Caled' – be delivered to Cathal's son, Áed.[237] 'Caled' was roughly coterminous with the barony of Rathline (Co. Longford), while 'Conmacni' alludes to Conmaicne Magh Réin, the polity in modern co. Leitrim. 'Ubriun', meanwhile, is a rendering of Uí Briúin, the branch of the ruling dynasty in Connacht which had established the kingdom of Bréifne in the seventh or eighth centuries.[238] In effect, Cathal was complaining that William had unlawfully seized the entirety of the kingdom of Uí Briúin Bréifne. The *crannóg* (island fortress) of Inis-Laodhachain may therefore be reasonably identified with 'Laghelachon' (from *Loch na Lachan*, 'lake of the ducks'), one

[233] K. W. Nicholls (ed.), 'Inquisitions of 1224 from the miscellanea of the exchequer', *Anal. Hib.* 27 (1972), 101–12, at 107–9.

[234] See Brown, 'Civil disobedience'.

[235] See Katharine Simms, 'The O'Reillys and the kingdom of east Breifne', *Bréifne* 5 (1979), 305–19.

[236] *ALC*, 1223.

[237] *Royal letters Hen. III*, i, 223; *CDI*, i, no. 1184. These lands were granted to Áed on 14 June: *RLC*, i, 604b; *CDI*, i, no. 1195.

[238] Orpen, *Normans*, 301n; Simms, 'O'Reillys', 305, 307.

of the territories restored to Walter de Lacy in 1215 and placed by Orpen at Loughan (*alias* Castlekieran, bar. Upper Kells), on the frontier between the lordship of Meath and Bréifne.[239]

It has been shown that the Irish mother of William de Lacy was probably a granddaughter of the king of Bréifne, Tigernán Ua Ruairc, slain by Hugh I de Lacy in 1172.[240] Some historic sense of entitlement to his great-grandfather's kingdom may help to explain William de Lacy's preoccupation with securing his own stake in Bréifne, in pursuit of which he would meet his death in 1233.[241] If, as will be argued, William aspired to becoming lord of Bréifne, he faced competition from the Gaelicised family of de Angulo, whose representative, Gilbert, had been expelled from Meath before 1191 for his mercenary service to Cathal Crobderg, usurper of William de Lacy's grandfather, Ruaidrí Ua Conchobair.[242] Gilbert was outlawed by King John in 1196 and his lands in Bréifne, at Lough Oughter (Co. Cavan), were transferred to Walter de Lacy in the next year.[243] Later, however, as the crown sought to establish more cordial relations with the king of Connacht, the de Angulos' unique connections to Cathal Crobderg became assets to be exploited. In 1207 Gilbert came to peace with Walter de Lacy and was retained in royal service, receiving from King John confirmation of his cantred of Maenmagh (Co. Galway), a gift of the king of Connacht.[244]

It is not unthinkable that this shift in royal policy, based on co-operation with William de Lacy's competitors in Bréifne and among the Uí Conchobhair, influenced William's alignment with Hugh de Lacy against the crown in 1210.[245] We have already seen that William's heritage could have influenced the earl of Ulster's acute appreciation of native Irish sensibilities of power.[246] Litigation heard before justices itinerant, c.1247, mentions the land of 'William de Lassi' near Ballymoney (Co. Antrim), from which we might also infer that he had acquired a stake in Ulster before his death in 1233, and possibly before 1210.[247]

239 *RLP*, 148b; *CDI*, i, no. 612; G. H. Orpen, 'Motes and Norman castles in Ireland', *EHR* 22, no. 86 (1907), 228–54, at 242. William de Lacy's subsequent operation in Bréifne renders this location more likely than those proposed by Veach (Lough Creggan, Co. Westmeath) or Otway-Ruthven (Ballyloughloe, Co. Westmeath): Veach and Verstraten Veach, 'William *Gorm* de Lacy', 73, following Margaret Dobbs, 'The territory and people of Tethba', *JRSAI* 68 (1938), 241–59, at 258; Otway-Ruthven, 'Partition', 414.

240 Veach and Verstraten Veach, 'William *Gorm* de Lacy', 64–5.

241 *AClon.*, 1233. On his death Hugh I de Lacy was described as 'king of Meath, and Bréifne, and Airgialla': *ALC*, 1186.

242 See above, 17. Gilbert is described in Irish sources as *Mac Goisdealbh* ('son of Jocelin', later Mac Costello).

243 *Gorm. reg.*, 7, 179; Orpen, *Normans*, 297.

244 *RLC*, i, 78b, 98; *Rot. chart.*, 173a; *CDI*, i, nos 254, 311, 363.

245 *RLP*, 128b, 131a; *CDI*, i, nos 536, 541.

246 See above, 60–2.

247 *Gorm. reg.*, 160, where 'Ballyboni' (rendered by the editor as Ballybom) may be a corruption of

William's fidelity was still under suspicion upon his release from royal custody in 1215, when Walter de Lacy and four other barons were compelled to give assurances that he would 'become the king's liege man, faithfully serve the king all the days of his life, and never part with his land in Ireland, save at the king's pleasure'.[248] By this time the de Angulos were once again operating in Bréifne, and seeking restitution of their estates in the lordship of Meath, which had been re-granted to Hugh de Lacy c.1190.[249] The crucial point is that both William and Hugh de Lacy had cause to resent the revival of the de Angulos' fortunes, while their elder brother Walter was principally concerned with preserving normative relations with Connacht.

In 1220 Walter de Lacy led a 'great hosting' into Bréifne, to Ua Ragallaig's *crannóg* at Lough Oughter (Co. Cavan), obtaining 'hostages and great power'.[250] If, as has been claimed, the lord of Meath was determined to reward William de Lacy with an appanage in the Irish midlands,[251] now was the opportune time to do so. Instead, Walter granted all the land of Ualgarc Ua Ruairc in Bréifne – from Lough Oughter (Co. Cavan) to the 'midst of the Shannon' on one side, and from Lough Erne (Co. Fermanagh) to Slieve Carbury (Co. Longford) on the other – to Philip de Angulo, for whom William de Lacy undertook to build three stone castles.[252]

The theory advanced by Veach and Verstraten Veach holds that, while de Angulo was being placed in the land of Ua Ruairc, William *Gorm* was to have his own stake in the territory of the Uí Ragallaig, dynastic rivals of the Uí Ruairc, in east Bréifne (Co. Cavan).[253] He had a 'vested interest' in the grant to de Angulo, which 'would serve to protect William's flank as he set about establishing himself in the lands of Ua Ragallaig'.[254] The shortcoming of this argument is that, in the grant of Lough Oughter, and with it the ancestral Ua Ragallaig *crannóg*, Walter de Lacy had awarded to Philip de Angulo the key power centre in the land of east Bréifne supposedly intended to provide for his brother. Indeed, the fact that William would subsequently use the occasion of Hugh de Lacy's revolt as a pretext to occupy the kingdom of Bréifne in its

Ballybony, the medieval name for the modern parish of Ballymoney, while 'Talachoor' is probably Tullaghgore (*alias* Forttown), a townland in the same parish: James O'Laverty, *Historical account of the diocese of Down and Connor* (5 vols, Dublin, 1878–95), iv, 119–21.

248 *RLP*, 128b; *CDI*, i, no. 536.

249 *ALC*, 1214; *Rot. oblatis*, 551; *CDI*, i, no. 673.

250 *ALC*, 1220.

251 Veach and Verstraten Veach, 'William *Gorm* de Lacy', 69–70.

252 *Calendar of the patent and close rolls of the chancery in Ireland, Henry VIII to 18th Elizabeth*, ed. James Morrin, (2 vols, Dublin, 1861–2), ii, 197.

253 Veach and Verstraten Veach, 'William *Gorm* de Lacy', 71.

254 Veach, *Lordship*, 184.

entirety would seem to suggest that he was dissatisfied with whatever division had been envisaged by Walter de Lacy in 1221.

If William *Gorm* was more interested in the failure than the success of de Angulo's operation in Bréifne, how then are we to interpret his commission to construct fortresses on Philip's behalf? He cannot have been acting as Walter de Lacy's representative because this office was being filled by one Nicholas fitz Leon, who witnessed the conveyance to de Angulo as 'seneschal of Meath'.[255] A more plausible reading may be that, in building castles for his rival, William was being forced into publicly submitting to his elder brother's plans for Bréifne. This was a disciplinary measure, sending a clear signal that private enterprise or dissent would not be tolerated.[256] The need for such punitive action becomes clearer in light of the straining of relations between the lord of Meath and Cathal Crobderg, the de Angulos' Irish patron, resulting from the construction of a castle by Walter at Athleague (co. Roscommon) in 1221.[257] This fortress was abandoned soon after in order to preserve the goodwill of the king of Connacht,[258] but the ensuing uneasy peace would be jeopardised if William de Lacy refused to cooperate in Bréifne.

Notably, it was also in 1221 that a son of Ruaidri Ua Conchobair, Diarmait, was killed by Thomas of Galloway while collecting a fleet in the Hebrides to contest 'the sovereignty of Connacht'.[259] Links to dynastic rivals gave Cathal Crobderg added incentive to block William de Lacy's ambitions in Bréifne. Here we have a plausible context for Walter de Lacy's advancement of Philip de Angulo, the king of Connacht's long-standing associate, and the concurrent obstruction of William de Lacy's aspirations to lordship in Bréifne. Moreover, it is in the frustration of William's pretensions to power in the midlands that we find the most reasonable explanation for his alliance with the recalcitrant Llywelyn ap Iorwerth in Wales, as well as his enlistment in Hugh de Lacy's impending rebellion in Ireland.

[255] It is possible that William acted as his elder brother's representative in Ireland after his release by the crown in 1215, when he 'came from England and tooke upon him the kingdome of Meath and government thereof': *AClon.*, 1215. Nicholas fitz Leon witnessed a charter of Hugh de Lacy to Walter Hose after 1227: appendix I, no. 22.

[256] William's seizure of the Ulster castles of Dundrum and Carlingford in 1217, for which Walter de Lacy was to make amends, may have been used by the justiciar of Ireland, Geoffrey de Marisco, as a pretext to delay Walter's full seisin in Meath: *Pat. rolls, 1216–25*, 26, 74, 77–8; *CDI*, i, nos 755, 791.

[257] *AFM*, 1220 [*recte* 1221]; *ALC*, 1221; *AClon.*, 1220 [*recte* 1221].

[258] *ALC*, 1221.

[259] Ibid.

The royal response

Hugh de Lacy's clandestine arrival in Ireland had probably owed something to the distraction of the minority council in England with the so-called 'Christmas crisis' of 1223.[260] At the root of this conflict was the resumption of royal demesne being advocated by Hubert de Burgh, a policy which alienated several important magnates, including Falkes de Bréauté, sheriff of Bedford, Oxford and Northampton. In November de Bréauté and the earls of Chester and Gloucester went so far as to attack the Tower of London, bringing England to the brink of civil war. By the end of the year the malcontents had agreed to give up the privileges and offices in question, leaving only de Bréauté in open opposition. Falkes would later claim by way of justification that his actions had been motivated by the treatment of two of his peers, Walter de Lacy and Ralph Musard, who had been summoned to the *curia regis* in early November and compelled to give up their respective shrievalties of Hereford and Gloucester.[261]

It is tempting to connect this curtailment of Walter's privileges with the actions of his brothers, by then active against the government in Ireland. But, as with almost everything involving the de Lacys, the circumstances are more complex than might first be appreciated. Ralph Musard was an intimate of William Marshal and therefore 'the last man whom Hubert [de Burgh] wished to offend'.[262] Accordingly, Carpenter has argued that Musard's treatment was a way for de Burgh to gauge the political temperature and coax his opponents into compliance with his policy of resumption through an exhibition of non-partisanship. By this time Walter de Lacy's daughter, Egidia, may already have been married to Hubert's nephew, Richard de Burgh,[263] and the lord of Meath could also have been targeted precisely because of his loyalty and pliability. The recalcitrance of his brother may have recommended Walter's selection as a test case in the resumption, but if any serious doubt existed as to the lord of Meath's fidelity, the crown's next move in the Irish war would be close to inexplicable.

In March 1224 Walter was dispatched to Ireland to deal with those of his vassals accused of harbouring Hugh de Lacy, pillaging and burning the king's land, and killing or holding the crown's men to ransom.[264] As part of his remit Walter surrendered his castles of Ludlow and Trim for two years, while the perpetrators in Ireland were to have their property confiscated for one

260 Carpenter, *Minority*, 316–70.

261 Daniel Power, 'Bréauté, Sir Falkes de (†1226)', in *ODNB*.

262 Carpenter, *Minority*, 316.

263 A royal mandate from 21 April 1225 mentions the land of Eóganacht Cashel in Munster which Walter de Lacy 'gave' (*dedit*) to Richard de Burgh in marriage to his daughter: *RLC*, ii, 35b; *CDI*, i, no. 1268.

264 *Pat. rolls, 1216–25*, 483; *CDI*, i, no. 1180.

year. Once he had dealt with the rebels, the king was to decide Walter's fate. However, if the lord of Meath was being held responsible for the actions of his tenants, Walter's personal allegiance cannot have been in question, having already proved himself in royal service against his brothers in the Welsh war. The temporary losses of Ludlow and Trim should also be weighed against royal mandates from 29 to 30 March, which granted Walter custody of the castles of Ratoath and Nobber – *capita* of Hugh de Lacy's baronies of Ratoath and Morgallion – and appointed his associate, Richard de Tuit, as custodian of Clonmacnoise.[265] The crown was also well enough disposed towards Walter to quit him of suits in Herefordshire and Shropshire for the duration of his service in Ireland.[266] Most telling is the statement in a further royal missive, that Walter was being dispatched to deal with 'enemies of the king *and of himself*'.[267]

The slow progress which Walter made against the rebels in the two months after his arrival in Ireland, around April, has been seen as evidence of some degree of complicity with his brothers.[268] On the other hand, an army large enough to intimidate the justiciar into a truce could not be easily subdued, and a substantial portion of the midlands was already in rebel hands. Walter was not afforded much in the way of equipment or money to carry out his brief, and it was only some months later that the Irish barons consented to render military service and material assistance for the war.[269] In 1207 Meiler fitz Henry's castle at Ardnurcher had held out for five weeks against Walter and Hugh de Lacy. It would not have been altogether surprising if the fortress at Ratoath – complete with bailey, fosses and ramparts – now proved equally redoubtable. Still, this 'magnificent specimen of a Norman earthwork',[270] with at least four other castles, had already been recaptured by Walter de Lacy by the time William Marshal assumed command of the royal forces in June.[271]

While his men garrisoned castles in the lordship of Meath, and William de Lacy was occupying Bréifne, Hugh de Lacy was attacking the lands of the

265 *Pat. rolls, 1216–25*, 432–3; *RLC*, i, 591; *CDI*, i, nos 1172–3, 1178.

266 *RLC*, i, 590b; *CDI*, i, nos 1175, 1177.

267 *RLC*, i, 591; *CDI*, i, no. 1176 (my emphasis).

268 Veach, *Lordship*, 203–4.

269 *Royal letters Hen. III*, i, 500–3; *CDI*, i, no. 1204.

270 Orpen, *Normans*, 180.

271 *Royal letters Hen. III*, i, 500–3; *CDI*, i, no. 1204 ('Rathune' is Rathline, Co. Longford; 'Rathfay' is Rathfeigh, bar. Skreen, north-east of Hugh de Lacy's former grange of Trevet; and the castles of Walter Sancmelle and William fitz John). For Rathline, one of the parts of Bréifne occupied by William de Lacy, see John Gorton and G. N. Wright, *A topographical dictionary of Great Britain and Ireland* (3 vols, London, 1833), iii, 23, and below. Walter Sancmelle held from Hugh II de Lacy at Cenél Enda (Co. Westmeath) and 'Gillemeston' (Kilmessan, bar. Ratoath): *CDI*, i, nos 495, 553, 957, 1313, 1467, 2894; Orpen, 'Earldom of Ulster (v)', 168–70. William fitz John held the manor of Crumlin (Co. Dublin) from the crown, but is not known to have held in Meath: *CDI*, i, no. 703.

Gallovidians in Ulster, who were otherwise engaged against Ólafr Guðrøðarson in the Isles. The summary of the Irish war in the Annals of Ulster begins:

> the son of Ugo De Lacy came into Ireland in despite of the king of the Saxons, until he came to Aedh O' Neill; so that they went together against the Foreigners of Ireland and destroyed much in Meath and in Leinster and in Ulidia and razed the castle of Cuil-rathain [Coleraine].[272]

The king of Cenél nEógain was seemingly in de Lacy's company from the early stages of the revolt, and forces from Tír Eógain may have taken part in the assault on Thomas of Galloway's castle at Coleraine, as well as a foray into Duncan of Carrick's lands around Larne, after which Hugh granted 'Balgeitheluah' (Ballygalley, near Glenarm, Co. Antrim) to one of his own men.[273] Hugh also targeted royal officers left to guard Ulster whose capture could be used to help finance his war. The knight, John de Tiwe, was taken prisoner and ransomed in early 1224, having seen his squire and cousin killed and his horses and arms commandeered.[274] The capture of Dundrum, the castle in de Tiwe's custody, may have prompted the hurried appointment of Roger Waspail to the stewardship of Ulster on 1 March.[275] Ulster's churchmen also suffered at de Lacy's hands. The bishop of Down would complain bitterly of the injuries to his see inflicted during the war, while the abbot of the Premonstratensian community at Carrickfergus, under the patronage of de Lacy's rival, Alan of Galloway, saw his house despoiled by the rebels 'because he had faithfully adhered to the king in the war', supplying the royal garrison at Carrickfergus castle as best he could.[276]

Henry of London was replaced by William Marshal as justiciar of Ireland in May.[277] Landing by 19 June, Marshal made his way to Trim, *caput* of the lordship of Meath, where he joined Walter de Lacy in besieging the castle.[278] Leaving his family in the security of his *crannóg* at Lough Oughter, William de Lacy set out to relieve the garrison but was overcome by a force of cavalry before he could reach the castle, abandoning his arms and fleeing to a nearby moor and the protection of the Irish. Trim was surrendered on 11 August after almost two months of resistance. Describing the siege, Marshal estimated the lands of the defenders to be worth little except those of William Sancmelle, which he had from his wife. As his followers had always been, de Lacy's rebels were

272 *AU*, 1222 [*recte* 1223/4]; *ALC*, 1221 [*recte* 1223/4]; *AFM*, 1221 [*recte* 1223/4].

273 *RLC*, i, 587a, 615; *CDI*, i, nos 1161, 1200–1.

274 *RLC*, i, 525b, 526, 590b; *CDI*, i, nos 1064, 1066, 1068, 1128, 1162, 1213, 1226.

275 Replacing William de Serland: *Pat. rolls, 1216–25*, 433; *RLC*, i, 588a; *CDI*, i, nos 1158, 1167.

276 *RLC*, i, 32a; *CDI*, i, nos 1225, 1264.

277 *Pat. rolls, 1216–25*, 437–8; *CDI*, i, nos 1186–8.

278 The ensuing sequence of events is related in two letters sent by William Marshal to England around the beginning of August: *Royal letters Hen. III*, i, 500–3; *CDI*, i, nos 1203–4.

apparently drawn from the lower social strata; men with the least to lose, but who recognised a rare chance to alter the tenurial landscape of the colony to their advantage.

In the meantime William Marshal had entered into an alliance with Ua Ragallaig, who recaptured the *crannóg* at Lough Oughter and the castle at Kilmore, and with them William de Lacy's wife, mother and half-brothers, Thomas and Henry Blund. In Ulster forty knights and armed men under the command of William le Gros arrived at Carrickfergus, where they found Hugh de Lacy besieging the castle. Approaching by sea, le Gros and his men were harassed by eight of Hugh's boats but managed to enter the castle unscathed, perhaps by the postern gate on the seaward side of the curtain wall. In no mood for a lengthy siege, and perhaps with the calamities at Beaucaire and Toulouse still fresh in his mind, Hugh cut his losses and abandoned the castle.[279]

William Marshal was meanwhile recruiting support from among the Irish, including the kings of Desmond and Thomond, and preparing to march on Ulster. The support of the new king of Connacht, Áed Ua Conchobair, was a particular boon for the royal army. Relations had been strained since the death of Cathal Crobderg on 28 May, and his son's 'speedy assumption of sovereignty'.[280] Mindful of the inevitable kin-strife which might throw up other claimants to the kingship, the Dublin administration had been reluctant to offer immediate support to Áed.[281] Ua Conchobair's attack on the castle of Lisardowlan (Co. Longford), in which he slew the entire garrison – 'both Foreigners and Gaeidhel' – only served to alienate him further from his Anglo-Norman neighbours, and a conference *in partibus Mauthie* (probably Meath) had been interrupted by William Marshal's arrival in June.[282] It was only through the mediation of Áed's cousin, the captive mother of William de Lacy, that Ua Conchobair returned to the king's peace.[283]

Echoing the initial progress of King John against Hugh de Lacy in the summer of 1210, twenty-four 'battalions' (*catha*) were led by William Marshal towards Dundalk, where they confronted the four 'battalions' of Hugh's, which were plundering the lands of Nicholas de Verdun.[284] This time, however, de Lacy was better prepared to impede his opponents. We might surmise that the war in the Isles had allowed Hugh's rebels to reoccupy Carlingford and its hinterland from the king of Man, preventing the royal army from taking the

279 McNeill, *Anglo-Norman Ulster*, 10, 11, 27.

280 *ALC*, 1224.

281 On 14 June it was agreed that the lands in Bréifne being detained by William de Lacy should be awarded to Áed: *RLC*, i, 604b; *CDI*, i, no. 1195.

282 *ALC*, 1224; *Royal letters Hen. III*, i, 500–3; *CDI*, i, no. 1204.

283 *Royal letters Hen. III*, i, 500–3; *CDI*, i, no. 1204.

284 *AU*, 1222 [*recte* 1224]; *ALC*, 1221 [*recte* 1224]; *AFM*, 1221 [*recte* 1224]; *RLC*, i, 618; *CDI*, i, no. 1210.

route northwards through the Cooley peninsula and into eastern Lecale (Co. Down), as King John had done in 1210. It was now that de Lacy's confederacy with the king of Tír Eógain proved its worth, cutting off the alternative route into Armagh. Hostages and sureties were demanded from the 'sons of Ugo' (presumably Hugh and William de Lacy), but not delivered. Then Áed Méith Ua Néill 'came with his Foreigners and Gaeidhel, whom he distributed on the passes of Sliabh-Fuaid and the "doors of Emhain", and on Fidh-Conaille, when he challenged the Foreigners to attack him in those places'.[285] 'Sliabh-Fuaid' was not a single peak but a mountain range (the Fews, from *na Feá/Feadha* – 'the woods') on the Armagh/Louth border, overlooking the approaches to Navan (*Emain Macha*), ancient pseudo-historical capital of the Ulaid kingdom.[286] The 'doors of Emhain' refers to the Dorsey, an earthwork and strip of land along the road leading south from Navan.[287] 'Fidh Conaill' ('the forest of Conaill') was presumably in the vicinity of Conaille Muirtheimne, the kingdom traditionally associated with the territory between Cooley and Dundalk.[288]

With Ua Néill holding the mountain and forest passes, the royal army's numerical advantage counted for little. 'When the Foreigners of Erinn saw that this protection was assured to them', the annals continue, 'the resolution they adopted was to make peace with the sons of Hugo, and to leave the conditions to the award of the king of the Saxons; and the Foreigners of Erinn separated without obtaining tribute or conditions from Aedh O'Neill'.[289]

From peace to restoration

The Irish war was over, but with no clear victor. William Marshal's decision to come to terms was not a difficult one given the inadequate support he was receiving from the minority council, which was still reeling from the losses of La Rochelle and Poitou to Louis VIII of France.[290] The justiciar was spending upwards of £16 per day, excluding expenses and the pay of foot soldiers, but had only received £20 since his arrival in Ireland.[291] William's sentiments probably mirrored those of his cousin, John Marshal, the beleaguered bailiff of Ulster, who requested permission to return to England in late summer, complaining

[285] *ALC*, 1224.
[286] L. P. Murray, 'An ancient poet's view from Sliabh-Fuaid', *JLAS* 8 (1933), 1–17.
[287] H. G. Tempest, 'The Dorsey: some notes on the large entrenchment in the townland of Dorsey in the south of the county of Armagh', *JLAS* 7 (1930), 187–240.
[288] D. E. Thornton, 'Early medieval Louth: the kingdom of Conaille Muirtheimne', *JLAS* 24 (1997), 139–50.
[289] *ALC*, 1224.
[290] Carpenter, *Minority*, 370–5.
[291] *Royal letters Hen. III*, i, 500–3; *CDI*, i, no. 1204.

that he was living at his own expense and had received next to nothing from his Irish lands.[292] Less immediately obvious is why Hugh de Lacy, under the protection of Áed Ua Néill and Cenél nEógain, saw fit to come to terms. The reality is that de Lacy's window of opportunity was closing; the Manx war could not distract Hugh's Gallovidian adversaries indefinitely, and Alan of Galloway had been informed of Marshal's truce with de Lacy on the very day that he had intended to set out with a fleet for Ireland.[293] With no obvious source of revenue beyond what could be obtained from plunder or ransom, the rebel army could not be kept in the field for much longer. If de Lacy was promised leniency by Marshal, as seems likely, conditional surrender may have been Hugh's only viable course of action.

For subsequent events we are again reliant on the Dunstable annalist, whose knowledge of court politics is quite remarkable, as is his appreciation of affairs in the Irish colony, of which he was able to report accurately that William Marshal's pursuit of Hugh de Lacy had been abruptly halted by 'densities of mountains and woods'.[294] Once Hugh had handed over his castles to the justiciar, he was conducted by John Marshal to England with supplicant letters and admitted into the king's presence after eight days. The archbishop of Canterbury, Stephen Langton, whose links to de Lacy have already been established, then absolved Hugh from his sentence of excommunication pronounced against him through the mediation of Henry of London for having 'rashly disturbed the realm of Ireland'.[295] Curiously, it was at the insistence of William Marshal, who had so recently campaigned against de Lacy in Wales and Ireland, that Hugh was offered an annuity of 200 marks for his maintenance, until more could be provided for him.[296] Even more puzzling is de Lacy's complimentary portrayal in the biography of the elder William Marshal, the compilation of which had begun prior to the crossing of William II to Ireland in 1224, and was completed by the end of 1226.[297] One plausible explanation for Marshal's willingness to advocate for his erstwhile enemy is that he was seeking to detach Hugh from his influential associates in Ireland, who were at that time attempting to usurp the king of Connacht and Marshal's confederate, Áed Ua Conchobair.

In 1225 Áed Méith Ua Néill helped to expel Áed Ua Conchobair from the kingship and set up in his stead another claimant, Toirdelbach, son of Ruaidrí Ua Conchobair.[298] In light of William de Lacy's own aspirations to lordship in

[292] *CDI*, i, no. 1205.

[293] Ibid., no. 1218; *CDS*, i, no. 890.

[294] *Ann. mon.*, iii, 91.

[295] Ibid., iii, 91–2, and above, 145.

[296] *RLC*, ii, 37b; *Ann. mon.*, iii, 92 (Dunstable annals).

[297] *HWM*, iii, 23–5.

[298] *AU*, 1225, 1226; *ALC*, 1224, 1225; *AFM*, 1225.

Connacht's 'Rough Third' of Bréifne, and the death of another of his relatives in 1221 while collecting a fleet to contest the kingship of Connacht, it would not be surprising if William was involved in the latest intrigue being orchestrated by his uncle.[299] It may be significant that the propagandistic poem composed in honour of Áed Ua Conchobair's succession in 1224, *Congaibh róm t'aghaidh, a Aodh*, sought to legitimise the son of Cathal Crobderg by calling attention to his royal lineage; juxtaposing the names of his kingly precursors with the names of the 'foreigners' – Henry, Hubock ('little Hubert') and William.[300] If the poem's intention was to point to Áed as the longed-for high-king portended by St Berchán, the slight to the 'Normanised' William de Lacy was surely intentionally, if obliquely made.

Ironically, it was only through the intervention of the deputy justiciar, Geoffrey de Marisco, and a force of 'foreigners', remunerated with generous wages for their trouble, that Áed Ua Conchobair was able to recover the kingship from Toirdelbach in 1225.[301] Meanwhile Richard de Burgh, recently appointed as steward of Munster and sensing an opportunity to revive his own claims to Connacht, led a force into the province.[302] Although ostensibly acting in support of Áed Ua Conchobair, the king 'disliked their coming into the district, for it was not he who had invited them; but when they heard of all the spoils the [deputy] justiciar with his foreigners had obtained, envy and jealousy seized them'.[303] As it happened the king of Connacht had every justification to suspect the motives of de Burgh, who was using Ua Conchobair's susceptibility to dynastic intrigue and his uncle's status as head of the Angevin minority government in order to promote his own candidacy for the position of royal agent beyond the Shannon. In June 1226 William Marshal was replaced in the justiciarship by Geoffrey de Marisco, who was instructed to confiscate Áed Ua Conchobair's land of Connacht and give seisin to Richard de Burgh, so long as the king's court in Ireland established the correctness of the decision.[304]

This abrupt reversal of royal policy brings into view the earlier decision of the minority council, made by 12 May, to commit to Walter de Lacy all of the lands and castles formerly held by Hugh de Lacy in Ulster, Meath and Uriel (except the fees of those installed in Ulster by King John); to be restored to

[299] *ALC*, 1221, and above.

[300] See Simms, *From kings to warlords*, 26–7.

[301] *AU*, 1225; *ALC*, 1225.

[302] In 1215, when King John had granted Connacht to Cathal Crobderg, he had also made a conflicting grant to Richard de Burgh of 'all the land of Connacht' which his father William had held of the king: *Rot. chart.*, 218–19. The second grant was likely to have been a safeguard in the event that Cathal Crobderg was deposed or forfeited his lands, and Richard made several attempts to have this grant enacted between 1219 and 1224: *RLC*, i, 401, 427, 551.

[303] *ALC*, 1225.

[304] *Pat. rolls, 1225–32*, 47–8; *Rot. chart.*, 219.

the king after three years unless in the meantime Hugh could obtain, of the king's grace, their restoration to himself.[305] This first meaningful step towards restitution to the earldom of Ulster had been impossible while Hugh's associates were intriguing with Uí Conchobhair malcontents against a royally sponsored king of Connacht. This obstacle was removed by the withdrawal of royal support from Áed Ua Conchobair. Now the crown's pressing concern was that the installation of Richard de Burgh should go unhindered. There can be little doubt that the way for Hugh de Lacy to obtain the *gratia regis* and restitution to his lands would be to place his weight behind the new project in the west. This implicit proposal aside, the prospect that Richard's grant might reactivate Hugh's own claim to the portion of Connacht previously awarded to him by William de Burgh surely provided de Lacy with added incentive to cooperate.[306] Notably, while William Marshal would come to the brink of rebellion in protest at the treatment of Áed Ua Conchobair, *fer caradraidh fein* ('his own friend'),[307] in 1228 Hugh de Lacy is reported to have played a part in Áed's assassination at the 'house' of Geoffrey de Marisco.[308]

The interim commitment of Hugh's lands to the custody of Walter de Lacy affects our understanding of the brothers' relationship in the aftermath of the Irish war. If already predisposed to the idea of an unshakeable fraternity, it would be tempting to envision this as a victory for 'the de Lacys', and a result of Walter's advocacy on his younger sibling's part, especially in light of Walter's further pledge that 'H[ugh], my brother, will faithfully serve the king'.[309] However, it is difficult to see an undertaking of this kind as evidence of intimacy when Walter had made a similar pledge regarding William de Lacy's future conduct in 1215, only for William afterwards to act to the detriment of his half-brother over Bréifne and during the revolt of 1223–24.[310] Indeed, that Walter had little confidence in his ability to ensure Hugh's fidelity may be inferred from the fact that the hostages which he offered as security can be safely categorised as his brother's men, namely Roger and Walter, Hugh's sons; the eldest son of Thomas fitz Leon; the eldest son of Thomas Blund; the nephew and heir of

[305] *Pat. rolls, 1225–32*, 31–2, 75–8; *CDI*, i, nos 1371–4.

[306] For Hugh's gift of five Connacht cantreds from Richard de Burgh, c.1234, see below, 190. For his earlier grants in the province from William de Burgh and the Lord John, see above, 28.

[307] ALC, 1227 [*recte* 1226], where Marshal is reported to have conducted Áed away from an ambush being prepared for him at Dublin. The new justiciar, Geoffrey de Marisco, claimed that Marshal's adherents had fortified royal castles against the king: *Royal letters Hen. III*, i, 290–3. See also, AC, 1227 [*recte* 1226]; AFM, 1227 [*recte* 1226]; *AClon.*, 1226.

[308] AC, 1228, and below, 196.

[309] In his charter confirming receipt of Hugh's lands and his acceptance of the terms of custody: *Pat. rolls, 1225–32*, 75–6; *CDI*, i, no. 1372. For a charter of Gilbert de Lacy, Walter's eldest son, signifying the same, see *Pat. rolls, 1225–32*, 76–8; *CDI*, i, no. 1373.

[310] See above, 151–4.

Walter Hose; and the eldest son of Ralph de Muntigny.[311] Walter would further disassociate himself from his responsibilities by abdicating custody of Ulster to William de Lacy by October 1226.[312]

Essentially, the detail of the 12 May mandate implies that Walter did not regard his royal commission so much as a diplomatic success as an unwelcome imposition. We could well understand Walter's reluctance to place himself at further risk on his brother's behalf, given the difficulties he had already incurred as a consequence of Hugh's revolt. A year before, in May 1225, the crown had made its decision in regard to the actions of Walter's rebellious tenants. By and large, things were restored to how they had been *ante bellum*, with Walter regaining custody of Trim and Ludlow and relinquishing Ratoath, Nobber and the bridge of Drogheda. The significant difference was the 3000-mark fine demanded of Walter to have the lands of his tenants since taken into the king's hand. Softening this financial blow, Walter was permitted to keep most of the personal fines offered by his vassals, but given the low social status of the rebels the sums recouped cannot have gone very far towards covering the lord of Meath's penalty.[313]

As in 1210 the elder brother was being made to suffer for the actions of the younger, although there was little else the crown could do to discipline Hugh de Lacy, who had no land in England to distrain nor any revenue of his own to siphon. Perhaps the most telling indictment of the de Lacy fraternity after the nadir of 1223–24 is that, when the king eventually mandated Hugh's restoration to his earldom and estates, on 20 April 1227, he wrote a separate letter to Walter de Lacy to the effect that, if Walter judged that Hugh *should not* be restored to the castles in his custody, then he was to deliver to Hugh only the plains without the castles.[314] In the context of a cohesive fraternal relationship such an offer would be absurd, but is perfectly understandable in light of the warning delivered by Plutarch's *De fraterno amore*, that 'when brothers have once broken the bonds of Nature, they cannot readily come together, and even if they do, their reconciliation bears with it a filthy hidden sore of suspicion'.[315]

[311] Thomas Blund had been captured by royal forces at Lough Oughter in 1224, along with the wife and mother of William de Lacy: see above, 157–8. 'Muntingy' could refer to Montigny-le-Bretonneux (dep. Yvelines) in the Île-de-France, from which many of Hugh de Lacy's companions on the Albigensian crusade had been drawn. For Thomas fitz Leon and Walter Hose, see appendix I, nos 19, 22, 28. It should be noted, however, that Nicholas fitz Leon, witness to one of Hugh de Lacy's comital charters (no. 22), was also Walter de Lacy's steward for Meath in 1221: *Calendar of the patent and close rolls of the chancery in Ireland*, ii, 197; above, 154.

[312] See the royal mandate concerning the lands of Richard fitz Roger confiscated by William de Lacy, who had 'seized custody of the lands we had conceded to Walter de Lacy in Ulster': *RLC*, ii, 140; *CDI*, i, no. 1448.

[313] *RLC*, i, 39b; *CDI*, i, no. 1289. For Walter's financial difficulties after 1227, see below, 170, 196.

[314] *Pat. rolls, 1225–32*, 118; *RLC*, ii, 182b.

[315] *Plutarch's Moralia, VI*, 266.

❖

James Bothwell has outlined several means by which disgraced nobles could return to royal favour.[316] Force of arms could sometimes bring the king to the table, and rapprochement with Henry III might never have been effected by Hugh de Lacy had he not given a demonstration of his clout in Wales and Ireland. Rebellion was a dangerous business, however, as Hugh had found to his cost in 1210. Military strength was no guarantee of reconciliation, and a noble might be compelled to throw himself upon the king's mercy, as did de Lacy in 1224. Influential middlemen were always useful, and both William Marshal and the archbishop of Canterbury were seemingly prepared to advocate for de Lacy in the wake of the Irish war. This said, if Hugh was now readmitted to the *pax regis*, he was scarcely any closer to regaining his earldom than he had been on his return from Occitania. Indeed, he was initially worse off, being offered nothing more by the crown besides an annuity of 200 marks, less than the 300 he had been offered in 1221.[317]

The subsequent revival of de Lacy's fortunes was only made possible by events outside his control. A noble's recovery could be brought closer by a shift in the political mood,[318] and it is hardly coincidental that Hugh's restoration to Ulster came just a few months after Henry III, who attained majority in January 1227, finally stepped out from the shadow of Hubert de Burgh. The second crucial factor was the reversal of royal policy regarding Connacht, which rendered the opposition of Hugh's affiliates to Áed Ua Conchobair no longer problematical. Richard de Burgh was confirmed in his grant of Connacht in May 1227 and the barons of Ireland massed for an expedition westwards.[319] We can be reasonably confident that among their banners and standards were those of Hugh de Lacy, who had been restored to his earldom and comital title after seventeen years in the political wilderness.[320]

316 Bothwell, *Falling from grace*, 178–81.

317 *Ann. mon.*, iii, 92 (Dunstable annals); above, 142.

318 Bothwell, *Falling from grace*, 185–6.

319 *CCHR, 1226–57*, 42; *CDI*, i, no. 1518.

320 *CCHR, 1226–57*, 36–7; *CDI*, i, no. 1505. Scutage was levied from those barons unable to join the campaign: *CDI*, i, no. 1581.

6

Restoration

Comes and colony, 1227–42

The chronicle of Matthew Paris reports a prodigy at Roche Abbey, Yorkshire, in 1236, whereby a ghostly company of mounted knights was seen to issue from the earth and array themselves as if taking part in a tournament. From the 'true account' obtained by Paris from the earl of Gloucester and others, it seems that the vision was seen even 'more plainly' across the Irish Sea, where, speaking to the psychology of the settler community in Ireland, the riders appeared, not equipped for sport, but 'as if coming from battle … severely wounded and bloody'. Beholding this supernatural host the people, seemingly more attuned to war than peace, 'fled before them in alarm, and betook themselves to the churches and castles, thinking that it was not an illusion, but a real battle'.[1]

By the time Hugh de Lacy was restored to the earldom of Ulster, in 1227, advances had been made by the Dublin administration in regard to communication, justice, finance and defence.[2] But we might doubt Orpen's assertion that the colonial community, for whom bloody violence was still a constant reality, had any sense that *pax Normannica* now reigned.[3] The 1230s saw the continued flexing of Anglo-Norman military muscle along familiar frontiers. The crown, meanwhile, continued to encourage factionalism as an extension of royal authority. It has been asserted that Henry III, blessed with a 'great aesthetic sensibility', had 'nothing of the cruel streak that was one of his father's many flaws'.[4] The implication of several leading magnates in the murder of Richard Marshal, however, shows that the royal apple had not fallen very far from the tree in regard to the promotion of 'aristocratic cannibalism'.[5]

In some ways, Hugh de Lacy's brand of power was now more assured than it had been before his exile. For the first time, Ulster's churchmen began to benefit from the earl's patronage, while the impulse towards self-promotion is tempered in Hugh's post-restoration *acta*, which make much less use of the

1 *Chron. maj.*, iii, 365; *Matthew of Paris's English history from the year 1235 to 1273*, trans. J. A. Giles (3 vols, London, 1889), iii, 367.

2 *NHI*, ii, 169–78.

3 Orpen, *Normans*, 279.

4 Michael Prestwich, *Plantagenet England, 1225–1360* (Oxford, 2005), 82.

5 Veach, 'Nobility and crown', 140.

majesterial plural or explicit dating clauses.[6] Instead, the earl sought to display his prestige in stone instead of parchment, commissioning new fortresses and religious houses. In 1205–10 Hugh had depended on his elder brother and the tenant community of Meath for support in consolidating his power. Now, the earl used the marriages of his own daughters as political currency, cementing new alliances within and outwith the Irish colony.

Overall, however, there is no real sense that lordship in Ireland had become any less demanding since de Lacy's expulsion in 1210. Robin Frame has claimed that inter-colonial and Anglo-Irish relations in the late 1230s 'were marked by a measure of harmony that had rarely if ever been known before'.[7] This would seem to overlook the less pacific state of affairs alluded to by Albert Suerbeer of Cologne, archbishop of Armagh (1240–46), who observed in 1242 that the two nations of English and Irish continued to 'persecute one other with an insatiable hatred'.[8] Alliance with Áed Méith Ua Néill permitted Hugh de Lacy to re-establish his position in Ulster in relative tranquillity, but the king of Tír Eógain's death in 1230 allowed for the appearance of new native leaders on the political scene and new challenges to Anglo-Norman overlordship. Despite the energy expended by the earl on defence, Ulster's frontier remained porous enough for the ascendant Uí hAnnluain to raid from Armagh as far as Antrim. In 1238 de Lacy was even temporarily expelled from his earldom by a coalition of disaffected satellite kings.[9]

Nothing better illustrates the different colour of the earl's lordship strategy than his diplomacy in the Irish Sea zone. In the first comital period Hugh had cultivated the Scottish crown as an ally in opposition to English royal policy. After 1227, de Lacy's rapprochement with Alan of Galloway set him at odds with King Alexander II of Scotland, disrupting Alexander's attempts to bring the autonomy of the Gallovidians to an end. As it had been before 1210, the nature of Hugh's relationship with the Scottish crown was to be his undoing. The improvement in Anglo-Scottish relations brought about by the Treaty of York (1237) made the earl of Ulster's political alignment with Gallovidian rebels diplomatically inconvenient for Henry III. Having basked briefly in the light of English royal favour, the years before his death would once again see Hugh consigned to the grey shade of the political periphery.

6 Appendix I, nos 19–30.

7 Robin Frame, *Colonial Ireland, 1169–1369* (Dublin, 1981), 62.

8 *Ir. cartul. Llanthony*, 25; Hogan, *Llanthony*, 307–9; Smith, *Colonisation and conquest*, 74.

9 *The poems of Giolla Brighde Mac Con Midhe*, ed. and trans. N. J. A. Williams, Irish Texts Society 51 (Dublin, 1980), 125–6; Smith, *Colonisation and conquest*, 53; Simms, 'O'Hanlons, O'Neills and Anglo-Normans', 79–80, and below, 199–200.

Consolidation

Rights, revenues and rivals

The charter effecting de Lacy's restitution to Ulster has not survived, denying us recourse to the specific terms by which Hugh was to hold his reconstituted earldom. The most pressing question, to which there can be no definite answer, is whether the crown had taken steps to prevent Ulster from passing to the earl's descendants. After Hugh's death, c.1242, Ulster would be taken back into the hand of the king and administered as royal demesne until 1263, when it was granted to the lord of Connacht, Walter de Burgh (†1271).[10] Three possible explanations for this reversion can be offered. The first is that the earldom was only granted for the duration of Hugh's life, but even for a magnate of such dedicated self-interest it seems almost inconceivable that de Lacy had willingly consented to the exclusion of his own progeny. In fact, the terms of the several post-restoration charters, which were to be observed by Hugh's 'heirs' or 'successors', would seem to imply that the earl fully expected his lands to pass to his kin.[11] Another possibility is that Hugh's sons were either illegitimate, and thus excluded from the succession, or predeceased their father. Two of de Lacy's sons, Walter and Roger, were alive in 1226,[12] but we hear no more of them afterwards, although one was perhaps the 'earl of Ulster's sone' killed in battle in 1239.[13] Even in the absence of male heirs, however, custom would have permitted the earl's daughters to inherit (as Walter de Lacy's female descendants did after 1241). That they did not do so must point to a third scenario: Ulster was re-granted to Hugh and *heredibus suis* in the normal fashion, as it had been in 1205, but these terms were simply disregarded by the crown in 1242.

The government had tightened its grip on the Irish liberties since de Lacy's flight from King John in 1210, and the earl could not hope to reclaim the same impressive array of jurisdictions with which he had been endowed in 1205. One of these was the right to try the pleas of the crown in the comital court. We have seen that this jurisdiction had been reserved in the revised charters issued for Meath and Leinster in 1208,[14] and in 1222 Walter de Lacy was appointed 'sheriff and keeper of pleas of the crown in his own lands, to answer therefore to the king in his court at Dublin'.[15] This restricted position, where the judgements of the liberty court were held subject to the supervision of royal justices,

10 See below, 175, 178, 204.
11 Appendix I, nos 19–22, 27–30.
12 Hugh's sons acted as hostages during the negotiations leading to his restoration: *Pat. rolls, 1225–32*, 75–6; *CDI*, i, no. 1372; above, 162.
13 *AClon.*, 1239.
14 See above, 56, 97–8.
15 *CCR, 1279–88*, 55; *CDI*, ii, nos 810, 1645; Otway-Ruthven, *Med. Ire.*, 159.

appears to have been analogous with that of the earl of Ulster after 1227. In 1309×10 it was found that Hugh had 'held the whole of Ulster exempt and separate from every county, and pleaded in his court all pleas which belong to justices and sheriffs'.[16]

But Ulster remained something of a special case. Against a general trend towards royal intrusion on private jurisdictions, the earl continued to preside over some serious crimes. Despite its prohibition in England, the trial by ordeal appears to have survived longer in Ireland, and judicial duel was still being used by archbishops of Dublin c.1257–63.[17] Somewhat earlier, before 1235, Hugh de Lacy granted Carlingford to his daughter, Matilda, along with 'judgement of hot iron and water, battle and gallows'.[18] Others would look back to a golden age of seigneurial liberty under Hugh de Lacy. In 1269 the king accused Earl Walter de Burgh of having wrongfully caused the archbishop of Armagh and the bishops of Ulster to answer in his court regarding their lands and other pleas belonging to the royal justices, 'as if they were subject to the earl, which they are not'.[19]Even the crown admitted uncertainty as to the earl's constitutional position subsequent to his restoration in 1227. After Hugh's death the king advised that de Lacy's manor of Nobber, in Meath, should be taken into the hand of the justiciar until he should be certified 'concerning the agreements made between the lord king and the same earl'.[20]

Restitution to Ulster offered a more immediate material advantage than the prestige of comital rank, providing Hugh with the regular profits of lordship denied him in the eight years since the loss of his Occitan lands. From the repeated petitions of those affected by de Lacy's Irish rebellion of 1223–24, we might be forgiven for thinking that Ulster was now little more than a wasteland. A very different impression is given by the inquisition taken by the justiciar in 1226 into the sums being recouped in Ulster by its steward, Robert de Vallibus.[21] Having previously been organised by cantreds, the record shows that the crown's demesne was now divided into five administrative territories, or bailiwicks: Antrim and Carrickfergus, in the south of modern Co. Antrim; Ards and Blathewic, covering the north of Co. Down, with the Ards peninsula; and Lecale, including Downpatrick and the southern part of Co. Down. The total sum for royal Ulster exceeded £900 in 1226, with the bailiwick of Antrim proving the most lucrative, at over £390. Carrickfergus and its vill, besieged by

16 *Cal. Carew* MSS, vi, 450.

17 Charles McNeill, 'The secular jurisdiction of the early archbishops of Dublin', *JRSAI* 45 (1915), 81–108.

18 Appendix I, no. 20; Bartlett, *Trial by fire and water*, 2, 24–5, 106–10.

19 *CDI*, ii, no. 860.

20 *Close rolls, 1242–7*, 23; *CDI*, i, no. 2616.

21 *RLC*, i, 205b; *CDI*, i, no. 1468.

de Lacy in 1224, rendered £230. The least profitable was Lecale, with just £62, but an impulse to blame de Lacy's war should be tempered by the fact that the bishop of Down's own extensive demesne lands must have been exempted from the bailiwick's account. There is no internal indication as to the time period being accounted for by de Vallibus, however, and so the annual sum which de Lacy could hope to recoup from his earldom remains a matter of conjecture.[22]

Hugh sought to supplement his comital income from an early stage. In August 1227 he was granted licence to hold three annual fairs: two in Meath, at his manors of Ratoath (21 July–4 August) and Nobber (10–24 November); and one in Ulster, at Carlingford (14–28 August).[23] James Davis has noted that the cost of hosting a fair could be significant, 'with regulation, hygiene, stalls and maintenance of the marketplace typically encroaching upon a lord's purse', although the outlay was usually outweighed by the benefits, including 'an outlet for demesne produce as well as income from tolls, rents, stallage and the profits of jurisdiction'.[24] The early evidence for fairs in Ireland is slender, but they appear to have operated on a relatively grand scale. In 1244 the royal seneschal in Meath was instructed to retain a range of goods from the fair at Trim, including wines, hides, wool, cloth, iron, wheat and dry oats.[25] A similar selection of produce was probably available at Hugh de Lacy's fairs at Ratoath and Nobber. As a sea-port, Carlingford could draw business from further afield, and merchants from important English trading centres like Bristol or Chester may have attended its fair.[26] In 1237 Hugh de Lacy was instructed to release merchandise seized from Scottish ships in his ports,[27] and the archaeological evidence points to trading contact with south-west France, from whence wine and green-glazed pottery were conveyed to Ulster.[28]

The reign of Henry III saw a proliferation of commercial licences, but those awarded to Hugh de Lacy in 1227 were remarkably liberal in scope. It was extremely unusual for fairs to run for a fortnight, and the grant of three such to a single beneficiary was unprecedented, reflecting either the degree to which de Lacy had restored himself in royal affections, or the earl's uncomfortable

22 Orpen believed the report to cover 'little more than a year prior to June 1226': Orpen, *Normans*, 409. This might be doubted given that Roger Pipard had rendered just £230 from Ulster for the period 1210–12: *Pipe roll Ire. 1211–12*, 53–65. By the late thirteenth century Ulster's annual revenue was around £500: McNeill, *Anglo-Norman Ulster*, 39.

23 *RLC*, i, 197a; *CDI*, i, no. 1544.

24 James Davis, *Medieval market morality: life, law and ethics in the English marketplace, 1200–1500* (Cambridge, 2012), 145–6.

25 *Close rolls, 1242–7*, 197; *CDI*, i, no. 2696.

26 A royal letter from 1251 mentions Irish wares being sold at Winchester by the burgesses of Southampton: *CPR, 1247–58*, 109; *CDI*, i, no. 3126.

27 *CPR, 1232–47*, 197; *CDI*, i, no. 2407.

28 McNeill, *Anglo-Norman Ulster*, 56, 92–3.

financial position.[29] Hugh's peers may well have resented his enfranchisement. One of the conditions for the licensing of fairs was that 'new foundations should not be a nuisance to neighbouring establishments (*nisi sit ad nocumentum*)'.[30] The two weeks of trade scheduled at Carlingford would almost certainly have impinged upon the franchises held by the burgesses of Drogheda and the monks of Mellifont Abbey.[31] Similarly, Hugh's fairs in Meath must have affected the volume of business conducted at Walter de Lacy's fair at Trim. Walter had even greater cause for resentment given that he was still heavily indebted to the crown, having been held responsible for the actions of his rebellious tenants in 1223–24.[32] As commercial franchises were held directly from the crown, Walter could not even use his status as chief tenant in Meath to claim any profits from his brother's fairs at Nobber and Ratoath.[33]

Much of the money gleaned from the earl's fairs must have gone towards rebuilding and improving Ulster's infrastructure. Barns, granges and mills were all required to set the economy on a firm footing, but Hugh's overriding concern was with defence, and the physical structures which acted as guarantors of security for those living under his sway. Razed by de Lacy in 1224, the castle at Coleraine was rebuilt in 1228,[34] a project more likely to have been directed by the earl of Ulster than by Thomas of Galloway.[35] Time and money were also spent in improving those fortresses which had been so easily overcome by King John's army in 1210. In doing so, the earl may have drawn upon his experiences of warfare outside the Irish colony. It was almost certainly de Lacy who updated the gatehouse at Dundrum and added the outer ward at Carrickfergus, with its own twin-towered gatehouse.[36] McNeill has pointed out that the gatehouse design at Carrickfergus, unique to Ireland in preferring circular to D-shaped towers, is also found at Chepstow, the seat of the Marshal lordship of Netherwent, in south-east Wales.[37] Previously thought to date from 1235–45,[38] recent work has shown that the gatehouse at Chepstow could have been

29 See those franchises granted to Richard de Burgh (1225), Nicholas le Petit (1226) and Nicholas de Verdun (1230), which were limited to seven days: *CDI*, i, nos 1310, 1381, 1830. One exception was the licence for a fortnight granted to Maurice fitz Gerald in 1234: ibid., no. 2182.

30 Davis, *Medieval market morality*, 145.

31 For these fairs, see *CDI*, i, nos 1550, 2881.

32 Hillaby, 'Colonisation, crisis-management and debt', 31–42.

33 I am grateful for the advice of Dr James Davis, Queen's University Belfast, on this matter.

34 *AU*, 1228.

35 Seán Duffy, 'The lords of Galloway, earls of Carrick, and the Bissets of the Glens: Scottish settlement in thirteenth-century Ulster', in David Edwards (ed.), *Regions and rulers in Ireland, 1100–1650: essays for Kenneth Nicholls* (Dublin, 2004), 37–50, at 45, and below, 172.

36 McNeill, *Castles in Ireland*, 88–92.

37 McNeill, *Anglo-Norman Ulster*, 27; David Sweetman, *The medieval castles of Ireland* (Cork, 1999), 58–9.

38 McNeill, *Castles in Ireland*, 88.

constructed as early as 1189.[39] If so, Hugh de Lacy could have seen the design at first-hand during his campaigns with Llywelyn against William II Marshal, and transplanted it to Ulster. More than a decade before de Lacy was warring in Wales, however, he had most likely been struck by the same innovative defensive design as part of the gatehouse of Porte St Honoré, incorporated into Philip Augustus's fortress at the Louvre, in Paris, not long before Hugh is likely to have visited the Île-de-France in exile.[40] Notwithstanding de Lacy's re-integration into the Angevin nobility, it remains an enticing possibility that the evolution of Carrickfergus castle after 1227 was modelled on the latest Capetian trends in architecture.

Perhaps the earl's greatest defensive undertaking was the construction of a fortress at Greencastle (Co. Down) on the eastern shore of Carlingford Lough, controlling the ferry crossing into de Lacy's estates in Louth, and providing extra security in the event that the king of Man should attempt to revive his claim to Carlingford.[41] Certainly constructed by the mid 1250s, we might follow McNeill's logic that a work of such magnitude should have left a trace in the royal records had it been begun by the crown, and so it is with reasonable confidence that we can date the castle's foundation to 1227–42, under Hugh de Lacy's supervision.[42] In fact, it seems likely that the fortress had already been built by 1237 to overlook de Lacy's vill of 'Heirinach' (later Greencastle), mentioned in a charter of the earl issued in that year to the Cistercians at Newry.[43]

The earl could not consolidate his position without money,[44] but neither could he impose his authority on Ulster *in absentia*. We have seen that Hugh's restoration was probably conditional on his participation in Richard de Burgh's hosting to Connacht in 1227. Two years later, in 1229, de Lacy was among the Irish barons summoned to join Henry III's continental expedition, being ordered to present himself, with five others (*se quinto*), at London on Palm Sunday in the following year.[45] In April 1230, however, Hugh's name was omitted from an extensive list of magnates (including his brothers Walter and

39 Rick Turner and Andy Johnson (eds), *Chepstow castle: its history and buildings* (Logaston, Herefordshire, 2006), 51–62.

40 Paul Duffy, 'The architecture of defiance', *Archaeology Ireland* 29, no. 1 (2015), 20–24.

41 This was another innovative structure, following the contemporary trend 'in not having a keep but relying on the curtain and its towers for defence': McNeill, *Anglo-Norman Ulster*, 22–7, at 27. See also, idem., *Castles in Ireland*, 88–91.

42 McNeill, *Anglo-Norman Ulster*, 23; Sweetman, *Medieval castles of Ireland*, 76.

43 Flanagan, *Irish royal charters*, 388–9; Gerard Stockman (ed.), *Place-names of Northern Ireland* (8 vols, Belfast, 1992–2004), iii, 45.

44 cf. Hugh's grant of common pasture to his burgesses of Nobber, on the understanding that they should undertake the expense of constructing a 'great causeway' between the castle and vill of Nobber: appendix I, no. 21.

45 *Close rolls, 1227–1231*, 255–6. Walter de Lacy was also instructed to come *se quinto*, and Maurice fitz Gerald *se tercio*, while the other barons were to simply to come *se alterio* or *solus*.

William) being granted security for their lands while on foreign service.[46] We can only infer that the king had seen fit to excuse Hugh from his obligation, the irony being that one of the most immediate threats to the earl's security was posed by others whose claims to portions of Ulster were under royal protection.

By the arrangements of May 1226, the lands of those installed in Ulster by the crown after 1210 were to be alienated from the reconstituted earldom, namely Alan and Thomas of Galloway; the royal *curiales*, William and Geoffrey de Serland and Francis de Bresne; and 'others' to whom King John had granted lands.[47] Of these, some fared better than others in competition with the earl. Sent to Ireland with William de Serland in 1223, Francis de Bresne had been awarded the fee which had belonged to William le Puinur in Ulster. Soon after Hugh de Lacy's restoration, however, Francis followed the king to Gascony and we hear no more of him in an Irish context.[48] In contrast, the de Serlands appear to have maintained their Ulster interests by forging new bonds with the earl's supporters, including the Shropshire family of fitz Warin. In 1305 Alan fitz Warin was impleaded by William de Mandeville in Earl Richard de Burgh's court at Carrickfergus. He then produced a charter of King John to William de Serland, Alan's great-grandfather, and a later charter to William fitz Warin, Alan's father.[49] We cannot know whether intermarriage between these two families took place during Hugh de Lacy's second comital period, but the record at least confirms that the de Serlands managed to preserve a foothold in Ulster after 1227.

The evidence surrounding the Gallovidian tenures is more ambiguous. Thomas of Galloway's lands may already have been overrun by 1224, when de Lacy razed Thomas's castle of Coleraine. An annuity of 100 marks, granted to Thomas in 1225 as compensation for his losses, went unpaid; in early January 1227 he complained again to the king of having being impoverished through carrying out the king's war in Ireland.[50] It would therefore be surprising if it was Thomas who met the cost for rebuilding Coleraine castle in 1228,[51] although it is only in 1241, when Hugh de Lacy granted his barony of Morgallion to the archbishop of Armagh, in exchange for land in the tenement of Coleraine, that we have definitive evidence of the earl's operation in Thomas of Galloway's portion.[52] The lands of Duncan of Carrick had not been expressly alienated from the reconstituted earldom of Ulster, but it is possible that he was implied in

46 *Pat. rolls, 1227–32*, 358–60.

47 *Pat. rolls, 1225–32*, 31–2, 75–8; *CDI*, i, nos 1371–4.

48 *CDI*, i, nos 1113, 1225, 1272; Frame, 'King Henry III', 39.

49 *Calendar of the justiciary rolls: or, proceedings in the court of the justiciar of Ireland preserved in the Public Record Office of Ireland*, ed James Mills (3 vols, Dublin, 1905), ii, 11, 63.

50 *Pat. rolls, 1225–32*, 5; *RLC*, i, 164b; *CDI*, i, nos 1334, 1473.

51 *AU*, 1228.

52 Appendix I, no. 30.

the general exemption of those 'others' enfeoffed by King John. The immunity would have been cosmetic in any case.[53] Hugh de Lacy had already awarded Ballygalley, near Larne, to one of his supporters in August 1224.[54] Duncan wrote to the king soon after complaining that nothing had been done by the justiciar to restore the land to him, and requesting that the king implore his representative to act in stronger terms.[55] There is no evidence to suggest that the earl of Carrick was able to recover his position in Ulster, and his estates around Larne would later pass into the hands of the de Mandevilles and Bissets, perhaps through Hugh de Lacy's patronage.[56]

The fate of Alan of Galloway's vast claim in north Antrim is less certain. McNeill has suggested that the region's later stability, evident by the time it emerged as the county of Twescard in accounts from the early 1260s, points toward Anglo-Norman colonisation directed by Hugh de Lacy after 1227.[57] The earl's grant to Robert Savage of land in 'Dalrod' (Dál Riata), the part of the later county of Twescard lying between the modern towns of Ballymena and Ballymoney (Co. Antrim), as well as his possible enfeoffment of William *Gorm* de Lacy around Ballymoney, lend support to McNeill's argument.[58] Even still, Hugh is unlikely to have been able to make early inroads on Alan's position. At the end of 1229 both Thomas and Alan of Galloway were summoned with other chief tenants from the Irish colony to join the royal campaign abroad, implying that they still had some kind of viable interest in Ireland.[59] The pivotal moment most likely came in 1229, with the marriage of the earl's daughter, Rose, to the lord of Galloway, as recorded in the Lanercost chronicle.

> Alan, the lord of Galloway, went with a large force into Ireland, where he took the daughter of Hugh de Lacy as his wife. On their return, the ship in which [he/she] was being carried was imperilled, [he/she] escaping with few others, the rest in it being drowned there.[60]

53 Duncan's position may have been similar to that of the king of Man, whose knight's fee at Carlingford was not specifically exempted, having already been reoccupied by de Lacy's forces.

54 See above, 157.

55 *RLC*, i, 615a, 640a; *CDI*, i, nos 1200–1.

56 See below, 192–3.

57 McNeill, *Anglo-Norman Ulster*, 22.

58 Appendix II, no. v, and above, 152–3.

59 Oram, *Galloway*, 124.

60 *Chronicon de Lanercost*, ed. Joseph Stevenson (Edinburgh, 1839), 40 (*Dominus Galweie Alanus cum ingenti comitatu profectus in Hiberniam ibi duxit filiam Hugonis de Lascy in uxorem. Unde rediens, navi in qua ipse continebatur periclitante, vix cum paucis evasit, ceteris qui in illa erant ibidem submersis*). For this late thirteenth-century Franciscan chronicle, adapted by the Augustinian canons at Lanercost, see A. G. Little, 'The authorship of the Lanercost chronicle', *EHR* 31, no. 122 (1916), 269–79. Rose may have been the same daughter of Hugh de Lacy entrusted to the wardship of Walter de Lacy in 1217: *Pat. rolls, 1216–25*, 49. For the view that the marriage could have taken

The entry is entirely ambiguous as to whether the union was part of a pre-arranged agreement, or followed from a confrontation between the forces of the earl and the lord of Galloway's *comitatus*. Either way, it does little to challenge the picture of aristocratic daughters in the thirteenth century as 'objects of exchange between male lineages'.[61] At least one member of the earl's inner circle accompanied his daughter across the North Channel. A charter from Bernard de Ripley, lord of Kirkandrews in Cumbria, to the priory of St Bees, lists 'Roesya de Lascy' as principal witness.[62] Among the other attestors we find both Lucian de Arquilla ('Luciano de Arkille'), who held from Hugh de Lacy at Dunover (near Ballywalter, Co. Down) and in the 'honor of Lober' (Nobber? bar. Morgallion) before 1210,[63] and one 'Robert de Lacy, *clericus*', of uncertain relationship to the earl of Ulster.

On de Lacy's part, rapprochement with the lord of Galloway is proof that the earl was willing to set aside old scores in the interests of security. For the lord of Galloway, although it probably meant relinquishing his stake in north Antrim, the revival of his political understanding with the earl harmonised with strategic interests in the Irish Sea province. Alan had backed the losing party in the dynastic struggle for kingship in Man, failing to prevent King Rögnvaldr's death at the hands of his brother, Ólafr, in 1229.[64] Oram has suggested that the loss of such an influential ally could have caused the lord of Galloway to make a friend of Hugh de Lacy.[65] But it may be that Alan hoped for more than the re-establishment of cordial relations across the North Channel. If Ulster had not merely been restored to de Lacy for life, and if Hugh had no legitimate heirs, Duffy has pointed out that Alan of Galloway stood to inherit the earldom of Ulster in the event that the earl predeceased him.[66] In fact, it would be Alan's premature death, in early 1234, which would see his father-in-law intrude on the Galloway succession.[67]

De Lacy faced no challenge to his authority from west of the Bann until after Áed Méith Ua Néill's death in 1230. Exactly what understanding existed between the two men is difficult to say, but the commemoration of Ua Néill in the annals of Connacht, as a king who 'never gave pledge or hostage or tribute

place as early as 1219, while Hugh de Lacy was still on crusade, see Stringer, 'Periphery and core', 93.

[61] The view of Georges Duby, as summarised in Theodore Evergates (ed.), *Aristocratic women in medieval France* (Philadelphia, PA, 1999), 1.

[62] *Reg. St Bees*, 98.

[63] *RLC*, i, 222b; *RLP*, 191a; *CDI*, i, nos 625, 704–5.

[64] McDonald, *Manx kingship*, 80–2.

[65] Oram, *Galloway*, 126–8.

[66] Duffy, 'The lords of Galloway', 45–6.

[67] See below, 191–5.

to Foreigner or Irishman',[68] is shown to be patently false by the Irish pipe roll of 1211–12, in which there are several references to fines and rents offered by Áed Méith to the English crown.[69] Simms also points to the later thirteenth century, when the de Burghs would demand material and military service from the native polities beyond the bounds of their earldom.[70] None of this is sufficient to prove that Hugh de Lacy acted as Áed Méith's overlord, however, and it is worth noting that, when the earl had tried to impose himself on Tír Eógain in 1206–07, his efforts had been unequivocally denounced in the annals as unsuccessful.[71] Perhaps the most we might say, following Simms, is that the dynamic between Ua Néill and his Anglo-Norman neighbours 'fluctuated from time to time between subordination and defiance'.[72] The picture is also clouded by the fact that after 1230 the 'Foreigners' – a group perhaps, but not automatically including Hugh de Lacy – chose not to place their weight behind Domnall, son of Áed Méith Ua Néill, but instead lent their support to the rival claimant to the kingship of Cenél nEógain, Domnall Ua Lochlainn.[73]

On Ulster's southern border de Lacy had regained Carlingford from the king of Man, but had still to contend with his brother-in-law, Nicholas de Verdun, whose long-running feud with the earl was no doubt fuelled by the latter's less than gallant treatment of his first wife, Lescelina, sister of Nicholas, whom de Lacy had abandoned at Carrickfergus in 1210. Lescelina was perhaps still alive in 1226,[74] but any notion of a marital reconciliation in exile would appear to be dispelled by the allegation in the well-informed Dunstable annals, that on the eve of his Irish rebellion in 1223, 'having dismissed his rightful wife, [Hugh de Lacy] took an adulteress to himself'.[75] Nicholas de Verdun had taken advantage of de Lacy's exile to expand his own territorial interests into provincial Ulster, granting twenty knights' fees 'in the south part of Armagh' to his son-in-law, Theobald Butler, c.1225.[76] Nicholas had also encroached on that portion of Uriel which Hugh claimed in right of his first marriage, and which was restored

68 AC, 1230.

69 *Pipe roll Ire. 1211–12*, 36, 66.

70 Simms, 'O'Hanlons, O'Neills and Anglo-Normans', 76–7.

71 See above, 61–2.

72 Simms, 'O'Hanlons, O'Neills and Anglo-Normans', 77.

73 *AU*, 1232.

74 In a charter of Walter de Lacy from 1226, acknowledging receipt of Hugh de Lacy's lands and castles, Lescelina is still referred to as Hugh's wife (*uxor*): *Pat. rolls, 1225–32*, 75–6; *CDI*, i, no. 1372.

75 *Ann. mon.*, iii, 91–2 (*dimissa legitima uxore, adulteram assumpsisset*). The identity of this *adultera* is not known, but perhaps some regret over the treatment of his first wife prompted Lescelina's inclusion in the dedication of de Lacy's grant to Newry Abbey (1237) '*pro...animabus comitissarum Lestelinae et Evelinae*': appendix I, no. 29. For Hugh's second wife, Emelina de Ridelisford, see below, 187, 198, 202, 208.

76 *Ormond deeds*, i, no. 863 (5), 366; Hagger, *De Verduns*, 66.

to de Lacy along with Ulster in 1227. Between 1220 and 1225 a charter of Nicholas to Henry de Wooton granted one knight's fee above Kane (bar. Upper Dundalk), where Hugh de Lacy had previously enfeoffed Henry de Audley.[77] De Verdun complained that his lands were laid waste during de Lacy's rebellion, but it is unclear whether he ever received the reparations which he sought.[78] In 1235, when Hugh quit-claimed his rights in Uriel to Nicholas's daughter, Rose, the agreement prescribed that all of de Lacy's tenants could continue to hold their lands in peace, except for those disseised by Nicholas for failure of service.[79] Hagger has argued that the clause alludes to fees transferred to Nicholas in compensation for the damages done to him in 1223–04.[80] Possibly, de Verdun's interests outside Ireland prevented him from obstructing de Lacy to any great extent after 1227. Nicholas was used by the justiciar to guard the marches during the expedition to Connacht in that year,[81] but he was otherwise preoccupied with his English estates until his death in 1231.[82]

We are further informed as to the conditions on Ulster's southern frontier by Hugh's charter to his daughter, Matilda, perhaps issued on the occasion of her marriage to David fitz William fitz William, baron of Naas (Co. Kildare), 1224×35, in which he granted:

> my castle of Carlingford with all its rights and appurtenances, with all the land which I had with [Matilda's] mother in 'Cole' (Cooley) and 'Ergalea' (Uriel) and in the cantred of Louth, with all their appurtenances. Likewise all the land of 'Machergallyng' (Morgallion), with the addition of 'Fithemunterrody' in the county of Meath.[83]

With the exception of his barony of Ratoath, in Meath, de Lacy was effectively relinquishing direct control over all of his territories south of, and including, his outpost at Carlingford. What occasioned such an extensive dowry? Simms has argued that 'disunity' arising from the struggle for succession to the kingship of Cenél nEógain, between 1230 and 1235, may have triggered Anglo-Norman expansion in Uriel.[84] Another interpretation may be proposed: before 1230,

77 *Chartul. St Mary's, Dublin*, i, 65; Hagger, *De Verduns*, 66. Kane was included in the list of Henry de Audley's possessions, as confirmed to him by the king in May 1227: appendix II, no. vii.

78 *RLC*, i, 643b; *CDI*, i, no. 1210.

79 Appendix I, no. 27, and below, 195–6.

80 Hagger, *De Verduns*, 67.

81 *Close rolls, 1227–31*, 28–9; *CDI*, i, no. 1581.

82 Hagger, *De Verduns*, 68–9.

83 Appendix I, no. 20. As de Lacy is not known to have held in Limerick, Otway-Ruthven suspected that *in can[tredo] Luuit* – 'in the cantred of Louth' – should be read in the place of *in comitatu Lim[er]it*, as rendered by the editor in *Gorm. reg.*: Otway-Ruthven, 'Partition', 405. For the cantred of Louth, see MacCotter, *Medieval Ireland*, 236.

84 Simms, 'O'Hanlons, O'Neills and Anglo-Normans', 77–8. Domnall Ua Lochlainn eventually killed his rival, Domnall Ua Néill, in 1234/35: *AU*, 1234, 1235; *AC*, 1235.

Áed Méith Ua Néill's sway over the native polities of north Louth must have allowed Hugh de Lacy to re-establish himself there with relative impunity. Ua Néill's death, and the subsequent weakening of Uí Néill leadership, may well have been to de Lacy's disadvantage, allowing for a reinvigoration of native opposition in the region. It may have been in this context that the earl saw fit to cede power in Uriel to his daughter and her husband, who, as a prominent Leinster tenant, was well placed to help shoulder the burden of lordship.[85] That Hugh was forced to quit-claim his rights in Uriel in 1235, however, would seem to indicate that his position had become untenable by that date. The probable construction of a fortress at Greencastle before 1237, in such close proximity to de Lacy's existing fortress at Carlingford, provides a further indication that the southern approaches to his earldom had been compromised.

Ecclesiastical patronage

In the first comital period the spectre of John de Courcy's lordship may have manifested in Hugh de Lacy a reluctance to sponsor the churchmen or religious institutions of his earldom. We see a marked difference in the years after 1227, during which de Lacy began to spread his patronage more liberally among Ulster's senior clergy, who appear by name for the first time in the earl's charters.[86] This is not to suggest that Hugh severed ties with religious communities outside Ulster with which he had a particular affinity. Before 1233 the earl granted a portion of his tenement of Donaghmore (bar. Ratoath, Co. Meath) to the canons of St Thomas in Dublin who had given him succour during the war of 1223–24, and who continued to guard and pray for the bodies of his father and mother.[87] Neither can we say with any certainty that de Lacy's relations with Ulster's churchmen were unblemished after 1227. As before, Hugh was confronted with an archbishop of Armagh who had every reason to be ill-disposed towards him. When Luke de Netterville died in April 1227, his successor at Armagh was Donatus Ua Fidabra (†1237), bishop of Clogher since 1218.[88] This was almost certainly the same Donatus who had been prior of St Mary's in Louth when, in 1205, that community had complained to the papal *curia* about encroachment on its property by one of Hugh de Lacy's knights.[89] This earlier incident may not have compromised the earl's relationship with

[85] Strongbow had awarded the cantred of Offelan (Ui Faelain), in north Kildare, to David's great-grandfather, Maurice fitz Gerald: Orpen, *Normans*, 336–7.

[86] Appendix I, nos 25–7, 29–30.

[87] Ibid., no. 26.

[88] *NHI*, ix, 274.

[89] *Pont. Hib.*, i, no. 63; *Cal. papal letters, 1198–1304*, 22; Gwynn, 'Armagh and Louth in the twelfth and thirteenth centuries', 31–2.

the archbishop, however, as in 1237 the 'lord primate Donatus' would attest de Lacy's charter to the abbey of Newry.[90]

Signalling a new era of co-operation with the church in Ulster, when de Lacy confirmed his vassal, Richard White, in his lands in Lecale (Co. Down), to hold from the Dublin priory of Holy Trinity (Christ Church), the grant was witnessed by both Thomas, bishop of Down (†1242), and 'W', prior of the cathedral church at Down.[91] It was probably not de Lacy who had originally endowed Holy Trinity with land in Ulster; there can be little doubt that Richard White's stake comprised part of the parish of Ballykinler, opposite Dundrum (Co. Down), which had been granted to the priory by John de Courcy, c.1200, to maintain a perpetual light for the cathedral church and its crucifix, the most venerated in Dublin.[92] If the bishop of Down was prepared to forgive de Lacy for the damage done to his property during the Irish war, for which Thomas was still seeking reparation in 1235, the incentive may have been provided by a new spirit of generosity on the earl's part.[93] Before 1234 Hugh granted to the bishop and his successors four carucates of comital demesne, with the land formerly belonging to John de Lennes (*alias* Leynes) and Richard fitz Serlonis, all in the Ards; with ten carucates in *Oueh* (Uíbh Echach, *alias* Iveagh, Co. Down), 'in a suitable place according to the oversight of his friends as well as of ours'.[94] It was possibly around the same time that the earl granted a fishing boat and net on the river Bann to the monks of St Patrick's at Down.[95] Certainly, the bishop of Down's association with de Lacy was more cordial than with the next earl of Ulster, Walter de Burgh, of whom Thomas would complain in 1269 that he was 'oppressed and harassed … with exactions which no earl ever demanded of his predecessors'.[96]

In terms of religious foundations, Hugh de Lacy's reputation has suffered in

90 Appendix I, no. 29.

91 Ibid. For White's charter from Holy Trinity, setting his rent at 20*s*., with the tithes reserved, and witnessed by Hugh de Lacy as earl of Ulster, see *Christ Church deeds*, ed. M. J. McEnery and Raymond Refaussé (Dublin, 2001), 81 (no. 238b). The Whites, later settled in bar. Dufferin (Co. Down), were probably de Lacy tenants in Meath, and perhaps synonymous with the family of 'Albus' who held around Donaghmore (bar. Ratoath): *Reg. St Thomas*, 28, 41, 59; Reeves, *Eccl. ant.*, 185.

92 Reeves, *Eccl. ant.*, 211–12. This was the same cross which, according to Giraldus, *testimonium perhibuit veritati*: *Gir. Camb. op.*, v, 128–9, 257, at 129.

93 *CDI*, i, nos 1264, 1360, 1492, 1685, 2275. The bishop's lands cannot have been completely wasted, as on 28 May 1226 Thomas obtained a licence to export corn, flour and other articles for a term of three years: ibid., no. 1377.

94 Appendix I, no. 19. The only place known to have been held by the bishop of Down in Iveagh was the early church site of Maghera, west of Dundrum Bay: Reeves, *Eccl. ant.*, 165n; *Med. relig. houses*, 198.

95 Appendix I, no. 25.

96 *CDI*, i, no. 2551.

comparison with that of his precursor, that most energetic of patrons. 'Unlike John de Courcy', McNeill has stated, Hugh 'founded no monasteries: although friaries were founded in his time in Ulster, their founders are unknown and they were the cheapest form of religious house'.[97] This ungenerous assessment does an injustice to the earl's outward piety after 1227. If friaries were relatively uncostly,[98] de Lacy's introduction of the Franciscans into Ulster is deserving of more attention than it has been given. McNeill's appraisal also fails to take into account the evidence pointing to the establishment of the Hospitallers in Lecale under de Lacy's patronage, as well as Hugh's desire to construct a new Cistercian abbey within the confines of his earldom.

Ware attributed the foundation of a friary at Downpatrick to the year 1240, and that of another at Carrickfergus to 1232, one year before the first certain evidence for a Franciscan community in Ireland, at Dublin.[99] No support was provided for this chronology, but the communities in question had certainly appeared by 1248, when the friars *de ordine Minorum* at Down and Carrickfergus were granted goods and garments to the value of ten marks by royal mandate.[100] According to the sixteenth-century *Annales Hiberniae*, however, there was already a community at Carrickfergus by the time of Hugh de Lacy's death and burial, c.1242, *apud Cragfergous in conventu Fratrum Minorum*.[101]

The evidence concerning the third Franciscan community, at Armagh, is also deserving of reassessment. The accepted date of foundation is 1264, when the annals of Ulster state that Archbishop Máel Pátraic Ó Sgannail made a ditch around the *civitas*, and brought Friars Minor to Armagh in the same year.[102] But in Hugh de Lacy's charter in favour of Archbishop Albert Suerbeer, from November 1241, the witness list is headed by two friars, Johannes de Alneto and Thomas of Barton.[103] These men are unlikely to have come to Ireland from Germany in

97 McNeill, *Anglo-Norman Ulster*, 27.

98 'Friary churches were generally long plain rectangles with few architectural details and little decoration': C. J. Lynn, Katharine Simms, T. G. F. Paterson, Donal Bateson and Michael Dolley, 'Excavation in the Franciscan friary church, Armagh', *UJA*, 3rd ser., 38 (1975), 61–80, at 65.

99 Sir James Ware, *The antiquities and history of Ireland…now first published in one volume, in English; and the life of Sir James Ware prefixed* (Dublin, 1705), 93–4; *Med. relig. houses*, 244, 247–8. The first Franciscans probably arrived in Ireland under the first minister-provincial, Richard of Ingworth, c.1231: Watt, *Two nations*, 177–80; C. N. Ó Clabaigh, *The Franciscans in Ireland, 1400–1534* (Dublin, 2002), 33–6.

100 *Close rolls, 1247–51*, 72; *CDI*, i, no. 2957.

101 *Chartul. St Mary's, Dublin*, ii, 315.

102 *AU*, 1264.

103 Appendix I, no. 30. Suerbeer, from Cologne, was awarded the archbishopric of Armagh through the mediation of the legate, Otto, after failing to secure the see of Riga. He spent much of his brief archiepiscopate (1240–46) seeking recognition of Armagh's rights and jurisdictions: M. T. Flanagan, 'Suerbeer, Albert (Albertus, Albrecht)', in James McGuire and James Quinn (eds), *Dictionary of Irish biography* (9 vols, Cambridge, 2009), ix, 143–4; Erwin Gatz and Clemens Brodkorb (eds), *Die Bischöfe des heiligen Römischen Reiches, 1198–1448* (Berlin, 2001), 647–8.

Suerbeer's company. Johannes, later bishop of Raphoe, probably belonged to the same family which provided tenants of the de Lacys in Meath, and whose representative, Adam de Alneto, witnessed the earl of Ulster's grant to the bishop of Down before 1234.[104] Thomas of Barton, whose patronym derived from an English manor belonging to the de Verduns, can also be tentatively tied to Hugh de Lacy. Arnold of Barton was the dapifer of Bertram de Verdun, and other members of the family might well have come into de Lacy's company through the latter's acquisition of de Verdun territory in Uriel.[105] If the Friars Minor had not yet been placed at Armagh by 1241, it is not implausible that the two Franciscan witnesses to the earl's charter in that year belonged to other communities in Ulster possibly founded under Hugh's direction, at Carrickfergus or Downpatrick. It seems that de Lacy, like John de Courcy before him, was staffing new religious foundations in his lordship with men from his own affective ambit.

After a decade crusading in Occitania, where he sponsored St Dominic's foundation at Prouille, it is somewhat surprising that Hugh made no apparent effort to install the Dominincans in Ulster, even though the Black Friars arrived in Ireland c.1224, a few years before their Franciscan counterparts.[106] This hesitancy is even more curious in light of the durability of Hugh's association with another religious order he had encountered on crusade. In 1212×15, binding himself as *confrater* of the order of St John, de Lacy had entrusted his property at Renneville, with his body and soul, to the Hospital at Toulouse.[107] Expulsion from Languedoc may have severed the connection with the Toulouse commandery, but Hugh's link with the Hospitallers appears to have been perpetuated in Ulster. Ware identified de Lacy as the founder of the order's preceptory at Castleboy (St John in Ards, Co. Down), which must be the *terram Hospitalariorum in Artea* mentioned in Hugh's charter to the bishop of Down as bordering on those of the bishop at Ardquin.[108] The foundation at Castleboy may even have represented one of the gifts which, according to the Hospitallers' *Usances* of c.1239, each *confrater* was bound to make to St John each year on his feast day.[109]

104 Appendix I, no. 19. In 1265 Pope Clement IV absolved Johannes de Alneto, 'a Friar Minor, living in Ireland, from the provision and mandate of Pope Urban, by whom he was appointed to the see of Raphoe, an incurable infirmity unfitting him for that office': *Cal. papal letters, 1198–1304*, 425.

105 Hagger, *De Verduns*, 43, 47, 156, 164–8, 170.

106 *Med. relig. houses*, 218–19. O'Sullivan asks whether the two Dominican foundations to appear in Ulster shortly after Hugh's death, c.1242, at Newtonards and Coleraine, could have been planned by de Lacy, 'as a tardy gesture of repentance for the lawless and evil life he had led': Benedict O'Sullivan, *Medieval Irish Dominican studies*, ed. Hugh Fenning (Dublin, 2009), 40.

107 Appendix I, no. 16.

108 Ibid., no. 19; *Ware's Antiquities*, 93; *CPR, 1340–3*, 508–9; Mac Niocaill, 'Cartae Dunenses', 422; Reeves, *Eccl. ant.*, 164–5.

109 Selwood, *Knights of the cloister*, 117–18.

It was the Cistercians to whom the earl considered making his greatest benefaction. In 1233 the order's general chapter considered a petition for the construction of a new abbey brought by the *nobilis comes Ultensis*. The business was delegated to the abbots of Grey Abbey (*Iugo Dei*), Inch (*Insula*) and Comber (*Cumba*), in Ulster, who were ordered to inspect the proposed location for the foundation and report back with their findings in the following year.[110] Possibly, now advanced in years, de Lacy was motivated by a genuine concern for his soul, but there is more likely to have been an element of *realpolitik* cloaked in piety. Hugh's earlier grant of Ballymascanlan to the abbey of Mellifont, 1195×1205, had utilised the Cistercian talent for colonising tracts of wilderness, placing the monks between his own property in north Louth and the Irish inhabiting the uplands and forests of Cooley.[111] An echo of the same strategy can be detected in de Lacy's petition of 1233.[112]

The death of Áed Méith Ua Néill in 1230 had further destabilised the region around the Armagh/Louth border in which Hugh de Lacy was already struggling to consolidate his extra-comital possessions. Moreover, whatever function the Cistercians had performed in regard to security for the remaining Anglo-Norman colonists had been severely compromised by the dispute which erupted soon after de Lacy's restoration in 1227 between Archbishop Donatus of Armagh and the monks of Mellifont. This centred on the revival of Armagh's claims to churches in Louth, in pursuit of which Donatus strenuously advocated the integration of Clogher diocese into his own ecclesiastical province.[113] Opposing the archbishop's plan was the former prior of Mellifont, Nehemias Ua Bracáin, forcing the monks of Mellifont into a choice between honouring their community's long-standing association with Armagh or supporting Nehemias. Most chose the latter, and when the abbot of Stanley in Wiltshire, Stephen of Lexington, made a visitation of the Irish Cistercian houses in 1228/9, by direction of the general chapter, he found Mellifont almost deserted and lying 'in a very bad and dangerous marchland between the English and the Irish'.[114] Elsewhere, writing to the bishop of Chichester, Stephen remarked that 'throughout the whole lordship of the Earl Marshal, or of lords W[alter] de Lacy and Earl H[ugh], his brother, there is no-one who resists or dares to

[110] *Statuta capitulorum generalium ordinis Cisterciensis, ab anno 1116 ad annum 1786: tome II, 1221–61*, ed. Josephus-Maria Canivez (Louvain, 1934), 116.

[111] Appendix I, no. 7, and above, 65.

[112] Fr. Colmcille's argument, that Ballymascanlan was the intended location for the abbey, is undermined by an incorrect dating of Hugh's charter to the same period as his petition to the Cistercian general chapter: Fr. Colmcille, 'Three unpublished Cistercian documents', *JLAS* 13 (1955), 252–78, at 253–5.

[113] Smith, 'The Armagh-Clogher dispute', 26–38; Watt, *Two nations*, 72–107.

[114] Stephen of Lexington, *Letters from Ireland, 1228–1229*, ed. and trans. L. W. O'Dwyer (Kalamazoo, 1982), no. 24.

make any move to rebel in any way at all against God and the commands of the order'.[115] Another of Stephen's letters confirms that monks at Newry, affiliated to Mellifont, had most certainly contravened the order's rules.[116] It would seem, therefore, that Stephen did not consider Newry – situated just north-west of Hugh de Lacy's manor at Carlingford – to be under the earl of Ulster's control.

It is de Lacy's obvious insecurity which provides the most convincing context for his proposed establishment of a new Cistercian abbey. Certainty is impossible, however, because the foundation never materialised. The general chapter's *statuta* for 1234 repeated the directive of the previous year, which was to be communicated by the abbot of Holm Cultram (mother house of Grey Abbey), in Cumbria. Still nothing had been done by 1235, when the abbot of Mellifont was entrusted with reminding the delegated abbots of their instructions. By 1236 the chapter's patience had been exhausted. It was found that the abbots of Inch, Grey Abbey and Comber, who had not reported to the general chapter about their commission, should be punished according to the laws set down in the Usages. However, if the abbot of Mellifont had been negligent in informing them of their responsibilities, the penalty was to be remitted.[117] There is no other indication as to why the chapter's wishes were not carried out, but the relevant abbots perhaps considered the chosen location for de Lacy's abbey to be uncomfortably close to that of their own houses, situated in a ring around Strangford Lough (Co. Down). While plans for his monastic foundation stalled, Hugh found himself caught up in events beyond Ulster, in which he would reprise the role he had made his own almost three decades before – that of the king's man.

Agent of the crown

The 'murder' of Richard Marshal, 1234

We have seen that relations between Hugh de Lacy and William II Marshal appear to have improved almost immediately following the conclusion of Hugh's revolt in 1224,[118] making it all the more difficult to comprehend the significant part played by the earl of Ulster in bringing about the demise of Marshal's brother and successor. Until the death of William II, in 1231, Richard Marshal controlled his family's lands in Normandy (at Longueville and Orbec), while maintaining an English interest in Buckinghamshire, Hampshire and

[115] Ibid., no. 69.
[116] Ibid., no. 50.
[117] *Statuta capitulorum generalium*, ed. Canivez, 130, 147, 158.
[118] See above, 160.

Northamptonshire.[119] As they had been for the elder William Marshal in 1205, Richard's French connections would prove to be a source of contention, and are problematic for those historians who have sought to portray him as a martyr for the cause of English liberty.[120] Tensions with Henry III emerged during the king's continental campaign of 1230, resulting in the seizure of Marshal's castle of Dinan, in Brittany. An unwillingness to sever ties with the *regnum Francorum* meant that Richard's succession was blocked by Henry III between Easter and August 1231.[121] This caused consternation among the lay and ecclesiastical communities in Ireland, to whom the king wrote on 31 May to explain his position.[122] We might suspect that Hugh de Lacy's sympathies initially resided with Marshal, being already ill-disposed towards Hubert de Burgh, head of the curial faction opposing Richard's succession.

In 1232, having been blamed for reverses in the Welsh march and on the continent, and for the poor state of the crown's finances, Hubert de Burgh was replaced as head of the royal council by the bishop of Winchester, Peter des Roches, recently returned from five years on crusade.[123] Overlooked in the division of de Burgh's estates, and cutting an ever-more isolated figure at court, Richard Marshal retired from court in the spring of 1233, and after a brief foray against Llywelyn ap Iorwerth in Wales, embarked for Ireland.[124] The renaissance of his long-standing advocate, Peter des Roches, gave Hugh de Lacy the chance to ingratiate himself further in royal favour, especially once Hubert's nephew, Richard, was replaced in the Irish justiciarship by Maurice fitz Gerald in August 1232.[125] Wary of Richard Marshal's increasing bellicosity, des Roches and King Henry needed allies in Ireland who could be relied upon to resist the lord of Leinster. To this end des Roches' nephew, Peter de Rivallis, was endowed with a series of privileges and offices in Ireland.[126] But de Rivallis's inexperience in Irish affairs was evident from the beginning, and native resurgence in Connacht

119 Daniel Power, 'Marshal, Richard, sixth earl of Pembroke (†1234)', in *ODNB*.

120 In Orpen's estimation, Marshal was a 'fearless knight, fighting for justice and the liberties of England against the autocracy of the crown and its alien advisers': Orpen, *Normans*, 315.

121 Power, 'Marshal, Richard, sixth earl of Pembroke'. For the view that King Henry was not unduly concerned about Marshal's fidelity at this stage, see David Crouch, 'Earl Gilbert Marshal and his mortal enemies', *Historical Research* 87, no. 237 (2014), 393–403, at 395–7.

122 *Pat rolls, 1225–32*, 435; *CDI*, i, no. 1892.

123 D. A. Carpenter, 'The fall of Hubert de Burgh', *Journal of British Studies* 19, no. 2 (1980), 1–17; Vincent, *Peter des Roches*, 259–309.

124 Vincent, *Peter des Roches*, 324–39. Marshal's chief grievance concerned Henry III's award of an extensive dowry to his sister, the widow of William II Marshal, which might have reduced Richard's English income by as much as a third: ibid., 327.

125 Ibid., 394–5. Hubert de Burgh had been justiciar of Ireland temporarily in June 1232: H. G. Richardson and G. O. Sayles, *The administration of Ireland, 1172–1377* (Dublin, 1963), 77.

126 *CCHR, 1226–57*, 166–7; *Pat. rolls, 1225–32*, 493–5; *Close rolls, 1231–4*, 102, 104; *CDI*, i, nos 1969–72.

almost caused Henry III to cross to Ireland personally in 1233.[127] The crown sought other willing agents of the royal will, and few other magnates possessed more expertise in the particularities of the Irish colony than the earl of Ulster.

If Hugh de Lacy's relationship with Peter des Roches commended him to the king, a prior affinity with the disgraced Hubert de Burgh may have counted against the earl of Ulster's elder brother, Walter.[128] When Richard Marshal made his 'reluctant lurch into insurgency'[129] in the summer of 1233, Walter's estates in the Welsh march were targeted by the rebels, but the lord of Meath was still among a group of barons compelled to deliver hostages to the crown as pledges of loyalty. Further, when Walter's castle of Ewyas Lacy was recovered from Marshal's forces, it was not returned to its lord, but instead handed over by the king to Peter de Rivallis.[130] The de Lacy brothers would both subsequently align against Richard Marshal in Ireland, but it does not automatically follow that they were of the same mind: the motive force for Walter was resentment over the permanent truncation of his Welsh hegemony; for Hugh, it was most likely the anticipation of reward.

The events leading to Richard Marshal's 'murder' on the Curragh (Co. Kildare) are well known,[131] but the earl of Ulster's complicity in the act is worthy of closer scrutiny. In early 1234, according to the contemporary chronicle of Roger of Wendover, a royal letter concocted by Peter des Roches and Peter de Rivallis was delivered to several of the barons in Ireland, including Hugh and Walter de Lacy, Maurice fitz Gerald, Geoffrey de Marisco and Richard de Burgh, requesting that they capture Richard Marshal *vivum vel mortuum* upon his arrival in Ireland, and further promising the division of Leinster among them.[132] While some details in Wendover's account can be called into question,[133] Peter des Roches had good reason to seek a swift resolution to the Marshal's rebellion, as English bishops sympathetic to Marshal's cause pressed the king to resist the

127 *Close rolls, 1231–4*, 315–18; Vincent, *Peter des Roches*, 385; Otway-Ruthven, *Med. Ire.*, 96.

128 See above, 143–5.

129 Crouch, 'Earl Gilbert Marshal', 397.

130 Veach, *Lordship*, 215–16.

131 Orpen, *Normans*, 310–18; Crooks, 'Divide and rule', 292–6.

132 *Flores hist.*, iii, 72–3; *Flowers of history*, ii, 582; Bertie Wilkinson, 'The council and the crisis of 1233–4', *Bulletin of the John Rylands Library* 27 (1942–3), 384–93. Wendover's account of the Marshal affair (*Flores hist.*, iii, 80–7) is amplified by his successor as official chronicler at St Albans, Matthew Paris: *Chron. maj.*, iii, 273–9, 289–90.

133 Such as the assertion that Geoffrey de Marisco refused to fight for Marshal because 'my wife is the sister of Hugh de Lacy and therefore I cannot fight against him with whom I am allied': *Flores hist.*, iii, 83; *Flowers of history*, ii, 589. There is no supporting evidence for this marriage, or Hugh de Lacy's alliance with de Marisco, who was taken prisoner at the Curragh: *CDI*, i, nos 2119, 2222, 2300; Orpen, *Normans*, 312, 314. During Hugh's rebellion of 1223–4, William Marshal asked that the king commend de Marisco, who had not conspired with the rebels (*H[ugoni] de Lascy et ipsius fautoribus nullum habuit consensum*): *Royal letters Hen. III*, i, 500; *CDI*, i, no. 1203.

influence of his 'alien' counsellors.[134] Wendover goes on to say that the recipients of the royal communiqué invaded Marshal's Irish lordship and carved it up among themselves.[135] There is nothing else to suggest such early intervention, and the Irish annals place the beginning of the war between the 'Foreigners' after Marshal's crossing to Ireland in early February.[136]

In any case, Hugh de Lacy was with the royal faction which subsequently marched on Leinster,[137] and the Irish pipe roll for 19 Henry III (29 September 1234 to 29 September 1235), now lost, alluded to horses delivered to the earl of Ulster for his use in the Leinster war.[138] It was Marshal who made the early running in the conflict, attacking Limerick and seizing castles in Connacht, in response to which the royalist faction, including Walter and Hugh de Lacy, attacked Richard's castle of Kildare.[139] The dramatic denouement came in early April: setting aside the colourful but untrustworthy detail in Wendover's chronicle,[140] it seems that fighting broke out during a parley at the Curragh, near Kildare castle, in which Marshal was killed or fatally wounded.[141] The outrage generated by the 'murder' in the wider aristocratic community can scarcely be overestimated. The earl of Ulster was denounced as a 'notorious traitor' by the (pro-Marshal) continuator of the annals of Margam,[142] while even an Irish commentator conceded that 'this was one of the worst deeds done in that age'.[143] If Peter des Roches had sought to engineer Marshal's downfall to save his own skin, the scheme backfired. In an attempt to distance himself from Marshal's death, the king ousted the bishop of Winchester and his creatures from court.[144] The expulsion of des Roches is often said to have ushered in a new era of personal kingship, but Henry had 'unquestionably proceeded *per voluntatem*' in his handling of the Marshal affair.[145] Privately, if the king had grown uncomfortable with des Roches' influence, he cannot have been displeased by the violent turn of events in Ireland.

134 Vincent, *Peter des Roches*, 429.

135 *Flores hist.*, iii, 73–4; *Flowers of history*, ii, 582–3.

136 ALC, 1234; AFM, 1234; AC, 1234.

137 ALC, 1234; AFM, 1234; AC, 1234; *Flores hist.*, iii, 82–3, *Flowers of history*, ii, 588–9.

138 *Thirty-fifth report of the deputy keeper of the Public Records in Ireland* (Dublin, 1903), 35.

139 M. J. Colker, 'The 'Margam chronicle' in a Dublin manuscript', *The Haskins Society Journal* 4 (1992), 123–48, at 140; Crouch, 'Earl Gilbert Marshal', 398.

140 *Flores hist.*, iii, 84–7; *Flowers of history*, ii, 589–92.

141 ALC, 1234; AFM, 1234; AC, 1234; MCB, 1234; Orpen, *Normans*, 312–13; Otway-Ruthven, *Med. Ire.*, 97; Vincent, *Peter des Roches*, 439.

142 Colker, 'Margam chronicle', 140.

143 AC, 1234; Crooks, 'Divide and rule', 292–3.

144 Vincent, *Peter des Roches*, 441–65. Des Roches was actually removed from office by 10 April, six days before Marshal's death: Wilkinson, 'The council and the crisis of 1233–4', 387n.

145 D. A. Carpenter, 'Kings, magnates and society: the personal rule of King Henry III, 1234–1258', *Speculum* 60 (1985) 39–70, at 41.

Hugh de Lacy had lost an ally at court in the form of Peter des Roches, but the earl of Ulster's conspicuous part in the Irish war was to count in his favour. In May 1234 Hugh was called to England with the bishops of Ferns and Meath to confer on the direction of royal policy in Ireland.[146] However, if de Lacy and his confederates had hoped to profit materially from Marshal's undoing, they were to be disappointed. There was no division of Leinster, and whatever had been seized by private enterprise during the war was soon surrendered. Despite his status as a clerical acolyte, Richard's brother, Gilbert, was swiftly granted seisin of the Marshal lands[147] and in September 1234 the earl of Ulster was instructed to release the castle of 'Cabry' (Carbury, Co. Kildare) to Gilbert's messenger.[148]

The negative corollary of Hugh's elevation in royal esteem was the damage to his relationship with those in his own affinity with links to the Marshal faction. Among those fined for having been against the king in 1234 were Hugh's son-in-law, David, baron of Naas,[149] and Henry Wallensis, who had been with de Lacy during his lean years on crusade and during the revolt of 1223–24.[150] Another of Hugh's affiliates may have gone to extreme lengths in defence of Richard Marshal's honour. In early May 1235, near Westminster, some men forced their way into a lodging house and murdered Henry Clement, a messenger of Maurice fitz Gerald.[151] The motive is not clear, but Matthew Paris attributed the killing to Clement's boast 'that he had been the cause of the death of Earl Richard the Marshal', whom he called 'a traitor and a cruel enemy of the king'.[152] A prime suspect in the crime was Geoffrey de Marisco, who was falsely rumoured to have betrayed Marshal on the Curragh.[153] Others believed to have been complicit in Clement's murder, as recorded on the close roll, included one *Walterus Sancmedl*; this was possibly the same Walter Sancmelle who had

146 *Close rolls, 1231–4*, 561; *CDI*, i, nos 2111–14. John of St John, the bishop of Ferns (1223–53), had been treasurer of Ireland from 1217 until 1232, when he was replaced by Peter de Rivallis: *NHI*, ix, 311. The bishop of Meath was Richard de la Corner (1231–52), a former canon of St Patrick's, Dublin: *NHI*, ix, 285.

147 *CPR, 1232–47*, 65–6; *CDI*, i, no. 2151; Vincent, *Peter des Roches*, 440–3; Crouch, 'Earl Gilbert Marshal', 400.

148 *CPR, 1232–47*, 70; *CDI*, i, no. 2175. For Carbury, see Orpen, *Normans*, 143, 330–1.

149 In a rare instance of G. H. Orpen having consulted administrative records then available in the Public Record Office of Ireland, the name of David, baron of Naas, was noticed in a list of magnates fined for their adherence to Marshal in the war, contained in the (lost) Irish pipe roll for 19 Henry III: Orpen, *Normans*, 315; *Thirty-fifth report of the deputy keeper*, 35.

150 *Close rolls, 1234–7*, 504; *CDI*, i, no. 2418.

151 F. M. Powicke, *King Henry III and the Lord Edward: the community of the realm in the thirteenth century* (Oxford, 1947), 740–59.

152 *Chron. maj.*, iii, 327; Powicke, *King Henry III and the Lord Edward*, 742. From 1235 Paris's chronicle is independent and draws from sources close to the centre of political events, including Hubert de Burgh and Peter des Roches: Gransden, *Historical writing in England*, 356–60.

153 See above, 184n.

fought for Hugh de Lacy in 1210, and again in 1223–24.[154] It has already been noticed that one of Walter's relatives had been an overlord of Archbishop Henry of Dublin,[155] whose niece was a daughter-in-law of Geoffrey de Marisco.[156] However, the possibility remains that Sancmelle was falsely implicated in the murder, especially considering that Walter would witness a charter of Hugh de Lacy in favour of Maurice fitz Gerald, Henry Clement's master, c.1236.[157]

Political affiliations had mutated significantly in the decade since Hugh de Lacy's Irish rebellion. In 1224 Walter II de Ridelisford, a prominent Leinster tenant, had taken the fortress of Ua Ragallaig at Lough Oughter against William *Gorm* de Lacy on William Marshal's behalf.[158] Ten years later, de Ridelisford aligned himself against Richard Marshal, being reproached by the king for extorting ransoms from prisoners taken in the Leinster war.[159] In April 1235 Gilbert Marshal complained to the king that de Ridelisford had occupied the vill of Comyn, *tempore ejusdem guerre*, and still retained it.[160] Walter's alignment was no doubt influenced by his tenure from the crown at Bray, near Dublin.[161] 'In Leinster, as elsewhere in Ireland', writes Brendan Smith, 'the pattern of conquest and land distribution engineered by the Angevin kings worked against strong honorial lordship and the possibility of effective rebellion'.[162] Whatever de Ridelisford's motivation in 1234, it is the background of confederacy against Richard Marshal which brings into focus Hugh de Lacy's second marriage to Walter's young daughter, Emelina (†c.1278), probably concluded around the same time.[163] Through this match, the earl of Ulster perhaps hoped to obtain the foothold in Leinster which Richard Marshal's destruction had failed to bring about.[164]

154 *Close rolls, 1234–7*, 180–1, and above, 76, 156n.
155 See above, 150.
156 Brooks, 'Archbishop Henry of London', 15.
157 Appendix I, no. 28.
158 See above, 158.
159 *Close rolls, 1234–7*, 166; *CDI*, i, no. 2253.
160 *Close rolls, 1234–7*, 70; *CDI*, i, no. 2255.
161 Orpen, *Normans*, 146, 315n.
162 Brendan Smith, 'Irish politics, 1220–1245', in Michael Prestwich, Richard Britnell and Robin Frame (eds), *Thirteenth century England VIII: proceedings of the Durham conference, 1999* (Woodbridge, 2001), 13–32, at 17. Highlighting the difficulty in inferring affinity from charter evidence, both Walter de Ridelisford and Maurice fitz Gerald witnessed an Irish charter of Richard Marshal dating from 1232: *Chartul. St Mary's, Dublin*, ii, 157, cited in Smith, 'Irish politics', 18; G. H. Orpen (ed.), 'Charters of Earl Richard Marshal of the forests of Ross and Taghmon', *JRSAI* 64 (1934), 54–63.
163 After her husband's death, Emelina received her dower from Hugh's lands and tenements in Ireland, except Ulster, which the justiciar was to retain in the king's hand: *CPR, 1247–58*, 425–6; *CDI*, i, no. 2663. She was subsequently constrained by the king to marry Henry III's cousin, Stephen Longespée: *Close rolls, 1242–7*, 60; *CDI*, i, no. 2600.
164 For evidence connecting the de Ridelisfords with lands in England controlled by the Pontefract

The reconquest of Connacht, 1235

The principal beneficiary of the Marshal affair was Richard de Burgh, whose loyalty restored him into royal favour. In May 1234 the king thanked de Burgh for his fidelity and stated his readiness to bestow an adequate reward. The prize was dependent on the advice of the 'beloved and faithful' Hugh de Lacy, who was called to court with Maurice fitz Gerald and the bishops of Ferns and Meath, and without whom the king professed reluctance to respond to the recent occurrences in Ireland, and the petitions of the justiciar and other barons. We cannot know exactly what council was given by the earl of Ulster, but with Anglo-Norman settlement under grave threat in the west, it appears that de Lacy and his fellow advisers recommended Richard de Burgh's restoration to his portion of Connacht, which was effected in September.[165]

The reverses suffered in Connacht since Richard de Burgh's suppression in 1232 were partly of the crown's own making. The two principal Irish claimants to the kingship were Áed (†1233), son of Ruaidrí Ua Conchobair, and Fedlimid (†1265), son of Cathal Crobderg. Having initially supported the latter, Richard de Burgh had taken Fedlimid prisoner at Meelick (Co. Galway) in 1231.[166] In August 1232 the king wrote to de Burgh demanding that he release his captive, whom he had treated disgracefully.[167] The royal intention appears to have been to use Fedlimid to subjugate Meelick, being held against the crown by de Burgh's forces, and to restore order to Connacht.[168] The policy was ill-considered, failing to take into account the propensity of Irish kings to use war against the 'Foreigners' as a legitimising strategy. In 1233 Fedlimid defeated and slew his rival, Áed.[169] He then used the opportunity of William *Gorm* de Lacy's renewed intrusion in Bréifne to lead a hosting into Co. Westmeath, burning the strongholds at Ballyloughoe and Ardnurcher. Then, with the king of Thomond, previously allied with the crown, he attacked the city of Limerick itself.[170] This affront to the crown demanded a strong response, and when Richard de Burgh set out for Connacht in 1235, he was joined by many of the other great magnates of Ireland. Mustered under the leadership of the justiciar, Maurice fitz Gerald, were Hugh de Lacy, leading a force from Ulster, and Hugh's

de Lacys, see Eric St John Brooks, 'The de Ridelisfords', *JRSAI* 81 (1951), 115–38.

165 *Close rolls, 1231–4*, 524–5, 561; *CDI*, i, nos 2112, 2114, 2189.

166 Orpen, *Normans*, 371–6.

167 *Close rolls, 1231–4*, 100–1; *CDI*, i, no. 1975.

168 Otway-Ruthven, *Med. Ire.*, 96.

169 *ALC*, 1233.

170 *AClon.*, 1234; *ALC*, 1235. For the death of William *Gorm* de Lacy, while warring in Bréifne, see *AClon.*, 1233.

father-in-law, Walter de Ridelisford, described by the Loch Cé annalist as *ard bharún Laigen* ('high baron' of Leinster).[171]

The spring/summer campaign, ranging from Loch Cé and the kingdom of Moylurg to the Atlantic coast, and from Thomond as far north as Tír Conaill, is described in vivid detail by several sets of annals.[172] War on such a grand scale could not be waged cheaply, and on 25 August Richard de Burgh was granted temporary respite from his fine for Connacht.[173] Arms, armour, horses and food had to be found for the 'many mail-clad Foreigners and great multitude of cavalry' making up the expeditionary force. A flotilla of ships and transports was constructed, with which the Anglo-Normans harried the islands of Clew Bay on the Mayo coast, while 'innumerable mercenaries' were hired to supplement the army, bringing 'great herds [of cows] with them … to meet the Foreigners'. Hugh de Lacy had perhaps exploited his familial link to the 'sons of Ruaidrí [Ua Conchobair]', who assumed command of these 'predatory bands'.[174] De Lacy's experience of siege warfare, hard-won in the crucible of the Albigensian crusade, may also have influenced the construction of stone-throwing engines for use against the walled enclosure on the island 'Rock' of Loch Cé.[175]

The maintenance of discipline was problematic with any force of such magnitude, and the leaders were anxious to avoid incidents which could exacerbate tensions with the local populations, or bring divine judgment against them. When some soldiers despoiled the Cistercian abbey of Boyle (Co. Roscommon), breaking open the sacristy and stealing 'all its valuable things', we are told that the expedition's leaders 'returned every article of them that was to be found; and they paid for the things that were not found'. Showing genuine or feigned deference to sacred objects had its practical advantages. Before the assault on the 'Rock' of Loch Cé, the Anglo-Norman leadership

[171] *ALC*, 1235. For the course of the expedition, see also AC, 1235; *AClon.*, 1235; *AFM*, 1235; Orpen, *Normans*, 372–3; Otway-Ruthven, *Med. Ire.*, 97–100.

[172] The most comprehensive accounts are found in *ALC*, 1235 and AC, 1235, but much of the detail is based on the contemporary Cottonian annals, which at the time of the expedition were being maintained at the Premonstratensian abbey at Holy Trinity island, on Loch Cé: see Freeman, 'The annals in Cotton MS Titus A. XXV', *s.a.* 1235; Robin Flower, 'The origins and history of the Cottonian annals', *Rev. Celt.* 44 (1927), 336–46; Gearóid Mac Niocaill, *The medieval Irish annals* (Dublin, 1975), 30–1; McCarthy, *Irish annals*, 15–16, 245–60.

[173] *Close rolls, 1234–7*, 134; *CDI*, i, no. 2283.

[174] *ALC*, 1235.

[175] *ALC*, 328, *s. a.* 1235; Freeman, 'The annals in Cotton MS Titus A. XXV', *s.a.* 1235; AC, 1235. The word *pirrél* indicates a small traction-trebuchet, while *gaillér* derives from the French *galerie*, a covered gallery protecting the siege-crew: Orpen, *Normans*, 373n; eDIL (Electronic dictionary of the Irish language), letters G, col. 23; P, col. 189 (http://www.dil.ie); Kieran O'Conor, Niall Brady, Anne Connon and Carlos Fidalgo-Romo, 'The Rock of Lough Cé, co. Roscommon', in Thomas Finan (ed.), *Medieval Lough Cé* (Dublin, 2010), 15–40. For the use and typology of siege engines in the Albigensian crusade, see Marvin, *Occitan war*, 48–9, 78, 110, 134, 301.

offered a general protection to Clarus, archdeacon of Elphin, and the canons residing on Trinity Island, in Loch Cé, and 'the chiefs of the Foreigners, went to see that place, and to pray there, and to show respect to it, in honour of the Holy Trinity'. The gesture earned the friendship of the archdeacon, who would later engineer the escape of the Anglo-Norman garrison placed at Loch Cé.[176]

In the aftermath of the campaign Richard de Burgh's claim to the greatest part of Connacht was acknowledged by Fedlimid, who in turn agreed to hold the 'king's cantreds' in Roscommon from the crown at a fixed rent.[177] Those who had aided de Burgh in his recovery were rewarded for their exertions with generous portions of his stake. Hugh de Lacy's leading role in the campaign is perhaps reflected in his own substantial award of five cantreds, comprising most of the modern county of Sligo – 'Korn' (Corran), 'Karbridrumclef' (Carbury-Drumcliff), 'Tirfichre Omoly' (Tireragh on the Moy), 'Lune' (Luigne) and 'Clefluueth' (Slieve Lugha) – for the service of ten knights and 100 marks of silver annually.[178] At first, responsibility for administering these new territories appears to have been delegated to Walter Hose, to whom the earl granted the marshalship and one cantred of his land in Connacht, on the occasion of Walter's marriage to Hugh's daughter, Avicia.[179]

One of the most perplexing aspects of the earl's lordship strategy after 1227 is that, despite the arrangement with Walter Hose and the fulfilment of Hugh's ambitions in the west, first fuelled by the grant made to him by the Lord John before 1199, Hugh appears to have granted away all of his stake in Connacht almost immediately after securing it.[180] To Maurice fitz Gerald de Lacy gave Carbury-Drumcliff and the northern part of Luigne.[181] Jordan of Exeter came to hold the southern portion of Luigne, half of which was granted by Jordan to Maurice fitz Gerald, c.1240. Corran would be held by Gerald de Prendergast, and Tireragh by Piers de Bermingham.[182] Most intriguingly, Slieve Lugha came into the possession of Miles de Angulo, with whose family Hugh had hitherto enjoyed a less than cordial association.[183] Under the year 1259 the annals of Loch Cé record the death of 'the daughter of the Ultonian earl', further identified in the entry as 'the wife of Milidh Mac Goisdelbh (Miles Mac Costello, *alias* de Angulo)'.[184] There does not seem to be any obstacle to Orpen's

[176] *ALC*, 1235; Freeman, 'The annals in Cotton MS Titus A. XXV', *s.a.* 1235.

[177] Otway-Ruthven, *Med. Ire.*, 99; Orpen, *Normans*, 373–4.

[178] *Gorm. reg.*, 143, 191; Orpen, *Normans*, 378–9; MacCotter, *Medieval Ireland*, 132–3, 137, 139, 146, 149–50.

[179] Appendix I, no. 22.

[180] *Rot. chart*, 139b–140a; *CDI*, i, no. 241.

[181] Appendix I, no. 28, II, no. x.

[182] For the distribution of Connacht, see Orpen, *Normans*, 379–82.

[183] Ibid., 382; above, 16–17, 152–4.

[184] *ALC*, 1259.

'probable conjecture' that the presumed grant of Lugha was made on the occasion of Miles' marriage to a daughter of Hugh de Lacy.[185] It may be that the union represented some kind of settlement over de Lacy's barony of Morgallion, which had first been held by the de Angulos. In any case, the alliance was surely only made possible by the death of William *Gorm* de Lacy, the de Angulos' competitor in Bréifne, in 1233.[186] Relinquishment of his Connacht lands helped Hugh to solidify ties with others in the Anglo-Norman aristocratic community. But another influential factor on the earl's munificence may have been the more urgent requirement of his resources and energy elsewhere.

Reverses and decline

The Galloway succession and the Treaty of York, 1234–37

The earl of Ulster's preeminence among the tenant community in Ireland endured until early 1237. On 25 April in that year de Lacy was summoned to court with Maurice fitz Gerald and Luke, archbishop of Dublin, to confer with the king *de agendis regis in Hybernia*.[187] However, the same year would also see the last appearance of the earl in the English chancery records until after his death, pointing to an apparent drift to the fringe of national politics. For what may have brought about this change, we must look again across the North Channel from Ulster, to Scotland.

The marriage of Rose de Lacy to Alan of Galloway, c.1229, signalled a new chapter in Ulster–Gallovidian relations, and underlined Hugh de Lacy's willingness to set old enmities aside in advancement of strategic interests, as first evidenced by his alliance with Áed Méith Ua Néill.[188] According to Matthew Paris, after Alan of Galloway's death in February 1234 it was the earl of Ulster to whom the Gallovidian nobility looked for aid against the king of Scots, Alexander II.[189]

> Several nobles and powerful men from the various provinces of the west, namely from Galloway, and the island which is called Man, and parts of Ireland, [assembled]

[185] Orpen, *Normans*, 382.
[186] Between 1231 and 1233 William de Lacy was held in high regard by the king, being used as a juror in the Welsh march and receiving gifts of wood from royal forests. He was also enfeoffed by Walter de Lacy at Britford in Wiltshire, perhaps at the king's behest: Frame, 'King Henry III', 37.
[187] *Close rolls, 1234–7*, 527; *CDI*, i, no. 2384. Whether de Lacy travelled to court or not is uncertain, and he was still in Ireland in September 1237, when he was instructed to release Scottish merchandise seized on his land: see below, 194, 195n. Hugh's charter to the abbey of Newry was issued in Ireland in 1237 (before October): appendix I, no. 29.
[188] See above, 157–60.
[189] *Chron. Lanercost*, 42, s.a. 1233 [*recte* 1234].

> through Hugh de Lacy, whose daughter had been married to Alan of Galloway, now deceased; that they all might restore Galloway to the illegitimate son of the said Alan, and annul the just disposition of the king of Scots, who had distributed the inheritance among [Alan's] three daughters, to whom it belonged by hereditary right.[190]

Hugh's link to the Scottish crown had been broken by William I's submission to King John at Norham, in 1209, but avenues were available for the earl should he have sought to re-establish contact with the Scottish court. De Lacy's old affiliate, William Malveisin, was still alive, but the bishop of St Andrews was by now of advanced age, perhaps infirm, and certainly detached from political life.[191] Hugh could also have exploited his familial link to the steward of Scotland, Walter II fitz Alan, whose Shropshire kinsmen had married a daughter of Hugh I de Lacy c.1175.[192] As previously stated, it was perhaps through the fitz Alans that Hugh II had encountered the earl of Lennox, Alwyn II (†1217), to whom de Lacy entrusted his sons in 1210, but there is no evidence that Hugh had any interaction with Alwyn's successor, Maldoven (†1250).[193]

De Lacy's principal diplomatic concern was to retain the favour of the king of England. Henry III's sister was married to Alexander II, but relations between the two monarchs were strained in the decade after 1227, as the Scots agitated for papal recognition of their ecclesiastical and secular independence from England.[194] The revival of Hugh de Lacy's alliance with Alan of Galloway is not likely to have sat well with the king of Scots. Alan's disastrous manoeuvrings in Man between 1226 and 1231 invited Norwegian attacks on the Isles, causing King Alexander to withdraw his support from his constable.[195] Instead, the king of Scots began to promote the interests of Alan's competitors in the west, principally the royal steward, Walter II fitz Alan, and his affiliate, the earl of Lennox.[196] Effectively, alignment with the Gallovidians set Hugh de Lacy against other potential allies in the Scottish ambit. The earl's Irish Sea diplomacy also affects how we perceive his secular patronage in the period after 1227. In particular, the closeness of the Bissets to the Scottish court in the 1230s, and their antipathy towards the ruling elite in Galloway, may imply that

190 *Chron. maj.*, iii, 364–5; *Matthew of Paris's English history*, i, 30–1. Thomas was married to a daughter of King Rögnvaldr of Man in 1226: *Chron. Mann*, *s.a.* 1226.

191 Watt, *Scottish graduates*, 374–9.

192 See above, 104.

193 For the earldom of Lennox in this period, see C. J. Neville, *Native lordship in medieval Scotland: the earldoms of Strathearn and Lennox, c. 1140–1365* (Dublin, 2005), 25–9.

194 Duncan, *Kingship*, 119–20; D. M. Williamson, 'The legate Otto in Scotland and Ireland, 1237–1240', *Scot. Hist. Rev.* 28, no. 105 (1949), 12–30.
14–16.

195 Oram, *Galloway*, 125–31; Stringer, 'Periphery and core', 95–7; McDonald, *Manx kingship*, 155–7.

196 Oram, *Galloway*, 133.

it was someone other than Hugh de Lacy who installed members of the Bisset family in Ulster, in areas once belonging to the Gallovidian lords.[197]

Alan of Galloway's unexpected death in 1234, without a legitimate male heir, presented an opportunity for the king of Scots to break up Alan's hegemony and bring pretensions towards Gallovidian autonomy to an end. Ignoring customary Gaelic succession law, by which even illegitimate sons were not precluded from inheritance, and the plea of the Gallovidian nobility to take the lordship into royal hands intact, Alexander proceeded to partition Galloway and the Lauderdale/Cunningham honor among Alan's three heiresses.[198] Hugh de Lacy's part in the ensuing and unsuccessful Gallovidian rebellion of 1235–37 is opaque, and Matthew Paris is the only contemporary writer to name the earl of Ulster as the orchestrator of resistance to Alexander II.[199] The chronicler of St Albans was conceivably embellishing the truth, seizing an opportunity to indict one of the villains of the Richard Marshal affair by associating de Lacy with the contravention of proper legal procedure and the questionable customs of the Gaelic nobility.[200] On the other hand, Hugh had a vested interest in the outcome of the rebellion: had Alan of Galloway fathered a male heir by his new wife, the earl of Ulster's grandson would have been well placed to succeed to the Gallovidian inheritance. Alan's death dispelled that possibility, but de Lacy might at least have pressed for a substantial widow's jointure.[201]

From a strategic perspective, Galloway's partition would jeopardise any help Hugh hoped to procure from the region in offsetting the danger to his earldom from Tír Eógain and the other native polities west of the Bann.[202] But the imposition of Scottish royal power in Galloway presented another threat to

[197] For an examination of the theories surrounding the Bissets' transplantation to Ulster, see Duffy, 'Lords of Galloway', 37–50.

[198] Oram, *Galloway*, 141–3; Duncan, *Scotland*, 530–1. For Gaelic law regarding marriage and inheritance, see Hector MacQueen, 'The laws of Galloway: a preliminary survey', in R. D. Oram and D. P. Stell (eds), *Galloway: land and lordship* (Edinburgh, 1991), 131–43, at 137–8.

[199] Other contemporary accounts are found in *Chronicon de Lanercost*, 42; *Chronica de Mailros e codice unico in bibliotheca Cottoniana servato, nunc iterum in lucem edita* (Edinburgh, 1835), 145–6. The latter is biased by Melrose abbey's links to Alexander II, but may have been based on a Cistercian account compiled in Galloway: Oram, *Galloway*, 143. See also, *The chronicle of Melrose Abbey*, 1–13.

[200] Paris describes a blood-drinking ritual entered into by the Gallovidians and their allies: *Chron. maj.*, iii, 365.

[201] No such jointure is recorded, but it might not necessarily have formed part of the Galloway lordship, and 'it is not unlikely that [Hugh] de Lacy claimed Alan's Ulster estates as his daughter's dower': Duffy, 'Lords of Galloway', 46. Alternatively, Alan's widow may have been denied her dower in accordance with the customs of Galloway, which, being analogous with those used in Gaelic Ireland, offered less protection to widows than did feudal law: see Gillian Kenny, 'Anglo-Irish and Gaelic marriage laws and traditions in late medieval Ireland', *Journal of Medieval History* 32 (2006), 27–42, at 36.

[202] Oram, *Galloway*, 144.

Hugh's security. King Henry's swift endorsement of Gilbert Marshal had not quite drawn a line under Richard Marshal's death, and fear of reprisals from the new earl of Pembroke would seem to contextualise the 'near state of panic' which afflicted the Irish colony in late 1235.[203] Hugh de Lacy was one of several barons to whom royal letters were directed, reassuring them that Henry would not suffer anyone seeking to attack or injure them in any way.[204] The Irish barons must have been especially concerned that Gilbert Marshal would use his marriage to a sister of Alexander II, celebrated on 1 August 1235 with the blessing of King Henry, to recruit Scottish help against them.[205]

The earl of Ulster had multiple motives for intruding in the Galloway revolt, but participation in the concurrent Connacht campaign may have prevented him from providing the rebels with any direct support. Instead, assistance may have been given more circuitously. At a later stage of the rebellion, according to John of Fordun's fourteenth-century narrative, Thomas, son of Alan of Galloway, crossed from Ireland to Scotland with 'a king's son'.[206] Oram posits Thomas's companion to have been 'one of [Hugh] de Lacy's Uí Néill allies, with his military retinue, presumably a reflection of west Ulster interest in the outcome of the rising'.[207]

Initially, de Lacy's alignment with the Gallovidians harmonised with the interests of Henry III, whose relationship with the king of Scots had been strained further by King Alexander's repeated demands for recognition of his rights, as defined by the 1209 Treaty of Norham.[208] Henry's mood can only have grown darker on discovering that two of Alexander's commanders in the Galloway campaign, Patrick and Walter Comyn, respective earls of Dunbar and Mentieth, were implicated in raids on merchants and ships in the Irish Sea conducted by William, son of Geoffrey de Marisco, in 1236–37, with accomplices from Scotland.[209] However, while Hugh de Lacy and others were impounding Scottish merchandise and ships in Ireland on account of de Marisco's piratical activities,[210] King Henry was busy engineering a rapprochement with the Scots.

Alexander II's wrangling had become an unwelcome distraction as the English crown confronted the twin problems of baronial opposition to administrative

203 Otway–Ruthven, *Med. Ire.*, 99.

204 *CDI*, i, nos 2284–5; Otway-Ruthven, *Med. Ire.*, 99–100.

205 Oram, *Galloway*, 144; Duncan, *Kingship*, 120. This tense state of affairs endured until at least August 1237, when the Pope instructed a group of Irish bishops to enforce a peace agreed between Marshal and the barons of Ireland: *Cal. papal letters, 1198–1304*, 165–6.

206 *Chronica gentis Scotorum*, ii, 286.

207 Oram, *Galloway*, 144.

208 Duncan, *Kingship*, 118–20.

209 *CPR, 1232–47*, 187, 447; *CDI*, i, no. 2397; Duncan, *Kingdom*, 535–6. De Marisco conducted his piracy from Lundy Island, near Bristol: Powicke, *King Henry III and the Lord Edward*, 747–51.

210 *CPR, 1232–47*, 197; *CDI*, i, no. 2407.

reforms and acute financial difficulty.[211] With Gilbert Marshal rumoured to be negotiating sedition with Llywelyn of Wales and the king of Scots,[212] Henry had little option but to bring Alexander to the table. By the terms of the Treaty of York, drawn up on 25 September 1237 under the supervision of the papal legate, Otto, the king of Scots conceded any claims arising from the Treaty of Norham in return for lands in Northumberland and Durham worth £200 annually.[213] Having 'bought off' his counterpart,[214] Henry was anxious to avoid anything which might jeopardise the delicate peace initiated at York. However instrumental Hugh de Lacy had been as a royal agent in Ireland, the earl of Ulster's association with the disaffected Gallovidian nobility was now a source of inconvenience for the English crown.

With this in mind, we return to King Henry's confirmation of Hugh's charter to St Andrews, made just five days after the conclusion of the York negotiations (30 September).[215] It has already been suggested that de Lacy's original grant could have been preserved in the *instrumenta* relating to the Norham treaty of 1209, which were mutually restored at York.[216] In light of Hugh's interference in Galloway, Henry's endorsement of St Andrews's rights begins to look like a gesture of solidarity with the Scots. The implication of the royal confirmation, meanwhile, corroborated by de Lacy's subsequent disappearance from the chancery records, is that the earl of Ulster's brief resplendence in the light of royal favour had come to an end.

The last years: losses and legacy

Seemingly unknown to King Henry, by 1237 the churches of Cooley which had comprised part of the original gift to St Andrews were no longer situated in territory to which the earl of Ulster had a legitimate claim. In 1235, at the hospital of St Mary in Drogheda, Hugh had made an agreement with Rose de Verdun by which he quit-claimed his rights to the portion of the de Verdun lands acquired through his first marriage, saving the rights of his heirs after his

211 Willamson, 'The legate Otto in Scotland and Ireland', 16–17. During the Easter parliament in 1236 Henry was compelled to take refuge in the Tower of London: *Chron. maj.*, iii, 362–3. Around the same time the Holy Roman emperor, Frederick II, was pressing Henry for payment of his sister's dowry: *CPR, 1232–47*, 145.

212 *Chron. maj.*, iii, 372–3.

213 *Anglo-Scottish relations*, ed. Stones, 38–53; Duncan, *Scotland*, 533–4; Williamson, 'The legate Otto in Scotland and Ireland', 17–20.

214 Duncan, *Kingdom*, 533.

215 *St A. lib.* 119.

216 See above, 102. De Lacy was still impounding Scottish merchandise in his land by 28 September, when he was instructed to desist by the king: *CPR, 1232–47*, 197; *CDI*, i, no. 2407.

death, 'if they acquire anything out of the former agreement [with Thomas de Verdun]'. In return, Hugh was to receive £200, payable within two years, in installments of £50 each Michaelmas and Easter.[217] Walter de Lacy, who set his seal to the accompanying chirograph along with Richard de Burgh, was probably called to attest the 1235 agreement because he had orchestrated his brother's original concord with Thomas de Verdun before 1199.[218] Indeed, the lord of Meath may even have appeared courtesy of his own affinity with Rose de Verdun, whose daughter had married Walter's grandson and namesake (†1240) before 1235.[219] But if the nadir of 1223–24 ensured that the de Lacy fraternity never regained the levels of intimacy or cohesion seen prior to the brothers' exile in 1210, it appears that the pursuit of mutual political goals after 1227 led to some kind of reconciliation.

The murder of Áed Ua Conchobair, king of Connacht, in 1228, was said by one set of Connacht-biased annals to have been committed 'at the instigation of Hugo de Lacy's sons and of William [de Marisco]'.[220] As well as the prospect of rewards beyond the Shannon, influential on the lord of Meath's thinking may also have been the death in 1230 of Gilbert, his son and heir, whom Walter had associated with the management of his English interests.[221] In the face of mounting debts to the crown and assorted Jewish creditors, as well as his own growing infirmity,[222] Walter could ill-afford any further outbreaks of dissent in his Irish lands such as that fermented by his younger siblings in 1223–24 as he resumed direct lordship in England. In one gesture of goodwill, William de Lacy was granted the once lucrative manor of Britford, in Wiltshire, which had belonged to Gilbert de Lacy before 1230, and which had been used as security by Walter in 1231 against his debts to 'certain Jews'.[223] As a sign of renewed political interaction, both William and Hugh de Lacy witnessed Walter's conveyance of the church of St Patrick at Trim to the Norman abbey of Beaubec before 1233,[224] and the earl of Ulster was well-enough disposed towards his elder brother to join him in besieging Richard Marshal's castle of Kildare in the next year.[225] Moreover, it was more likely Walter, not William *Gorm*, who

217 Appendix I, no. 27.

218 Ibid., no. 4.

219 *Reg. St Thomas*, 420; Hagger, *De Verduns*, 72, 218–19.

220 AC, 1228.

221 See Veach, *Lordship*, 211–13.

222 For Walter's Jewish debts, see Hillaby, 'Hereford gold (ii)', 231–9. In 1237 Walter's proposed crossing to Ireland was cancelled owing to his ill-health: *Close rolls, 1237–42*, 11; *CDI*, i, no. 2451. According to Matthew Paris, Walter's death in 1241 followed his 'privation of sight and many other bodily afflictions': *Chron. maj.*, iv, 90.

223 Hillaby, 'Colonisation, crisis management and debt', 39, and above, 191n.

224 BL, Add. Charter 19803.

225 See above, 185.

was the '*dominus* W. de Lacy' appearing as principal witness to Hugh de Lacy's grant to Walter Hose (1227×1241).[226]

It is difficult to reconcile Hugh's quit-claim to Rose de Verdun with his anterior grant to his daughter, Matilda, which had included, with the comital castle and borough of Carlingford, 'all the land which [Hugh] had with her mother in 'Cole' (Cooley) and 'Ergalea' (Uriel)'.[227] It may be significant that Matilda's husband, David of Naas, had been on Richard Marshal's side in the Leinster war. Hugh's relationship with the de Verduns was hardly one of *bonhomie*, as demonstrated by the inclusion of an excommunication clause in the concord of 1235.[228] But as uncertainty continued to surround Gilbert Marshal's intentions in Ireland, de Lacy may have regretted empowering a Marshal sympathiser in Ulster's hinterland. The deterioration of relations with his son-in-law would also help to explain why, in November 1241, Hugh made a grant of Morgallion (Co. Meath) to Archbishop Albert Suerbeer of Armagh,[229] when he had already granted this barony to his daughter along with the de Verdun moiety.

Alternatively, de Lacy may have judged his earlier delegation of power to David of Naas, through his daughter, to be insufficient security for his earldom's borders. As suggested above, the death of Hugh's ally, Áed Méith Ua Néill, led to a loosening of Uí Néill control in Uriel and corresponding native Irish resurgence in the region. One of those to take advantage was the king of Oirthir (south-east Co. Armagh), Gilla Pátraic Ua hAnnluain. At some point before Ua hAnnluain's death in 1243, the poet, Giolla Brighde Mac Con Midhe, commemorated his military successes, including victories against the Anglo-Normans: 'East and west the settlements of the Foreigners of Ulster and Uriel were plundered by him; the settlements of the Foreigners of Midhe and their market, the chief of Line (Moylinny, Co. Antrim) were utterly plundered.'[230] The chronology is uncertain but it may have been Uí hAnnluain aggression which moved Rose de Verdun to build the fortress of Castleroche in 1236, close to Hugh de Lacy's former manor of Kane (bar. Upper Dundalk), something, it was noted at the time, 'which none of her predecessors was able

[226] Appendix I, no. 22.

[227] Ibid., no. 20.

[228] The party to break the agreement (and presumably an oath) would be excommunicated by Richard de la Corner, bishop of Meath, who set his seal to the chirograph.

[229] Appendix I, no. 30.

[230] *The poems of Giolla Brighde*, 125–6; Smith, *Colonisation and conquest*, 53; Simms, 'O'Hanlons, O'Neills and Anglo-Normans', 79–80. Giolla Brighde's poem aimed to assuage the anger of the king of Oirthir, who had previously been satirised by an unnamed bard; as such, Gilla Pátraic's prowess may be exaggerated. The 'chief of Line' was Ua Flainn Line, king of Uí Thuitri, settled to the east of Lough Neagh: *The poems of Giolla Brighde*, 303n. The market in Meath closest to Oirthir may have been that licensed to Hugh de Lacy at Nobber in 1227: see above, 169–70.

to do'.[231] Agitation in Oirthir might also have lain behind Maurice fitz Gerald's construction, as justiciar, of a new castle at the *civitas* of Armagh in the same year.[232]

If Rose de Lacy's transplantation to Galloway sustains the idea of medieval women as conduits of power, the experience of her namesake and heir to the de Verdun lordship betrays the ongoing involvement of women 'in the male domains of controlling property, dispensing justice, enforcing peace and waging war'.[233] Such a degree of agency was only possible outside marriage, however. As a widow, Hagger has noted, Rose 'had her own independent legal identity which would be retained provided that she did not marry again. She could inherit and administer her lands and bring lawsuits against those who infringed her rights'.[234] Although a surprising number of women did not remarry after their husband's death,[235] the more property and status they could convey to a new union, the more likely it was that the widow would be compelled into doing so. Rose de Verdun herself had been pressured by the crown to take Theobald Butler (†1230) as her second husband.[236] After Hugh de Lacy's death, in 1243 King Henry instructed Maurice fitz Gerald that if Emelina de Lacy would not take Stephen Longespée for her husband, as the king had requested, then Maurice should cause her to comply by distraining her.[237] This directly contravened the terms of Magna Carta (1225) which had preserved the clause contained in Henry III's 1216 version, also extended to Ireland, prescribing that 'no widow shall be caused to marry, while she wishes to live without a husband'.[238] Too much of the Irish colony was in the hands of heiresses for the rights of widows to remain inalienable.

By relinquishing his unprofitable and unmanageable estates in Uriel, in return for a money payment, Hugh de Lacy invited Rose de Verdun to re-establish Anglo-Norman control in the area south of Carlingford, leaving the earl to concentrate on improving his more northerly defences. It was perhaps

[231] *CCHR, 1234–7*, 364; *CDI*, i, no. 2334; Hagger, *De Verduns*, 78–81; Simms, 'O'Hanlons, O'Neills and Anglo-Normans', 77; Smith, *Colonisation and conquest*, 46.

[232] *AClon.*, 1236; Simms, 'O'Hanlons, O'Neills and Anglo-Normans', 78.

[233] Evergates (ed.), *Aristocratic women*, 5.

[234] Hagger, *De Verduns*, 72–8.

[235] Only 17 of 48 widows in the period 1225–1307 went on to re-marry: ibid., 83.

[236] *RLC*, ii, 60.

[237] *Close rolls, 1242–7*, 60; *CDI*, i, no. 2600.

[238] *Magna Carta*, ed. J. C. Holt (2nd edn, Cambridge, 1992), 504; H. G. Richardson, 'Magna Carta Hiberniae', *IHS* 3 (1942), 31–3. See also, Robin Dudley Edwards, 'Magna Carta Hiberniae', in John Ryan (ed.), *Féil-sgríbhinn Eóin Mhic Néill* (Dublin, 1940), 307–18. Possibly, King Henry intended the Countess Emelina's marriage to Longespée, later seneschal of Gascony and justiciar of Ireland (1258–60), to appease Stephen's elder brother, William II Longespée, whose long-standing claim to the earldom of Salisbury was finally denied in 1243: Simon Lloyd, 'Longespée, Sir William (II) (c. 1209–1250)', in *ODNB*.

around this time that work was undertaken on a new fortress overlooking the comital borough of Heirinach (Greencastle), on the northern shore of Carlingford Lough.[239]

A concern for security contextualises the generous charter drawn up by the earl in 1237 in favour of the Cistercian abbey of Newry. This confirmed to the monks there 'all reasonable gifts which Muirchertach Mac Lochlainn and Magnus Mac Duinn Sléibe and Murchad Ua Cerbaill and other lawful men before the advent of the English in Ireland, gave to them'; with the castle of 'Athcruthain' (Sheepstown, par. Newry); four burgages in 'Heirinach' (Greencastle), with twenty-four appurtenant acres, and fishery rights.[240] As at Ballymascanlan before 1205, de Lacy seems to have envisaged the establishment of a kind of ecclesiastical force field along the militarised frontier.[241] Such an extensive grant is indicative of urgency, an understandable mood in the context of Giolla Brighde's poetic celebration of the king of Oirthir, in which the Uí hAnnluain are described as having penetrated to the very heart of the earldom of Ulster:

> [Gilla Pátraic] took from Leath Cathail (Lecale, co. Down) with its white stones booty which disgraced the Ulaidh.
>
> He took great plunder from Magh C[o]bha (near Newry, co. Down); every man will have his trophy; he made a remarkable foray into the Aird (the Ards, co. Down); he plundered pale Magh Line (Moylinny) completely.[242]

These incursions, while uncomfortable for the Anglo-Norman settler community, were ostensibly directed against Irish targets. For the most part, the satellite kings of Ulster were content with a relationship of subordination to the earl, rendering tribute or service in return for nominal control over their lands and dependants.[243] But under the tentative understanding between the settler and native communities lay a thinly veiled hostility, and a simmering resentment on the part of the Irish towards their Anglo-Norman suzerains which could overspill at any moment. Alone among the annals, *Mageoghagan's book* records how, in response to an act of reckless violence by the earl of Ulster's men, Hugh

239 Appendix I, no. 29.
240 Ibid.
241 See above, 65.
242 *The poems of Giolla Brighde*, 127, 294, 304. The Anglo-Norman castle at Magh Cobha, in existence by 1211–12, may have been destroyed by the Irish during Hugh de Lacy's second comital incumbency, being rebuilt by the crown in 1252: G. H. Orpen, 'The earldom of Ulster (i)', 35; *Pipe roll Ire. 1211–12*, 60–1. For the identification of the castle with Seafin, on the Upper Bann, see H. C. Lawlor, 'The identification of the castle of Magh Cobha', *UJA*, 3rd ser., 1 (1938), 84–9.
243 McNeill, *Anglo-Norman Ulster*, 98–115.

de Lacy was temporarily expelled from his lands in 1238 by a confederation of disgruntled native kings:

> McGillemorie (Mac Gilla Muire), a good chieftaine of Ulster, was killed by some of the people of Hugh Delacie, earl of Ulster, as he was going to the earles house, whereupon Donnslewe (Donn Sléibe) the king of Ulster's son, Melaghlen (Domnall Ua Lochlainn) prince of Kinell owen (Cenél nEógain), and all the chieftains of Ulster took armes and banished the said earle of Ulster out of the whole province.[244]

The earl's emphatic response was to call together 'all the English of Ireland', with whom he 'went the second tyme to Ulster, where he possessed himself of all the lands again in the three months of harvest'.[245]

At this point *Mageoghagan's book* catches up with the other Irish annals in noting de Lacy's efforts to deal decisively with the threat posed by the king of Tír Eógain, Domnall Ua Lochlainn, who had ill-repaid the support previously given to him by certain among the Anglo-Normans by joining in the dissension against the earl of Ulster. With the justiciar, Maurice fitz Gerald, Hugh led an expeditionary force into Tír Eógain and Tír Conaill, expelling Ua Lochlainn into Connacht and setting up Brian, nephew of Áed Méith Ua Néill, in his stead.[246] The Anglo-Norman coalition also succeeded in taking the hostages of Cenél nEógain and Cenél Conaill, something de Lacy had failed to achieve in his campaigns of 1206–07.[247] It was probably also around the same time that, in return for his help against Ua Lochlainn, Maurice fitz Gerald was granted Hugh de Lacy's (purely nominal) claims as earl of Ulster over Tír Conaill.[248]

The earl's position was not yet decisively improved, and Domnall Ua Lochlainn managed to regain the kingship of Tír Eógain temporarily after the battle of Carnteel (Aughnacloy, Co. Tyrone) in 1239.[249] Hugh suffered an even greater blow when, in the same year, according to *Mageoghagan's book*, 'the earl of Ulster's sone was killed by the Ulstermen, and twenty eight men in shirts

244 *AClon.*, 1238. The murdered 'chief' was the king of Uí Derca Céin, settled in bar. Castlereagh (Co. Down): Orpen, *Normans*, 135. Where this information came from is unclear. While some post–1227 material in *Mageoghagan's book* (*AClon.*) may be derived from Maoilín Ó Maoil Chonaire's text, another annalistic compilation based on the same source (AC) does not contain the detail concerning Hugh de Lacy's expulsion. We might therefore tentatively conclude that the entry above represents an interpolation by Conell Mageoghagan, using as yet unidentified source material: see McCarthy, *Irish annals*, 287–93.

245 *AClon.*, 1238.

246 Brian Ua Néill would remain a nuisance to the crown in Ulster until his own death at Down in 1260, at the hands of Anglo-Normans, earning him the moniker *Brian catha an Dúin* (Brian of the battle of Down): Orpen, *Normans*, 415–19.

247 *AClon.*, 1238; *ALC*, 1238; *AC*, 1238; Simms, 'O'Hanlons, O'Neills and Anglo-Normans', 78.

248 Appendix I, no. 23. Along with the land already granted to him by de Lacy in Connacht, Maurice fitz Gerald now had a claim to an expanse of territory stretching from Sligo to Inishowen.

249 *AU*, 1239; *ALC*, 1239; *AC*, 1239; *AFM*, 1239.

of maile with him'.[250] This could have been Walter or Roger, de Lacy's sons who had served as hostages during the negotiations prior to his restoration in 1227.[251] But in 1241, at the battle of Caimeirghe (near Omagh, Co. Tyrone), Ua Lochlainn and many of his kin were killed by Brian Ua Néill, extinguishing the claims of the Uí Lochlainn to the kingship of Cenél nEógain, along with any encouragement being offered by Domnall to dissenting native factions in Ulster.[252]

The death of his son aside, de Lacy had some cause to feel satisfied with his work by 1242. The satellite polities within the bounds of his earldom had been subdued. Further west, one of his allies had been installed as king of Tír Eógain, while another, Maurice fitz Gerald, occupied the attention of Cenél Conaill as he attempted to make good on his gifts from the earl. Meanwhile Rose de Verdun was making inroads against the Irish in north Louth, providing respite for Hugh's garrisons along Ulster's southern frontier. The death of Walter de Lacy in 1241 cemented the earl's standing as the most senior magnate in the Irish colony, in terms of longevity at least. But Hugh had little time to enjoy his supremacy. By February 1243 he was dead, and the earldom of Ulster reverted into the hands of the crown.[253]

However many revolutions it had performed, the movement of the *rota Fortunae* was halted by death. But for contemporary writers like Gerald of Wales, if dying was a daunting prospect 'for those men whose attributes all seem to die with them', there was less to fear 'for those whose fame cannot die'.[254] The dynamism displayed by Hugh de Lacy in the period 1227–42 must be at least partly attributable to a concern for posterity. The foundation of fortresses or friaries left visible reminders of the lord's presence after his demise. Similarly, de Lacy's energetic prosecution of the crown's agenda earned him a level of royal recognition denied him since his departure from King John's court in the summer of 1205.

Might the earl have hoped for a more enduring legacy? His renaissance in royal esteem was fleeting, undermined by his activities in the Irish Sea province, and it was his elder brother, Walter, who was 'head of the council of the English in Ireland' by 1241.[255] No male heirs are known to have resulted from his second

250 *AClon.*, 1239.
251 See above, 162–3.
252 *AU*, 1241; *ALC*, 1241; *AC*, 1241; *AFM*, 1241.
253 *Close rolls, 1242–7*, 60; *CDI*, i, no. 2600; *AU*, 1242; *ALC*, 1243; *Annales Hiberniae*, 35.
254 *Expug. Hib.*, 48–9.
255 *AFM*, 1241.

marriage to Emelina de Ridelisford, and Hugh's sons from his first marriage were either illegitimate or predeceased their father. 'Who now will rule my lands and great honours after I am dead?', inquired the fictional count of Brabant in one recension of the *roman* of Guy of Warwick, revealing the aristocratic obsession with dynasty.[256] We might well imagine the ageing earl of Ulster pondering the same question, even as he relinquished his territorial claims in Connacht, Uriel, Meath and Tír Conaill. The answer, though perhaps de Lacy never knew it, was not his own progeny, but that of the king of England.[257]

[256] *Gui de Warewic: roman du XIII*[e] *siècle*, ed. Alfred Ewert (2 vols, Paris, 1932), ii, ll 7039–40, cited in Crouch, *Nobility*, 132.
[257] In February 1254 Henry III granted to the future Edward I all the land of Ireland, including Ulster: Michael Prestwich, *Edward I* (Berkeley, 1988), 11–14.

Conclusion

In the award of a comital title, the most coveted prize available to the Angevin nobility, Hugh II de Lacy had achieved something which none of his colonial peers had managed.[1] Even still, not even possession of Ireland's first earldom was enough to guarantee deference to his memory. While *Mageoghagan's book* provided glowing obituaries for the earl's brothers, William *Gorm* ('the hardiest and strongest hand of any Englishman from the Nicene seas to this place') and Walter ('the bountifullest Englishman for horses, cloaths, mony and goold that ever came before his tyme'), the same chronicle passed over the death of Hugh de Lacy entirely.[2] There was perhaps a sense, at least from an Irish perspective, that the earl of Ulster had not managed to surpass the achievements of his celebrated father. 'Hugo de Laci, earl of Uladh, *mortuus est*', is the simple statement in the annals of Loch Cé for 1243, with a telling explanatory note: 'He was not the first Hugo, whom Gilla-gan-inathair killed at Durmhagh-Choluim-Chille (Durrow), but the last Hugo.'[3] It was John de Courcy's conquest of Ulster which would burn brighter in the collective memory of the Anglo-Irish community, thanks largely to his very positive portrayal in the writings of Giraldus Cambrensis, which were widely disseminated among the later colonists. In the sixteenth century Hugh de Lacy (in fact, a loosely historical composite of Hugh I and II) is presented in the *Book of Howth* as a cypher for an intrusive English administration, purveyor of 'evil and mischief' and devious conspirator against that '*alter Ercules*', John de Courcy.[4]

It was perhaps safer to take personal charge of one's legacy. In a Gaelic lament composed for the 'Red Earl' of Ulster, Richard Óg de Burgh (†1326), the Irish bard professed regret that he was unable to follow his illustrious patron into death's vale.[5] Others were as effusive with their praise without pay. Friar Clyn's contemporary annals celebrated de Burgh as the very image of the chivalric

1 The next novel comital creation in Ireland was to be the earldom of Carrick, conferred on Edmund Butler by Edward II (1315). The other fourteenth-century creations were the earldom of Kildare, for John FitzGerald (1316); Louth, for John de Bermingham (1319); Ormond, for James Butler (1328); Desmond, for Maurice FitzGerald (1329); and Cork, for Edward of Norwich, earl of Rutland (c.1394).

2 *AClon.*, 1233, 1241.

3 *ALC*, 1243.

4 *Cal. Carew MSS*, vi, 87, 116.

5 *Catalogue of Irish manuscripts in the British Museum*, ed. S. H. O'Grady and Robin Flower (2 vols, London, 1926–53), i, 338; Miri Rubin, *The hollow crown: a history of Britain in the late Middle Ages* (London, 2005), 107.

lord: 'a prudent and witty knight, wealthy, wise and full of days' (*miles prudens, facetus, dives et sapiens, plenus dierum*).[6] It would be unfair to use the chance survival of subjective eulogies by annalists, bards or chroniclers as indicators of a career's success or failure. Nevertheless, it could be credibly argued that it was only under the de Burgh earls of Ulster (1263–1333), and especially under the Red Earl (1280–1326), that reality was given to Hugh de Lacy's pretensions of power.[7] Richard Óg was lord of Connacht as well as earl of Ulster, while Hugh's persistent attempts to make good on claims north of the Shannon had met with only the most fleeting of successes. For all his military dynamism, the boundaries of de Lacy's Ulster, defended by outlying fortresses, were not radically altered from those which had defined John de Courcy's twelfth-century lordship. Richard de Burgh's expanding hegemony, meanwhile, is evident from his new castles and acquisitions in Inishowen, as well as his retention of comital demesne in territories formerly controlled by the Irish.[8] At every step Hugh de Lacy's achievements are, on first appearance, eclipsed by those of the Red Earl. De Lacy's daughter married the lord of Galloway; de Burgh's wed the king of Scots, Robert the Bruce. Aside from a brief period in the late 1230s, Hugh's influence at the English court was never great, and his comital title was actively suppressed by the crown for twenty-two years. Richard de Burgh, once groom to Edward I, was reminded by the king in 1301 that he 'relies on him more than any other man in the land [of Ireland]', as 'his good servant' (*son bon nourri*).[9]

Lauded by Orpen as the true expression of *pax Normannica*,[10] Richard de Burgh's earldom of Ulster is held up by Robin Frame as the clearest illustration of the reality underpinning colonial Ireland after 1300: that 'power lay not so much within the clear-cut boundaries of units of royal administration as in the less stable and definable supremacies of the lords'.[11] In many ways, however, it was Hugh de Lacy who can be seen to have laid the foundations for the 'promising civilisation'[12] presided over by Richard de Burgh, prior to its wasting by the Scottish army of Edward Bruce (1315–18). Which components of this later comital autonomy were not present, at least in nascent form, under the

6 *The annals of Ireland by Friar John Clyn*, ed. Bernadette Williams (Dublin, 2007), *s.a.* 1326.

7 For overviews of Ulster under the de Burghs, see Orpen, *Normans*, 421–7, 500–59; McNeill, *Anglo-Norman Ulster*, 30–8. For Richard de Burgh, see Seán Duffy, 'Burgh, Richard de, second earl of Ulster (†1326)', in *ODNB*.

8 Orpen, *Normans*, 507–8.

9 *CDI*, iv, 849; Duffy, 'Burgh, Richard de'.

10 'In the time of Earl Richard, up to 1315, was comparative peace both in Ulster (in the large sense of the term) and in Connaught. The districts occupied by the English were no longer liable to the raids of Irish tribes … It seemed as if the *pax Normannica* was at last beginning to extend over the entire north of Ireland': Orpen, *Normans*, 513.

11 Robin Frame, 'Power and society in the lordship of Ireland, 1272–1377', in idem, *Ireland and Britain*, 191–220, at 195.

12 Orpen, *Normans*, 508.

first earl? There can be no doubt, as Frame suggests, that the de Burghs had an enviable 'jurisdictional independence'.[13] However, when in 1306 Richard Óg attempted to exercise authority over the crossed lands of Ulster, claiming '*dominium* of the temporalities, and certain services in the temporalities, which the king ought to have, and not the earl',[14] he may not have been making some novel assertion of comital freedom, but rather harkening back to the generous terms by which his precursor, Hugh de Lacy, first held his earldom from the crown.

Under Hugh de Lacy, just as in later years, the core of the *comitatus* was represented by the expanding proto-urban centres at Carrickfergus, Antrim, Downpatrick and Greencastle, from which the earl and his military tenants dominated the landscape and amassed the resources to wage war on their enemies. After 1263 the local Irish 'treated the de Burghs as their lords, holding their lands of them in return for a specified number of troops'.[15] This satellite relationship was more evidently one of formalised subjugation by the fourteenth century, but was hardly much different to the previous century, when the interaction between Áed Méith Ua Néill and Hugh de Lacy was akin to that of 'vassal and over-king'.[16] Frame rightly argues that the colonists' supremacy in Ulster 'depended on the presence, warlike energy and diplomatic skills of the earls',[17] but Hugh de Lacy's force of personality was no less compelling than that of his de Burgh successors. The murder of the 'Brown Earl', William de Burgh, in 1333, may have heralded the end of colonial ascendancy in the north,[18] but the earlier re-constitution of the earldom of Ulster for Walter de Burgh in 1263 was itself tacit recognition by the crown that its influence in Ulster relied on the brand of strong local lordship provided by Hugh de Lacy.

Viewed through a long lens, the period spanned by Hugh de Lacy's career constituted a unique epoch in the history of the Angevin colony. After the initial free-for-all which had marked the first wave of conquest, this was a time when private enterprise was still possible; when the extension of English law into the great lordships and liberties was not a foregone conclusion. The received view has been that the great freedoms of the first Anglo-Norman adventurers were

13 Frame, 'Power and society', 195.

14 *Cal. justiciary rolls*, ii, 195–6.

15 Frame, 'Power and society', 196.

16 Simms, 'O'Hanlons, O'Neills and Anglo-Normans', 77.

17 Frame, 'Power and society', 196.

18 Inquisitions held subsequent to William's murder, a crime thought to have been carried out by the de Logans and de Mandevilles, testify to the large numbers of once profitable manors and granges now fallen to ruin or abandoned: Orpen, 'The earldom of Ulster (i–v)'. Even in the earl's demesne at Carrickfergus, three carucates and forty acres 'formerly under the lord's plough and worth 4d. an acre', were now 'worth nothing, because they lie waste and unfilled owing to the destruction of the war of the Irish, and want of tenants': Orpen, 'The earldom of Ulster (i)', 137.

gradually undermined by their jealous royal masters. According to this paradigm all means at the crown's disposal – the encouragement of inter-baronial factionalism, the re-definition of legal jurisdictions in its favour or the extension of powers to royal deputies – were exploited in order to bring the constituent parts of the conquest more firmly under the king's control. The creation of the earldom of Ulster explodes the theory of consistent royal attrition of private power, in light of the fact that Hugh de Lacy was more liberally enfranchised than the notoriously autonomous John de Courcy. De Lacy's comital promotion also provides an antidote to the often parochial historiography on medieval Ireland, showing that the political context for key developments in the colony could be found far away from Irish shores. It was not John de Courcy's self-aggrandisement but that of the king of France, and King John's obsession with the continental war, which paved the way for Hugh de Lacy's belting in the splendid setting of a Whitsunday *coronatio*.

Events in Ireland, conversely, could resonate loudly at the Angevin court. At a time when the eighth centenary of Magna Carta is the topic *célèbre* among English historians, it remains to be seen how much attention will be retrained on the earlier legal summation transplanted to Ireland by King John after his Irish expedition of 1210, prescribing that (in Brand's words) English common law was to be henceforth recognised in Ireland.[19] It should be remembered that the definition of the legal framework was first brought about by the testing of its frailties and limitations by a combative colonial aristocracy, chief among whom in this period was the earl of Ulster. Nevertheless, it would be wholly incorrect to suggest that Hugh de Lacy and his cohorts were opposed to royal overlordship or institutions *per se*; de Lacy was equally content to fight in the name of the Capetian monarchy in Languedoc as he was to advise Henry III on Irish affairs. Much of the value of the comital title which Hugh so prized was located in its connotations of proximity to the royal personage. It was only when access to that dignity came under threat that the earl became politically dissident.

Unsurprisingly, for someone so dedicated to the attainment and recovery of personal honour, Hugh de Lacy's career causes us to look again at the question of identity. In an English context, David Crouch has pointed to a growing sophistication in the use of aristocratic insignia, heraldry and symbols, arguing that the dawn of the thirteenth century saw nobility becoming 'a matter of self-conscious expression'.[20] In Ireland, too, the language of power began to be voiced in individual cadences, and the capacity for self-invention is nowhere better illustrated than in the earl of Ulster's earlier comital *acta*, couched in quasi-regal style. As historians continue to debate the validity of

19 Brand, *Making of the common law*, 445–63, at 446.

20 Crouch, *Image of aristocracy*, 346.

terms describing different people-groups in the Middle Ages, the experience of Hugh de Lacy, who as earl or exile moved fluidly between allegiances and geo-political boundaries, reminds us that collective taxonomies tend to disguise the mutability of individual identities.

From the beginning the settlers in Ireland recognised that a certain cultural flexibility was vital for their political survival. Part of this acclimatisation involved inter-marriage with the greater Irish dynasties, and a familial link to the Uí Chonchobair provided the earl of Ulster with access to the cultural currency of the Gaelic world. Just as de Lacy could project the image of English courtly sophisticate by means of charter diplomatic, he could claim legitimacy as lord of Ulster by waging war in the manner of a marauding Irish king. For all the 'insatiable hatred' which Archbishop Albert of Armagh perceived between the 'English' and Irish nations in 1242,[21] it is remarkable that only one known insurrection against de Lacy's comital overlordship was made by the native kingdoms under his dominion (in 1238).[22] The earl's Irish connections were perhaps as powerful a statement of authentic lordship as John de Courcy's promotion of the Patrician cult.

In exile de Lacy took on yet another identity, joining the ranks of predominantly northern French, Christian warriors. As a member of Simon de Montfort's inner circle, de Lacy's prestige and seigneurial freedoms were naturally less pronounced than they had been as *comes Ultonie*. Nevertheless, it was only after the conclusion of the Albigensian crusade by the Treaty of Paris (1229) that integration into the kingdom of France began to reform Languedoc's reputation as the ideal setting for personal advancement through violence, a strategy so familiar to Hugh de Lacy as a frontiersman in Ireland. Had we only the list of prohibitions set out in the Statutes of Pamiers (1212), we might reasonably conclude that de Montfort's crusader-lords exercised only the smallest degree of autonomy over their hard-won territories. The remarkable testimonies later extracted by Dominican inquisitors, however, tell a different story. Whereas the ideologues among the crusade's leadership demanded the expulsion of heretics from God's land, under Hugh de Lacy the 'good men' and 'good women' of the Lauragais were merely kept at arm's-length, living within sight of their orthodox friends and families. Hugh's violation of his seigneurial remit underlines a feature of successful lordship often invisible in contemporary sources preoccupied with violence and the disturbance of peace, namely the sensitivity required of a lord to those under his dominion. While reasonable rule could be tolerated by a subjugated people, it was only after some of Hugh de Lacy's men unjustly murdered the king of Uí Derca Céin (Castlereagh, Co.

[21] *Ir. cartul. Llanthony*, 25.

[22] *AClon.*, 1238.

Down),[23] 'a good chieftaine of Ulster', as he travelled to the earl's 'house' in 1238, that a coalition of outraged native leaders effected de Lacy's temporary expulsion from his earldom.[24]

To his own advantage, Hugh de Lacy operated in the space between selves. The ability to choose one's identity, however, remained largely a preserve of the male aristocratic elite. On one hand, Rose de Verdun's energetic and successful competition with Hugh de Lacy provides support for the recent conclusion that 'it is no longer possible to depict well-born women as powerless in medieval society'.[25] Yet Henry III could still compel Hugh's second wife, Emelina, to remarry a man of the king's choosing; her decision to keep the name de Lacy, and with it the dignity of a countess, was the kind of small revolt against their treatment which aristocratic women could afford. Men and women could still be equal in the eyes of Fortune, however, with the fates of both genders being determined by the accident of birth. In the same way as Hugh II de Lacy could have felt unjustly supplied in the division of his father's lands, might the earl's own daughter, Avicia, having seen her sisters married to the lords of Naas and Galloway, have hoped for a better match than her father's marshal? For the most part, it is difficult to assess the agency available to those women close to the earl. Was it Matilda de Lacy or her husband, the lord of Naas, who truly wielded the ordeals of fire, water, battle and gallows over the manor of Carlingford? Was Rose de Lacy 'taken away' (*duxit*) across the North Channel by Alan of Galloway with force? Either way, Rose cannot have had much more choice than would Matilda, daughter of the Red Earl, first betrothed to the future earl of Louth, John de Bermingham, only to be selected by the earl of Gloucester's representatives, being considered more beautiful than her sister, Avelina.[26]

The corollary to the new stress placed on the thirteenth-century individual was the corrosion of collective identity, as part of political or family groups. By the late twelfth century the practice of tenants holding from more than one lord was already a destabilising factor in the English honorial structure, undermining the effectiveness of the territorial unit as 'a weapon of social control and local power'.[27] Across the Irish Sea a preoccupation with survival may have initially helped to preserve a sense of settler solidarity. Soon, however, the same fault lines began to appear in Ireland. The defection of the Ulster barons in 1204–05 had as much to do with Hugh de Lacy's and John de Courcy's overlapping affinities as with the threats of violence levelled by the king against their hostages. Just as in England, where 'tenants can be proved to have switched attention

23 Orpen, *Normans*, 135.
24 Ibid.
25 Evergates (ed), *Aristocratic women*, 4.
26 Duffy, 'Burgh, Richard de'.
27 Crouch, *Nobility*, 289–90.

when it suited them from one of their lords to another',[28] an approaching royal army saw some of Hugh de Lacy's most influential tenants abandon their lord. Even members of the earl's own family prized self-preservation over social bonds.

It would be a mistake to underplay the importance of the kin-group as a source of political support, and a study of Hugh de Lacy's affinity reveals a hitherto unrecognised degree of interaction between the Pontefract and Herefordshire familial branches, a solidarity fuelled as much by common ancestry as by shared political goals. However, the medieval *familia* was itself an abstraction, 'defined operationally'[29] and meaning very different things for different members at different times. Clearly, the mutual support provided by Hugh and Walter de Lacy in their early careers did not preclude later competition, catalysed by differentials in personal status and political objectives. It was from outside his own immediate kin-group that the earl recruited more loyal confederates. What caused members of the Sancmelle family, having chanced their lives and lands in support of de Lacy's first ill-fated revolt against the crown in 1210, to do so again in 1223? The earl's charisma must have played a part, as might the personal connections forged during Hugh's early career as a baron of Meath. Or, perhaps some members of the settler community with the least to lose simply saw in de Lacy, himself once an ambitious cadet, an opportunity to better their circumstances, no matter the risk.

Above all, Hugh de Lacy's career adds to our understanding of how magnates revolved on Fortune's wheel. A fast track to success might come in service to the king, sometimes at the expense of others. Even if nobles served the crown in the anticipation of some future reward, however, it is unlikely that Hugh de Lacy expected his conquest of Ulster to yield so glittering a prize as a comital title. The waxing or waning of a noble's fortunes could have little to do with his own personal qualities, as is evident from the political gamesmanship surrounding the Winchester *coronatio* in May 1205. De Lacy's swift estrangement from the king, meanwhile, shows how injured aristocratic dignity could cause a breakdown in crown/noble relations as easily as arbitrary financial demands or encroachment on baronial freedoms. When a lord's stock was low at court, he might look elsewhere for support. Ulster may have been vulnerable to the grasping of other lords of the Irish Sea world, but its littoral position granted Hugh de Lacy access to a series of useful alliances. Operation in this maritime arena, knit together by convoluted kin relationships, required careful negotiation: enemies of enemies were cultivated as friends; seemingly indefatigable opponents could become tools for future advancement. De Lacy's horizons stretched considerably further than the bounds of his earldom, his network of

28 Ibid., 285.

29 Bouchard, *Those of my blood*, 2–7, at 3.

contacts extending beyond the North Channel region as far as Orkney and Norway, underlining the fact that a restricted territorial purview was no insurmountable barrier to effective diplomacy.

❖

In Edwardian society the growing popularity of heraldic display went hand in hand with an ever increasing demand for illustrious lineage.[30] The deeds of Hugh de Lacy may not have been commemorated in bardic verse, as were Richard de Burgh's, but they must have been kept alive by his own colonial kinsmen. Once masters of Meath and Ulster, by the fourteenth century the de Lacys were peripheral figures in the Irish colony, whose most prominent representatives were the cadet branch settled at Rathwire (Co. Westmeath), descendants of the Robert de Lacy enfeoffed there by Hugh I after 1172.[31] In 1308 the heads of this collateral branch, Hugh and Walter de Lacy, were admitted into aristocratic society when, during a 'solemn feast' held at Trim (Co. Meath), they were knighted by the Red Earl of Ulster.[32] The event was a self-conscious, if pale imitation of the 'Feast of the Swans', orchestrated two years previously by Edward I, at Pentecost, when close to three hundred young men were knighted *en masse* by the king at Westminster Abbey.[33] For all their glittering appeal,[34] we might well wonder to what extent such occasions merely illuminated the glass vault separating the knightly and noble classes.[35] The newly knighted de Lacys must have been only too painfully conscious of their own humble positions relative to the lords of the great Irish liberties, both present and past. Possibly, Hugh de Lacy of Rathwire, knighted at Pentecost in 1308, was also aware that his ancestor and namesake had received his comital sword and charter from King John at the same festival, 103 years previously. Did the burden of lineage weigh as heavily on the latter Hugh as it had on the former?

If heraldry was one mechanism through which aristocrats displayed continuity with their lineage, another was to demonstrate that the same blood flowed through one's veins. In 1332 the mayor, coroners and sheriffs of Chester heard an appeal against the sentence of outlawry passed against Hugh de Lacy, 'knight of Ireland', for having supported the intrusion into Ireland (1315–18) of Edward

30 'Heraldry was a living presence. It was used to advertise the relationship between families, primarily through kinship and affinity': Cross, 'Knighthood, heraldry and social exclusion', 39–68, at 56.

31 *Deeds of the Normans*, lines 3148–9; *Song of Dermot*, lines 3150–1.

32 *Annales Hiberniae*, 55.

33 Strickland, 'Treason, feud and the growth of state violence', 104–8.

34 Cross, 'Knighthood, heraldry and social exclusion', 60–1.

35 Ibid., p. 68.

Bruce, brother of King Robert of Scotland.[36] Among the allegations levelled at Hugh were that he had harboured and brought troops to Bruce, engaged in mounted raids (*chivincha*) along with the Scots, with his banner displayed against the king's peace, and had committed 'arceouns, robberies et homicides' against the king's faithful men. After Edward's death at the battle of Faughart (1318), Hugh passed into Scotland with these felons, and stayed with them, for which he was expelled and outlawed from the king's lands by the process of law.[37]

The parallels with the plaintiff's ancestor, Hugh II, are unmistakable; indeed, so much so that it seems scarcely possible that the reputation of the first earl of Ulster – a two-time rebel whose alliance with the enemies of King John had led to his own banishment and flight to Scotland – did not influence the willingness of his fourteenth-century namesake to assume the role of political malcontent. Within medieval society there was always a 'strong current of opinion which disapproved of social mobility'.[38] Nevertheless, was Hugh II de Lacy's greatest legacy to the later colonists in Ireland a refusal to accept a place in a social hierarchy determined by birth? Ambition is the red thread running through de Lacy's career, as *juvenis*, earl or exile. What set Hugh apart from his peers and familial imitators, however, was not his drive, but the startling degree to which his aspirations were realised. Even more remarkable is that, despite the reversals of banishment and disgrace, those ambitions were fulfilled a second time.

[36] *CDS*, v, no. 726. Hugh and Walter de Lacy were first accused and acquitted of treason in 1315, but again indicted in July 1317: *Chartul. St Mary's, Dublin*, ii, 298, 407–12.

[37] *CDS*, v, no. 726.

[38] John Gillingham, *The English in the twelfth century: imperialism, national identity and political values* (Woodbridge, 2000), 259.

Appendices

The *acta* of Hugh de Lacy, 1189–1242

Appendix I

Extant charter-texts

Charter-texts are organised chronologically, on the basis of earliest possible issue (secure dates given without square brackets); in the case of matching chronologies, grants to secular beneficiaries are given precedence. Sources are indicated in the following manner: M (manuscript or archival source); P (Latin texts in printed volumes); T (translated versions); C (calendared versions). Dates of manuscript sources are indicated according to the following convention: s. xvii = seventeenth century; in. = early; ex. = late. As witnesses are indexed separately, information is only provided for those whose attestation has a bearing on dating. Punctuation, spelling and capitalisation are standardised, with the exception of the sole contemporary version (no. 16).

(1)

Hugh de Lacy confirms to Geoffrey Faber of Ratoath (Co. Meath), for his homage and service, Lagore (bar. Ratoath) with all its appurtenances, for one carucate of land as divided and perambulated in the time of grantor's father, Hugh (I) de Lacy, and with the same land that increase which grantor himself gave to him (Geoffrey). To hold by Geoffrey's heirs from Hugh and his heirs for the service of one tenth of a knight's fee, freely and quietly (etc.), in all liberties and free customs.

[1189×29 May 1205][1]

M: London, BL, Add. MS 4792, fo 188r [transcript in the collection of Sir James Ware, s. xvii].

[1] Absence of comital style. *Post quem* from Hugh II de Lacy's sub-enfeoffment by Walter de Lacy in bar. Ratoath and Morgallion (1189×91).

Sciant presentes et futuri quod ego Hugo de Laci dedi et concessi et hac presenti carta mea confirmavi Galfrido Fabro[a,2] de Rattoued[3] pro homagio et servitio suo Lochogoue[4] cum omnibus [pertin]ent[iis][b] suis pro una carucata terre sicut ei divisa et perambulata fuit tempore patris mei Hugonis de Lacy et cum continenti ejusdem terre illud incrementum quod ego ipse ei dedi, habendum et tenendum heredibus suis de me et heredibus meis in feudo et hereditate per servitium decime partis unius feodi militis pro omni servitio libere et quiete plene et integre in terris et hominibus in bosco et plano in pratis in pascuis in viis et semitis in aquis et molendinis et in moris et mariscis et in omnibus libertatibus et liberis consuetudinibus. Hiis testibus: Rob[erto] de Laci, Rob[erto] Flandrensi, Baldwino de Kair[merdin],[5] Elia de Sei, Stephano Pilate, Will[elmo] de Warewic, Willelmo Delmans et multis aliis.[c]

[a] M: marginal rubric 'Fabio' (nominative 'Faber'). [b] M: marginal note, 'vel tenementis, vel pertinentiis'. [c] M: note of 'sigillum Hugonis de Laci cum effigie armati'.

(2)

Hugh de Lacy, son of Hugh de Lacy, confirms to the canons of Llanthony all reasonable donations which his father had given to them in England, Wales and Ireland; and the church of St Peter of Drogheda in Uriel (Co. Louth), with all its appurtenances, and the church of Weobley (Herefordshire), and other churches and property which Walter de Lacy, grantor's brother, confirmed to them. Hugh takes the aforesaid canons and possessions under his protection and wishes his men and friends to uphold the aforesaid canons and their affairs in his court.

[1189×29 May1205][6]

2 'Faber' (nominative), deriving from the Latin for 'craftsman', is more likely than 'Fabius' (see n[a]), and is favoured in Eric St John Brooks, 'The grant of Castleknock to Hugh Tyrel', *JRSAI* 63 (1933), 206 20, at 215. One Galfridus Faber witnessed a charter of William Clut, a de Lacy tenant, granting the church of Killegland (bar. Ratoath) to the church and canons of St Thomas, Dublin: *Reg. St Thomas*, 45.

3 Ratoath (Co. Meath).

4 For the *crannóg* of Lagore (Loch Gabhair), an island-fortress and royal centre of the southern Uí Néill dynasty in the pre-Anglo-Norman period, see Hugh Hencken, Liam Price and L. E. Start, 'Lagore Crannog: an Irish royal residence of the seventh to tenth centuries', *PRIA* C 53 (1950), 1–247. In 1213 another de Lacy tenant, John fitz Leon, granted rights on the water of 'le Goure' to St Thomas's, Dublin: *Reg. St Thomas*, 282–3, and above, 127.

5 See below, nos 3, 5, 6, 11.

6 Absence of comital style indicates an *ante quem* of 1205. *Post quem* from Walter de Lacy's seisin of Meath, in 1189, after which time Walter could have made the grant(s) alluded to in the present charter-text.

M: *a*. Kew, TNA, C 115/80, fo 27 [cartulary, Llanthony Prima, s. xv in.].
b. Kew, TNA, C 115/75, fo 2 [cartulary, Llanthony Secunda, s. xiv. ex.].
P: *Ir. cartul. Llanthony*, 82–3, 216. T: Hogan, *Llanthony*, 248.

Hugo de Lacy filius Hugonis de Lacy omnibus ad quos presens carta peruenerit presentibus et futuris salutem. Sciatis me pro salute anime patris mei et matris mee et antecessorum meorum et pro salute anime mee concessisse et hac presenti carta mea confirmasse Deo et sancte Marie et sancto Iohanni Baptiste et canonicis de Lanthonia omnes racionabiles donaciones quas pater meus eis dedit in Anglia in Wallia et in Hibernia et nominatim ecclesiam sancti Petri de Druchdale in Vryel[7] cum omnibus pertinenciis suis et ecclesiam de Webbeleya[8] et alias ecclesias et possessiones quas dominus Walterus de Lacy frater meus eis confirmauit. Quare volo ut sciatis me esse protectorem et manutectorem prefatorum canonicorum et prefatarum possessionum suarum et volo ut homines mei et amici mei eos et res eorum in iure suo manuteneant. Testibus: domino Waltero de Lacy, Willelmo de Salcei, Nicholao de Dilun, Willelmo de Lacy, Willelmo de Warewyk, Roberto Fuget, Petro de Minton, Jordano coco et multis aliis.

(3)

Hugh de Lacy confirms to the canons of Llanthony all the land of Ballybin (Greater Ballybin, par. Cookestown, bar. Ratoath), with all appurtenances, as held by Roger Lych on the day when he became a canon, when Roger himself donated it to the canons. Additionally, all the land which brother Cradok held at Ratoath when he assigned it to the same canons with himself (i.e. upon entering the house). To hold well and in peace (etc.), in all liberties and free customs which Hugh has there or is able to give.

[1189×29 May1205][9]

M: Kew, TNA, C 115/80, fo 26 [cartulary, Llanthony Prima, s. xv in.].
P: *Ir. cartul. Llanthony*, 81. T: Hogan, *Llanthony*, 247–8.

7 Drogheda (in Uriel). In 1186×89 the Lord John had confirmed to the canons of Llanthony the church of St Peter, of Newbridge (Drogheda), as they held it from the gift of Hugh I de Lacy: *Ir. cartul. Llanthony*, 239; Hogan, *Llanthony*, 241. Despite the duplication of Hugh II's grant (above) in both Llanthony registers, it appears that the church of St Peter was administered by canons from Llanthony Prima, as rectors of the church: Hogan, *Llanthony*, 248.

8 Weobley, caput of the family's Herefordshire honor.

9 Absence of comital style. *Post quem* from Hugh II de Lacy's sub-enfeoffment in Meath (1189×91). Ralph Petit, later bishop of Meath (1227–30) and principal witness to the present grant, was archdeacon of Meath before 1191: Veach, 'A question of timing', 95.

[a]Sciant presentes et futuri quod ego Hugo de Lacy dedi et concessi et hac presenti carta mea confirmaui canonicis Lanthonie pro salute mea et heredum meorum et pro anima patris mei et matris mee et antecessorum meorum in puram et perpetuam elemosinam totam terram de Balybyn[10] cum omnibus pertinenciis suis sicud melius eam Rogerus Lych[11] habuit et tenuit die qua habitum mutauit et sicud ipse eisdem canonicis eam donauit et concessit. Concessi insuper canonicis prenominatis totam terram quam frater Cradok habuit et tenuit apud Rathouere[12] et quam idem Cradoc secum contulit illis. Quare volo et precipio ut idem canonici teneant et possideant predictam terram cum omnibus pertinenciis ut predictum est, bene et in pace integre et quiete et ab omni seculari seruicio libere in terris et hominibus in viis et semitis in aquis et molendinis in pratis et pascuis et in omnibus libertatibus et liberis consuetudinibus quas ibi habeo vel dare possum. Testibus: Radulfo archdiacono Midie, Willelmo Paruo, Nicholao Paruo, Galfrido de Kusac, Martino de Mandeuille, Baldewino de Kaermerdin, magistro Willelmo de Rodeach, Luciano.

[a] M: in rubric, 'Carta H de Lacy de [villa marinorum] terra [minoris] Balybyn' (words in square brackets struck through).

(4)

Agreement in chirograph form between Thomas de Verdun and Hugh de Lacy, whereby Thomas has given to Hugh half of all his lands of Ireland in Uriel, in free marriage to his sister, Lescelina de Verdun; retaining to Thomas the castle of Dundalk (co. Louth) with five knights' fees nearest the castle, on whatever side Thomas shall choose, and the harbour on the water of 'Athlon'. Thomas has exchanged with Hugh two-and-a-half knights' fees, in a suitable place, for the same number around the castle of Dundalk. Whatever Thomas and Hugh can conquer in the land of war, in their parts of Uriel, will be divided equally between them as they have divided the land of peace. Hugh and any heirs from the marriage will make a charter to Thomas for his portion of land, thereupon both parts of the present chirograph will be broken. Thomas, Hugh

10 The grange of Greater Ballybin (par. Cookstown, bar. Ratoath): Murphy and Potterton (eds), *Dublin region*, 82. For confirmation of this grant by Walter de Lacy (1189×1205), see *Ir. cartul. Llanthony*, 84; Hogan, *Llanthony*, 248.

11 During the minority of Walter de Lacy (1186–9), the Lord John had granted 'all the land of Ballybyn and two carucates of land with all of its appurtenances which belonged to Roger Lych' to the canons of Llanthony: *Ir. cartul. Llanthony*, 84; Hogan, *Llanthony*, 237.

12 As earl of Ulster, Hugh de Lacy confirmed to Llanthony Prima the territory 'near the land which was of William Cradoc, which Gilbert of Ballybin held of said prior and convent of Llanthony': below, no. 8. This was the grange of Lesser Ballybin (par. Ratoath): Murphy and Potterton (eds), *Dublin region*, 82; *Ir. cartul. Llanthony*, 76, 141.

and Walter de Lacy have sworn and pledged friends to faithfully observe the above. Thomas will entreat Count John (of Mortain, lord of Ireland), giving money or in any other way he can, to give consent to said marriage and agreement. Seals of Thomas de Verdun, Hugh and Walter de Lacy attached to each part of the chirograph.[13]

[1194×99][14]

M: Dublin, NLI, MS 1646, fos 189v–90r [Gormanston register, s. xiv ex.–s. xv in.]. P: *Gorm. reg.*, 192–3. C: *Gorm. reg.*, 144.

Hec est convencio[15] facta inter Thomam de Verdoun et Hugonem de Lacy scilicet quod Thomas dedit eidem Hugoni de Lascy cum Leselina de Verdone[16] sorore sua totam medietatem terre sue de Hibernia in Erigallo[17] in leberum [*sic*] maritagium cum omnibus pertinenciis suis in bosco et plano in viis et semitis in aquis et molendinis in pratis et pascuis et pascis in lacubus et mariscis et venacionibus in portibus maris et piscacionibus et hominibus et in omnibus aliis rebus et locis et libertatibus que ad prefatam terram suam de Ergallo pertiniant tam in mari quam in terra excepto quod idem Thomas de Verdon retinet sibi et heredibus suis integre et impartite castelum [*sic*] de Dondalc[18] et quinque feoda militum viciniora et propinquiora eidem castello versus mare et versus terram de quacumque parte eidem Thome placuuerit [*sic*] et portum que est super aquam de Athlon[19] quantum ad terram suam pertinet. T[homas] autem Verdon dedit prefato Hugoni de Lascy duo feoda militum et dimidium in loco competenti in escambium duarum feodarum militum et dimidii que retinuit in manu sua sibi et heredibus suis circa prefatum castellum de Dondalc. Et quicquid prefati Thomas et Hugo de Lacy poterint conquirere in terra gwerre in partibus suis terre de Ergallo totum inter se dimidiabunt sicut dimidiauerunt

13 For context, see above, 18–19.

14 Thomas de Verdun succeeded to his father Bertram's lands in 1194 and died in 1199: Hagger, *De Verduns*, 57–9. The first witness, Thomas (of Woodstock), is attested as abbot of Croxden, a Cistercian monastery patronised by the de Verduns in Staffordshire, between 1178 and 1229: M. W. Greenslade, *A history of the county of Stafford, vol.* 3 (London, 1970), 226–30.

15 For Hugh de Lacy's quitclaim to Rose de Verdun of the territories and rights conveyed by this agreement, c.1235, see below, no. 27.

16 Lescelina, first countess of Ulster: see above, 18, 49, 113, 175–6; below, no. 29.

17 Uriel (Airgialla).

18 The motte and bailey castle erected by Bertram de Verdun (perhaps adapting the native fortification implied by the Irish root-name, Dún Dealgan), controlled the ford over the Castletown river, and therefore the avenue north into Ulster via the Moyry Pass: Gosling, 'From Dún Delca to Dundalk', 253. Despite the reservation in Hugh's marriage-agreement, de Lacy would later grant to St Thomas's Abbey, Dublin, the parish church at Dundalk with *obventionibus castellarie de Dundalc que ad nos pertinent*: below, no. 11.

19 Áth Lethan ('the broad ford'), probably situated at the mouth of the Castletown river, the most likely location for the *portus* (harbour) of the present charter-text, serving the original proto-urban settlement at Dundalk: Gosling, 'From Dún Delca to Dundalk', 265; Hagger, *De Verduns*, 52–3.

inter se terram pacis. Hugo vero et heredes sui qui de ipso et de prefata Lecelina de egrediant de parte terre que eum contingit et quando carta ea traditur tunc confringguntur utreque partes cyrograffi. Thomas vero de Verdon et Hugo de Lascy et Walterus de Lascy frater ejus jurauerunt et affidauerunt et quidam amici eorum ex utraque parte ad ipsum affidauerunt quod hanc convencionem fideliter et inviolabiliter et sine malo ingenio inter se obseruabunt. Et predictus Thomas de Verdon affidauit quod tantum faciet versus comitem Johannem pro pecunia danda vel quocunque modo poterit quod dominus comes maritagium et predictam conuencionem concedet. Et Hugo de Lascy bonam voluntatem causa inde habebit. Et ut hec conuencio rata et inconcussa permaneat tam Thomas de Verdon quam Hugo de Lascy et etiam Walterus de Lascy utrique parti hujus sirograffi [*sic*] sigillum apposuit. Hiis testibus: Th'e Alb'e de Crolk,[20] magistro V. de Verdon, Roberto deb'e, Radulpho etc.

(5)

Hugh de Lacy confirms to the church of St Thomas the martyr of Dublin, in which Hugh's mother, Rose of Monmouth, is buried, and the canons serving God there, the grange and land beside Dunshaughlin, as his father, Hugh (I) de Lacy, had assigned it to them. Additionally the church of Dunshaughlin (bar. Ratoath, Co. Meath) and all parochial rights pertaining to it, and the church of Ratoath, with a messuage and its burgages, excepting the lord's right in those burgages. Likewise the church of the vill of Ballymaglasson, with appurtenances; the church of Killegland, with appurtenances; the church of Donaghmore, with appurtenances and the chapel of 'Baliokedin'; and the church of Greenoge, with appurtenances. To hold in pure and perpetual alms, well and in peace (etc.), with all liberties and free customs.

[1192×29 May1205][21]

M: Oxford, Bodleian Library, MS Rawlinson B 500, fo 2r [cartulary, St Thomas's Abbey, Dublin, s. xiii ex.]. P: *Reg. St Thomas*, 7–8.

Hugo de Lasci omnibus tam clericis quam laicis presentes litteras inspecturis salutem. Noverit universitas vestra me divini amoris intuitu et pro salute anime mee et domini patris mei Hugonis de Lasci et matris mee Rohes de Munomua[22] necnon antecessorum et successorum meorum concessisse et hac presenti carta mea confirmasse Deo et ecclesie beati Thome martiris de Dublinia in qua

[20] Thomas, abbot of Croxden, Staffordshire: see above, n. 14.

[21] Absence of comital style. *Post quem* from the attestation of Simon de Rochfort, bishop of Meath (1192–1224): *NHI*, ix, 285.

[22] Rose of Monmouth, first wife of Hugh I de Lacy (†before 1180): see above, 11, 78.

corpus predicte Rohes matris mee requiescit et canonicis ibidem Deo servientibus grangiam et terram juxta Dunenach Scahalin[23] sicut dominus pater meus H[ugo] de Lasci eis dedit perambulavit et assignavit. Preterea etiam ecclesiam de Dunenach Scahelin cum omnibus ad eam de jure parochiali spectantibus et ecclesiam de Ratouethe[24] cum libero et quieto mesuagio et burgagiis suis salvo tamen jure domini in eisdem burgagiis ecclesiam quoque de villa Macglassewein[25] cum pertinenciis et ecclesiam de Kilegelan[26] cum pertinenciis ecclesiam de Dunenachmor[27] cum pertinenciis et capellam de Baliokedin et ecclesiam de Grenach[28] cum pertinenciis habendas et tenendas in puram et perpetuam elemosinam bene et in pace integre et plenarie pacifice et quiete libere honorifice absque omni seculari servicio et exactione humana, in bosco in plano in pratis in pascuis communibus cum omnibus libertatibus et liberis consuetudinibus. Hiis testibus: domino S. Midensi episcopo, domino W. de Lasci, Roberto de Lasci, Ricardo de Tuit, Baldewino de Kaermurthin, Matheo de Clere, Willelmo de Garbe, Philippo de Nugent, Hugone de Ardis, Willelmo de Warewich, Luca, archidiacono Imelacensi, magistro Ricardo, magistro Simone, Luciano et multis aliis.

(6)

Hugh de Lacy confirms to the church of St Thomas of Dublin, where the body of his mother, Rose of Monmouth, is lying, and the canons serving God there, certain land beside Dunshaughlin (bar. Ratoath, Co. Meath): namely, between the great road extending from the stream to the church and the path extending from said road to the stone ford. To hold in pure and perpetual alms, freely and quietly (etc.). Sealing clause.

[1192×29 May1205][29]

23 The grange of Dunshaughlin (bar. Ratoath), probably co-extensive with the lands of the pre-Anglo-Norman monastery between Dunshaughlin and Lagore, was granted to St Thomas's by Hugh I de Lacy along with the chapel of Ratoath: *Reg. St Thomas*, 254. For Walter de Lacy's confirmation of the same benefices, with Hugh II de Lacy as principal witness, see ibid., 11–12. The charters of Walter and Hugh II sought to overturn anterior grants to St Thomas's (1186×89) by Robert Poer, curial favourite of the Lord John: ibid., 26–7, 224, 270, 273.

24 Ratoath (Co. Meath).

25 Ballymaglasson (bar. Ratoath), held by the Cruise family in the later thirteenth century: Murphy and Potterton (eds), *Dublin region*, 93.

26 Killegland, near Ashbourne (bar. Ratoath), where (c.1400) a tower-house may have replaced a much earlier stone castle: ibid., 133–4, 139, 420–1.

27 Donaghmore (bar. Ratoath): see below, no. 26.

28 Greenoge (bar. Ratoath), retained as seigneurial demesne, where the parish church was attached to a motte castle overlooking the Broad Meadow river: Murphy and Potterton (eds), *Dublin region*, 126.

29 As above, no. 5.

M: Oxford, Bodleian Library, MS Rawlinson B 500, fo 2r [cartulary, St Thomas's Abbey, Dublin, s. xiii ex.]. P: *Reg. St Thomas*, 13.

Sciant tam presentes quam futuri quod ego H[ugo] de Lascy dedi et concessi et hac presenti carta confirmavi Deo et ecclesie sancti Thome de Dublinia et canonicis ibidem Deo servientibus pro salute anime mee et domini patris mei Hugonis de Lasci et matris mee Roeis de Munemune[30] cujus corpus in predicta ecclesia requiescit quondam terram juxta Dunelinsahkelin[31] scilicet illam que est inter magnam viam que tendit per vadum ad ecclesiam et semitam que tendit a predicta via ad vadum lapicinum. Quare volo et precipio quod predicti canonici prefatam terram habeant et in puram et perpetuam elemosinam teneant libere et quiete absque omni seculari servicio et exactione humana. Ut autem hec mea donacio inposterum rata et inconcussa perseveret eam presenti scripto et sigilli mei apposicione corroboravi. Hiis testibus: domino Symone Midensi episcopo, W. de Lasci fratre meo, R. de Lasci, R. Pipard, R. de Tuit, W. Parvo, G. de Keusac, H. de Guteres, magistro S. persona de Adbui, Leonisio de Bromhard, P. de Multun, R. Figet, Willelmo de Kermerdin et multis aliis.

(7)

Hugh de Lacy confirms to the monks of the Cistercian order of Mellifont, Ballymascanlan (Co. Louth), with all the land between the Flurry and Black rivers, as each extends to the sea, and as the Flurry river extends from the sea to Glenmore (Co. Louth), and as the Black river extends from the sea to a fosse beyond 'Munardnebrac', until it returns to the same river at the mill of 'Hukinhocled', and to 'Ynesmoil lither' as far as 'Banuela' and Kilnasagart (Co. Armagh), and by the great road to 'Crosmoy' and by the mountains to 'Algarchan'. To hold by them and their successors, in pure and perpetual alms, freely and quietly (etc.), as well as any frankalmoign may be given or possessed. Sealing clause.[32]

[1194×29 May1205][33]

M: London, BL, Cotton MS Titus B XI, fo 258 [records and papers relating to Ireland, Edward I (1272–1307) to Mary I (1553–1558); s. xvi ex. transcript].[34] P: Fr. Colmcille, 'Three unpublished Cistercian documents',

30 Rose of Monmouth: see above, no. 5.

31 Dunshaughlin (bar. Ratoath): see above, no. 5.

32 For context, see above, 65.

33 Absence of comital style. *Post quem* from de Lacy's earliest possible acquisition in Uriel: see above, no. 4.

34 With an English translation, in same (s. xvi ex.) hand, as printed in Mac Íomhair, 'The lordship of Ballymascanlan', 79.

254–5. T: *Irish patent rolls of James I: facsimile of the Irish Record Commission's calendar, prepared prior to 1830 by George Hatchell*, ed. M. C. Griffith (Dublin, 1966), 275–6, no. lxxii [patent roll, 12 James I (1614)] C: *Irish patent rolls of James I*, 275–6, no. lxxii.

Universis sancti matris ecclesie filiis tam presentibus quam futuris ad quos presens carta pervenerit Hugo de Lacy salutem. Noverit universitas vestra me pro salute anime mee et antecessorum et successorum meorum concessisse et hac presenti carta mea confirmasse Deo et beate Marie et monachis Cisterciensis ordinis de Mellifonte[35] Balindascanlan[a] cum tota terra inter aquam quod vocatur Adbui et rivulum qui vocatur Aduneme[b][36] sicut utraque aqua cadit in mari et sicut aqua qui vocatur Adbui[c] extendit a mari usque ad Algarchan[37] et sicut rivulus de Aduneme extendit a mari usque ad fossetum unum quod extendit a rivulo illo ultra Munardnebrac usque in eundem rivulum iterum ubi fuit molendinum Hukinhocled[38] et sic per rivulum illum usque ad Ynesmoil lither et sic per directum usque ad Banauela[d][39] et sic usque ad Kilsagart[40] et sic per magnam viam usque ad Crosmoy[41] et sic per montes usque ad Algarchan iterum. Tenendum et habendum sibi et successoribus suis in puram et perpetuam elimosinam libere et quiete pacifice in omnibus libertatibus et liberis consuetudinibus ad eandem spectantibus, in bosco et plano in pratis et pasturis in ecclesiis et capellis in aquis in stagnis et molendinis et piscariis in moris et mariscis et turbariis in aquis dulcibus et salcis et in omnibus aliis libertatibus que infra terram illam sunt vel fieri possunt sicut aliqua elimosina melius et liberius dari vel possideri potest. Et ut hec nostra concessio rata et inconcussa permaneat [ ][e] eam sigillo meo appocicione munivi. Hiis testibus:[f] domino Waltero de Lacy, Roberto de Lacy, Rogero Pippard,[g] Gaufrido de Costetin[h] et Dardis, Philippo de Nugent, Nycholo de Nutrevile, Roberto de Mandeville, Henrico filius Hay, Henrico

[35] Mellifont Abbey (*Fons Mellis*, fd 1142), near Drogheda (Co. Louth): *Med. relig. houses*, 139–40.

[36] The Flurry and Black rivers, respectively the eastern and western boundaries of the lordship of Ballymascanlan: Mac Íomhair, 'The lordship of Ballymascanlan', 80–1.

[37] Glenmore (Co. Louth): Colmcille, 'Three unpublished Cistercian documents', 255.

[38] The townland of Whitemill, adjoining Annies (par. Ballymascanlan), may preserve the memory of this *molendinum*: Mac Íomhair, 'The lordship of Ballymascanlan', 81.

[39] An inquisition of 1606 mentions the 'ford of Aghbanavela alias Belarevin'; ie. a crossing (áth) on the river dividing the baronies of Upper and Lower Dundalk: ibid., 257. Fr. Colmcille speculated that the seventeenth-century translator (in C) was aware of this crossing, and that 'Advanaucla' represents a misreading of 'usque ad Banauela', joining preposition and place name: ibid., 256. In any case, 'Banauela' is still probably synonymous with the Belarevin, although Mac Íomhair suggests another etymology, from *Bun na buaile* ('foot of the pasture ground'): Mac Íomhair, 'The lordship of Ballymascanlan', 81.

[40] Kilnasagart (Co. Armagh): Colmcille, 'Three unpublished Cistercian documents', 256.

[41] Between Jonesborough and Meigh (Co. Armagh): Mac Íomhair, 'The lordship of Ballymascanlan', 81.

Beg, Ric[ardo] filius Humphrie, Thoma sacerdote, Philippo sacerdote, Willelmo Noell et multis aliis.

[a] M: underlined; in margin, 'Ballymascandlan'; C: 'Ballim[c]Scanlan'. [b] C: 'Awneure or Advneure'. [c] P: om., 'Adbui'. [d] C: 'Advanaucla'. [e] M: illegible; P: 'reper...'. [f] M: witness list contains nominative and ablative cases. [g] C: 'Peppard'. [h] C: 'Cosketin'.

(8)

Hugh de Lacy, earl of Ulster, confirms and releases in exchange to the prior and convent of Llanthony Prima (Gwent) all the land that Mulko Nolemi held in the 'New Vill' (Newtown Trim, Co. Meath), as it has been divided and as it extends: namely, from the land of John the clerk to the east as far as the land of Roger Palmer to the west, and from the land of Heneges Latimer to the south as far as the land which was William Brusebone's to the north, near the land which was William Cradok's that Gilbert of Ballybin held from said prior and convent. To hold in perpetual exchange, well and in peace (etc.), in all liberties and free customs which Hugh has there or is able to give. Sealing clause.

[29 May 1205×10] or [2 May 1227×42][42]

M: Kew, TNA, C 115/80, fo 26v [cartulary, Llanthony Prima, s. xv in.]. P: *Ir. cartul. Llanthony*, 81–2. T: Hogan, *Llanthony*, 260.

Sciant presentes et futuri quod ego Hugo de Lacy comes Vltonie dedi et concessi et in excambium tradidi priori et conuentui Lanthonie prime totam terram quam Mulko Nolemi tenuit in Noua Villa[43] per diuisas suas sicud se extendit, videlicet a terra Iohannis clerici ex parte orientali usque ad terram Rogeri Palmerii que iacet ex parte occidentali et de terra Heneges Latimer ex parte meridionali usque ad terram que fuit Willelmi Brusebone ex parte septentrionali propter terram suam que fuit Willelmi Cradoc[44] quam Gilbertus de Balybyn[45] tenuit de dictis priore et conuentu Lanthonie prime. Tenendam et habendam in perpetuum eschambium, bene et in pace integre et quiete et ab omni seruicio libere in terris et hominibus in viis et semitis in aquis et

[42] Based on comital style. Brooks gives a date of 1200×05, without support: *Ir. cartul. Llanthony*, 81–2.

[43] The settlement at Newtown Trim (bar. Upper Navan, Co. Meath) came into being after 1202, when Simon de Rochfort, bishop of Meath (1192–24), transferred the see of Meath to a new site on the river Boyne, east of Walter de Lacy's *caput* at Trim: Watt, *Two nations*, 60–1.

[44] In Lesser Ballybin (par. Ratoath): see above, no. 3.

[45] Ballybin (bar. Ratoath).

molendinis in pratis et pascuis et in omnibus libertatibus et liberis consuetudinibus quas ibi habeo vel dare possum. Et in huius rei testimonium ne alicui in posterum hoc veniat in dubium presenti carte sigillum meum apposui. Hiis testibus: domino Hugone de Ardys, domino Henrico Walensi, Willelmo filio fabri, Hamundo de Welyntone, [ ] Coco, Waltero le Rey, Wimundo de Scotard, Iohanne filio fabri et multis aliis.

(9)

Hugh de Lacy, earl of Ulster, confirms to the church of St Andrew the apostle in Scotland, and the canons serving God there, for those who have died or who may die in Hugh's service, the church of Rooskey and the church of Carlingford (bar. Lower Dundalk, Co. Louth), in Ireland, with all churches and all chapels of all of Cooley (Cooley peninsula, Co. Louth), and with all tithes, obventions and all other ecclesiastical benefices pertaining to said churches by right, as well and as fully as Gilbert de Lacy, Hugh's brother, possessed said benefices. Sealing clause.[46]

[29 May 1205×10][47]

M: Edinburgh, NRS, GD 45/27/8, fo. 52v [cartulary, St Andrews cathedral priory; s. xiii copy]. P: *St A. lib.*, 118.

Hugo de Lascy comes Ultonie omnibus sancte matris ecclesie filiis presens scriptum visuris vel audituris salutem. Noverit universitas vestra nos divini amoris intuitu et pro animabus antecessorum nostrorum et successorum et eorum qui in nostro servicio mortui sunt vel morientur dedisse et concessisse et hac presenti carta nostra confirmasse Deo et beate Marie et ecclesie sancti Andree apostoli in Scocia et canonicis ibidem Deo servientibus et servituris in puram et perpetuam elemosinam in Hybernia ecclesiam de Ruskach[48] et ecclesiam de Karlingeford[49] cum omnibus ecclesiis et capellis tocius Coling[50]

46 Confirmed by King Henry III on 30 September 1237: *St A. lib.*, 119. For context, see above, 101–8, 191–5.

47 See Brown, 'Power and patronage', 3–5, and above, 101–2.

48 The remains of the church at Rooskey are located three kilometres southwest of Carlingford (bar. Lower Dundalk), with a souterrain indicating some early importance attached to the site: H. G. Tempest, 'Rooskey priory', *JLAS* 6 (1928), 263–4; V. M. Buckley, *Archaeological inventory of county Louth* (Dublin, 1986), 236; *Med. relig. houses*, 368.

49 The church of Carlingford was either Holy Trinity, on an elevated site near the original town walls, or the parish church of St Mary (with appurtenant chapel of St Michael), both referred to in a will from 1485: Gosling, *Carlingford town*, 18; Oliver Davies, 'Old churches in County Louth', *JLAS* 10 (1941), 5–23, at 11; *Dowdall deeds*, ed. Charles McNeill and A. J. Otway-Ruthven (Dublin, 1960), 205–7.

50 Cooley (Co. Louth), later granted with Carlingford by Hugh de Lacy to hs daughter, Matilda

et cum omnibus decimis et obvencionibus et omnibus aliis ecclesiasticis beneficiis ad predictas ecclesias et capellas de iure pertinentibus sicut melius et plenius Gillebertus de Lascy frater noster dicta beneficia possedit.[51] Et ut hec donacio nostra in posterum rata et inconcussa permaneat eam presentis scripti testimonio et sigilli nostri apposicione communivimus. Hiis testibus: domino Waltero de Lascy fratre nostro, Gilleberto de Lascy, Willelmo de Lascy, Ricardo de Tuyt, Mathia de thurth, Huberto Hose, Willelmo clerico.

(10)

At the request of Hugh de Lacy, earl of Ulster, the canons of St Thomas of Dublin have allowed to the lepers of St. Mary Magdalene, at Ratoath, their cemetery to bury all their lepers, to be consecrated having observed in everything the indemnity of the mother-church of Ratoath, in tithes and first fruits as well as obventions, as sworn by the head of the brothers serving there, as well as the chaplain. Alongside his own seal, and to ensure greater ecclesiastical authority, Hugh has requested the attachment of the seal of his beloved in Christ, S[imon], bishop of Meath.

[29 May 1205×10][52]

M: Oxford, Bodelian Library, MS Rawlinson B 500, fo 8v [cartulary, St Thomas's Abbey, Dublin, s. xiii ex.]. P: *Reg. St Thomas*, 48–9.

Universis sancte matris ecclesie filiis presentes litteras inspecturis Hugo de Lasci comes Ultonie salutem. Noveritis canonicos sancti Thome de Dublinia ad instanciam et peticionem nostrum concessisse leprosis sancte Marie Magdalene de Rathowa[53] cimiterium suum ad sepeliendum ibi tantum leprosos suos consecrari observata in omnibus indempnitate matricis ecclesie de Rathowa[54] tam in decimis et fructibus quam in obventionibus ita quod tam major fratrum quam capellanus ibidem deserviens corporaliter prestent juramentum se in omnibus et per omnia sicut predictum est indempnitatem matricis ecclesie observaturos. Ut autem istud omnibus innotescat litteris presentibus sigilli nostri appositione munitis protestamur. Ad majorem ecclesiasticam protestacionis

(1224×35): below, no. 20.

[51] See below, no. iii.

[52] Comital style. Simon de Rochefort was bishop of Meath until 1224, ruling out the second comital period (1227–42): *NHI*, ix, 285.

[53] The Augustinian house dedicated to St Mary Magdalen at Ratoath, seized of 40 acres of land in 1385 and attested in 1485, was surely the hospital alluded to above, maintained by the regular canons of St Thomas's, Dublin: *Med. relig. houses*, 191.

[54] The church of Ratoath was granted by Hugh II de Lacy to St Thomas's before 1205: see above, no. 5.

auctoritatem sigillum dilecti in Christo patris nostris S. Midensi episcopi apponi impetravimus.

(11)

Hugh de Lacy, earl of Ulster, confirms to the church of St Thomas of Dublin, and the canons serving God there, the church of Dundalk (Co. Louth), with the appurtenances, offerings, and obventions of the castlery of Dundalk, as they pertain to Hugh, in pure and perpetual alms, for the canons' own use.

[12 May 1206×12 May1210][55]
Dundalk (Co. Louth)

M: Oxford, Bodelian Library, MS Rawlinson B 500, fo 1r [cartulary, St Thomas's Abbey, Dublin, s. xiii ex.]. P: *Reg. St Thomas*, 9.

H[ugo] de Lasci comes Ultonie omnibus presentes litteras visuris salutem. Noveritis nos divini amoris intuitu concessisse et presenti carta confirmasse Deo et ecclesie sancti Thome de Dublinia et canonicis ibidem Deo servientibus pro salute anime mee et patris et matris mee ecclesiam de Dundalc[56] cum suis pertinenciis oblationibus et obventionibus castellarie de Dundalc que ad nos pertinent[57] in puram et perpetuam elemosinam in proprios usus habendam. Hiis testibus: W. de Lasci, R.[a] de Lasci,[58] W.[b] Parvo, Ricardo de Tuit, Willelmo de Mauns, Willelmo clerico de Kermerdin, et multis aliis. Datum per manum nostram apud Dundalc duodecimo die Maii comitatus nostri anno[c] [ ].

[a] P: 'Ricardo'. [b] P: 'Willelmo'. [c] M: punctus (baseline).

[55] Internal date ['*Datum per manum nostram apud Dundalc duodecimo die Maii comitatus nostri anno* ( )']. Hugh de Lacy was created earl of Ulster on 29 May 1205, giving a *post quem* of 12 May 1206, while Richard de Tuit's death in 1211 implies a date prior to de Lacy's expulsion from Ulster, in 1210: *ALC*, 1211; *AClon.*, 1210 [*recte* 1211]; *Chartul. St Mary's, Dublin*, ii, 312. The punctus (baseline) immediately following the dating clause in M (see n[c]), however, could imply that there is no missing year, and that the original charter-text, as transcribed in St Thomas's cartulary, implied 'the year of [the creation of] our earldom' (i.e. 12 May 1206). See, however, the form of the dating clause in nos 12–13.

[56] Almost certainly the church which was located on an elevated site near the castle of Dundalk at Castletown Mount, replaced by a late-medieval building and abandoned by the seventeenth century: Gosling, 'From Dún Delca to Dundalk', 254–5.

[57] For the specific reservation of the castle of Dundalk by Thomas de Verdun, as part of his agreement with Hugh de Lacy (1194×99), see above, no. 4.

[58] Richard de Lacy (see n[a]) is otherwise unknown, whereas there were at least three individuals with the name Robert de Lacy to be found in Ireland during the period 1205–10: see above, 12n, 16n, 66, 99, 210.

(12)

Hugh de Lacy, earl of Ulster, confirms to Roger Pipard, for his homage and service, in Ulster, one cantred of land, namely Dufferin (Co. Down), with all its appurtenances, saving to Hugh all rabbit-warrens. To hold from Hugh and his heirs for the service of five knights for all service. Roger and his heirs shall hold from Hugh and his heirs the said cantred with all its appurtenances, excepting rabbit-warrens, for the aforesaid service, well and in peace (etc.), saving to Hugh the pleas pertaining to his sword (i.e. criminal jurisdictions).[59]

13 January 1207[60]
Rathbeggan (Co. Meath)

M: Dublin, NLI, MS D 971 [inspeximus of Henry IV, 24 April 1401].
C: *Ormond Deeds*, i, 365–6, no. 863 (2).

Hugo de Lascy comes Ultonie omnibus hominibus presentibus et futuris salutem. Noverit universitas vestra nos dedisse et hac presenti carta mea confirmasse Rogero Pipard[61] pro homagio et servicio suo in Ultonia unum cantredum terre s[c]ilicet Duffian[62] cum omnibus pertinenciis suis salvis nobis cuningaris omnibus illi et heredibus suis tenendum et habendum de nobis et heredibus nostris iure hereditario per servicium quinque militum pro omni servicio. Quare volumus et firmiter precipimus ut idem Rogerus et heredes sui habeant et teneant de nobis et heredibus nostris iure hereditario totum suprамemoratum cantredum cum omnibus pertinenciis suis exceptis cuningaris memoratis per prenominatum servicium bene et in pace libere et quiete plenarie integre et honorifice cum ecclesiis et capellis in bosco et plano in pratis et pascuis in viis et semitis in aquis et molendinis in stagnis et ripariis in vivariis et piscariis in moris et mariscis in omnibus libertatibus ad liberam terram pertinentibus salvis nobis placitis ad nostrum gladium pertinentibus. Hiis testibus: Waltero de Lascy, Roberto de Lascy, Willelmo de Lascy, Ricardo del Tuit, Willelmo Parvo, Henrico de Astitlee, Waltero Sa[nc]melle, Jacobo Hose, Huberto Hose, Willelmo Hose, Waltero de Logan, Ricardo fist [*sic*] Roberti, Reginaldo Haket, Willelmo clerico.

59 For context, see above, 55, 65–6, 69, 71–2, 178.

60 Internal date [‘*Data per manum nostram propriam apud Radbegan, terciodecimo die Januari comitatus nostri anno secundo*’ (29 May 1206–28 May 1207)].

61 Brother-in-law to Hugh II and Walter de Lacy through his marriage to Alice, a daughter of Hugh I de Lacy: see above, 68.

62 Dufferin (from *Duibthrian* = ‘the black third’), later the bailiwick of Blathewyc (from ‘Uí Blaithmeic’, covering north Co. Down) which also absorbed the bailiwick of Ards (the Ards peninsula): MacCotter, *Medieval Ireland*, 232.

Data per manum nostram propriam apud Radbegan,[63] terciodecimo die Januari comitatus nostri anno secundo.

(13)

Hugh de Lacy, earl of Ulster, confirms to Hugh Hose, for his homage and service, 'in Omcht Maygarb et Schagh Clogh', with four knights' fees surrounding, to hold by grantee and his heirs from Hugh and his heirs by hereditary right, for the service of a half-knight, well and in peace (etc.), with all liberties pertaining to free land.

2 March 1207[64]
Galtrim (Co. Meath)

M: London, BL, Add. MS 4797, fo 45r [transcript in collection of Sir James Ware, s. xvii].[65] P: Brown, 'A charter of Hugh de Lacy, earl of Ulster, to Hugh Hose', 509–10.

Hugo de Lacy com[es] Ultonie omnibus hominibus presentibus et futuris salutem. Noverit universitas vestra nos dedisse et concessisse et hac presenti charta nostra confirmasse Hugoni Hose[66] pro homagio et servicio suo in Omcht[67] Maygas[68] et Schagh Clogh[69] cum quatuor feodis militum pertin[enciis] in circuitu illi et heredibus suis tenendum et habendum de nobis et heredibus nostris iure hereditario per servicium dimidii militis pro omni servicio. Quare volumus et firmiter precipimus [ut] idem Hug[o] Hose et heredes sui habeant et teneant de nobis et heredibus nostris iure hereditario omnes supramemoratos quatuor feod[os] milit[um] per dictum servicium bene et in pace libere et quiete plenarie integre honorifice in ecclesiis et capellis in bosco et plano in pratis et pascuis in viis et semitis in aquis et molendinis in stagnis et ripariis in vivariis et piscariis in moris et mariscis et in omnibus libertatibus ad liberam terram pertinentibus.

63 Rathbeggan, near Ratoath (Co. Meath), classed as a 'manorial village' in Graham, 'Anglo-Norman settlement in county Meath', appendix. The Anglo-Norman seigneurial centre, which most likely superseded a native fotification (as indicated by the prefix, *ráith*), was probably located at the site of the extant 'oval flat-topped mound … with traces of wide fosse', serviced to the south by the Tolka river, and adjacent to the medieval church attested in the ecclesiastical taxation of 1302–4: M. J. Moore, *Archaeological inventory of county Meath* (Dublin, 1987).

64 Internal date ['*Data per manum nostram propriam apud Galletrum, secundo die Martii, comitatus nostri anno secundo*' (29 May 1206 to 28 May 1207)].

65 In same copy-book as no. 22.

66 Lord of Deece (Co. Meath) and Penkridge (Staffordshire), †1226: see Brown, 'A charter of Hugh de Lacy, earl of Ulster, to Hugh Hose', 504–8, and above, 65–7, 74, 76, 94n, 150n.

67 Uí Méith (Macha)?, Co. Monaghan: see above, 66–8.

68 Moygashel?, Co. Tyrone: see above, 66–8.

69 Skeagh townland?, par. Drumsnatt, Co. Monaghan: see above, 67.

Hiis testibus: domino Waltero de Lascy, Willelmo de Lascy, Roberto de Lascy, Ricardo de Tuyt, Willelmo Parvo, Ricardo Tirell, Rogero Pipard, Henrico de Auditleg, Henrico de Gulous, Matheo de Clere, Radulfo de Mutton, Galfrido de Mutton, Willelmo clerico. Data per manum nostram propriam apud Galletrum,[70] secundo die Martii, comitatus nostri anno secundo.

(14)

Hugh de Lacy, earl of Ulster, confirms to Geoffrey Sancmelle the seargeantship of 'Liskenane' (Liskenna?, Co. Monaghan), with five ploughlands, divided by certain waters, as Geoffrey Weylur had more fully held them. To hold by Geoffrey of Hugh and his heirs by hereditary right for the service of one sixth of a knight, freely (etc.), in all appurtenant liberties, saving to Hugh all matters pertaining to his sword (ie. criminal jurisdictions).

6 June 1207[71]

M: Dublin, NLI, MS 6136, fo 7 [abstracts of title deeds of the de Mandeville family, s. xvii in.]. P: Nicholls, 'Abstracts of Mandeville deeds', 14, no. 28.

Hugh de Lassey Earle of Ulter [*sic*] by his deede bearinge date the sixt daye of Junie in the third yeare of his Earldome did give and graunt unto Geofrey Samell[72] the sergeantshipp of Liskenane[73] together with five plowlands in circuit by certein meeres divided as Geofrey Weylur more fullie and effectually them before held. To be hold[en] of the said Earle and of his heires by the sixt parte of a knights Fee for all mann[er o]f services which the said Earle by his daid deed willed and graunted the said Geofr[ey] and his heires to have and enioye of the said Earle, and of his heires in inherit[ance] Right for ever, vidzt. the forementioned five ploughlands by the said services [ ] and freely, quietlie, fullie, honorablie, in Churches, Chappells, in [ ] grounde, in meadowes and pastures, in highe Wayes and by parts, in [ ]M……s, in Pooles and Ryvers,

70 Galtrim (from Irish, Calatruim), caput of Hugh Hose's barony of Deece (Co. Meath), had been part of the pre-Anglo-Norman kingdom of Deiscert Breg. The motte and bailey castle was abandoned in 1176 'for fear of the Cenél nEógain', but must have been reoccupied before the drafting of the present charter: *AU*, 1176; Orpen, *Normans*, p. 184; MacCotter, *Medieval Ireland*, 206.

71 Internal date.

72 For the family of Sancmelle, tenants of Hugh II de Lacy in Meath, see above, 76, 156–7, 186–7.

73 Possibly Liskenna, a Mac Cionaoith (McKenna) stronghold in Trough barony (Co. Monaghan), where native univallate ringforts could have been adopted for Anglo-Norman use: Ó Dufaigh, 'Medieval Monaghan', 23–6; Brindley (ed.), *Archaeological inventory of county Monaghan*, 69. For the meaning of 'seargeantship', see above, 76n.

in vavaries and fisheings, in Moores and Marrish [ ] in all other liberties to the same belonginge (onely saveing unto us all matters Concerninge and Appertayninge to the honowr of the sworde).

(15)

H[ugh] de Lacy, earl of Ulster, notifies all his bailiffs in Ireland that he has taken into his protection the church of St Thomas of Dublin, [with its] canons, properties, lands and possessions. Hugh orders said bailiffs to maintain, protect and defend said church, property, lands and possessions, permitting no molestation or crime to be inflicted on them. If any one of the earl's men will remove anything from them, it should be restored without delay.[74]

8 March 1210[75]
Dublin

M: Oxford, Bodleian Library, MS Rawlinson B 500, fo 8v [cartulary, St Thomas's Abbey, Dublin, s. xiii ex.]. P: *Reg. St Thomas*, 49.

H[ugo] de Lasci comes Ultonie omnibus ballivis suis in Hybernia ad quos presentes littere pervenerint salutem. Noverit universitas vestra nos in protectionem nostram suscepisse ecclesiam sancti Thome Dublinie canonicos res terras et possessiones suas. Unde vobis mandamus precipientes quatinus ecclesiam illam res terras et possessiones suas manuteneatis protegatis et defendatis nullam molestiam aut gravamen eis inferentes vel inferri permittentes sed si quis ex nostris eis in aliquot forisfecerit id eis sine dilacione emendari faciatis. Valete. Teste me ipso apud Dubliniam octavo die Marcii comitatus nostri anno quinto.

(16)

Hugh de Lacy, lord of the Lauragais, donates his soul and body to the lords, the poor and the brothers of the house of the hospital of Jerusalem, and to B[ernard] de Capoulège, prior of [the Hospitallers at] Toulouse, declaring his wish to assume the habit of their order, to the exclusion of any other. Hugh will not yet assume the habit, but if it should happen that his body is overtaken by death, he prays that it will be honourably conveyed to the nearest house of said order. Out of a similar regard for piety, and for the remission of his sins, Hugh also grants the garrison and fortification

74 For context, see above, 110.

75 Internal date ['*Teste me ipso apud Dubliniam octavo die Marcii comitatus nostri anno quinto*' (29 May 1209 to 28 May 1210)].

of Renneville (dép. Haute-Garonne), withholding nothing pertaining to dominion or right. B[ernard], prior of Toulouse, with the counsel and consent of his fellow brothers, receives Hugh de Lacy into all the benefices, past, present and future which may be in the said hospital from its foundations until the end of the world; and if by divine grace it should happen that Hugh wishes to assume their habit, he will be allowed bread, water and humble clothing according to the regulations of the house.[76]

[1212×15][77]

M: Toulouse, AD Haute-Garonne, Serie H, Ordre de Malte, Renneville 1 [records of Hospitallers, Toulouse]. Single sheet parchment, in contemporary s. xiii in. hand. P: *Histoire du grand-prieuré de Toulouse*, ed. Du Bourg, *pièces justificatives*, xviii–xix.

[78]. In nomine patris . et filii . et spiritus sancti . Tam presentibus quam futuris . notificatur quod Ego Ugo de lasces lauragensis[79] dominus reddo et dono animam meam et corpus meum domino deo . et beate virgini marie . et sancto Johanni . et dominis pauperibus et fratribus sancte domus hospital[is] ihu[ersu] litaris[a] et tibi fratri . B. de Capolegio priori tol[os]e[b] in vita et in morte ita quod divinitus inspiratus cum habitum religionis recipere velim predicte sancte[c] domus habitum me profiteor et assero receptarum et ad nullum alium habitum profiteor me posse extendere propter ipsum . Int[er]im[d] verum[e] habito scilicet nondum assumpto si forte contingeret quod corpus meum morte preoccuparetur[f] ipsum ad propinquiorem[g] domus antedicti hospital[is] rogo et supplico[h] deferendum . Ibidem similiter pietatis Intuitu cum predicto dono pro anime mee salute et omnium peccatorum meorum remissione erogo[i] iamdictis dominis pauperibus et fratribus prefate sancte domus . et tibi fratri . B. de Capolegio priori Tol[os]e forcium et municionem Ranaville[80] . homines . scilicet et feminas . terras . herbas . et prata . cultum et incultum . aquas et nemora . egressus et[j] ingressus . et quicquid ibi pertinet vel pertinere debet . nullo mihi penitus et omnibus predictis retento dominio vel alio iure que omnia ut predictum est laudo et approbo et in perpetuum concedo iamdictis dominis pauperibus . et fratribus et prefato priori Tol[os]e . in pace possidenda. Et ego frater. B. humilis

76 For context, see above, 134, 180.

77 From the beneficiary of de Lacy's grant, Bernard de Capoulège, prior of the Hospitallers at Toulouse (1212–15): *Histoire du grand-prieuré de Toulouse*, ed. Du Bourg, 24; Power, 'Who went on the Albigensian crusade', 1063n.

78 In most instances abbreviations are expanded silently, but punctuation and capitalisation have been retained.

79 The Lauragais plain, extending east of Toulouse into déps. Haute-Garonne, Aude and Tarn.

80 For the Hospitallers' commandery at Renneville (dép. Haute-Garonne), one of the *castra* confiscated from Aimery of Montréal, see *Histoire du grand-prieuré de Toulouse*, ed. Du Bourg, ch. 4, and above, 121, 124–5, 130, 134.

prior Tol[os]e de consilio et consensu nostrorum fratrum Colligo et[k] recipio te Ugonem de lasces in omnibus beneficiis preteritis[l] presentibus et futuris . que in[m] prefato hospitali a principio usque in finem mundi facta sunt vel ad unanimitate domino fient in propria parte[n] velut nostrum fratrem . et cum divina gratia proveniente[o] habitum nostrum summere volueris in pretaxata domo panem et aquam atque pannos humiles tibi concedimus diligenter.[p]

[a] P: 'Iherosolimitari'. [b] P: 'Tholosae'. [c] M: 'sancte', repeated; om. in P. [d] P: 'introitum'. [e] P: om., 'verum'. [f] P: 'occuparetur'. [g] P: 'cimiterium'. [h] P: 'porego'. [i] P: 'dono et pago'. [j] P: om., 'et'. [k] P: om., 'et'. [l] P: om., 'preteritis'. [m] P: om., 'in'. [n] P: om., 'vel ad unanimitate domino fient in propria parte'. [o] P: 'preveniente'. [p] M: text is followed by alphabet in capitals, in same hand, terminating with punctus elevatus.

(17)

Hugh de Lacy, lord of Castelnaudary and Laurac, grants to blessed Mary of Prouille (cant. Fanjeaux) and the brothers and sisters serving God and blessed Mary there, the place of Agassens (cant. Salles-sur-l'Hers), with all its appurtenances, men and fields, cultivated and uncultivated, and all woods and waters, and all rights pertaining to said place, and pasture for animals and wood in the forest of Pech-Luna (cant. Belpech) for firewood and for building dwellings at Agassens. To hold freely and in perpetuity, and Hugh warrants this against all living persons. Sealing clause.[81]

[June 1214][82]

M: Paris, Bibliothèque Nationale de France, Doat 98, fo 53r–v [documents copied by Jean Doat from archives in Languedoc, 1663–70]. P: *a. Monumenta diplomatica S. Dominici*, ed. V. J. Koudelka and R. J. Loenertz, *Monumenta ordinis fratrum praedicatorum historica 25* (Rome, 1966), 50; *b. Cart. Prouille.*, ii, 135. C: Molinier, 'Catalogue des actes de Simon et d'Amauri de Montfort', 470.

Notum sit presentibus et futuris quod ego Ugo de Lascin dominus Castrinovi et Lauriacensis[83] do pro remedio anime mee et predecessorum meorum locum de Agascens[84] cum omnibus pertinenciis suis hominibus et agris cultis et incultis

[81] For context, see above, 125, 131.

[82] Internal date ['*Datum mense Junii anno Domini millesimo ducentesimo decimo quarto*'].

[83] Castelnaudary and Laurac (dép. Aude).

[84] La Grange d'Agassens (com. Payra-sur-l'Hers, cant. Salles-sur-l'Hers), today a cluster of buildings on an elevated site, surrounded by cultivated fields. On 8 October 1215 Pope Innocent III confirmed what Simon de Montfort and other crusaders had granted to Prouille, including *apud*

nemoribus aquis et omnibus juribus ad predictum locum pertinentibus et pascua animalibus domus[a] et ligna ad comburendum et ad edificandum domos in loco de Agascens in foresta de Podiolunar[85] do inquam Deo et beate Marie de Proliano[86] et fratribus et sororibus presentibus et futuris[b] ibidem Deo et beate Marie servientibus presentibus et futuris libere et inperpetuum possidendum et ego faciam vobis guirentiam ab omni vivente. Et ut ratum permaneat omni tempore presentem paginam sigilli nostri munimini roboramus. Hujus rei sunt testes: Radulfus Pel-de-Loup, Ugo de Campania, Baulabertus de Belfort, Hubertus Oyse, Bernardus de Sancto Juliano et Rogerius frater ejus, et Bernardus de Sancto Goyrico. Datum mense Junii anno Domini millesimo ducentesimo decimo quarto.

[a] *Pb*: 'animalia, domos'. [b] *Pb*: om., 'et futuris'.

(18)

Hugh de Lacy, lord of Laurac and Castelnaudary, acknowledges his grant to the Lord God and blessed Mary of Prouille (cant. Fanjeaux), and Natalis, prior, and the brothers and sisters of said monastery, of the vill of Agassens (cant. Salles-sur-l'Hers), with all its rights and appurtenances, as outlined in the instrument reinforced with Hugh's seal, and clearly defined by the present charter: namely, of the 'condomina' formerly belonging to Roger d'Orsans; and all the lands formerly belonging to Arnald de Cugurone and his brother, B. Mondi, and Arnald de Sales, all in the 'decimarius' of St Peter of Agassens; and all lands and right within said 'decimarius' which pertain or ought to pertain to Hugh. Additionally, Hugh grants saplings in the forest of Pech-Luna (cant. Belpech) to build dwellings at Agassens and for firewood, with his guarantee and without any fraud. Any men of Payra, Payranel or Brésil (cant. Salles-sur-l'Hers) with lands in said 'decimarius' will render to said grantees whatever portions of service or use they had owed to Hugh. If, however, grantees' men hold anything in the 'decimarii' of said granges (i.e. Payra, Payranello or Verazillo), they will return their portions of service or use to Hugh or his [delegates]. The animals of Agassens may graze in the waste at Verazillo, but not in the cultivated fields, as the animals of Verazillo may graze in the waste at Agassens. Conceded, confirmed and certified before Hugh and his heirs, without any other reservation. Sealing clause.

Agascons Hugo de Lasci: *Monumenta diplomatica*, 59; *Cart. Prouille*, i, 2. The papal confirmation is more likely to pertain to Hugh's general grant of the locus of Agassens (no. 17), than the more specific conveyance of rights in the *decimarius* of Agassens, made before 1217, when they were certified by de Lacy in no. 18, below.

[85] The small hill-top commune of Pech-Luna ('Moon-Hill', cant. Belpech) still commands views of surrounding woodland.

[86] Prouille (*alias* Prouilhe), fd c.1207 by St Dominic of Osma: see above, 125, 129, 180.

27 February 1217[87]
Castelnaudary (dép. Aude)

P: *a. Cartulaire ou histoire diplomatique de Saint Dominique*, ed. François Balme, Paul Lelaidier and Joachim Collomb (3 vols, Paris, 1893–1901), ii, 167–9 [from copy in the possession of the family Capella, s. xvii in., as copied by Édilbert de Teule in *b*.];[88] *b*. Édilbert de Teule, *Annales du prieuré de Notre Dame de Prouille* (Carcassonne, 1902), part ii, 7–8; *c*. *Monumenta diplomatica*, 88–90; *d*. *Cart. Prouille*., ii, 135–6.

Noverint universi presentem paginam inspecturi quod ego Ugo de Laci dominus Lauraci et Castrinovi[89] recognosco et concedo quod donavi Domino Deo et beate Marie de Prolliano[90] et Natali priori[91] et fratribus et sororibus ejusdem monasterii tam presentibus quam futuris villam de Agassensis[92] cum omnibus juribus suis et pertinentiis suis sicut continetur in instrumento quod sigilli mei munimine roboravi[93] et expressum in presenti est hac carta. Dono Domino Deo et B. Marie de Prulliano et tibi Natali priori et fratribus et sororibus ejusdem monasterii tam presentibus quam futuris condominam que fuit Rogerii d'Orsans[94] que est in decimario sancti Petri[95] de Agassensis et omnes illas terras que fuerunt Arnaldi de Cugurone[96] et fratrum suorum que sunt in decimario predicto et omnes illas terras que fuerunt B. Mondi[a][97] que sunt in eodem decimario et omnes illas terras que fuerunt Arnaldi de Sales[98] que sunt in eodem decimario et omnes illas terras que sunt infra predictum decimarium que ad me pertinent et pertinere debent et omne jus quod illic habeo ad omnem voluntatem vestram in perpetuum faciendam. Insuper dono predictis fratribus talivum[b] in nemore

87 Internal date ['*Hoc actum est apud Castrumnovum ii die a fine mensis Februarii feria iii anno Verbi incarnati M°CC°XVII*'].

88 The copy (s. xvii) followed in *Pa*. was collated with the original instrument by royal notaries, and the original returned to the abess of Prouille, Antoinette de Voisins (1597–1604): *Monumenta diplomatica*, xxxi.

89 Laurac (cant. Fanjeaux) and Castelnaudary.

90 Prouille (cant. Fanjeaux).

91 Brother Natalis (Noël) succeeded Dominic of Osma as prior of Prouille by 2 March 1215: *Cart. Prouille*, ii, 189–90. He drowned in 1218, and was succeeded as prior by William Claret: *Cartulaire de Saint Dominique*, ii, 248–9, 284.

92 The vill at Agassens, granted to Prouille by Hugh de Lacy in June 1214: above, no. 17.

93 Above, no. 17.

94 Commune of Orsans (cant. Fanjeaux): Sabarthès, *Dict. top. de l'Aude*, 285; Toulouse, Bib. Mun., MS 609, fos 43b–44b, 152b, 154, 158, 160a, 164, 200, 201a. For 'condomina', see above, 126.

95 Tithe-land of the church of St Peter at Agassens: Sabarthès, *Dict. top. de l'Aude*, 413.

96 Cucurou, near Castelnaudary: ibid., 113; Toulouse, Bib. Mun., MS 609, fos 3b, 17a, 143–144a.

97 Toulouse, Bib. Mun., MS 609, fos 4a, 9a.

98 Commune (and cant.) of Salles-sur-l'Hers: Sabarthès, *Dict. top. de l'Aude*, 425; Toulouse, Bib. Mun., MS 609, fos 87b, 93b, 96b, 191a.

de Podio Lunari[99] scilicet ad domos ediffícandas de Agassensis et ad focum vestrum necessarium in eternum. Predicte donationis ero tibi Natali et fratribus et sororibus ejusdem monasterii tam presentibus quam futuris bonus guirens semper ab omnibus amparatoribus sine omni nostro nostrorumque dolo. Tamen si homines de Payrano[100] et Payranello[101] et Verazillo[102] habent aliquas terras infra decimarium sancti Petri de Agassensis habeant illas et possideant ita quod reddant vobis portiones servicia et usaticos sicut michi faciebant pro illis terris. Item si homines vestri de Agassensis habent aliquas terras in decimariis predictarum villarum similiter habeant illas et possideant reddendo mihi vel meis portiones servicia et usaticos pro illis terris. Item sciendum est quod animalia de Agassensis debent pascere in eremis de Verazillo si voluerint tamen non in cultis et animalia de Verazillo debent pascere in eremis de Agassensis eodem modo sicut vestra ut supra. Predicta concedo confirmo et aprobo pro me et heredibus meis sine alio aliquo retentu quem ibi non facio et ut ratum sit presentem cartam sigilli mei munimine corroboro. Hoc actum est apud Castrumnovum[103] ii die a fine mensis Februarii feria iii anno Verbi incarnati M°CC°XVII Philipo rege Francorum Simone comite Tholose.[104] Hujus rei sunt testes: dominus Henricus Vualensis et dominus Henricus, filius Leonini,[c] et dominus Willelmus de Amiel et magister Germanus et Petrus Amelli.[d]

[a] *Pb*: 'huismodi'. [b] *Pa*: 'talivium'; *b*. 'talinum'. [c] *Pb*: 'Lernini'. [d] *Pa*: note of description in s. xvii copy, of green wax seal attached with a cord of a different colour.

(19)

Hugh de Lacy, earl of Ulster, confirms to Thomas, bishop of Down, and his successors, four carucates of land in Hugh's demesne in the bailiwick of Ards (Co. Down), lying in one direction between the land of Ardquin (Co. Down) of said bishop and the land of the hospital in Ards, and in the other direction between the land formerly belonging to Ralph fitz William of 'Lunwahr' and Hugh's land of 'Arhen'. Hugh also grants to said bishop and his successors the land formerly belonging to John de Lennes in Ards, and one carucate which Robert fitz Serlonis held from Hugh next

[99] Pech-Luna (cant. Belpech): see above, no. 17n.
[100] Commune of Payra (cant. Salles-sur-l'Hers): Sabarthès, *Dict. top. de l'Aude*, 294.
[101] Payranel (com. Payra): ibid., 294.
[102] The church of St Etienne at 'Verazillo' (Brésil-Haut, Brésil-Bas, com. Payra), with that of St Peter at Agassens, formed part of the bishop of Saint Papoul's possessions after 1317, as Saint-Pierre-de-la-Rivière: Sabarthès, *Dict. top. de l'Aude*, 47, 413.
[103] Castelnaudary.
[104] Toulouse (dép. Haute-Garonne).

to Strangford (Co. Down), with the homage and service of their heirs. Additionally, Hugh grants to said bishop and his successors ten carucates of land in Iveagh (Co. Down), in a place deemed suitable by view of friends of Hugh and said bishop, to be held by Thomas and his successors in all liberties, as freely as any frankalmoign may be given and quietly possessed. Hugh and his heirs will warrant all said lands to said bishop and his successors against all men. Sealing clause.

[1227×34][105]

M: Kew, TNA, C 66/207, *m*. 17 [patent roll; royal inspeximus of Edward III, 24 August 1342]. P: *a*. MacNiocaill, 'Cartae Dunenses', 422; *b*. Reeves, *Eccl. ant.*, 164–5. C: *CPR*, *1340–43*, 508–9.

Universis has litteras visuris vel audituris Hugo de Lascy comes Ultonie salutem in Domino. Sciatis me[a] dedisse et concessisse et hac presenti carta nostra confirmasse venerabili patri nostro in Christo Thome Dunensi episcopo et eius successoribus in puram et perpetuam elemosinam pro salute anime nostre et antecessorum nostrorum quatuor carucatas terre de dominico nostro in Arte[106] jacentes ex una parte inter terram predicti episcopi de Ardwhum[b][107] et terram hospitaliorum[c] in Arte[108] ex altera et ex parte alia inter terram que fuit quondam Radulfi filii Willelmi de Lunwahr[109] et ex alia parte terram nostram de Arhen.[110] Concessimus eciam eidem episcopo et eius successoribus in puram et perpetuam elemosinam terram que fuit Johannis de Lennes in Arte cum homagio et servicio heredum suorum et unam carucatam terre quam Robertus filius Serlonis tenuit de nobis in Arte iuxta Stranford[111] cum homagio et servicio heredum suorum. Preterea concessimus eidem episcopo et eius successoribus decem carucatas terre in Oueh[112] in loco competenti secundum visum tam

105 Comital style. *Post quem* from the attestation of Thomas, bishop of Down (1224–42): *NHI*, ix, 280. *Ante quem* from Geoffrey de Marisco, opposed to Hugh de Lacy from at least the baronial war of 1234: see above, 184, 186, 194.

106 The bailiwick of Ards, covering the peninsula in modern Co. Down, was established before 1226: see above, 168.

107 Ardquin (Co. Down): Reeves, *Eccl. ant.*, 21, 164–5.

108 The preceptory of Hospitallers at Castleboy (St John in Ards, Co. Down): *Med. relig. houses*, 335, and above, 180. The strip of land between Ardquin and Castleboy, granted by the present charter, constitutes the townlands of Ballyward and Dunevly (par. Ardkeen): Reeves, *Eccl. ant.*, 21, 164–5.

109 Possibly at 'Sithe' (*alias* 'le Syth'), appearing alongside Ardquin in the ecclesiastical taxation of 1306: ibid., 21–2, 164–5.

110 The castle of 'Archen' ('Ardkene' in 1306, now par. Ardkeen) had been granted to Black Abbey (St Andrew in the Ards) by John de Courcy, exempting its tithes: Dugdale, *Mon. Ang.*, vi, pt. 2, 1019; Reeves, *Eccl. ant.*, 21–2; 164–5.

111 Strangford (Co. Down).

112 Uíbh Echach (Iveagh, Co. Down). These carucates would appear to have been at Maghera, near Dundrum, the only episcopal manor in Iveagh: Reeves, *Eccl. ant.*, 165.

amicorum nostorum quam suorum, tenendas et habendas ei et successoribus suis in omnibus libertatibus sicut aliqua elemosina liberius potest conferri et quiecius possideri. Nos vero et heredes nostri omnes dictas terras dicto episcopo et eius successoribus contra omnes homines warantizabimus. In testimonium autem huius rei presenti scripto sigillum nostrum apposuimus. Hiis testibus: Galfrido de Mariscis, Gilberto de Lascy, Waltero de Ridlesford,[d] Nicholao Parvo, Waltero de Mariscis, Johanne Parvo, Adam de Alneto, Johanne Flandrensi et multi aliis.

[a] *Pb*: 'nos'. [b] *Pb*: 'Arwhum'. [c] *Pb*: 'Hospitalariorum'. [d] *Pb*: 'Bidlesford'.

(20)

Hugh de Lacy confirms to Matilda, his daughter, his castle of Carlingford (Co. Louth), with all its rights and appurtenances, with all the land which Hugh had with her mother in Cooley and Uriel, and in the cantred of Louth, with all their appurtenances, and likewise all the land of Morgallion, with the addition of 'Fithemunterrody', in the 'comitatus' (ie. in the earl's lands) of Meath. To hold from Hugh and his heirs by Matilda and her heirs for the service of five knights, as freely and fully as Hugh held it, fully, wholly (etc.), in all liberties and free customs pertaining to said castle and land, with judgement of hot iron and water, battle and gallows. Sealing clause.[113]

[1227×35][114]

M: Dublin, NLI, MS 1646, fo 191v [Gormanston register, s. xiv ex.–s. xv]. P: *Gorm. reg.*, 195–6. C: *Gorm. reg.*, 146.

Sciant presentes et futuri quod ego Hugo de Lascy dedi concessi et hac presenti carta mea confirmaui Matilde filie mee castrum meum de Carlingford cum omnibus juribus suis et pertinenciis cum tota terra quam habui cum matre sua in Cole et Ergalea[115] ac in comitatu Limit'[116] cum omnibus suis pertinenciis et

[113] The charter's probable context was the occasion of Matilda's marriage to David, baron of Naas: see above, 176.

[114] Absence of comital style allows for a date prior to Hugh's restoration in 1227, but subsequent to his return to Ireland in 1223. However, the present instrument would appear to have been issued prior to no. 21, which implies Hugh de Lacy's ongoing direct lordship in Morgallion, and in which the comital title is employed. *Ante quem* from de Lacy's chirograph with Rose de Verdun, quitclaiming his rights in Uriel: below, no. 27.

[115] The Cooley peninsula (Co. Louth) and Uriel. For the cantred of Louth, see MacCotter, *Medieval Ireland*, 236.

[116] Possibly Louth: Otway-Ruthven, 'Partition', 405 ('I am inclined to suspect that the original charter read *in can[tredo] Luuit* rather than *in comitatu Lim[er]it*: the copyist who compiled the register might easily have misread the minims').

similiter totam terram de Machergallyng[117] cum incremento de Fithemunterrody[118] in comitatu Midie,[119] habendas et tenendas de me et heredibus meis sibi et heredibus suis per seruicium quinque militum pro omni seruicio adeo libere et quiete sicut ego liberius et plenius ea tenui, integre plenarie et quiete in dominicis dominiis homagiis seruiciis wardis relauiis escaetis in castris fortelescis burgis willis hominibus ecclesiis cappellis molendinis et omnibus aliis libertatibus et liberis consuetudinibus que ad castrum et terram predictam pertinent vel pertinere poterint inperpetuum cum judicio ignis et aque duelle et furcarum. Ut autem hec mea donacio concessio et confirmacio robur firmitatis opteniat [*sic*] presentem cartam sigilli mei munimine roboraui. Hiis testibus: maiustro [*sic*] Alexandro de Nottyngam et domino Waltero le Bryt, domino Willelmo de Bewys, Petro capellano et Alexandro clerico et multis aliis.

(21)

Hugh de Lacy, earl of Ulster, confirms to his burgesses of Nobber (bar. Morgallion, Co. Meath), four carucates of his land in the common pasture, as lying between the vill of Nobber and the great wood towards the western part, and having been divided by right boundaries and perambulated. To hold of Hugh and his heirs by hereditary right, freely and quietly (etc.), making a great causeway between the castle and vill of Nobber for all services and demands. And because Hugh wishes said burgesses and all merchants of said vill, poor as well as rich, to have and enjoy said pasture, the present charter is reinforced by his seal.

[1227×November 1241][120]

M: Dublin, NLI, MS 1646, fo 209v [Gormanston register, s. xiv ex.–s. xv]. P: *Gorm. reg.*, 202. C: *Gorm. reg.*, 162–3.

Sciant presentes et futuri quod ego Hugo de Lascy comes Ultonie dedi concessi et hac presenti carta mea confirmaui burgencibus meis de Nobire[121] iiij carucatas terre mee in communem pasturam sicut jacent inter villam de Nobire

[117] The barony of Morgallion (Co. Meath), granted to Hugh de Lacy with Ratoath by Walter de Lacy in 1189×91. In 1241 de Lacy made a competing grant of Morgallion, with its *caput* of Nobber, to Albert Suerbeer, archbishop of Armagh (below, no. 30).

[118] 'Fid Muintir Rodaigh'? ('the wood of the people of Rodaigh'); possibly synonymous with the 'thueth of fithd Winterwod', part of Hugh's grant from Walter de Lacy in 1189×91: see above, 16.

[119] i.e. lands of the earl in Meath.

[120] Comital style. *Ante quem* from de Lacy's exchange of Nobber, with Morgallion, for land held from the archbishop of Armagh (below, no. 30). Presumably also anterior to no. 20, in which Morgallion was granted by de Lacy to his daughter, Matilda (1227×35).

[121] Nobber (bar. Morgallion, Co. Meath).

et magnum boscum versus occidentem partem[a] per rectas et diuisas metas ac perambulatas tenendas et habendas de me et heredibus meis sibi et heredibus suis iure hereditario libere et quiete integre et plenarie facientibus magnam causeam inter castellum et magnam villam de Nobire pro omni seruicio et demanda. Et quia volo quod dicti burgenses et omnes mercatores dicte ville tam pauperes quam diuites predictam communem pasturam habeant[b] et gaudeant presentem cartam meam sigillo meo coroboraui. Hiis testibus: domino Dau[id] e, barone de Nas, Michale le Gros, Roberto Schallowhed, Radulfo Bellew, Nicholao de Stoce et aliis.

[a] M: 'partem', interpolated in same hand. [b] M: 'habeant', interpolated in same hand.

(22)

Hugh de Lacy, earl of Ulster, confirms to lord Walter Hose, in marriage to his daughter, Avicia, Hugh's whole marshalship and one cantred of land in Connacht, as soon as Hugh shall obtain it. To hold from Hugh and his heirs by Walter and any heirs proceeding from his marriage to Avicia, freely and quietly (etc.), with all liberties and free customs pertaining or which will pertain to so much land. Grantor's seal attached.[122]

[1227×41][123]

M: London, BL Add. MS 4797, fo 45v [transcript in collection of Sir James Ware, s. xvii].[124]

Sciant omnes tam presentes quam futuri quod ego Hugo de Lascy comes Ultonie dedi et concessi et hac presenti carta mea confirmaui domino Waltero Hoose[125] in maritagio Auicie filie mee[126] totam mariscalciam meam et unam cantereth de terra mea in Connatia[127] quamcito eam perquisiero tenendam et habendam de me et heredibus meis sibi et heredibus suis de predicta Auicia filia mea exeuntibus libere et quiete plene et integre et honorifice cum omnibus libertatibus et liberis consuetudinibus ad pred[ictam] terram pertinentibus faciendo inde seruicium quod ad tantam terram pertinet. Et ut hec mea concessio et donatio

[122] For context, see above, 190.
[123] Absence of majesterial style is consistent with other of de Lacy's acta from the second comital period (1227–42). The principal witness, 'W. de Lacy', could refer either to Walter (†1241) or William Gorm (†1233), giving an *ante quem* of 1241.
[124] In same copy-book as no. 13.
[125] Presumed relative of Hugh Hose, lord of Deece and beneficiary of no. 13.
[126] Otherwise unattested: see above, 190.
[127] For Hugh de Lacy's claims in Connacht, see above, 28, 34–5, 38, 190.

rata et inconcussa permaneat presenti scripto sigillum meum apposui. Hiis testibus: domino W. de Lascy, domino Nich[ola]o filio Leonisi [*sic*], Radulpho Sendelue, Willelmo de S[a]ngnne, Roberto de Sangnne, Ricardo de Cliffordia, Roberto Saluagio et multis aliis.

(23)

Hugh de Lacy, earl of Ulster, confirms to Maurice fitz Gerald, for his homage and service, Tír Conaill (Co. Donegal), with all its [appurtenances,] having been divided by right boundaries between Cenél nEógain and Tír Conaill. To hold from Hugh and his heirs by Maurice and his heirs, freely, quietly (etc.), with all liberties and free customs pertaining to free land, for the service of four knights for all service, exactions and demands. Sealing clause.

[1227×42][128]

M: Dublin, NLI, MS 5769, fo 5v ['photostat' copy of *Red book of Kildare*; deeds relating to the Leinster FitzGeralds, s. xvi in.]. P: *Red bk Kildare*, 26, no. 21.

Sciant presentes et futuri quod ego Hugo de Lascy comes Ultonie dedi, concessi et hac presenti carta mea confirmavi Mauricio filio Geraldi[129] pro homagio et servicio suo Tirconyll[130] cum omnibus suis [pertinenciis] per rectas metas et divisas inter Keneleon[131] et Tirconyll, tenendam et habendam de me et heredibus meis sibi et heredibus suis libere quiete integre et plenarie pacifice et honorifice iure hereditario cum omnibus libertatibus et liberis consuetudinibus ad liberam terram pertinentibus, faciendo inde ipse et heredes sui michi et heredibus meis servicium quatuor militum[132] pro omni servicio exaccione et demanda. Et ut hec mea donacio concessio et confirmacio perpetuum robur

128 Smith suggests a date of c.1238, from the joint expedition of Maurice fitz Gerald and Hugh de Lacy into Tír Eógain and Tír Conaill: see Brendan Smith, 'Fitzgerald, Maurice (c.1194–1257)', in ODNB; above, 200. Definitive *post quem* from Maurice's majority as lord of Offaly, in 1215, modified by comital style to the year of de Lacy's restoration (1227): Smith, 'Fitzgerald, Maurice (c.1194–1257)'.

129 Maurice fitz Gerald, lord of Offaly (†1257) and justiciar of Ireland (1232–45): Smith, 'Fitzgerald, Maurice (c.1194–1257)'; *NHI*, ix, 471. For Hugh de Lacy's grant of Carbury-Drumcliff (Co. Sligo) to the same beneficiary, see below, no. 28. See also, below, no. x.

130 The four *tríchas* of Tír Conaill recorded in Irish sources, co-extensive with the diocese of Raphoe (Co. Donegal), represent the four cantreds found in Anglo-Norman records (Tír Énna, Tír Lugdach, Trícha Esa Ruaid, and Tír Bóguine): MacCotter, *Medieval Ireland*, 222–3. The king of Tír Conaill (1207–41) at this time was Domnall Mór mac Éicnecháin: *NHI*, ix, 214.

131 Cenél nEógain.

132 Presumably calculated on the basis of one knight from each of Tír Conaill's four cantreds.

optineant presentem cartam sigilli mei munimine roboravi. Hiis testibus: dominis Johanne de Cogan, Petro de Bermegham, Symone de Clyfford, Roberto de Cruys, Johanne le Chen, Johanne de Crauyll, Roberto de Capella, Thoma de Capella, Willelmo capellano et aliis.

(24)

Hugh de Lacy, earl of Ulster, confirms to Richard White the land of Ballykinler in Lecale (Co. Down), to hold as he holds from the prior and convent of Holy Trinity (Dublin).

[1227×42][133]

C: *Christ Church deeds*, 42, no. 35 [photographic reproduction of McEnery's calendar].

Hugh de Lacy, earl of Ulster, grants to Richard White,[134] the land of the Cross of Holy Trinity, Dublin, in Lechkachel,[135] to hold as he holds[136] from the prior and convent of Holy Trinity. Witnesses: lord Thomas, bishop of Down, W., prior of St Patrick's, Down, Robert de Mandeville, Robert Talbot, Henry the Welshman, Ralph Pel de Lu, Thomas fitz Bishop, William Sancmolle, William de Stokes, Richard de Petraponte, Nicholas de Dunmal.

(25)

H[ugh] de Lacy, earl of Ulster, confirms to the prior and monks of St Patrick of Down one boat and one free net for the fishing of the (River) Bann, in perpetuity, [free] from all demands pertaining to Hugh or his heirs. Sealing clause.

[1227×42][137]

[133] *Post quem* from the attestation of Thomas, bishop of Down (1224–42): *NHI*, ix, 280. Modified by comital style to the year of de Lacy's restoration to Ulster (1227).
[134] Possibly from the family of 'Albus', de Lacy tenants in Meath, later settled at Dufferin (Co. Down): see above, 178n.
[135] Ballykinler (bar. Lecale, Co. Down), opposite Dundrum, was granted by John de Courcy to Holy Trinity c.1200, to maintain a perpetual light for the cathedral church and its crucifix: Reeves, *Eccl. ant.*, 211–12, and above, 178. The bailiwick of Lecale, including south Co. Down, with Downpatrick, was established before 1226: *RLC*, i, 205b; *CDI*, i, no. 1468, and above, 168–9, 178.
[136] By a coeval charter, witnessed by Hugh de Lacy as earl of Ulster, the prior and convent of Holy Trinity, Dublin, granted to Richard White the land of the Cross of Holy Trinity in Lecale, for a rent of 20s., reserving tithes: *Christ Church deeds*, 80–1, no. 238(b).
[137] As above (no. 24).

M: Kew, TNA, C 66/278, *m*. 11 [patent roll; royal inspeximus of Edward III, 24 November 1368]. P: *a*. MacNiocaill, 'Cartae Dunenses', 422; *b*. Dugdale, *Mon. Ang.*, vi, pt. 2, 1124–5. C: *CPR*, *1367–70*, 177.

Universis ad quos presens scriptum pervenerit H[ugo] de Lacy comes Ultonie salutem in Domino. Universitati vestre significamus nos divine pietatis intuitu et pro salute anime nostre et omnium antecessorum nostorum dedisse et concessisse et presenti carta nostra confirmasse priori et monachis sancti Patricii de Duno[138] ibidem Deo et sancto Patricio servientibus unum batellum et unum rete libera ad piscacione[a] de Banna[b][139] imperpetuum ab omni demanda ad nos vel heredes nostros pertinente. Et ut hec nostra donacio et confirmacio perpetuam optineat firmitatem presenti scripto sigillum nostrum apposuimus. Hiis testibus: T. Dunensi episcopo, Henrico Wallensi,[c] Radulfo Pendelu, Willelmo de Duillers,[d] Willelmo Ponmeur, Roberto Ponmeur, Willelmo de Stokys, Michaelo de Waletun clerico nostro, Philippo filio David et aliis.

[a] *Pb*: 'piscationem'. [b] *Pb*: 'Banne'. [c] *Pb*: 'Wellensi'. [d] *Pb*: 'de Avillers'.

(26)

Hugh de Lacy, earl of Ulster, confirms to the canons of St Thomas beside Dublin, his dear brothers and friends in Christ, the land which Walter de Escotot, by agreement and consent of John fitz Leon, gave to them and recorded by charter in fee and perpetual farm, in the tenement of Donaghmore (bar. Ratoath, Co. Meath), next to Greenoge (bar. Ratoath), with all its appurtenances. To hold by them or their successors as freely and quietly (etc.) as Walter de Escotot gave, granted and confirmed it to them with his charter, saving the external service owing to Hugh or his heirs. Additionally, Hugh confirms out of the same gift of Walter de Escotot, insofar as it pertains to Hugh, the church of Trevet (bar. Skreen, Co. Meath), with all its appurtenances. Hugh wishes said canons to enjoy and possess said lands and whatever else they have in his demesne, free from all impediment, opposition or vexation. Sealing clause.

[1231×33][140]

M: Oxford, Bodleian Library, MS Rawlinson B 500, fo 1v [cartulary, St Thomas's Abbey, Dublin, s. xiii ex.]. P: *Reg. St Thomas*, 9–10.

[138] For the Benedictine cathedral priory at Downpatrick (Co. Down), see *Med. relig. houses*, 168–9, and above, 32, 81, 139, 178.

[139] River Bann.

[140] Richard de la Corner was bishop of Meath from 1231, while William Gorm de Lacy, witness, died in 1233: *AClon.*, 1233; *Reg. St Thomas*, 10; *NHI*, ix, 285.

Universis Christi fidelibus ad quos presens scriptum pervenerit H[ugo] de Lasci comes Ultonie salutem. Noveritis nos concessisse et hac presenti carta confirmasse dilectis fratribus nostris et amicis in Christo karissimis canonicis sancti Thome juxta Dubliniam totam terram quam Walterus de Escotot[141] de consensu et voluntate Johannis filii Leonisii[142] eis dedit et incartavit in feudo et ad perpetuam firmam in tenemento de Dunenachmor juxta Grenoch[143] cum omnibus suis pertinenciis, tenendam et habendam eis et eorum successoribus ita libere et quiete sicut jamdictus Walterus de Escotot eam eis melius plenius et liberius dedit concessit et carta sua confirmavit[144] salvo servicio forinesco ad nos et heredes nostros pertinente.[145] Confirmavimus autem eis ex dono ejusdem Walteri de Escotot quantum ad nos pertinet ecclesiam de Treuet[146] cum omnibus suis pertinenciis. Quare volumus et firmiter precipimus quod jamdicti canonici omnia supranominata et cetera quecumque in nostro habent dominio bene plenarie et in pace absque omni impeditione contradictione et vexatione nostrorum heredum nostorum et omnium teneant habeant gaudeant et possideant. Ut autem cuncta supranominata perpetuo eis rata firma et inconcussa permaneant presentem cartam sigilli nostri impressione roboravimus. Hiis testibus: domino R[icardo] Midensi episcopo, domino T[homa] Donensi episcopo, S[imone] Midensi archidiacono, A[dam] Parvo Cenanensi archidiacono, magistro L. tunc temporis officiali Midensi, magistro R. de Bureford, Willelmo de Lascy, R. Pendelon, T. filio Johannis filii Leonisii, W. et J. filiis Fabri et multis aliis clericis et laicis.

141 The family of de Escotot were tenants of Hugh I de Lacy in Herefordshire and Shropshire, centred on King's Pyon (near Weobley, Herefordshire): Robert Bartlett, 'Colonial aristocracies of the high Middle Ages' in Angus McKay and Robert Bartlett (eds), *Medieval frontier societies* (Oxford, 1992), 23–47, at 38–40. For the Irish branch, with lands at Donaghmore (bar. Ratoath) and Trevet (bar. Skreen), see *Reg. St Thomas*, 10, 12–20, 22–4, 48, 65–7, 262, 283.

142 See above, no. 2n.

143 For Donaghmore and Greenoge, see above, no. 5.

144 This anterior grant of Walter de Escotot to St Thomas's, made in the hundred court at Bristol, c.1214, stipulated that the beneficiaries should pay five silver marks every Michaelmas (29 September) in St Augustine's church, Bristol, notwithstanding any contrary winds, tempestuous seas, or piratical attacks: *Reg. St Thomas*, 15–17; Bartlett, 'Colonial aristocracies', 38–9.

145 'External service' indicated military service normally belonging to the king, rather than to the chief lord. Walter de Escotot had reserved external service in granting Donaghmore to St Thomas's, c.1214, so the meaning of the present clause appears to be that Walter would continue to provide the service owed to Hugh de Lacy by the terms of his original tenure, towards de Lacy's own obligation to the king: *Reg. St Thomas*, 17. For the participation of the Hiberno-Norman baronage in Henry III's foreign expedition of 1230 (and Hugh de Lacy's possible exemption), see above, 171–2.

146 The grange of Trevet was located in bar. Skreen, but formed part of Hugh II de Lacy's sub-tenancy in Meath: see above, 15.

(27)

Agreement between Hugh de Lacy, earl of Ulster, and the lady Rose de Verdun, whereby Hugh quitclaims all right, claim and complaint concerning that moiety of land which he demanded from Rose, by right of the agreement between Hugh and Thomas de Verdun, for all the days of Hugh's life, saving the right of his heirs if they are able to claim anything out of the former agreement. If Hugh's heirs wish to dispute the present agreement, he will annul their actions. Rose concedes that none of Hugh's tenants will be disturbed, rendering their services to Rose and her heirs, except for those disseised by Nicholas de Verdun, father of the said Rose, for failure of service. Rose gives to Hugh £200, to be paid within two years, by installments of £50 at Michaelmas (29 September) and Easter in the first year, and similarly in the second year. Made at Drogheda (Co. Louth) in the house of the hospital of St Mary outside the gate, in the nineteenth year of the reign of King Henry III. Rose has found pledges to observe said agreement, who are named in another instrument which Hugh has. Hugh and Rose pledge themselves to faithful observance, upon pain of excommunication by the bishop of Meath. If Hugh should die within the [two-year] term, the money will be fully repaid to his executors and assigns, and his heirs will hold the land as he held it on the day said agreement was made. Seals of R[ichard], bishop of Meath, Walter de Lacy and Richard de Burgh attached to the present writing, in the form of a chirograph.

[28 October 1234×27 October1235][147]

M: Dublin, NLI, MS 1646, fos 207v–8r [Gormanston register, s. xiv ex.–s. xv]. C: *Gorm. reg.*, 161–2.

Hec est convencio facta inter Hugonem de Lassy comitem Ultonie ex una parte et dominam Roesiam de Verdonne ex altera parte videlicet quod predictus Hugo de Lassy dimisit et quietum clamavit totum ius et clameum et querelam quod habuit et quod habere potuit in illam dimidietatem terre quam petiit domina Roesia de Verdonne iure convencionis quondam facte inter dictum comitem et Thomam de Verdune[148] quantum in eo est omnibus diebus vite sue salvo iure heredum suorum. Post decessum suum si quid adhipissi [*sic*] poterunt ex tali convencione inter dominum comitem et predictum Thomam quondam terram ita videlicet quod prefata Roesia de Verdun et heredes sui teneant et possideant totam illam medietatem terre quam dictus comes petiit ab illa Roesia tota vita ipsius comitis. Et si ita contigisset quod heredes dicti comitis eo vivente versus dictam Roesiam de Verdune vel heredes suos in aliquo reclamare voluissent vel quest[ionem] racionabiliter movere super dictam terram per dictam

[147] Internal date [‘*anno nonodecimo regni regis Henrici Anglie tercii*’ (19 Henry III)].
[148] See above, no. 4.

convencionem dictus comes omnino illud adnichilabit. Concessit autem prefata Roesia quod omnes feodati per ipsum comitem teneant et possideant bene et in pace facientibus eidem Roesie et heredibus suis serviciis quantum illis pertinet faciend[um] exceptis illis quorum terre seisita fuerunt in manum domini Nicolai de Verdun patris prefate Roesie sic aliter in manu sua maxime per defectum servicium. Pro hac autem concessione et quieta clamancia prefata Roesia dedit dicto domino Hugoni de Lassy ducentas libras argenti ita quod dicta pecunia paccabitur infra duos annos proximos sequentes post ipsam convencionem factam videlicet primo anno ad festum sancti Michaelis quinquaginta libras et ad Pasca quinquaginta libras et in secundo anno similiter ad festum sancti Michaelis quinquaginta libras et ad Pasca quinquaginta libras. Hec autem convencio facta fuit apud Drohedah[149] in domo hospitalis beate Marie extra portam[150] anno nonodecimo regni regis Henrici Anglie tercii. Et ad hos predictos terminos firmiter et fideliter observandos prefata Roesia salvos plegios invenit quorum nomina dictus comes in alio scripto habet nominatos. Ad hanc vero convencionem firmiter et fideliter observandam sepedictus Hugo de Lassy et prefata Roesia affidaverunt et etiam ad maioram huius rei securitatem dictus iterum Hugo de Lassy et dicta Roesia se obligaverunt quod si quis eorum contra hoc nemius presumpserit a domino episcopo Midens[i] sit excommunicatus et pro excomunicato se habeat quousque tam parti uni quam alteri fuerit emendatum. Et si fortasse dictus Hugo de Lassi infra dictum terminum infata decesserit pecunia prenominata executoribus et assignatis suis plenarie reddatur per predictam obligacionem. Predictus autem Hugo de Lassy et heredes sui tenebunt plene et integre totam terram sicud ille tenuit die convencionis facte. Et in cuius rei testimonium tam dictus Hugo de Lassy quam dicta Roesia una cum testimonium sigillorum domini R. Midens[is] et domini Walteri de Lassy et domini Ricardi de Burg[o] presenti scripto in modum cirografi confecto sigillum suum apposuit. Hiis testibus: domino R. Midens[i] episcopo, domino Waltero de Lassy, domino Ricardo de Burgo, Willelmo Grasso seniori, Nicolao Parvo, Milone de Verdune, Ada de Kusake, Henrico Walens[is], Henrico de Wotton, Ricardo de Wotton et aliis.

149 Drogheda (Co. Louth).

150 The absence of the qualification 'Magdalene' (in contrast to above, no. 10) implies that the hospital in question was that of St Mary (d'Urso), located outside Drogheda's west gate, founded by Ursus de Swemele c.1214, rather than the Dominican priory and hospital of St Mary Magdalen, situated to the north of the city: see Eoin Halpin, 'Excavations at St Mary d'Urso, Drogheda, county Louth', *JLAS* 23 (1996), 452–509; *Med. relig. houses*, 211, 224.

(28)

Hugh de Lacy, earl of Ulster, confirms to Maurice fitz Gerald, for his homage and service, the cantred of Carbury-Drumcliff (Co. Sligo), with all its appurtenances. To hold by Maurice and his heirs from Hugh and his heirs by hereditary right, freely and quietly (etc.), and in all liberties and free customs which Hugh or his heirs are able to give or warrant to said Maurice or his heirs, who will provide Hugh and his heirs with the service of two knights, and will render twenty marks per annum, by payments of ten marks at Easter and at Michaelmas, with one sore (unmewed) hawk at said feast of St Michael, or a half-mark, for all service, exactions and demands pertaining to Hugh or his heirs. Sealing clause.

[1235×42][151]

M: Dublin, NLI, MS 5769, fo 5v ['photostat' copy of *Red book of Kildare*; deeds relating to the Leinster FitzGeralds, s. xvi in.]. P: *Red bk Kildare*, 26–7, no. 22.

Sciant presentes et futuri quod ego Hugo de Lascy comes Ultonie dedi concessi et hac presenti carta mea confirmavi Mauricio filio Geraldi[152] pro homagio et servicio suo cantredum de Carebre Drumclef[153] cum omnibus suis pertinenciis, tenendum et habendum sibi et heredibus suis de me et heredibus meis iure hereditario, libere et quiete plene integre et honorifice bene et in pace in bosco et plano in viis et semitis in pratis et pascuis in moris et mariscis in aquis et stagnis et molendinis in castris et forcelestis in rivariis vivariis et piscariis in ecclesiis et capellis et in[a] omnibus libertatibus et liberis consuetudinibus quas ego vel heredes mei dicto Mauricio vel heredibus suis dare vel warrantizare poterimus, faciendo inde ipse et heredes sui michi et heredibus meis servicium duorum militum necnon et reddendo viginti marcas annuas ad duos terminos videlicet decem marcas ad Pascha et decem marcas ad festum sancti Michaelis et unum ancipitrem sorum ad idem [festum] vel dimidiam marcam pro omni servicio exaccione et demanda ad me vel heredes meos pertinente. Et ut hec mea donacio concessio et confirmacio futuris temporibus perpetue firmitatis robur optineat illam presenti scripto et sigilli mei munimine roboravi. Hiis testibus: Ricardo de Tuyt, Radulfo de Picheford, Hugone Tirell, Thoma filio Leonis, Johanne de Cogan, Johanne Pincerna, Waltero Sanmell, Ricardo de

[151] Carbury was one of five Connacht cantreds (with Corran, Tireragh on the Moy, Luigne, and Slieve Lugha) granted to Hugh de Lacy by Richard de Burgh, subsequent to the Anglo-Norman expedition of 1235: see above, 190.

[152] See above, no. 23; below, no. x.

[153] Carbury-Drumcliff, which formed the main part of the Geraldine manor of Sligo: see MacCotter, *Medieval Ireland*, 132–3.

Wodynton, Petro de Bermegham, Waltero Hosee, Johanne le Chen et multis aliis.

[a] M: large ink blotch; no apparent syntactic interruption.

(29)

Hugh de Lacy, earl of Ulster, confirms to God and blessed Mary and St Patrick of Newry (Co. Down), and the abbot L., and the monks serving God there, all reasonable gifts which Muirchertach Mac Lochlainn and Magnus Mac Duinn Sléibe and Murchad Ua Cerbaill and other lawful men gave to them before the coming of the English to Ireland. In addition, Hugh confirms the castle of 'Athcruthain' (Sheeptown, par. Newry), with all the island and its appurtenances. Grantees will supply three priests for the souls of Hugh's mother and father; of his ancestors and successors; and of the countesses Lescelina and Emelina. Said abbot and convent have granted in advance all their land of 'Cremkayl' (Cranfield, par. Kilkeel), with all its appurtenances, retaining to them the tithes, revenues, offerings and obventions of that land, which Hugh and his successors will warrant to said monks in perpetuity against all men. Hugh has also granted to said convent and abbot four burgages in his vill of 'Heirinach' (Greencastle, Co. Down), with twenty-four acres beyond his demense towards the mill of Ua Dimegain to the northern side, and of the same tenement and with the fishery. After the death of the parson, Cristinus, Hugh shall grant to said monks the whole parsonage of 'Cluainfechragh' and of 'Ofirg', with greater tithes of Hugh's fishery of 'Herenach' (Greencastle). Sealing clause.

[1237 (before 17 October)][154]

M: London, BL, Add. MS 4821, fo 145 [transcript in collection of Sir James Ware, s. xvii]. P: Flanagan, *Irish royal charters*, 388–9.

Omnibus Christi fidelibus has litteras inspecturis vel audituris Hugo de Lascy comes Ultonie salutem. Noverit universitas vestra nos pro salute anime nostre necnon et animarum patrum et matrum nostrarum et animabus comitissarum Lesteline[155] et Eveline[156] et pro animabus omnium antecessorum et successorum nostrorum confirmasse domui Dei et beatae Marie et sancti Patricii de Viridi

[154] Internal date ['*anno ab incarnatione domini m.cc.xxxvii*']. The principal witness, Donatus Ua Fidabra, archbishop of Armagh, died before 17 October 1237: *NHI*, ix, 269.

[155] Lescelina de Lacy (née de Verdun), first wife of Hugh de Lacy, was possibly still alive in 1226: see above, 175.

[156] Emelina de Lacy (née de Ridelisford, †c.1276), second wife of Hugh de Lacy: see above, 22, 187, 198, 202, 208.

Ligno[157] et L. abbati[158] et monachis ibidem Deo servientibus omnia rationabilia dona que Murciertach Maglachlain[159] et Magnus mac Donslebe[160] et Murchad O Kerbail[161] et viri alii legales ante adventum Anglicorum ad Hyberniam eis dederunt secundum consuetudinem regni Hibernie tam in terris quam in grangiis edificiis piscariis et in locis aliis. Confirmamus etiam castrum de Athcruthain[162] cum tota insula et pertinenciis suis. Dicti vero abbas et conventus de Viridi Ligno invenient 3 sacerdotes ad divina celebranda in perpetuum pro animabus omnium innominatorum. Et sciendum est quod prefatus abbas et conventus nobis concesserunt totam terram suorum de Cremkayl[163] cum omnibus pertinenciis suis remanentibus sibi decimis oblationibus et obventionibus eiusdem terre que nos et successores nostri dictis monachis contra omnes homines in perpetuum warrantizabimus. Donavimus etiam sepedicto conventui et abbati 4 burgagia in villa nostra de Heirinach[164] cum 24 acris terre extra dominicum nostrum versus molendinum O Dimegain de parte aquilonali et de eodem tenemento et cum piscaria. Post decessum vero Cristini personae donabimus predictis monachis totum personatum de Cluainfechragh et de Ofirg cum decimis maioris piscarie nostre de Herenach. Hec autem donatio et confirmatio facte fuerunt anno ab incarnatione domini m.cc.xxxvii. Et ut hec nostra donatio et confirmatio rate inconcusse et stabiles permaneant presens scriptum sigilli nostri munitione roboravimus. Hiis testibus domino D. primato, domino T. Dunensi episcopo, G. Dromorensi episcopo, I. et G. de Jugo Dei et Ines abbatibus, R. priore de Duno, R. Talebot, H. Wallensis, M. clerico, H. Pastelew et multis aliis.

157 Newry Abbey (fd c.1153): *Med. relig. houses*, 142.

158 Not found in the abbatial list provided by Gearóid Mac Niocaill, *Na manaigh liatha in Éirinn, 1142–c.1600* (Dublin, 1959), 168–70.

159 For the confirmation and grant of protection to Newry, c.1157, by Muirchertach Mac Lochlainn, king of Cenél nEógain (1136–43, 1145–66) and high-king of Ireland (1156–66), see Flanagan, *Irish royal charters*, 107–24, 291–305.

160 This grant by Magnus Mac Duinn Sléibe, king of Ulaid (1166–71), to Newry, has not survived: ibid, appendix 1, no. 8.

161 Murchad Ua Cerbaill, king of Airgialla (1168–89), who, along with his father, Donnchad (†1168), gave permission for Muirchertach Mac Lochlainn's confirmation and grant of protection to Newry, c.1157: ibid., 293–4.

162 'Athcruithin' (Áth Cruithne: *AU*, 926), located in the townland of Sheepstown (par. Newry) was confirmed to Newry Abbey by Muirchertach Mac Lochlainn, c.1157: Flanagan, *Irish royal charters*, 292–3; *Place-names of Northern Ireland*, i, 37–8. This location may be synonymous with the fortress on the Newry River, known as 'Crown Mound', whose name derives from 'Cruithen' (i.e. of the Cruithin): *Place-names of Northern Ireland*, i, 36.

163 'Cromcaill', identified with Cranfield (par. Kilkeel, bar. Mourne), was also subject to confirmation by Muirchertach Mac Lochlainn: Flanagan, *Irish Royal Charters*, 292–3; *Place-names of Northern Ireland*, iii, 33.

164 Greencastle (par. Kilkeel): *Place-names of Northern Ireland*, iii, 42–5, and above, 177, 199, 204.

(30)

Hugh de Lacy, earl of Ulster, confirms to Albert [Suerbeer], archbishop of Armagh, primate of all Ireland, and his successors, all the land of Morgallion (Co. Meath) and Hugh's manor of Nobber (caput of bar. Morgallion), with demesnes, homages and all their appurtenances, to possess in perpetuity, in exchange for the lands which Hugh held of the church of Armagh, or anyone else of his name. To hold by Albert and his successors from Hugh and his heirs, freely, quietly (etc.), and in all other liberties and free custums or other things pertaining to said land and manor, retaining nothing to Hugh or his heirs, causing to be rendered by way of external service (i.e. service not owing to an intermediate overlord) one pound of wax annually at Easter for all demands and secular exactions. Hugh and his heirs after him will also warrant to said archbishop and his successors said land and manor, with all their appurtenances, for said render, before all in perpetuity. Sealing clause.[165]

[November 1241][166]

M: Belfast, PRONI, MS DIO/4/2/2, fo 48 [register of Nicholas Fleming, archbishop of Armagh (1404–16)]. P: *a*. Smith (ed.), *Register of Nicholas Fleming*, 201–2; *b*. *Chartae, privilegia et immunitates: being transcripts of charters and privileges to cities, towns, abbeys and other bodies corporate, 1171–1395* (Dublin, 1889), 24 [from the Irish plea rolls, destroyed in the Dublin PROI fire, 1922]. C: H. J. Lawlor, 'A calendar of the register of Archbishop Fleming', *PRIA* C 30 (1912/13), 94–190, at 150.

Sciant presentes et futuri quod ego Hugo de Lacy comes Ultonie dedi et concessi et hac presenti carta mea confirmavi pro me et heredibus meis venerabili patri Alberto archiepiscopo Armachane[a][167] totius Hibernie primati eiusque successoribus totam terram de Machergalyn[b] et manerium meum de Nobyr[c][168]

[165] For context, see above, 179.

[166] Internal dating in reference to the pontificate of Pope Gregory IX ['*actum anno gratie M°CC° quadragesimo primo, mense Novembris, pontificatus Domini Gregorii pape Noni anno quintodecimo*'], implies drafting by a clerk among Archbishop Suerbeer's familia. The notary was seemingly unaware of Gregory's death on 22 August 1241, nor the swift demise of Gregory's successor, Celestine IV, on 10 November 1241.

[167] Albert Suerbeer of Cologne, archbishop of Armagh (1240–46): see above, 179n.

[168] The barony of Morgallion (Co. Meath), with its *caput* at Nobber, had already been granted by Hugh de Lacy to his daughter, Matilda, before 1235 (above, no. 20). Some confusion surrounded Nobber's status after the earl's death in 1242 (see above, 168), while a later legal dispute reveals that de Lacy had reneged on the terms of the present grant. In 1302, a plaint brought by Nicholas Mac Máel Ísu, archbishop of Armagh (1270–1303), against one Nicholas de Netterville, for one messuage, one mill, 200 acres and 40s. of rent at Nobber, was opposed by Matilda (wife of William of London), great-granddaughter of Hugh II de Lacy. Although jurors in the case eventually found in favour of Matilda, and debarred Archbishop Nicholas from further action for his own lifetime,

cum dominiis homagiis et omnibus suis pertinentiis perpetuo possidenda in compensationem videlicet omnium terrarum quas ego ab ecclesia Armachana[d] tenui vel aliquis nomine meo[169] tenenda et habenda sibi suisque successoribus de me et heredibus meis, libere quiete integre et plenarie in bosco et plano pratis et pasturis in moris et mariscis in stagnis et vivariis in aquis et molendinis in ecclesiis et capellis et in omnibus aliis libertatibus et liberis consuetudinibus vel rebus aliis ad prefatam terram et manerium pertinentibus adeo etiam libere integre et quiete sicut ego unquam predictam terram et manerium cum eorum pertinentibus quibuscunque integris liberius et quietus tenui et possedi sine aliquo retinemento[e] mei vel [ ][f] heredum meorum, faciendo inde forinsecum[g] servicium reddendo nichilominus inde singulis annis pro se et successoribus suis michi et heredibus meis unam libram cere ad Pascha pro omni servicio demanda et exactione seculari. Ego autem et heredes mei post me predicto archiepiscopo et suis successoribus predictam terram et manerium cum omnibus pertinentiis suis pro predicto redditu contra omnes warentizabimus in perpetuum. Actum [ ][h] anno gratie M°CC° quadragesimo primo mense Novembris pontificatus Domini G[re]g[orii] pape Noni anno quintodecimo. Ut autem hec mea donatio concessio confirmatio et warentizatio perpetuis temporibus robur fortitudinis optineant presentem cartam sigilli mei munimine roboravi. Hiis testibus: Johanne de Alnato[i] et Thoma de Bartoun fratribus minoribus, Simone de Clifford, Roberto de Cruis, Johanne de Clintoun, Rogero Thalin[j] et Galfrido filio Philipi, militibus, Willelmo capellano comitis, Rogero de Kenley,[k] Roberto de Capella, Simone de Drogheda[l] et Eudone de Lindeseya,[m] clericis[n] et multis aliis.

[a] *Pb*: 'Ardm~'. [b] *Pb*: 'mathergalyng'. [c] *Pb*: 'del Nober'. [d] *Pb*: 'Ardm~'. [e] *Pb*: 'retenemento'. [f] M: scored out. [g] *Pb*: 'forincecum'. [h] M: 'anni', scored out. [i] *Pb*: 'Alucco'. [j] *Pb*: 'Talon'. [k] *Pb*: 'Kenlys'. [l] *Pb*: 'Drotheda'. [m] *Pb*: 'Lyndeseya'. [n] *Pb*: om., 'clericis'.

the record also stated that Albert Suerbeer had been seised of the disputed tenements 'in right of his church of Armagh, and was unjustly disseised by Hugh de Lacy': *Cal. justiciary rolls*, i, 432–9, at 436. For Nicholas de Netterville, see Smith, *Colonisation and conquest*, 81–2.

169 On 15 July 1301 Archbishop Nicholas of Armagh resigned any claim to the tenement of 'Coulrath (Coleraine, Co. Londonderry) in Touscard (county of Twescard)', originating 'from the time when Hugh de Lacy gave to Albert, archbishop of Armagh, our successor, our manor of Nobber in compensation for said tenement': *Chart. privil. immun.*, 40. Orpen identified the lands in question as the *villa monasterii* ('grange of the monastery'), assessed by the *custos* of Twescard in 1262: Orpen, *Normans*, 424–5.

Appendix II

Lost *acta* of Hugh de Lacy*

(i)

Grant by Hugh de Lacy to H. de Say, knight of the diocese of Armagh, of 'Balimerlongfortan' in Uriel.[1]

[1194×1202][2]

M: Vatican, *Regesta* 7, fo 24r [Papal register, 8–9 Innocent III, 1205–7].
P: *Pont. Hib.*, i, no. 63. C: *Cal. papal letters*, i, 22.

Letter of Pope Innocent III addressing a dispute between the canons of St Mary's, Louth, and one H. de Say, knight of the diocese of Armagh. On foot from a gift of Hugh de Lacy, de Say had occupied the land of 'Balimerlongfortan',[3] previously given to the canons of St Mary's by the king of 'Eriel' (Uriel), notwithstanding the admonishment of John of Salerno, then papal legate to Ireland. 6 June 1205.

* The following list includes only those acta which can be explicitly attributed to Hugh de Lacy (excluding, for example, grants of land which might be inferred from later tenure, but where a dispositive act is not alluded to in the documentary evidence).

1 For context, see above, 82, 84–5, 177.

2 *Ante quem* from the legation of John of Salerno to Ireland (1202): see above, 32–3, 82, 84. *Post quem* from Hugh de Lacy's earliest acquisition of land in Uriel: see above, no. 4.

3 Stephenstown? (formerly Stephenstown de Say, Co. Louth): Otway-Ruthven, 'Partition', 404.

(ii)

Grant by Hugh de Lacy to Henry de Audley, of Dunleer (Co. Louth), with appurtenances.[4]

[1194×2 May 1227][5]

M: *a*. Kew, TNA, C 53/18 [charter roll, 11 Henry III, pt 1, *m*. 6]; *b*. Kew, TNA, E 326/12466 [Augmentation Office, Ancient Deeds]. C: *a*. *CCHR, 1226–57*, 36–7; *b*. *CDI*, i, 1505; Paul Dryburgh and Brendan Smith, 'Calendar of documents relating to medieval Ireland in the series of Ancient Deeds in the National Archives of the United Kingdom', *Anal. Hib*. 39 (2006), 1, 3–61, at 57.

King Henry III confirms to Henry 'de Aldithele' (Audley)[6] various lands and tenements in England and Ireland, including the town called 'Dunlir' (Dunleer, Co. Louth), of the gift of Hugh de Lacy, earl of Ulster. 2 May 1227.

(iii)

Grant by Hugh de Lacy, earl of Ulster, to Gilbert de Lacy, grantor's brother, of the churches of Rooskey and Carlingford (Co. Louth), and the churches of Cooley (Co. Louth), with tithes and obventions.[7]

[29 May 1205×10][8]

M: Edinburgh, NRS, GD 45/27/8, fo 52v [cartulary, St Andrews cathedral priory; s. xiii in. copy]. P: *St A lib.*, 118.

Charter of Hugh de Lacy, as earl of Ulster, confirming to the church of St Andrew in Scotland and the canons serving there, a grant of churches in Ireland, as well and as fully as Gilbert de Lacy,[9] Hugh's brother, possessed said benefices.

4 Granted with the lands and constableship previously held from Hugh de Lacy by Henry's brother, Adam de Audley (below, no. vii). For context, see above, 73, 143, 176.

5 *Post quem* from Hugh de Lacy's earliest acquisition of land in Uriel: see above, no. 4.

6 For Henry de Audley, see above, 143n, 176.

7 Contained in no. 9, above.

8 See above, no. 9.

9 See above, 14, 75, 144n.

(iv)

Grant by Hugh de Lacy to Ralph Pedelowe, of Larne and Drumaliss (Co. Antrim).[10]

[29 May 1205×10] or [1223×42][11]

M: Kew, TNA, C 53/18 [charter roll, 29 Henry III, *m.* 2]. C: *CCHR, 1226–57*, 287.

King Henry III confirms to Ralph 'Pel de Lu' (Pedelowe)[12] the land of 'Inver' and 'Dumnal' (Larne and Drumaliss, Co. Antrim),[13] which he has of the gift of Hugh de Lacy, late earl of Ulster. 24 September 1245.

(v)

Grant by Hugh de Lacy to Robert Savage of the tuath of 'Kineltweuthel' in 'Dalrod' (Dál Riata, north Antrim).[14]

[29 May 1205×10] or [2 May 1227×42][15]

M: London, BL Add. MS 6041 [rubrics of charters and documents relating to the inheritance of Philippa, wife of Edmund Mortimer (†1381), third earl of March and earl of Ulster *jure uxoris*]. P: Robin Frame, 'A register of lost deeds concerning the earldom of Ulster, c.1230–1376', in Duffy (ed.), *Princes, prelates and poets*, 85–106, at 94.

'La chartre Hugh de Lacy counte duluestre par quele il ad done a Robert Salvage[16] la Tweuth qest appellez Kineltweuthel en Dalrod (Dál Riata).[17] saunz date'.

10 For context, see above, 127.
11 Although Hugh was only officially restored to his comital lordship in 1227, the grant to Ralph Pedelowe could conceivably have been made in the preceding four years, subsequent to de Lacy's return to Ireland in 1223: see above, 150.
12 See above, 127, 150.
13 Reeves, *Eccl. ant.*, 54–5.
14 For context, see above, 71, 173.
15 Based on comital style. For evidence pointing to an issue date subsequent to de Lacy's restoration in 1227, see above, 173.
16 See above, 71, 173.
17 The cantred of 'Dalrod' (*alias* Dalrede, Dalrethe), later absorbed by that of Twescard, is identified with the pre-Anglo-Norman kingdom of Dál Riata, the bounds of which roughly extended from the River Bush to the Ravel Water: MacCotter, *Medieval Ireland*, 230–1.

(vi)

Grant of Hugh de Lacy to lord Dominic, canon of Osma, and the brothers and ladies of Prouille (Fanjeaux, dép. Aude), of land at Villenouvette (dép. Aude, cant. Estissac), between Pech-Luna (cant. Belpech) and Villepinte (cant. Estissac).[18]

[1211×May1213][19]

P: *a*. *Monumenta diplomatica*, 44–5; *b*. *Cart. Prouille*, i, 54; c. Jean Giffre (de Réchac), *La vie du glorieux patriarche Sainte Dominique* (Paris, 1647), 203–4; *d*. Jean-Jaques Percin, *Monumenta conventus Tolosani ordinis F.F. praedicatorum primi* (Toulouse, 1693), 13. C: Molinier, 'Catalogue des actes de Simon et d'Amauri de Montfort', 467.

Charter of Simon de Montfort, as viscount of Béziers and Carcassone, by the assent and wish of his wife, Alice de Montmorency (†1221) and first-born, Amaury de Montfort (†1241), confirming that which Hugh de Lacy, lord of Laurac and Castelnaudary (dép. Aude), has given to the lord Dominic, canon of Osma, and the brothers and ladies of Prouille, now and in perpetuity: namely, those lands which Hugh has and ought to have at 'Villamnovetam' (Villenouvette, dép. Aude),[20] between 'Podium Suiranum' and 'Villam Pictam' (Pech-Luna and Villepinte). Carcassonne, May 1213.

(vii)

Grant of Hugh de Lacy to Henry de Audley, of the lands that Adam de Audley, grantee's brother, held from grantor, with the constabulary of all of Hugh's lands of Ulster and of all his conquests, with Killard (Co. Down) and Kane (Co. Louth).[21]

[1223×2 May 1227][22]

M: *a*. Kew, TNA, C 53/18 [charter roll, 11 Henry III, pt 1, *m*. 6]; *b*. Kew, TNA, E 326/12466 [Augmentation Office, Ancient Deeds]. C: *a*. *CCHR, 1226–57*, 36–7; *b*. *CDI*, i, 1505; c.Dryburgh and Smith, 'Calendar of documents in the series of Ancient Deeds', 57.

18 For context, see above, 125.

19 *Post quem* from Simon de Montfort's confirmation; *ante quem* from Hugh's likely arrival on the Albigensian crusade: see above, 118–19.

20 Cazes, 'Un village castral de la plaine lauragaise: Lasbordes (Aude)', 4–5.

21 For context, see above, 73n, 176, 197.

22 First comital period ruled out by Adam de Audley's death, c.1211: Philip Morgan, 'Audley family (c.1130–1391)', in ODNB. *Post quem* from Hugh de Lacy's return to Ireland in 1223: see above, 141–2.

King Henry III confirms to Henry de Audley various lands and tenements in England and Ireland, including the town of Dunleer in Louth (above, no. ii), and all the lands which Adam de Audley,[23] brother of Henry, held from Hugh de Lacy, with the constabulary of Hugh's land in Ulster and of all his conquests, with 'Ledcathel Rinles' (Killard, Audleystown, Co. Down)[24] and 'Hurielkien' (Kane, Co. Louth).[25] 2 May 1227.

(viii)

Grant of Hugh de Lacy to an unknown beneficiary, of Ballygalley (Co. Antrim).[26]

[c.1224 (before August)][27]

M: Kew, TNA, C 54/31, 32 [close roll, 8 Henry III, pt 3, *m.* 8; pt 2, *m.* 8]. P: *RLC*, i, 587a, 615. C: *CDI*, i, no 1200.

King Henry III to William Marshal, justiciar of Ireland. King John had granted to Duncan (earl) of Carrick the land called 'Balgeitheluah',[28] of which Hugh de Lacy has disseised Duncan and conferred the land on another. 4 August 1224.

(ix)

Concord between Donatus (Ua Fidabra), archbishop of Armagh, and the dean and cathedral chapter [of Armagh], and Hugh de Lacy, concerning various arrangements made between them.[29]

[1227×37][30]

M: London, BL Add. MS 6041 [rubrics of charters and documents relating to the inheritance of Philippa, wife of Edmund Mortimer (†1381), third earl of March and earl of Ulster *jure uxoris*]. P: Frame, 'Register of lost deeds', 93.

23 See above, 73, 143n.
24 Reeves, *Eccl. ant.*, 39.
25 Otway-Ruthven, 'Partition', 404.
26 For context, see above, 157, 173.
27 See above, 157.
28 See above, 157, 173.
29 For context, see above, 177–8, 181.
30 Donatus Ua Fidabra was archbishop of Armagh from 1227 until his death in 1237 (before 17 October): *NHI*, ix, 269.

'Lescrit entre Donat' Ercevesque darm[agh] et le deon et le chapitre illeqe et Hugh de Lacy de divers composicions entre eux faitz. saunz date.'

(x)

Grant of Hugh de Lacy to Jordan of Exeter, of a moiety of the half-cantred of Luigne, in Connacht.[31]

[1235×10 September 1240][32]

M: Dublin, NLI, MS 5769, fo 62v [*Red book of Kildare* ('photostat' copy); deeds relating to the Leinster FitzGeralds, s. xvi in.]. P: *Red bk Kildare*, 167.

Chirograph between Maurice fitz Gerald, justiciar of Ireland, and Jordan of Exeter, at Ardrahan (Co. Galway), 10 September 1240. Jordan gives to Maurice the moiety of the half-cantred of 'Luyna' (Luigne) which Jordan holds from the earl of Ulster, to hold for the service of one knight by returning 100s. annually.[33]

[31] For context, see above, 28, 190.

[32] *Post quem* from Hugh de Lacy's acquisition of Luigne, subsequent to the Anglo-Norman re-conquest of Connacht: see above, 190.

[33] The moiety of southern Luigne retained by Jordan of Exeter, lord of Affane (Co. Waterford), included most of the barony of Gallen (Co. Mayo), excluding the manor retained by Hugh de Lacy at Meelick: Orpen, *Normans*, 380–1; MacCotter, *Medieval Ireland*, 139–40, and above, 190. As well as the territory specified by the present grant, Maurice fitz Gerald also held the half-cantred of northern Luigne, together making up the later barony of Leyney (Co. Sligo). The northern portion was perhaps a gift from Hugh de Lacy (see above, nos 23, 27), but no such grant is alluded to in the charter of Richard de Burgh (dated c.1235/6 by Mac Niocaill) which confirmed to Maurice *suo dimidium cantredum de Luyne*: *Red bk Kildare*, 28.

Appendix III

Index of persons in charter-texts

Key: **witness/(beneficiary)**/mentioned

Appendix IV

Index of place names in charter-texts

Bibliography

Manuscripts consulted

Belfast

PRONI, MS DIO/4/2/2 (register, Nicholas Fleming, archbishop of Armagh, 1404–16)

Dublin

NLI, MS 1646 (Gormanston register)
NLI, MS 5769 (Red book of Kildare)
NLI, MS 6136 (abstracts of title deeds, de Mandeville family)
NLI, MS D 971 (inspeximus of Henry IV, 24 April 1401)

Edinburgh

NRS, GD 45/27/8 (cartulary, St Andrews cathedral priory)

Kew

TNA, C 66/207 (patent rolls, Edward III)
TNA, C 66/278 (patent rolls, Edward III)
TNA, C 53/18 (charter rolls, Henry III)
TNA, C 54/31, 32 (close rolls, Henry III)
TNA, C 115/75 (cartulary, Llanthony Secunda)
TNA, C 115/80 (cartulary, Llanthony Prima)
TNA, E 164/2 (King's remembrancer, Red book of the exchequer)
TNA, E 326/12466 (Augmentation Office, Ancient Deeds)

London

BL, Add. Charter 19803 (grant, Walter de Lacy to Beaubec Abbey, Normandy)
BL, Add. MS 4792 (Ware collection)
BL, Add. MS 4797 (Ware collection)
BL, Add. MS 4821 (Ware collection)
BL, Cotton MS Titus B XI (records relating to Ireland, 1272–1558)

Oxford

Bodleian Library, MS Rawlinson B 500 (cartulary, St Thomas's Abbey, Dublin)
Magdalen College, MSS Wanborough, 6a, 19, 20a, 22, 23, 24, 25, 31a, 33, 36a, 48a, 56a, 57a, 58a, 59a, 66 (Wanborough deeds)

Paris

Bibliothèque Nationale de France, Doat 98 (Doat collection, Languedoc, 1663–70)

Toulouse

AD Haute-Garonne, Serie H, ordre de Malte, Renneville 1 (order of Hospitallers, Toulouse)

Published primary sources

The acts and letters of the Marshal family: marshals of England and earls of Pembroke, 1145–1248, ed. David Crouch, Camden Fifth Series 47 (Cambridge, 2015)
The acts of Welsh rulers, 1120–1283, ed. Huw Pryce (Cardiff, 2005)
Amis and Amiloun, Robert of Cisyle and Sir Amadace, ed. Edward Foster (2nd edn, Kalamazoo, 1997)
Anglo-Scottish relations: some selected documents, ed. E. L. G. Stones (2nd edn, Oxford, 1970)
Annála Connacht: the annals of Connacht, A.D. 1224–1544, ed. A. M. Freeman (Dublin, 1970)
Annala rioghachta Eireann: annals of the kingdom of Ireland by the Four Masters from the earliest period to the year 1616, ed. John O'Donovan (7 vols, Dublin, 1851)

Annala Uladh. Annals of Ulster, otherwise Annala Senait, Annals of Senat; a chronicle of Irish affairs, A.D. 431–1131, 1155–1541, ed. Bartholomew Mac Carthy (4 vols, Dublin, 1893)

Annales Cambriae, ed. John Williams ab Ithel, Rolls Series (London, 1860)

Annales Cambriae, trans. Paul Martin Remfry (Shrewsbury, 2007)

Annales monastici, ed. H. R. Luard, Rolls Series (5 vols, London, 1864–9)

Annals and antiquities of Lacock Abbey, in the county of Wiltshire, ed. W. L. Bowles and J. G. Nichols (London, 1835)

The annals of Clonmacnoise, being annals of Ireland from the earliest period to A.D. 1408, ed. Denis Murphy, trans. Conell Mageoghagan (Dublin, 1896)

The annals of Inisfallen (MS Rawlinson B 503), ed. Seán Mac Airt (Dublin, 1951)

The annals of Ireland by Friar John Clyn, ed. Bernadette Williams (Dublin, 2007)

The annals of Loch Cé. A chronicle of Irish affairs from A.D. 1014 to A.D. 1590, ed. W. M. Hennessy, Rolls Series (2 vols, London, 1871)

Annals of the reigns of Malcolm and William, kings of Scotland, ed. A. C. Lawrie (Glasgow, 1910)

Binchy, D. A., *Corpus iuris Hibernici* (6 vols, Dublin, 1978)

Boethius, *The consolation of philosophy*, trans. Richard Green (Indianapolis, 1962)

Brown, Daniel J. F., 'Select document: a charter of Hugh II de Lacy, earl of Ulster, to Hugh Hose', *IHS* 38, no. 151 (2013), 492–510

Calendar of the Carew manuscripts preserved in the archiepiscopal library at Lambeth, 1515–74 [etc.] (6 vols, London, 1867–73)

Calendar of the charter rolls, 1226–57 [etc.] (6 vols, London, 1903–1927)

Calendar of the close rolls, 1272–9 [etc.] (47 vols, London, 1892–1963)

Calendar of documents preserved in France, illustrative of the history of Great Britain and Ireland, A.D. 918–1206, ed. J. H. Round (London, 1889)

Calendar of documents relating to Ireland preserved in Her Majesty's Public Record Office, London, 1171–1251 [etc.], ed. H. S. Sweetman and G. F. Handcock (5 vols, London, 1875–86)

Calendar of documents relating to Scotland preserved in Her Majesty's Public Record Office, London, 1108–1272 [etc.], ed. Joseph Bain (4 vols, Edinburgh, 1881–8)

Calendar of entries in the papal registers relating to Great Britain and Ireland: papal letters, 1198–1304 [etc.] (12 vols, London, 1893–1933)

Calendar of the Gormanston register: from the original in the possession of the Right Honourable the viscount of Gormanston, ed. James Mills and M. J. McEnery (Dublin, 1916)

Calendar of the justiciary rolls: or, proceedings in the court of the justiciar of Ireland preserved in the Public Record Office of Ireland, ed. James Mills (3 vols, Dublin, 1905)

Calendar of the patent and close rolls of the chancery in Ireland, Henry VIII to 18th Elizabeth, ed. James Morrin (2 vols, Dublin, 1861–2)

Calendar of the patent rolls, 1232–47 [etc.] (London, 1901–16)

The cartae antiquae rolls, 11–20, printed from the original MSS in the Public Record Office, ed. James Conway Davies, Pipe Roll Society (London, 1960)

Cartulaire de Notre-Dame de Prouille, ed. Jean Guiraud (2 vols, Paris, 1907)

Cartulaire Normand de Philippe-Auguste, Louis VIII, Saint-Louis et Philippe-le-Hardi, ed. Léopold Delisle (Paris, 1882)

Cartulaire ou histoire diplomatique de Saint Dominique, ed. François Balme, Paul Lelaidier and Joachim Collomb (3 vols, Paris, 1893–1901)

Catalogue of Irish manuscripts in the British Museum, ed. S. H. O'Grady and Robin Flower (2 vols, London, 1926–53)

Cert cech ríg co réil, ed. and trans. Tadhg O'Donoghue, in Osborn Bergin and Carl Marstrander (eds), *Miscellany presented to Kuno Meyer* (Halle, 1912), 258–77

Chārtae, privilegia et immunitates: being transcripts of charters and privileges to cities, towns, abbeys and other bodies corporate, 1171–1395 (Dublin, 1889)

The charters of the Anglo-Norman earls of Chester, c. 1071–1237, ed. Geoffrey Barraclough (Chester, 1988)

Charters of the honour of Mowbray, 1107–91, ed. D. E. Greenway (London, 1972)

Chartularies of St Mary's Abbey, Dublin: with the register of its house at Dunbrody and annals of Ireland, 1162–1370, ed. J. T. Gilbert, Rolls Series (2 vols, London, 1884–6)

The chartulary or register of the abbey of St Werburgh, Chester, ed. James Tait (2 vols, Manchester, 1920–3)

Christ Church deeds, ed. M. J. McEnery and Raymond Refaussé (Dublin, 2001).

Chronica de Mailros e codice unico in bibliotheca Cottoniana servato, nunc iterum in lucem edita (Edinburgh, 1835)

Chronica magistri Rogeri de Houedene, ed. William Stubbs, Rolls Series (4 vols, London, 1869–71)

The chronicle of Melrose Abbey: a stratigraphic edition. Volume 1: introduction and facsimile edition, ed. Dauvit Broun and Julian Harrison (Woodbridge, 2007)

Chronicle of the kings of Mann and the Isles, ed. and trans. George Broderick and Brian Stowell (Edinburgh, 1973)

The chronicle of William of Puylaurens: the Albigensian crusade and its aftermath, ed. and trans. W. A. Sibly and M. D. Sibly (Rochester, NY, 2003)

Chronicles of the reigns of Stephen, Henry II and Richard I, ed. Richard Howlett, Rolls Series (4 volumes, London, 1884–9)

Chronicon de Lanercost, ed. Joseph Stevenson (Edinburgh, 1839)

Chronicon Galfridi le Baker de Swynebroke, ed. E. M. Thompson (Oxford, 1889)

Chronique [de] Guillaume de Puylaurens: chronica magistri Guillelmi de Podio Laurentii, ed. Jean Duvernoy (Paris, 1976)

Close rolls of the reign of Henry III, 1227–31 [etc.] (14 vols, London, 1892–1963)

Colgan, John, *Acta triadis thaumaturgae* (Louvain, 1647)

Colmcille, Fr., 'Three unpublished Cistercian documents', *JLAS* 13 (1955), 252–78

Crouch, David, 'The complaint of King John against William de Briouze (c. September 1210)', in J. S. Loengard (ed.), *Magna Carta and the England of King John* (Woodbridge, 2010), 168–179

Curia regis rolls of the reigns of Richard I and John, preserved in the Public Record Office (7 vols, London, 1922–35)

The deeds of the Normans in Ireland: la geste des Engleis en Yrlande, ed. Evelyn Mullally (Dublin, 2002)

Documents illustrative of English history in the thirteenth and fourteenth centuries, selected from the records of the Queeen's remembrancer of the exchequer, ed. Henry Cole (London, 1844)

Dowdall deeds, ed. Charles McNeill and A. J. Otway-Ruthven (Dublin, 1960)

Dryburgh, Paul and Brendan Smith, 'Calendar of documents relating to medieval Ireland in the series of Ancient Deeds in the National Archives of the United Kingdom', *Anal. Hib.* 39 (2006), 1, 3–61

Dugdale, William, *Monasticon Anglicanum* (6 vols in 8, London, 1846)

Earldom of Gloucester charters: the charters and scribes of the earls and countesses of Gloucester to A.D. 1217, ed. R. B. Patterson (Oxford, 1973)

Early sources of Scottish history, A.D. 500–1286, ed. A. O. Anderson (2 vols, Edinburgh, 1922)

Early Yorkshire charters: being a collection of documents anterior to the thirteenth century made from the public records, monastic chartularies, Roger Dodsworth's manuscripts and other available sources, ed. William Farrer (3 vols, Edinburgh, 1914–16)

English episcopal acta, VI: Norwich, 1070–1214, ed. Christopher Harper-Bill (Oxford, 1990)

English episcopal acta, XI: Exeter, 1046–1184, ed. Frank Barlow (Oxford, 1996)

Extracts from the MS liber Luciani de laude Cestrie written about the Year 1195 and now in the Bodleian Library, Oxford, ed. M. V. Taylor, *The Record Society of Lancashire and Cheshire* 64 (1912)

Félire Óengusso ('the martyrology of Óengus'), ed. and trans. Whitley Stokes, Henry Bradshaw Society 29 (London, 1905)

Flanagan, M. T. (ed.), *Irish royal charters: texts and contexts* (Oxford, 2005)

Foedera, conventiones, litterae, et cujuscunque generis acta publica, inter regis Angliae et alios quosvis imperatores, reges, pontifices, principes, vel communitates, ed. Thomas Rymer (4 vols in 7, London, 1816–30)

Frame, Robin, 'A register of lost deeds concerning the earldom of Ulster, c.1230–1376', in Seán Duffy (ed.), *Princes, prelates and poets in medieval Ireland: essays in honour of Katharine Simms* (Dublin, 2013), 85–106

Freeman, A. M., 'The annals in Cotton MS Titus A. XXV', *Rev. Celt.* 41 (1924), 301–30; 42 (1925), 281–305; 43 (1926), 358–84; 44 (1927), 336–61)

Gesta Stephani, ed. K. R. Potter and R. H. C. Davis (2nd edn, Oxford, 1976)

Giffre (de Réchac), Jean, *La vie du glorieux patriarche Sainte Dominique* (Paris, 1647)

Giraldi Cambrensis opera, ed. J. S. Brewer, J. F. Dimock and G. F. Warner, Rolls Series (8 vols, London, 1861–91)

Giraldus Cambrensis, *Expugnatio Hibernica: the conquest of Ireland*, ed. A. B. Scott and F. X. Martin (Dublin, 1978)

— *The history and topography of Ireland*, ed. J. J. O'Meara (Mountrath and Harmondsworth, 1982)

Grace, James, *Annales Hiberniae*, ed. Richard Butler, Irish Archaeological Society (Dublin, 1842)

The great roll of the pipe for the fifth year of the reign of King John, ed. D. M. Stenton, Pipe Roll Society (London, 1938)

The great roll of the pipe for the fourteenth year of the reign of King John, ed. P. M. Barnes, Pipe Roll Society (London, 1955)

The great roll of the pipe for the seventh year of the reign of King John, ed. Sidney Smith, Pipe Roll Society (London, 1941)

The great roll of the pipe for the third year of the reign of King John, ed. D. M. Stenton, Pipe Roll Society (London, 1936)

The great roll of the pipe for the thirteenth year of the reign of King John, ed. D. M. Stenton, Pipe Roll Society (London, 1953)

The great roll of the pipe for the thirty-third year of the reign of King Henry II, A.D. 1186–7, ed. J. H. Round, Pipe Roll Society (London, 1915)

Gui de Warewic: roman du XIIIe siècle, ed. Alfred Ewert (2 vols, Paris, 1932)

Henry de Bracton, *De legibus et consuetudinibus Angliae*, ed. G. E. Woodbine, trans. S. E. Thorne (4 vols, Cambridge, MA, 1968–77)

Histoire des ducs de Normandie et des rois d'Angleterre, ed. Francisque Michel (Paris, 1840)

The historical works of Gervase of Canterbury, ed. William Stubbs, Rolls Series (2 vols, London, 1879–90)

Historic and municipal documents of Ireland, 1172–1320: from the archives of the city of Dublin, ed. J. T. Gilbert, Rolls Series (London, 1870)

The history of William Marshal, ed. A. J. Holden, Stewart Gregory and David Crouch (3 vols, London, 2002–6)

Ingulf's chronicle of the abbey of Croyland with the continuation of Peter of Blois, trans. H. T. Riley (London, 1854)

The Irish cartularies of Llanthony Prima and Secunda, ed. Eric St John Brooks (Dublin, 1953)

Irish patent rolls of James I: facsimilie of the Irish Record Commission's calendar, prepared prior to 1830 by George Hatchell, ed. M. C. Griffith (Dublin, 1966)

'The Irish pipe roll of 14 John, 1211–1212', ed. Oliver Davies and D. B. Quinn, *UJA*, 3rd ser., 4, suppl. (1941), 53–69

Johannis de Fordun chronica gentis Scotorum, ed. W. F. Skene (2 vols, Edinburgh, 1871–2)

*La chanson de la croisade Albigeoise, tome II: le poème de l'auteur anonyme (I*re *partie)*, ed. and trans. Eugène Martin-Chabot (Paris, 1957)

Lawlor, H. J., 'A calendar of the register of Archbishop Fleming', *PRIA* C 30 (1912/13), 94–190

Liber cartarum prioratus Sancti Andree in Scotia, ed. Thomas Thomson, Bannatyne Club (Edinburgh, 1841)

Liber feodorum, the book of fees commonly called testa de Nevill reformed from the earliest MSS by the deputy keeper of the records (3 vols, London, 1920)

Mac Niocaill, Gearóid, 'Cartae Dunenses', *Seanchas Ard Mhacha* 5, no. 2 (1970), 418–24

Magna Carta, ed. J. C. Holt (2nd edn, Cambridge, 1992)

Matthew of Paris's English history from the year 1235 to 1273, trans. J. A. Giles (3 vols, London, 1889)

Memoriale fratris Walteri de Coventria, ed. William Stubbs, Rolls Series (2 vols, London, 1872–3)

Miscellaneous Irish annals, A.D. 1114–1437, ed. Séamus Ó hInnse (Dublin, 1947)

Molinier, Auguste, 'Catalogue des actes de Simon et d'Amauri de Montfort', *Bibliothèque de l'École des Chartes* 34 (1873), 153–203, 445–501

Percin, Jean-Jaques, *Monumenta conventus Tolosani ordinis F.F. praedicatorum primi* (Toulouse, 1693)

Monumenta diplomatica S. Dominici, ed. V. J. Koudelka and R. J. Loenertz, *Monumenta ordinis fratrum praedicatorum historica 25* (Rome, 1966)

Nicholls, K. W. (ed.), 'Inquisitions of 1224 from the miscellanea of the Exchequer', *Anal. Hib.* 27 (1972), 101–12

— 'Abstracts of Mandeville deeds', *Anal. Hib.* 32 (1985), 1, 3–26

— 'Anglo-French Ireland and after', *Peritia* 1 (1982), 370–403

Oeuvres de Froissart, publiées avec les variantes des divers manuscrits, ed. Kervyn de Lettenhove (Brussels, 1867–77)

Ordre de Malte: histoire du grand-prieuré de Toulouse, ed. Antoine du Bourg (Toulouse, 1883)

The Orkneyinga saga, ed. A. B. Taylor (Edinburgh, 1938)

Orpen, G. H. (ed.), 'Charters of Earl Richard Marshal of the forests of Ross and Taghmon', *JRSAI* 64 (1934), 54–63

Otway-Ruthven, A. J. (ed.), 'Dower charter of John de Courcy's wife', UJA, 3rd ser., 12 (1949), 77–81

Paris, Matthew, *Chronica majora*, ed. H. R. Luard, Rolls Series (7 vols, London, 1872–83)

— *Historia Anglorum, ed. Frederic Madden, Rolls Series (3 vols, London, 1866–9)*

Paris, William, *Life of St Christina of Bolsena*, in Sherry Reames (ed.) *Middle English legends of women saints* (Kalamazoo, 1995)

Patent rolls of the reign of Henry III, 1216–25 [etc.] (2 vols, London, 1901–3)

Peter des Vaux-de-Cernay, *Historia Albigensis*, trans. W. A. Sibly and M. D. Sibly (Woodbridge, 1998)

Plutarch's Moralia, VI, ed. and trans. W. C. Helmbold (London, 1939)

The poems of Giolla Brighde Mac Con Midhe, ed. and trans. N. J. A. Williams, Irish Texts Society 51 (Dublin, 1980)

Pontificia Hibernica: medieval papal chancery documents concerning Ireland, A.D. 640–1261, ed. M. P. Sheehy (2 vols, Dublin, 1962–5)

Ralph of Coggeshall, *Chronicon Anglicanum*, ed. Joseph Stevenson (London, 1875)

Recueil des actes de Henri II, roi d'Angleterre, et duc de Normandie, ed. Léopold Delisle and Élie Berger (3 vols, Paris, 1923)

Recueil des actes de Philippe Auguste roi de France publié sous la direction de M. Charles Samaran membre de l'institut, tome III, années du règne XXVIII à XXXVI, ed. M. J. Monicat and M. J. Boussard (3 vols, Paris, 1916–66)

Recueil des historiens des Gaules et de la France, tome XIX, ed. Michel-Jean-Joseph Bril and Léopold Delisle (New edn, Paris, 1880)

The red book of the earls of Kildare, ed. Gearóid Mac Niocaill (Dublin, 1964)

The red book of the exchequer, ed. Hubert Hall (3 vols, London, 1896)

Reeves, William (ed.), Ecclesiastical antiquities of Down, Connor and Dromore (Dublin, 1850)

The register and records of Holm Cultram, ed. Grainger Francis and W. G. Collingwood, Cumberland and Westmorland Antiquarian and Archaeological Society Record Series 7 (1929)

The register of Milo Sweteman, archbishop of Armagh, 1361–80, ed. Brendan Smith (Dublin, 1996)

The register of Nicholas Fleming, archbishop of Armagh, 1404–1416, ed. Brendan Smith (Dublin, 2003)

Register of the abbey of St Thomas, Dublin, ed. J. T. Gilbert, Rolls Series (London, 1889)

The register of the priory of St Bees, ed. James Wilson (Durham, 1915)

Richardson, H. G., 'Magna Carta Hiberniae', *IHS* 3 (1942), 31–3

Roger of Wendover's Flowers of history, comprising the history of England from the descent of the Saxons to A.D. 1231 formerly ascribed to Matthew Paris, trans. J. A. Giles (2 vols, London, 1849)

Rogeri de Wendover liber qui dicitur Flores historiarum, ed. H. G. Hewlett, Rolls Series (3 vols, London, 1886–9)

Rotuli chartarum in Turri Londinensi asservati, 1199–1216 (London, 1837)

Rotuli de liberate ac de misis et praestitis regnante Johanne, ed. T. D. Hardy (London, 1844)

Rotuli de oblatis et finibus in *Turri Londinensi asservati tempore regis Johannis*, ed. T. D. Hardy (London, 1835)

Rotuli litterarum clausarum, 1204–27 [etc.], ed. T. D. Hardy (2 vols, London, 1833–44)

Rotuli litterarum patentium, 1201–16, ed. T. D. Hardy (London, 1835)

Rotuli Normanniae in Turri Londinensi asservati, ed. T. D. Hardy (London, 1835)

Rotulorum patentium et clausorum cancellariae Hiberniae calendarium, ed. Edward Tresham (4 vols, Dublin, 1828)

Royal and historical letters illustrative of the reign of Henry III, from the originals in the Public Record Office, ed. W. W. Shirley, Rolls Series (2 vols, London, 1862–6)

Scotia Pontificia: papal letters to Scotland before the pontificate of Innocent III, ed. Robert Somerville (Oxford, 1982)

Scotichronicon, by Walter Bower, ed. D. E. R. Watt (9 vols, St Andrews, 1994)

Scottish annals from English chroniclers, 500–1286, ed. A. O. Anderson (London, 1908)

Sheehy, M. P., 'Cairteacha Meán-Aoiseacha do Mhainistir Fhobhair (XII–XIII Céad)', *Seanchas Ard Mhacha* 4 (1960), 171–5

The song of the Cathar wars: a history of the Albigensian crusade, ed. and trans. Janet Shirley (Aldershot, 2000)

The song of Dermot and the earl: an Old French poem from the Carew manuscript no. 596 in the archiepiscopal library at Lambeth palace, ed. and trans. G. H. Orpen (Oxford, 1892)

Statuta capitulorum generalium ordinis Cisterciensis, ab anno 1116 ad annum 1786: tome II, 1221–61, ed. Josephus-Maria Canivez (Louvain, 1934)

Stephen of Lexington, *Letters from Ireland, 1228–1229*, ed. and trans. L. W. O'Dwyer (Kalamazoo, MI, 1982)

Teule, Édilbert de, *Annales du prieuré de Notre Dame de Prouille* (Carcassonne, 1902)

Thirty-fifth report of the deputy keeper of the public records in Ireland (Dublin, 1903)

Transcripts of charters relating to the Gilbertine houses of Sixle, Ormsby, Catley, Ballington and Alvingham, ed. F. M. Stenton, *Lincoln Record Society Publications* 52 (Horncastle, 1922)

Treharne, R. F., 'The Franco-Welsh treaty of alliance in 1212', *Bulletin of the Board of Celtic Studies* 18, no. 1 (1958), 60–75

Secondary works

Anglo-Norman studies, ed. R. A. Brown, Christopher Harper-Bill, Marjorie Chibnall *et al.* (Woodbridge, 1978–)

Arnold, J. H., *Inquisition and power: catharism and the confessing subject in medieval Languedoc* (Philadelphia, PA, 2001)

Aurell, Martin, *The Plantagenet empire*, trans. David Crouch (Harlow, 2007)

Barber, Malcolm, 'Catharism and the Occitan nobility: the lordships of Cabaret, Minerve and Termes', in Christopher Harper-Bill and Ruth Harvey (eds), *The ideals and practice of knighthood III: papers from the fourth Strawberry Hill conference* (Woodbridge, 1990), 1–19

— *The Cathars: dualist heretics in Languedoc in the high Middle Ages* (Abingdon, 2014)

Barrell, A. D. M., *Medieval Scotland* (Cambridge, 2000)

Bartlett, Robert, 'Colonial aristocracies of the high Middle Ages', in Angus McKay and Robert Bartlett (eds), *Medieval frontier societies* (Oxford, 1992), 23–47

— *'Cults of Irish, Scottish and Welsh saints in twelfth-century England', in Brendan Smith (ed.), Britain and Ireland, 900–1300: insular responses to medieval European change (Cambridge, 1999), 67–86*

— *England under the Norman and Angevin kings, 1075–1225* (Oxford, 2000)

— *Trial by fire and water: the medieval judicial ordeal* (Oxford, 1986)

Bellamy, J. G., *The law of treason in England in the later Middle Ages* (Cambridge, 1970)

Bhreathnach, Edel, 'Authority and supremacy in Tara and its hinterland, c. 950–1200', *Discovery Programme Reports* 5 (Dublin, 1999), 1–25

Biddle, Martin, 'Seasonal festivals and residence: Winchester, Westminster and Gloucester in the tenth to twelfth centuries', in *ANS* 8, 51–63

Birkett, Helen, *The saints' lives of Jocelin of Furness: hagiography, patronage and ecclesiastical patronage* (York, 2010)

Blumenthal, Uta-Renate, *The investiture controversy: church and monarchy from the ninth to the twelfth century* (Philadelphia, PA, 1988)

Bothwell, James, *Falling from grace: reversal of fortune and the English nobility, 1075–1455* (Manchester, 2008)

Bouchard, Constance Brittain, *Those of my blood: constructing noble families in medieval Francia* (Philadelphia, PA, 2001)

Bourin, Monique, 'Peasant elites and village communities in the south of France, 1200–1350', *Past & Present, suppl. 2* (2007), 101–14

Brady, Ciaran, Mary O'Dowd and Brian Walker (eds), *Ulster: an illustrated history* (London, 1989)

Brand, Paul, *The making of the common law* (London, 1992)

Brindley, A. L. (ed.), *Archaeological inventory of county Monaghan* (Dublin, 1986)

Bronstein, Judith, *The Hospitallers and the Holy Land: financing the Latin east, 1187–1274* (Woodbridge, 2005)

Brooks, Eric St John, 'Archbishop Henry of London and his Irish connections', *JRSAI* 60 (1930), 1–22

— 'The de Ridelisfords', *JRSAI* 81 (1951), 115–38; 82 (1952), 45–61

— 'The grant of Castleknock to Hugh Tyrel', *JRSAI* 63 (1933), 206–20

Broun, Dauvit, 'The presence of witnesses and the writing of charters', in idem (ed.), *The reality behind charter diplomatic in Anglo-Norman Britain* (Glasgow, 2011), 235–90

Brown, Daniel J. F., 'The citizens and archbishop of Dublin during Hugh de Lacy's Irish rebellion, 1223–4', in Seán Duffy (ed.), *Medieval Dublin XVII: proceedings of the Friends of Medieval Dublin symposium, 2015* (Four Courts Press, forthcoming)

— 'Power and patronage across the North Channel: Hugh de Lacy, St Andrews and the Anglo-Scottish crisis of 1209', *Scot. Hist. Rev.* 94, no. 1 (2015), 1–23

Buckley, V. M., *Archaeological inventory of county Louth* (Dublin, 1986)

Byrne, F. J., *Irish kings and high-kings* (London, 1973)

Carpenter, D. A., 'The English royal chancery in the thirteenth century', in Adrian Jobson (ed.), *English government in the thirteenth century* (Woodbridge, 2004), 49–69

— 'The fall of Hubert de Burgh', *Journal of British Studies* 19, no. 2 (1980), 1–17

— '*In testimonium factorum brevium*: the beginnings of the English chancery rolls', in Nicholas Vincent (ed.), *Records, administration and aristocratic society in the Anglo-Norman realm: papers commemorating the 800th anniversary of King John's loss of Normandy* (Woodbridge, 2009), 1–29

— 'Kings, magnates, and society: the personal rule of King Henry III, 1234–1258', *Speculum* 60 (1985) 39–70

— *Magna Carta* (London, 2015)

— *The minority of Henry III* (London, 1990)

— 'The second century of English feudalism', *Past & Present* 168 (2000), 30–71

Cazes, Jean-Paul, 'Structures agraires et domaine comtal dans la bailie de Castelnaudary en 1272', *Annales du Midi* 99, no. 180 (1987), 453–77

— 'Un village castral de la plaine Lauragaise: Lasbordes (Aude)', *Archéologie du Midi Médiéval* 8–9 (1990), 3–25

Church, S. D., 'The 1210 campaign in Ireland: evidence for a military revolution?', in *ANS* 20, 45–57

— *The household knights of King John* (Cambridge, 1999)

Clanchy, M. T., *From memory to written record: England, 1066–1307* (3rd edn, Chichester, West Sussex, 2013)

Clyne, Miriam, 'The founders and patrons of Premonstratensian houses in Ireland', in Janet Burton and Karen Stöber (eds), *The regular canons in the medieval British Isles* (Turnhout, 2011), 145–72

Cockayne, G. E., *The Complete Peerage of England, Scotland, Ireland, Great Britain and the United Kingdom*, ed. Vicary Gibbs, H. A. Doubleday, Duncan Warrand, Lord Howard de Walden, G. H. White and R. S. Lea (2nd edn, 8 vols, London, 1910–59)

Cohen, J. J., *Hybridity, identity, and monstrosity in medieval Britain: on difficult middles* (Basingstoke, 2006)

Colker, M. J., 'The 'Margam chronicle' in a Dublin manuscript', *The Haskins Society Journal* 4 (1992), 123–48

Cook, William and Ronald Herzman, *The medieval world view: an introduction* (Oxford, 2004)

Coulson, Charles, 'Fortress-policy in Capetian tradition and Angevin practice: aspects of the conquest of Normandy by Philip II', in *ANS* 6, 13–39

Cowan, I. B. and D. E. Easson, *Medieval religious houses: Scotland* (2nd edn, London, 1976)

Crawford, Barbara, 'Haraldr Maddaðarson, earl of Caithness and earl of Orkney (1133/4–1206)', in *ODNB*

— 'Peter's Pence in Scotland', in G. W. S. Barrow (ed.), *The Scottish tradition: essays in honour of Ronald Gordon Cant* (Edinburgh, 1974), 14–23

Crooks, Peter, 'Divide and rule: factionalism as royal policy in the lordship of Ireland, 1171–1265', *Peritia* 19 (2005), 263–307

Cross, Peter, 'Knighthood, heraldry and social exclusion in Edwardian England', in idem and Maurice Keen (eds), *Heraldry, pageantry and social display in medieval England* (Woodbridge, 2002), 39–68

Crouch, David, 'The administration of the Norman earldom', in A. T. Thacker (ed.), *The earldom of Chester and its charters: a tribute to Geoffrey Barraclough*, *Journal of the Chester Archaeological Society* 71 (1991), 69–96

— *The birth of nobility: constructing aristocracy in England and France, 900–1300* (Harlow, 2005)

— 'Earl Gilbert Marshal and his mortal enemies', *Historical Research* 87, no. 237 (2014), 393–403

— 'Earls in Wales and Ireland', in idem and Doherty (eds), *The earl in medieval Britain* (Cambridge University Press, forthcoming)

— *The image of aristocracy in Britain, 1000–1300* (London, 1992)

— *'Strategies of lordship in Angevin England and the career of William Marshal', in Christopher Harper-Bill and Ruth Harvey (eds), The ideals and practice of medieval knighthood II: papers from the third Strawberry Hill conference (Woodbridge, 1988), 1–25*

— *William Marshal: knighthood, war and chivalry, 1147–1219* (2nd edn, London, 2002)

Curtis, Edmund, *A history of medieval Ireland* (London, 1923)

Davies, Oliver, 'Old churches in County Louth', JLAS 10 (1941), 5–23

Davis, James, *Medieval market morality: life, law and ethics in the English marketplace, 1200–1500* (Cambridge, 2012)

Dobbs, Margaret, 'The territory and people of Tethba', *JRSAI* 68 (1938), 241–59

Donaldson, Gordon, 'The bishops and priors of Whithorn', *TDGNHAS*, 3rd ser., 27 (1948–9), 127–54

Dowden, John, *The bishops of Scotland*, ed. J. M. Thomson (Glasgow, 1912)

Duby, Georges, 'Youth in aristocratic society', in idem, *The chivalrous society*, trans. Cynthia Postan (London, 1977), 113–22

Duffy, Paul, 'The architecture of defiance', *Archaeology Ireland* 29, no. 1 (2015), 20–24

— '"*Ung sage et valent home*": Hugh de Lacy and the Albigensian crusade', *JRSAI* 141 (2014), 66–90

Duffy, Seán, 'Burgh, Richard de, second earl of Ulster (†1326)', in *ODNB*

— *'The first Ulster plantation: John de Courcy and the men of Cumbria', in T. B. Barry, Robin Frame and Katharine Simms (eds), Colony and frontier in medieval Ireland: essays presented to J. F. Lydon (London, 1995), 1–27*

— 'John and Ireland: the origins of England's Irish problem', in S. D. Church (ed.) *King John: new interpretations* (Woodbridge, 1999), 221–45

— 'King John's expedition to Ireland, 1210: the evidence reconsidered', *IHS* 30, no. 117 (1996), 1–24

— 'The lords of Galloway, earls of Carrick, and the Bissets of the Glens: Scottish settlement in thirteenth-century Ulster', in David Edwards (ed.), *Regions and rulers in Ireland, 1100–1650: essays for Kenneth Nicholls* (Dublin, 2004), 37–50

— 'The prehistory of the galloglass', in idem (ed.), *The world of the galloglass: kings, warlords and warriors in Ireland and Scotland, 1200–1600* (Dublin, 2007), 1–23

— 'Town and crown: the kings of England and their city of Dublin', in Michael Prestwich, Richard Britnell and Robin Frame (eds), *Thirteenth century England X: proceedings of the Durham conference, 2003* (Woodbridge, 2005), 95–117

Duggan, A. J., 'The power of documents: the curious case of *Laudabiliter*', in Brenda Bolton and Christine Meek (eds), *Aspects of power and authority in the Middle Ages*, *International Medieval Research* 14 (Turnhout, 2007), 251–76

Duncan, A. A. M., 'The foundation of St Andrews cathedral priory', *Scot. Hist. Rev.* 84, no. 217 (2005), 1–37

— 'John king of England and the kings of Scots', in S. D. Church (ed.) *King John: new interpretations* (Woodbridge, 1999), 247–71

— *The kingship of the Scots, 842–1292: succession and independence* (Edinburgh, 2002)

— 'Roger of Howden and Scotland, 1187–1201', in Barbara Crawford (ed.), *Church, chronicle and learning in medieval and early Renaissance Scotland: essays presented to Donald Watt on the occasion of the completion of the publication of Bower's Scotichronicon* (Edinburgh, 1998), 135–59

— *Scotland: the making of the kingdom* (2nd edn, Edinburgh, 1996)

Edwards, Robert, 'Exile, self, and society', in María-Inés Lagos-Pope (ed.), *Exile in literature* (Bucknell, PA, 1988), 15–32

Edwards, Robin Dudley, 'Anglo-Norman relations with Connacht, 1169–1224', *IHS* 1, no. 2 (1938), 135–53

— 'Magna Carta Hiberniae', in John Ryan (ed.), *Féil-sgríbhinn Eóin Mhic Néill* (Dublin, 1940), 307–18

Empey, C. A., 'The settlement of the kingdom of Limerick', in J. F. Lydon (ed.), *England and Ireland in the later Middle Ages: essays in honour of Jocelyn Otway-Ruthven* (Dublin, 1981), 1–25

Evergates, Theodore (ed.), *Aristocratic women in medieval France* (Philadelphia, PA, 1999)

Eyton, R. W., *Antiquities of Shropshire* (12 vols, London, 1854–60)

Farrer, William, *History of the county of Lancaster, vol.* 6 (London, 1911)

Federico, Sylvia, 'Shifting horizons of expectation: the late medieval family (preface to section)', in Isabel Davis, Miriam Müller and Sarah Rees Jones (eds), *Love, marriage and family ties in the later Middle Ages* (Turnhout, 2003), 121–8

Fitzpatrick, Elizabeth, *Royal inauguration in Gaelic Ireland, c. 1100–1600: a cultural landscape study* (Woodbridge, 2004)

Flanagan, M. T., 'Anglo-Norman change and continuity: the castle of Telach Cail in Delbna', *IHS* 28, no. 112 (1993), 385–9

— 'Defining lordships in Angevin Ireland: William Marshal and the king's justiciar', in Martin Aurell and Frédéric Boutoulle (eds), *Les seigneuries dans l'Espace Plantagenêt, c. 1150–1250* (Bordeaux, 2009), 41–59

— 'Defining nations in medieval Ireland', in Hirokazu Tsurushima (ed.), *Nations in medieval Britain* (Donington, 2010), 104–21

— 'Fitz Henry, Meiler (†1220)', in *ODNB*

— *Irish society, Anglo-Norman settlers, Angevin kingship: interactions in Ireland in the late twelfth century* (Oxford, 1989)

— 'Jocelin of Furness and the cult of St Patrick in twelfth-century Ulster', in Clare Downham (ed.), *Jocelin of Furness: proceedings from the 2011 conference* (Donington, 2013), 45–66

— *'John de Courcy, the first Ulster plantation and Irish church men', in Smith (ed.), Britain and Ireland, 154–79*

— 'Poer, Robert (†1178?)', in *ODNB*

— 'Strategies of lordship in pre-Norman and post-Norman Leinster', in *ANS* 20, 107–26

— 'Suerbeer, Albert (Albertus, Albrecht)', in James McGuire and James Quinn (eds), *Dictionary of Irish biography* (9 vols, Cambridge, 2009), ix, 143–4

— *The transformation of the Irish church in the twelfth century* (Woodbridge, 2010)

Flanders, Steve, *De Courcy: Anglo-Normans in Ireland, England and France in the eleventh and twelfth centuries* (Dublin, 2008)

Flower, Robin, 'The origins and history of the Cottonian annals', *Rev. Celt.* 44 (1927), 336–46

Frame, Robin, 'Aristocracies and the political configuration of the British Isles', in R. R. Davies (ed.), *The British Isles, 1100–1500: comparisons, contrasts and connections* (Edinburgh, 1988), 142–59

— *Colonial Ireland, 1169–1369* (Dublin, 1981)

Robin Frame, 'England and Ireland, 1171–1369', in idem, *Ireland and Britain, 1170–1450* (London, 1998), 15–30

— 'King Henry III and the shaping of a peripheral lordship', in idem, *Ireland and Britain, 1170–1450* (London, 1998), 31–58

— 'Lordship and liberties in Ireland and Wales, c. 1170–c. 1360', in Huw Pryce and John Watts (eds), *Power and identity in the Middle Ages: essays in memory of Rees Davies* (Oxford, 2007), 125–52

Ganshof, F. L., *Feudalism* (New York, 1961)

Garnett, George, *Conquered England: kingship, succession and tenure, 1066–1166* (Oxford, 2007)

Gatz, Erwin and Clemens Brodkorb (eds), *Die bischöfe des heiligen Römischen Reiches, 1198–1448* (Berlin, 2001)

Gaydon, A. T. (ed.), *A history of the county of Shropshire, vol. 2* (London, 1973)

Gillingham, John, *The English in the twelfth century: imperialism, national identity and political values* (Woodbridge, 2000)

— 'Normanizing the English invaders of Ireland', in Pryce and Watts (eds), *Power and identity in the Middle Ages*, 85–97

— 'The travels of Roger of Howden and his views of the Irish, Scots and Welsh', *ANS* 20, 151–69

Gogarty, Thomas, 'St Mary's Abbey, Louth. With an account of the lives of St Mochta, Cristin, bishop of Louth and Donatus, prior of Louth', *JLAS* 4, no. 2 (1917), 169–89

Gorton, John and G. N. Wright, *A topographical dictionary of Great Britain and Ireland* (3 vols, London, 1833)

Gosling, Paul, *Carlingford town: an antiquarian's guide* (Newry, 1992)

— 'From Dún Delca to Dundalk: the topography and archaeology of a medieval frontier town, A.D. 1187–1700', *JLAS* 22, no. 3 (1991), 223–353

Graham-Leigh, Elaine, *The southern French nobility and the Albigensian crusade* (Woodbridge, 2005)

Graham, B. J., 'Anglo-Norman settlement in county Meath', *PRIA* C 75 (1975), 223–49

Gransden, Antonia, *Historical writing in England, c. 550–1307* (London, 1974)

Gray, James, *Sutherland and Caithness in saga-time* (Edinburgh, 1922)

Green, J. A., *The aristocracy of Norman England* (Cambridge, 1997)

Greenslade, M. W., *A history of the county of Stafford, vol. 3* (London, 1970)

Greeves, Ronald, 'The Galloway lands in Ulster', *TDGNHAS*, 3rd ser., 36 (1957–58), 115–21

Guida, Saverio, 'L'autore della seconda parte della canso de la crotzada', *Cultura Neolatina* 63 (2003), 255–82

Gundacker, Jay, 'Absolutions and acts of disobedience: excommunication and society in fourteenth-century Armagh', *Traditio* 64 (2009), 183–212

Gwynn, Aubrey and R. N. Hadcock, *Medieval religious houses: Ireland* (London, 1970)

Gwynn, Aubrey, 'Armagh and Louth in the twelfth and thirteenth centuries', Seanchas Ard Mhacha 2 (1955), 17–37

— *'Armagh and Louth in the twelfth century', Seanchas Ard Mhacha 1 (1954), 1–11*

— *'Henry of London, archbishop of Dublin: a study in Anglo-Norman statecraft', Studies: an Irish quarterly review 38 (1949), 297–306*

Hagger, Mark, *The fortunes of a Norman family: the de Verduns in England, Ireland and Wales, 1066–1316* (Dublin 2001)

Halpin, Eoin, 'Excavations at St Mary d'Urso, Drogheda, county Louth', *JLAS* 23 (1996), 452–509

Hamlin, Ann, 'The early church in county Down to the twelfth century', in Lindsay Proudfoot (ed.), *Down history and society: interdisciplinary essays on the history of an Irish county* (Dublin, 1997), 47–70

Hartland, Beth, 'English landholding in Ireland', in Michael Prestwich, Richard Britnell and Robin Frame (eds), *Thirteenth century England X: proceedings of the Durham conference, 2003* (Woodbridge, 2005), 119–29

Healy, John, *History of the diocese of Meath* (2 vols, Dublin, 1908)

Helle, Knut, 'Anglo-Norwegian relations in the reign of Hákon Håkonsson (1217–63)', *Mediaeval Scandinavia* 1 (1968), 101–14

Helmholz, R. H., 'Excommunication in twelfth-century England', *Journal of Law and Religion* 11, no. 1 (1994–5), 235–53

Hencken, Hugh, Liam Price and L. E. Start, 'Lagore Crannog: an Irish royal residence of the seventh to tenth centuries', *PRIA* C 53 (1950), 1–247

Heslop, T. A., 'The seals of the twelfth-century earls of Chester', in Thacker (ed.), *Chester and its charters*, 179–97

Hillaby, Joe, 'Colonisation, crisis management and debt: Walter de Lacy and the lordship of Meath, 1189–1241', Ríocht na Mídhe: records of the Meath Archaeological and Historical Society 8, no. 4 (1992/3), 1–50

— *'Hereford gold: Irish, Welsh and English land', Transactions of the Woolhope Field Club (Herefordshire) 44, no. 3 (1984), 358–419; 45, no. 1 (1985), 193–270*

Hogan, Arlene, *The priory of Llanthony Prima and Secunda in Ireland, 1172–1541: lands, patronage and politics* (Dublin, 2008)

Hogan, Edmund, *Onomasticon Goedelicum: locorum et tribuum Hiberniae et Scotiae. An index, with identifications, to the Gaelic names of places and tribes* (Dublin, 1910)

Holden, Brock, 'King John, the Braoses, and the Celtic fringe, 1207–1216', *Albion* 33 (2001), 1–23

— *Lords of the central marches: English aristocracy and frontier society, 1087–1265* (Oxford, 2008)

Holdsworth, Christopher, 'Langton, Stephen (c.1150–1228)', in *ODNB*

Hoskins, Peter, *In the steps of the Black Prince: the road to Poitiers, 1355–6* (Woodbridge, 2013)

Howard, Matthew, '"We are broderen": fraternal bonds and familial loyalty within the fifteenth-century romance of Generydes', in Isabel Davis, Miriam Müller and Sarah Rees Jones (eds), *Love, marriage and family ties in the later Middle Ages* (Turnhout, 2003), 129–42

Hudson, John, 'Diplomatic and legal aspects of the charters', in Thacker (ed.), *Chester and its charters*, 153–78

Hurlock, Katherine, 'The crusades to 1291 in the annals of medieval Ireland', *IHS* 37, no. 148 (2012), 517–35

Hurnard, N. D., 'The Anglo-Norman franchises', *EHR* 64, no. 252 (1949), 289–327

Jolliffe, J. E. A., *Angevin kingship* (2nd edn, London, 1963)

Kay, Richard, 'Walter of Coventry and the Barnwell chronicle', *Traditio* 54 (1999), 141–67

Keck, Christine, 'L'entourage de Simon de Montfort pendant la croisade Albigeoise et l'établissement territorial des *crucesignati*', in *La croisade*

Albigeoise: actes du colloque du Centre d'Études Cathares, Carcassonne, Octobre 2002, sous la présidence de Michel Roquebert (Balma, 2004), 236–43

Keefe, T. K., *Feudal assessments and the political community under Henry II and his sons* (Berkeley, CA, 1983)

Kenny, Gillian, 'Anglo-Irish and Gaelic marriage laws and traditions in late medieval Ireland', *Journal of Medieval History* 32 (2006), 27–42

King, Edmund, 'William fitz Alan (c. 1105–1160)', in *ODNB*

Kingsford, C. L., 'Lacy, Roger de (†1211)', *rev.* Paul Dalton, in *ODNB*

Knowles, David and R. N. Hadcock, *Medieval religious houses: England and Wales* (London, 1971)

Kosto, Adam, *Hostages in the Middle Ages* (Oxford, 2012)

Kuttner, Stephen and Antonio Garcia y Garcia, 'A new eyewitness to the Fourth Lateran Council (1215)', *Traditio* 20 (1964), 115–78

Lambdin, R. T. and L. C. Lambdin (eds), *Encyclopedia of medieval literature* (Westport, CT, 2000)

Lapidge, Michael, *The cult of St Swithun: Winchester studies 4.ii: the Anglo-Saxon minsters of Winchester* (Oxford, 2003)

Lawlor, H. C., 'The identification of the castle of Magh Cobha', *UJA*, 3rd ser., 1 (1938), 84–9

— 'Mote and mote-and-bailey castles in de Courcy's principality of Ulster (i)', *UJA*, 3rd ser., 1 (1938), 155–64; (ii), 2 (1939), 46–54

— 'The vassals of the earls of Ulster (ii)', *UJA* 3rd ser., 4 (1941), 23–7

Leslie, James and Henry Swanzy, *Biographical succession lists of the clergy of diocese of Down* (Enniskillen, 1936)

Little, A. G., 'The authorship of the Lanercost chronicle', *EHR* 31, no. 122 (1916), 269–79

Lloyd, J. E., *A history of Wales from the earliest times to the Edwardian conquest* (3rd edn, 2 vols, London, 1939)

— 'Who was Gwenllian de Lacy?', *Archaeologia Cambrensis* 19 (1919), 292–8

Lloyd, Simon, 'Longespée, Sir William (II) (c. 1209–1250)', in *ODNB*

Logan, F. D., *Excommunication and the secular arm in medieval England: a study in legal procedure from the thirteenth to the sixteenth century* (Toronto, 1968)

Lydon, J. F., 'The defence of Dublin in the Middle Ages', in Seán Duffy (ed.), *Medieval Dublin IV: proceedings of the Friends of Medieval Dublin symposium, 2002* (Dublin, 2003), 63–79

— *The lordship of Ireland in the Middle Ages* (Revised edn, Dublin, 2003)

— *The making of Ireland: from ancient times to the present* (London, 1998)

Lynn, C. J., Katharine Simms, T. G. F. Paterson, Donal Bateson and Michael Dolley, 'Excavation in the Franciscan friary church, Armagh', *UJA*, 3rd ser., 38 (1975), 61–80

McCarthy, D. P., *The Irish annals: their genesis, evolution, and history* (Dublin, 2008)

MacCotter, Paul, 'Functions of the cantred in Medieval Ireland', *Peritia* 19 (2005), 308–32

— *Medieval Ireland: territorial, political and economic divisions* (Dublin, 2008)

McDonald, R. A., 'Dealing death from Man: Manx sea power in and around the Irish Sea, 1079–1265', in Seán Duffy (ed.), *The world of the galloglass: kings, warlords and warriors in Ireland and Scotland, 1200–1600* (Dublin, 2007), 45–76

— *Manx kingship in its Irish Sea setting, 1187–1229: King Rögnvaldr and the Crovan dynasty, 1187–1229* (Dublin, 2007)

McFarlane, K. B., *The nobility of later medieval England: the Ford lectures for 1953 and related studies* (Oxford, 1973)

McGowan-Doyle, Valerie, *The book of Howth: Elizabethan conquest and the old English* (Cork, 2011)

Mac Íomhair, Diarmuid, 'The lordship of Ballymascanlan', *JLAS* 17, no. 2 (1970), 79–83

McKay, Patrick (ed.), *A dictionary of Ulster place-names* (Antrim, 1999)

McNeill, Charles, 'The secular jurisdiction of the early archbishops of Dublin', *JRSAI* 45 (1915), 81–108

MacNeill, Eoin, Celtic Ireland (2nd edn, Dublin, 1981)

— Phases of Irish history (Dublin, 1920)

McNeill, T. E., Anglo-Norman Ulster: the history and archaeology of an Irish barony (Edinburgh, 1980)

— *Carrickfergus castle* (Belfast, 1981)

— *Castles in Ireland: feudal power in a Gaelic world* (London, 1997)

— 'The Premonstratensian houses of Carrickfergus, White Abbey and Woodburn', *Peritia* 2 (1983), 265–6

Mac Niocaill, Gearóid, *The medieval Irish annals* (Dublin, 1975)

— *Na manaigh liatha in Éirinn, 1142–c.1600* (Dublin, 1959)

MacQueen, Hector, 'The laws of Galloway: a preliminary survey', in R. D. Oram and D. P. Stell (eds), *Galloway: land and lordship* (Edinburgh, 1991), 131–43

Maddicott, J. R., *Simon de Montfort* (Cambridge, 1994)

Maitland, F. W., 'The introduction of English law into Ireland', *EHR* 4 (1889), 516–17

Maitland, F. W. and Frederick Pollock, *The history of English law* (2nd edn, 2 vols, Cambridge, 1923)

Mallory, J. P. and T. E. McNeill, *The archaeology of Ulster: from colonisation to plantation* (Belfast, 1991)

Marenbon, John (ed.), *Routledge history of philosophy, vol. 3: medieval philosophy* (London, 2003)

Marvin, L. W., *The Occitan war: a military and political history of the Albigensian crusade, 1209–1218* (Cambridge, 2008)

Mazlish, Bruce, 'Leader and led, individual and group', in idem (ed), *The leader, the led and the psyche: essays in psychohistory* (Hanover, NH, 1990), 249–66

Mertes, Kate, *The English noble household, 1250–1600: good governance and politic rule* (Oxford, 1988)

Milsom, S. F. C., *The legal framework of English feudalism* (Cambridge, 1976)

Moody, T. W., T. D. Williams, J. C. Beckett and F. X. Martin (eds), *A new history of Ireland, under the auspices of the Royal Irish Academy* (9 vols, Dublin, 1968–2008)

Moore, M. J., *Archaeological inventory of county Meath* (Dublin, 1987)

Morgan, Philip, 'Audley family (c.1130–1391)', in *ODNB*

Mortimer, Richard, *Angevin England, 1154–1258* (Oxford, 1994)

Murphy, Margaret and Kieran O'Conor, 'Castles and Deer parks in Anglo-Norman Ireland', *Eolas: Journal of the American Society of Irish Medieval Studies* 1 (2006), 53–70

Murphy, Margaret and Michael Potterton (eds), *The Dublin region in the Middle Ages: settlement, land-use, and economy* (Dublin, 2010)

Murphy, Margaret, 'Balancing the concerns of church and state: the archbishops of Dublin, 1181–1228', in T. B. Barry, Robin Frame and Katharine Simms (eds), *Colony and frontier in medieval Ireland: essays presented to J. F. Lydon* (London, 1995), 41–56

Murray, Alexander, *Reason and society in the Middle Ages* (Oxford, 1978)

Murray, L. P., 'An ancient poet's view from Sliabh-Fuaid', *JLAS* 8 (1933), 1–17

— 'Omeath', *JLAS* 3, no. 3 (1914), 213–31

Neville, C. J., *Native lordship in medieval Scotland: the earldoms of Strathearn and Lennox, c. 1140–1365* (Dublin, 2005)

Ní Úrdail, Meidhbhín, 'Some observations on the "Dublin annals of Inisfallen"', Ériu 57 (2007), 133–53

Norgate, Kate, *John Lackland* (London, 1902)

Ó Clabaigh, C. N., *The Franciscans in Ireland, 1400–1534* (Dublin, 2002)

O'Conor, Kieran, Niall Brady, Anne Connon and Carlos Fidalgo-Romo, 'The Rock of Lough Cé, co. Roscommon', in Thomas Finan (ed.), *Medieval Lough Cé* (Dublin, 2010), 15–40

Ó Corráin, Donnchadh, 'Creating the past: the early Irish genealogical tradition, Carroll Lecture 1992', *Peritia* 12 (1998), 177–208

Ó Dubhthaigh, Bearnárd, 'A contribution to the history of Drumsnat', *Clogher Record* 6, no. 1 (1966), 71–103

Ó Dufaigh, Seosamh, 'Medieval Monaghan: the evidence of place-names', *Clogher Record* 16, no. 3 (1999), 7–23

Ó Riain, Padraig, *A dictionary of Irish saints* (Dublin, 2011)

— 'The "crech ríg" or "royal prey"', Éigse 15 (1973), 24–30

O'Laverty, James, *Historical account of the diocese of Down and Connor* (5 vols, Dublin, 1878–95)

O'Rahilly, Cecile, *Táin bó* Cúailnge: recension 1 (Dublin, 1976)

O'Rahilly, T. F., 'Some instances of vowel shortening in Modern Irish', *Ériu* 13 (1942), 128–34

O'Sullivan, Benedict, *Medieval Irish Dominican studies*, ed. Hugh Fenning (Dublin, 2009)

Oram, R. D., 'In obedience and reverence: Whithorn and York, c. 1128–c. 1250', *The Innes Review* 42, no. 2 (1991), 83–100

— *The lordship of Galloway* (Edinburgh, 2000)

Orpen, G. H., 'The earldom of Ulster (i)', *JRSAI* 43 (1913), 30–46, 133–43; (ii) 44 (1914), 51–66; (iii) 45 (1915), 123–42; (iv) 50 (1920), 167–77; (v) 51 (1921), 68–76

— *Ireland under the Normans, 1169–1333 (4 vols, Oxford, 1911–20; 1 vol. repr., Dublin, 2005)*

— 'Motes and Norman castles in Ireland', *EHR* 22, no. 86 (1907), 228–54

Otway-Ruthven, A. J., A history of medieval Ireland (2nd edn, London, 1980)

— 'Anglo-Irish shire government in the thirteenth century', *IHS* 5, no. 17 (1946), 1–28

— 'Knight service in Ireland', *JRSAI* 89 (1959), 1–15

— 'The partition of the de Verdon lands in Ireland in 1332', *PRIA* C 66 (1967–8), 401–55

Owen, D. D. R., *William the lion: kingship and culture, 1143–1214* (East Linton, 1997)

Painter, Sidney, *The reign of King John* (Baltimore, MD, 1949)

— *William Marshall: knight-errant, baron and regent of England* (Baltimore, MD, 1933)

Pegg, Mark, *The corruption of angels: the great inquisition of 1245–46* (Princeton, NJ, 2001)

Perros, Helen, 'Crossing the Shannon frontier: Connacht and the Anglo-Normans, 1170–1224', in T. B. Barry, Robin Frame and Katharine Simms (eds), *Colony and frontier in medieval Ireland: essays presented to J. F. Lydon* (London, 1995), 117–39

Phillips, J. R. S., 'The Anglo-Norman nobility', in J. F. Lydon (ed.), *The English in medieval Ireland* (Dublin, 1984), 87–104

Pollock, M. A, 'Rebels of the West, 1209–1216', *Cambrian Medieval Celtic Studies* 50 (2005), 1–30

— *Scotland, England and France after the loss of Normandy, 1204–1296: 'auld amitie'* (Woodbridge, 2015)

Power, Daniel, 'Bréauté, Sir Falkes de (†1226)', in *ODNB*

— 'Marshal, Richard, sixth earl of Pembroke (†1234)', in *ODNB*

— 'Who went on the Albigensian crusade?', *EHR* 128, no. 524 (2013), 1047–85

Powicke, F. M., *King Henry III and the Lord Edward: the community of the realm in the thirteenth century* (Oxford, 1947)

— *The loss of Normandy, 1189–1204: studies in the history of the Angevin Empire* (3rd edn, Manchester, 1999)

— *The thirteenth century, 1216–1307 (Oxford, 1953)*

Prestwich, Michael, *Edward I* (Berkeley, 1988)

— *Plantagenet England, 1225–1360* (Oxford, 2005)

Prioreschi, Plinio (ed.) *A history of medicine, vol. 6: Renaissance medicine* (Omaha, NE, 2007)

Pryce, Huw, *Native law and the church in medieval Wales* (Oxford, 1993)

Reuter, Timothy, 'Nobles and others: the social and cultural expression of power relations in the Middle Ages', in A. J. Duggan (ed.), *Nobles and nobility in medieval Europe: concepts, origins, transformations* (Rochester, NY, 2000), 85–100

Reynolds, Susan, *Fiefs and vassals: the medieval evidence reinterpreted* (Oxford, 1994; repr. 2001)

Richardson, H. G. and G. O. Sayles, *The administration of Ireland, 1172–1377* (Dublin, 1963)

Richardson, H. G., 'The coronation in medieval England', *Traditio* 16 (1960), 111–202

Rodger, N. A. M., *The safeguard of the sea: a naval history of Britain, 660–1649* (London, 1997)

Rosenthal, Joel, *Patriarchy and families of privilege* (Philadelphia, PA, 1991)

Ross, Alasdair, 'Moray, Ulster and the Mac Williams', in Seán Duffy (ed.), *Princes, prelates and poets in medieval Ireland: essays in honour of Katharine Simms* (Dublin, 2013), 24–44

Ross, Leslie, *Medieval art: a topical dictionary* (Westport, CT, 1996)

Rubin, Miri, *The hollow crown: a history of Britain in the late Middle Ages* (London, 2005)

— 'Identities', in Rosemary Horrox and W. M. Ormrod (eds), *A social history of England, 1200–1500* (Cambridge, 2006), 383–412

Sabarthès, Antoine, *Dictionnaire topographique du département de l'Aude comprenant les noms de lieux anciens et modernes* (Paris, 1912)

Selwood, Dominic, *Knights of the cloister: Templars and Hospitallers in central-southern Occitania, c. 1100–c. 1300* (Woodbridge, 2002)

Shirley, E. P., *The history of the county of Monaghan* (London, 1879)

Simms, Katharine, *From kings to warlords: the changing political structure of Gaelic Ireland in the later Middle Ages* (Woodbridge, 1987)

— 'Frontiers in the Irish church: regional and cultural', in T. B. Barry, Robin Frame and Katharine Simms (eds), *Colony and frontier in medieval Ireland: essays presented to J. F. Lydon* (London, 1995), 177–200
— *Medieval Gaelic sources* (Dublin, 2009)
— 'The O'Hanlons, the O'Neills and the Anglo-Normans in thirteenth-century Armagh', *Seanchas Ard Mhacha* 9 (1978–9), 70–94
— 'The O'Reillys and the kingdom of East Breifne', *Bréifne* 5 (1979), 305–19
Smith, Brendan, 'The Armagh-Clogher dispute and the "Mellifont conspiracy": diocesan politics and monastic reform in early thirteenth-century Ireland', *Seanchas Ard Mhacha* 14 (1991), 26–38
— *Britain and Ireland, 900–1300: insular responses to medieval European change* (Cambridge, 1999)
— *Colonisation and conquest in medieval Ireland: the English in Louth, 1170–1330* (Cambridge, 1999)
— 'Fitzgerald, Maurice (c.1194–1257)', in *ODNB*
— 'Irish politics, 1220–1245', in Michael Prestwich, Richard Britnell and Robin Frame (eds), *Thirteenth century England VIII: proceedings of the Durham conference, 1999* (Woodbridge, 2001), 13–32
— 'Lacy, Hugh de, earl of Ulster (†1242)', in *ODNB*
— 'Tenure and locality in north Leinster in the early thirteenth century', in T. B. Barry, Robin Frame and Katharine Simms (eds), *Colony and frontier in medieval Ireland: essays presented to J. F. Lydon* (London, 1995), 29–40
— 'Review of Colin Veach, *Lordship in four realms: the Lacy family, 1166–1241* (Manchester, 2014)', *IHS* 39, no. 154 (2015), 338–9
Spence, John, *Re-imagining history in Anglo-Norman prose chronicles* (Woodbridge, 2013)
Stacey, Robin Chapman, *The road to judgement: from custom to court in medieval Ireland and Wales* (Philadelphia, PA, 1994)
Stenton, F. M., *The first century of English feudalism, 1066–1166 (2nd edn, Oxford, 1961)*
Stockman, Gerard (ed.), *Place-names of Northern Ireland* (8 vols, Belfast, 1992–2004)
Stokes, Whitley and John Strachan (eds), *Thesaurus paleohibernicus: a collection of Old-Irish glosses, scholia, prose and verse* (3 vols, Cambridge, 1901–10)
Strickland, Matthew, 'Against the Lord's anointed: aspects of warfare and baronial rebellion in England and Normandy, 1075–1265', in John Hudson and George Garnett (eds), *Law and government in medieval England and Normandy* (Cambridge, 1994), 56–79
— 'Treason, feud and the growth of state violence: Edward I and the 'war of the earl of Carrick', 1306–7', in Chris Given-Wilson, Ann Kettle and Len Scales

(eds), *War, government and aristocracy in the British Isles, c. 1150–1500: essays presented to* Michael Prestwich (Woodbridge, 2008), 84–113

— *War and chivalry: the conduct and perception of war in England and Normandy, 1066–1217* (Cambridge, 1996)

Stringer, K. J., 'The charters of David, earl of Huntingdon and lord of Garioch: a study in Anglo-Scottish diplomatic', in idem (ed.), *Essays on the nobility of medieval Scotland* (Edinburgh, 1985), 72–101

— *Earl David of Huntingdon: a study in Anglo-Scottish history* (Edinburgh, 1985)

— 'The early lords of Lauderdale, Dryburgh Abbey and St Andrew's priory at Northampton', in idem (ed.), *Essays on the nobility of Medieval Scotland*, 44–71

— 'Periphery and core in thirteenth-century Scotland: Alan son of Roland, lord of Galloway and constable of Scotland', in Alexander Grant (ed.), *Medieval Scotland: crown, lordship and community* (Edinburgh, 1998), 82–113

Sumption, Jonathan, *The Albigensian crusade* (London, 1978)

Sweetman, David, *The medieval castles of Ireland* (Cork, 1999)

Taylor, Claire, 'Pope Innocent III, John of England and the Albigensian crusade (1209–16)', in J. C. Moore (ed.), *Pope Innocent III and his world* (Aldershot, 1999), 205–28

Tempest, H. G., 'The Dorsey: some notes on the large entrenchment in the townland of Dorsey in the south of the county of Armagh', *JLAS* 7 (1930), 187–240

— *'Rooskey priory', JLAS 6 (1928), 263–4*

Thornton, D. E., 'Early medieval Louth: the kingdom of Conaille Muirtheimne', *JLAS* 24 (1997), 139–50

Timbal, Pierre-Clément, *Un conflit d'annexion au Moyen-Âge: l'application de la coutume de Paris au pays Albigeois* (Paris, 1950)

Topping, Patrick, 'Harald Maddadson, earl of Orkney and Caithness, 1139–1206', *Scot. Hist. Rev.* 62, no. 174 (1983), 105–20

Turner, Ralph, *King John* (London, 1994)

— 'Longchamp, William de (†1197)', in *ODNB*

— *Men raised from dust: administrative service and upward mobility in Angevin England* (Philadelphia, PA, 1988)

Turner, Rick and Andy Johnson (eds), *Chepstow castle: its history and buildings* (Logaston, Herefordshire, 2006)

Veach, Colin, 'A question of timing: Walter de Lacy's seisin of Meath, 1189–94', *PRIA* C 109 (2009), 165–94

— 'Henry II's grant of Meath to Hugh de Lacy in 1172: a reassessment', *Ríocht na Mídhe: records of the Meath Archaeological and Historical Society* 18 (2007), 67–94

— 'King and magnate in medieval Ireland: Walter de Lacy, King Richard and King John', *IHS* 37, no. 146 (2010), 179–202

— 'King John and royal control in Ireland: why William de Briouze had to be destroyed', *EHR* 129, no. 540 (2014), 1051–78
— *Lordship in four realms: the Lacy family, 1166–1241* (Manchester, 2014)
— 'Nobility and crown: the de Lacy family in Ireland, England and Normandy, 1172–1241', (Ph.D. thesis, University of Dublin, 2010)
Veach, Colin and Freya Verstraten Veach, 'William *Gorm* de Lacy, "chiefest champion in these parts of Europe"', in Seán Duffy (ed.), *Princes, prelates and poets in medieval Ireland: essays in honour of Katharine Simms* (Dublin, 2013), 63–84
Vincent, Nicholas, 'The court of Henry II', in Christopher Harper-Bill and Nicholas Vincent (eds), *Henry II: new interpretations* (Woodbridge, 2007), 278–335
— 'England and the Albigensian crusade', in Björn Weiler and Ifor Rowlands (eds), *England and Europe in the reign of Henry III, 1216–1272* (Aldershot and Burlington, 2002), 67–97
— 'King Henry III and the blessed Virgin Mary', in R. N. Swanson (ed.), *The church and Mary: papers read at the 2001 summer meeting and the 2002 winter meeting of the Ecclesiastical History Society* (Woodbridge, 2004), 126–46
— *Peter des Roches: an alien in English politics, 1205–1238* (Cambridge, 1996)
— 'Why 1199? Bureaucracy and enrolment under John and his contemporaries', in Jobson (ed.), *English government in the thirteenth century*, 17–49
— 'The record of 1204', in idem (ed.), *Records, administration and aristocratic society in the Anglo-Norman realm: papers commemorating the 800th anniversary of King John's loss of Normandy* (Woodbridge, 2009)
Vodola, Elizabeth, *Excommunication in the Middle Ages* (London, 1986)
Wakefield, W. L., 'Heretics and inquisitors: the case of Le Mas-Saintes-Puelles', *The Catholic Historical Review* 69, no. 2 (1983), 209–226
Walker, R. F., 'Audley, Henry (†1246)', in *ODNB*
Ware, James, *The antiquities and history of Ireland…now first published in one volume, in English; and the life of Sir James Ware prefixed* (Dublin, 1705)
— *Antiquities of Ireland*, ed. Walter Harris (Dublin, 1764)
Warren, W. L., 'Church and state in Angevin Ireland', *Peritia 13 (1999), 259–75*
— 'The historian as "private eye"', in J. G. Barry (ed.), *Historical Studies, IX* (Belfast, 1974), 1–18
— 'John in Ireland, 1185', in John Bossy and Peter Jupp (eds), *Essays presented to Michael Roberts, sometime professor of modern history in the Queen's University of Belfast* (Belfast, 1976), 11–23
— *King John* (2nd edn, London, 1978)
— 'King John and Ireland', in Lydon (ed.), *England and Ireland in the later Middle Ages*, 26–42

— 'Painter's King John – forty years on: an address to the Haskins Society conference, 1988', *The Haskins Society Journal* 1 (1989), 1–9

Watt, D. E. R., *A biographical dictionary of Scottish graduates to A.D. 1410* (Oxford, 1977)

Watt, J. A., *The church and the two nations in medieval Ireland* (Cambridge, 1970)

— *The church in medieval Ireland* (Dublin, 1972)

Webber, M. T. J., 'The scribes and handwriting of the original charters' in Thacker (ed.), *Chester and its charters*, 137–51

Weiler, Björn, 'Symbolism and politics in the reign of Henry III', in Michael Prestwich, Richard Britnell and Robin Frame (eds), *Thirteenth century England IX: proceedings of the Durham conference, 2001* (Woodbridge, 2003), 15–41

Wightman, W. E., *The Lacy family in England and Normandy, 1066–1194* (Oxford, 1966)

Wilkinson, Bertie, 'The council and the crisis of 1233–4', *Bulletin of the John Rylands Library* 27 (1942–3), 384–93

Williams, Bernadette, 'The Dominican annals of Dublin', in *Medieval Dublin II: proceedings of the Friends of Medieval Dublin symposium, 2000*, ed. Seán Duffy (Dublin, 2001), 142–68

Williamson, D. M., 'The legate Otto in Scotland and Ireland, 1237–1240', *Scot. Hist. Rev.* 28, no. 105 (1949), 12–30

Wolff, Robert and Harry Hazard (eds), *A history of the crusades, II: the later crusades* (Philadelphia, PA, 1962)

Woods, Susan, *The proprietary church in the medieval west* (Oxford, 2006)

Zečević, Nada, 'Brotherly love and brotherly service: on the relationship between Carlo and Leonardo Tocco', in Davis, Müller and Rees Jones (eds), *Love, marriage and family ties*, 143–56

Internet resources

Brown, Daniel J. F., 'Civil disobedience: the citizens and archbishop of Dublin during Hugh de Lacy's Irish rebellion, 1223–4', 'Fine of the month' (December 2012), 'Henry III Fine Rolls Project' (www.finerollshenry3.org.uk)

eDIL (Electronic dictionary of the Irish language) (http://www.dil.ie)

National sites and monuments record, no. MO013–002001 (http://www.archaeology.ie/smrmapviewer/mapviewer.aspx)

Oxford dictionary of national biography (60 vols, Oxford, 2004); online version (www.oxforddnb.com)

Transcript, Toulouse, Bib. Mun., MS 609 (www.jean.duvernoy.free.fr)

Index